Andrew Murray Devotional

Andrew Murray

Whitaker House

Includes excerpts from these other books by Andrew Murray:
God's Best Secrets
A Life of Power
Full Life in Christ
Divine Healing (also previously titled *Healing Secrets)*
Waiting on God
The Inner Life

Publisher's note:
Andrew Murray's selection of Bible versions has been retained whenever possible, including the Revised Version when it was originally cited. The text of this book, however, has been abridged and updated for the modern reader. Words, expressions, and sentence structure have been revised for clarity and readability.

Unless otherwise indicated, all Scripture quotations are taken from the King James Version of the Holy Bible. Scripture quotations marked (RV) are taken from the Revised Version of the Holy Bible.

Andrew Murray Devotional

ISBN-13: 978-0-88368-778-9
ISBN-10: 0-88368-778-X
Printed in the United States of America

Whitaker House
1030 Hunt Valley Circle
New Kensington, PA 15068
www.whitakerhouse.com

Library of Congress Cataloging in Publication Data

Murray, Andrew.
Andrew Murray devotional / by Andrew Murray.
p. cm.
Summary: "A year-long devotional of Bible passages and excerpts compiled from the writings of Andrew Murray, which have been adapted and abridged to fit the daily one-page format"—Provided by publisher.
ISBN-13: 978-0-88368-778-9 (trade pbk. : alk. paper)
ISBN-10: 0-88368-778-X (trade pbk. : alk. paper) 1. Devotional calendars. I. Title.
BV4811.M793 2006
242'.2—dc22
2006027028

3 4 5 6 7 8 9 10 11 12 18 17 16 15 14 13 12 11

A Note from the Publisher

For several generations of believers, the writings of Andrew Murray have stirred hearts, minds, and souls toward deeper devotion to God, to the Lordship of Jesus Christ, and to the powerful ministry of the Holy Spirit. It became evident to us that a devotional of Murray's writings, divided into daily readings and Scripture meditations, would be a cherished item for loyal readers of his many books.

Thus, we have endeavored to select the meatiest insights from several of Andrew Murray's books and cut them into daily bite-sized morsels. It is our prayer that these readings will enrich the daily moments you spend with your Creator.

The Publisher
Whitaker House
New Kensington, PA

Contents

January

January 1

From Day to Day

Yet the inward man is renewed day by day.
—2 Corinthians 4:16

There is one lesson that all young Christians should learn, and that is the absolute necessity of fellowship with Jesus each day. This lesson is not always taught at the beginning of the Christian life, nor does the new convert always understand it. He should realize that the grace he has received—the forgiveness of his sins, his acceptance as God's child, his joy in the Holy Spirit—can only be preserved by daily renewal in fellowship with Jesus Christ Himself.

Many Christians backslide because this truth is not clearly taught. They are unable to stand against the temptations of the world and of their old nature. They strive to do their best to fight against sin and to serve God, but they have no strength. They have never really grasped the secret that the Lord Jesus in heaven will continue His work in them every day, but only on one condition: every soul must give Him time each day to impart His love and His grace. Time alone with the Lord Jesus each day is the indispensable condition of growth and power.

Read Matthew 11:25–30. Christ says, *"Come unto me…and I will give you rest.…Learn of me…and ye shall find rest unto your souls"* (vv. 28–29). The Lord will teach us just how meek and humble He is. Bow before Him, tell Him that you long for Him and His love, and He will let His love rest on you. This is a thought not only for new Christians, but also for all who love the Lord.

If you desire to live this life of fellowship with Christ, if you wish to enjoy this blessed experience each day, then learn the lesson of spending time each day, without exception, in fellowship with your Lord. In this way, your inner man will be renewed from day to day.

January 2

Fellowship with God

He that loveth me shall be loved of my Father, and I will love him, and will manifest myself to him.
—John 14:21

The three persons in the Godhead are the Father, the Son, and the Holy Spirit. Each one is different from the others, just as each one of us is an individual. God desires to reveal Himself as a person; He will reveal Himself, and it is our holy calling to enter into fellowship with Him.

God greatly desires this fellowship with man. But sin has come between man and his God. Even in the Christian, who thinks he knows God, there is often great ignorance of and even indifference to this personal relationship of love for God.

People believe that at conversion their sins are forgiven, that God accepts them so that they may go to heaven, and that they should try to do God's will. But the idea is strange to them that they may and must each day have this blessed fellowship with God, just as a father and his child on earth have pleasure in fellowship.

God gave us Christ, His Son, in order to bring us to Himself. But this is only possible when we live in close fellowship with Jesus Christ. Our relationship to Christ rests on His deep, tender love for us. We are not able in ourselves to reciprocate this love to Him. But the Holy Spirit will do the work in us. For this we need to separate ourselves each day from the world and turn in faith to the Lord Jesus, so that He may pour out His love in our hearts (see Romans 5:5), and so that we may be filled with a great love for Him.

Dear soul, meditate quietly on this thought. Take time to believe in this personal fellowship. Tell God of your love. Say to Him, "Lord, You have loved me dearly; therefore, I earnestly desire to love You above all others."

January 3

Jesus

Thou shalt call his name JESUS: for he shall save his people from their sins.
—Matthew 1:21

Because the Lord Jesus was a person, He had His own individual name. His mother, His disciples, and all His friends called Him by this name, Jesus. But they probably thought little of what that name meant. And the majority of Christians today hardly know what a treasure is contained in that name, Jesus: *"He shall save his people from their sins."*

Many think of His death on the cross or of His work in heaven as our Intercessor, but they do not realize that Jesus is a living person in heaven who thinks of us each day and longs to reveal Himself. He desires us to bring Him our love and adoration each day.

Christians pray to Christ to save them from their sins, but they know very little how the blessed work is done. The living Christ reveals Himself to us, and through the power of His love, the love of sin is expelled. It is through personal fellowship with Him that Jesus saves us from our sins. I must come as an individual, with my heart and all the sin that is in it, to Jesus as an almighty personal Savior in whom God's holiness dwells. And as He and I commune together in the expression of mutual love and desire, by the work of His Holy Spirit in my heart, His love will expel and conquer all the sin.

O Christian, you will find the secret of happiness and holiness in fellowship with Jesus each day. Your heart will long for the hour of prayer as the best hour of the day. As you learn to take time to be alone with Him each day, you will experience His presence, enabling you to love Him, to serve Him, and to walk in His ways throughout the day. Through this unbroken fellowship, you will learn the secret of the power of a truly godly life.

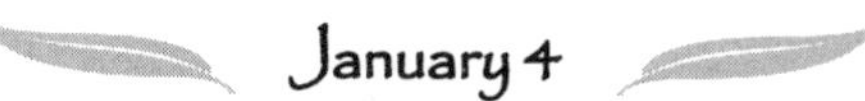
January 4

The Inner Chamber

When thou prayest, enter into thine inner chamber, and having shut thy door, pray to thy Father which is in secret, and thy Father which seeth in secret shall recompense thee.
—Matthew 6:6 (RV)

Have you ever thought what a wonderful privilege it is that everyone each day, and each hour of the day, has the liberty of asking God to meet them in the inner chamber to hear what He has to say? We imagine that every Christian uses such a privilege gladly and faithfully. But how many really do take advantage of the privilege?

"When thou prayest," said Jesus, *"enter into thine inner chamber, and having shut thy door, pray to thy Father which is in secret."* This means two things. First, shut the world out and withdraw from all worldly thoughts and activities. Second, shut yourself in alone with God to pray to Him in secret. Let this be your chief aim in prayer: to realize the presence of your heavenly Father. Let your watchword be, "Alone with God."

This is only the beginning. As you take time to realize His presence with you and to pray to *"thy Father which seeth in secret,"* you can do so in the full assurance that He knows how you long for His help and guidance, and that He will incline His ear to you.

Then follows the great promise: *"Thy Father which seeth in secret shall recompense thee."* The Father will see to it that your prayer is not in vain. All through the activities of a busy day, the answer to your prayer will be granted. Prayer in secret will be followed by the secret working of God in your heart.

The Lord Jesus has given us the promise of His presence, and He shows us the way to the inner chamber. Therefore, He will surely be with us to teach us to pray. It is through Him that we have access to the Father. (See John 14:6.) Be childlike and trustful in your fellowship with Christ. Confess each sin; bring your every need. Offer your prayer to the Father in the name of Christ. Prayer in fellowship with Jesus cannot be in vain.

January 5

Faith

Only believe.
—Mark 5:36

We have here a lesson of the greatest importance. When we are alone in the inner chamber, we must send up our petitions, trusting implicitly in the love of God and in the power of the Lord Jesus. Take time to ask yourself the question, Is my heart full of a great and steadfast faith in God's love? If this is not the case, do not begin to pray just yet. Faith does not come of itself.

Consider quietly how impossible it is for God to lie. He is ready with infinite love to give you a blessing. (See Psalm 29:11.) Take some passage of Scripture in which God's power, faithfulness, and love are revealed. Take hold of the words and say, "Yes, Lord, I will pray in firm faith in You and in Your great love."

It is a mistake to limit the word *faith* to the forgiveness of sins and to our acceptance as children of God. Faith includes far more than this. We must have faith in all that God is willing to do for us. We must have faith each day according to our special needs. God is so infinitely great and powerful, and Christ has so much grace for each new day, that our faith must reach out afresh each day according to the need of the day.

When you enter into the inner chamber, even before you begin to pray, ask yourself, Do I really believe that God is here with me and that the Lord Jesus will help me to pray? Do I believe that I can expect to spend a blessed time in communion with my God?

Jesus often taught His disciples how indispensable faith was to true prayer. He will teach you this lesson, too. Remain in fellowship with Him, and ask Him to strengthen your faith in His almighty power. Christ says to you and to me, as He did to Martha, *"Said I not unto thee, that, if thou wouldest believe, thou shouldest see the glory of God?"* (John 11:40).

January 6

The Word of God

Man shall not live by bread alone, but by every word that proceedeth out of the mouth of God.
—Matthew 4:4

In the verse above, our Lord compares the Word of God to our daily bread, thereby teaching us a great lesson. We know bread is indispensable to life. We all understand this. However strong a person may be, if he has no nourishment, he will grow weaker, and he will die. If an illness prevents me from eating, I will die. It is the same with the Word of God. The Word contains a heavenly principle and works powerfully in those who believe.

Bread must be eaten. I may know all about bread. I may have bread and give it to others. I may have bread in my house and on my table in great abundance, but that will not help me unless I eat it. Similarly, a mere knowledge of God's Word and even the preaching of it to others will not benefit me. It is not enough to think about it. Rather, I must feed on God's Word and take it into my heart and life. In love and obedience I must take hold of the words of God and let them take full possession of my heart. Then they will indeed be words of life.

Bread must be eaten daily, and the same is true of God's Word. The psalmist wrote, *"Blessed is the man...*[whose] *delight is in the law of the LORD; and in his law doth he meditate day and night"* (Psalm 1:1–2); *"O how love I thy law! it is my meditation all the day"* (Psalm 119:97). To secure a strong and powerful spiritual life, an intake of God's Word every day is indispensable.

When He was on earth, the Lord Jesus learned, loved, and obeyed the Word of the Father. If you seek fellowship with Him, you will find Him in His Word. Christ will teach you to commune with the Father through the Word, just as He did on earth. You will learn, like Him, to live solely for the glory of God and the fulfillment of His Word.

January 7

How to Read God's Word

Blessed is the man...[whose] delight is in the law of the LORD; and in his law doth he meditate day and night.
—Psalm 1:1–2

Here are some simple rules for Bible reading. First, read God's Word with great reverence. Meditate a moment in silence on the thought that the words come from God Himself. Bow in deep reverence. Be silent before God. Let Him reveal His Word in your heart.

Second, read with careful attention. If you read the words carelessly, thinking that you can grasp their meaning with your human understanding, you will use the words superficially and will not enter into their depths. When someone tries to explain anything wonderful or beautiful to us, we give our entire attention to try to understand what is said. How much higher and deeper are God's thoughts than our thoughts! *"For as the heavens are higher than the earth, so are...my thoughts than your thoughts"* (Isaiah 55:9). We need to give our undivided attention to understand even the superficial meaning of the words. How much harder it is to grasp the spiritual meaning!

Next, read with the expectation of the guidance of God's Spirit. It is God's Spirit alone that can make the Word a living power in our hearts and lives. Read Psalm 119. Notice how earnestly David prayed that God would teach him, open his eyes, give him understanding, and incline his heart to God's ways. As you read, remember that God's Word and God's Spirit are inseparable.

Finally, read with the firm purpose of keeping the Word day and night in your heart and in your life. The whole heart and the whole life must come under the influence of the Word. David said, *"O how love I thy law! It is my meditation all the day"* (Psalm 119:97). In the same manner, in the midst of his daily work, the believer can cherish God's Word in his heart and meditate on it. Read Psalm 119 again, until you accept God's Word with all your heart. Pray that God may teach you to understand it and to carry out its precepts in your life.

January 8

The Word and Prayer

Quicken me, O LORD, according unto thy word.
—Psalm 119:107

Prayer and the Word of God are inseparable and should always go together in the quiet time of the inner chamber. In His Word, God speaks to me; in prayer, I speak to God. If there is to be true fellowship, God and I must both take part. If I simply pray without using God's Word, I am apt to use my own words and thoughts. To really give prayer its power, I must take God's thoughts from His Word and present them before Him. Then I am enabled to pray according to God's Word. How indispensable God's Word is for all true prayer!

When you pray, you must seek to know God correctly. It is through the Word that the Holy Spirit gives you right thoughts of Him. The Word will also teach you how wretched and sinful you are. It reveals to you all the wonders that God will do for you and the strength He will give you to do His will. The Word teaches you how to pray with strong desire, with firm faith, and with constant perseverance. The Word teaches you not only what you are, but also what you may become through God's grace. Above all, it reminds you each day that Christ is the great Intercessor, and allows you to pray in His name.

O Christian, learn this great lesson, to renew your strength each day in God's Word, and thereby pray according to His will.

Now let us turn to the other side: prayer. We need prayer when we read God's Word: prayer to be taught by God to understand His Word, prayer that through the Holy Spirit we may rightly know and use God's Word, prayer that we may see in the Word that Christ is all in all, and will be all in us.

Blessed inner chamber, where I may approach God in Christ through the Word and prayer! There I may offer myself to God and His service and be strengthened by the Holy Spirit, so that His love may be poured out in my heart (see Romans 5:5) and I may daily walk in that love.

January 9

Obedience

Obey my voice...and I will be your God.
—Jeremiah 11:4

God gave this command to Israel when He gave them the law. But Israel had no power to keep the law. So God gave them a new covenant, to enable His people to live a life of obedience. We read, *"I will put my law in their inward parts, and write it in their hearts"* (Jeremiah 31:33); *"I will put my fear in their hearts, that they shall not depart from me"* (Jeremiah 32:40); *"I will...cause you to walk in my statutes"* (Ezekiel 36:27). These wonderful promises gave Israel the assurance that obedience would be their delight.

See what the Lord Jesus said about obedience: *"He that hath my commandments, and keepeth them, he it is that loveth me"* (John 14:21); *"If a man love me, he will keep my words: and my Father will love him, and we will come unto him, and make our abode with him"* (v. 23); *"If ye keep my commandments, ye shall abide in my love"* (John 15:10). These words are an inexhaustible treasure. Through faith we can firmly trust Christ to enable us to live such a life of love and obedience.

No father can train his children unless they are obedient. No teacher can teach a child who continues to disobey him. No general can lead his soldiers to victory without prompt obedience. Pray that God will imprint this lesson on your heart: the life of faith is a life of obedience. As Christ lived in obedience to the Father, so we, too, need obedience for a life in the love of God.

But so many people think, "I cannot be obedient; it is impossible." Yes, impossible to you, but not to God. He has promised to *"cause you to walk in* [His] *statutes"* (Ezekiel 36:27). Pray and meditate on these words, and the Holy Spirit will enlighten your eyes, so that you will have power to do God's will. Let your fellowship with the Father and with the Lord Jesus Christ have this as its one aim: a life of quiet, determined, unquestioning obedience.

January 10

Confession of Sin

If we confess our sins, he is faithful and just to forgive us our sins, and to cleanse us from all unrighteousness.
—1 John 1:9

Too often the confession of sin is superficial, and often it is quite neglected. Few Christians realize how necessary it is to be sincere about the matter. Some do not feel that an honest confession of sin gives power to live the life of victory over sin. But we, in fellowship with the Lord Jesus, need to confess with sincere hearts every sin that may be a hindrance in our Christian lives.

Read what David said: *"I acknowledged my sin unto thee....I said, I will confess my transgressions unto the LORD; and thou forgavest the iniquity of my sin....Thou art my hiding place....Thou shalt compass me about with songs of deliverance"* (Psalm 32:5, 7). David spoke of a time when he was unwilling to confess his sin. *"When I kept silence...thy hand was heavy upon me"* (vv. 3–4). But when he had confessed his sin, a wonderful change came.

Confession means not only that you confess your sin with shame, but also that you hand it over to God, trusting Him to take it away. Such a confession implies that you are wholly unable to get rid of your guilt, but by an act of faith you depend on God to deliver you. This deliverance means, in the first place, that you know your sins are forgiven, and secondly, that Christ undertakes to cleanse you from the sin and keep you from its power.

O Christian, if you are seeking to have fellowship with Jesus, do not fear to confess each sin in the confident assurance that there is deliverance. Let there be a mutual understanding between the Lord Jesus and yourself that you will confess each sin and will obtain forgiveness. Then you will know your Lord as Jesus, who saves His people from their sins. (See Matthew 1:21.) Believe that there is great power in the confession of sin, for the burden of sin was borne by our Lord and Savior.

January 11

The First Love

Nevertheless I have somewhat against thee, because thou hast left thy first love.
—Revelation 2:4

In the verses preceding Revelation 2:4, eight signs are mentioned that show the zeal and activity of the church at Ephesus. But there was one bad sign, and the Lord said, *"I will come unto thee quickly, and will remove thy candlestick out of his place, except thou repent"* (v. 5). And what was this sign? *"Thou hast left thy first love."*

We find the same lack in the church of the present day. There is zeal for the truth, there is continuous and persevering labor, but what the Lord values most is still missing: the tender, fervent love for Himself.

This is a thought of great significance. A church, or even an individual Christian, may be an example in every good work, and yet the tender love for the Lord Jesus in the inner chamber is missing. There is no personal, daily fellowship with Christ, and all the manifold activities with which people satisfy themselves are nothing in the eyes of the Master Himself.

Dear brother or sister in Christ, this book speaks of the fellowship of love that we can have with Christ in the inner chamber. Everything depends on this. Christ came from heaven to love us with the love with which the Father loved Him. (See John 17:26.) He suffered and died to win our hearts for this love. His love can be satisfied with nothing less than a deep, personal love on our part.

Christ considers this of the highest importance. Let us have the same thought. Many ministers, missionaries, and Christian workers confess with shame that, in spite of all their zeal in the Lord's work, their prayer lives are defective because they have left their first love. I pray that you will write this down on a piece of paper and remember it continually: the

love of Jesus must be all—in the inner chamber, in all our work, and in our daily lives.

January 12

The Holy Spirit

He shall glorify me: for he shall receive of mine, and shall show it unto you.
—John 16:14

Our Lord, on the last night that He was with His disciples, promised to send the Holy Spirit as a Comforter. Although His bodily presence was removed, they would realize His presence in them and with them in a wonderful way. The Holy Spirit would so reveal Christ in their hearts that they would experience His presence with them continually. The Spirit would glorify Christ and would reveal the glorified Christ in heavenly love and power.

How little do Christians understand, believe, and experience this glorious truth! Ministers would fail in their duties if, in a book like this or in their preaching, they encouraged Christians to love the Lord Jesus without at the same time warning them that it is not a duty they can perform in their own strength. No, that is impossible; it is God, the Holy Spirit alone, who will pour out His love in our hearts (see Romans 5:5) and will teach us to love Him fervently. Through the Holy Spirit we may experience the love and abiding presence of the Lord Jesus throughout the day.

But let us remember that the Spirit of God must have entire possession of us. He claims our hearts and our entire lives. He will strengthen us with might in the inner man (see Ephesians 3:16), so that we may have fellowship with Christ, keep His commandments, and abide in His love.

Once we have grasped this truth, we will begin to feel our deep dependence on the Holy Spirit and will ask the Father to send Him in power into our hearts. The Spirit will teach us to love the Word, to meditate on it, and to keep it. He will reveal the love of Christ to us, so that we may love Him *"with a pure heart fervently"* (1 Peter 1:22). Then we will begin to see that having the love of Christ in the midst of our daily lives and distractions is a glorious possibility and a blessed reality.

January 13

Christ's Love for Us

Even as the Father hath loved me, I also have loved you: abide ye in my love.
—John 15:9–10 (RV)

In fellowship between friends and relatives, everything depends on their love for each other. Of what value is great wealth if love is lacking between husband and wife, or between parents and children? And in our religion, of what value is all knowledge and zeal in God's work, without the knowledge and experience of Christ's love? (See 1 Corinthians 13:1–3.) O Christians, the one thing needed in the inner chamber is to know by experience how much Christ loves you, and to learn how you may abide and continue in that love.

Think of what Christ said: *"As the Father hath loved me"*—what a divine, everlasting, wonderful love—*"I also have loved you."* It was the same love with which He had loved the Father and that He always bore in His heart, which He now gave into the hearts of His disciples. He yearns that this everlasting love will rest upon us and work within us, so that we may abide in it day by day. What a blessed life! Christ desires every disciple to live in the power of the very same love of God that He Himself experienced. Do you realize that in your fellowship with Christ in secret or in public, you are surrounded by and kept in this heavenly love? Let your desire reach out for this everlasting love. The Christ with whom you desire fellowship longs unspeakably to fill you with His love.

Read all that God's Word says about the love of Christ. Meditate on the words, and let them sink into your heart. Sooner or later you will begin to realize, "The greatest happiness of my life is that I am loved by the Lord Jesus. I may live in fellowship with Him all day long." Let your heart continually say, "His love for me is unspeakable; He will keep me abiding in His love."

January 14

Our Love for Christ

**Jesus Christ: whom not having seen ye love; on whom, though now ye see him not, yet believing, ye rejoice greatly with joy unspeakable and full of glory.
—1 Peter 1:8 (RV)**

What a wonderful description of the Christian life! People had never seen Christ, yet they truly loved Him and believed in Him, so that their hearts were filled with unspeakable joy. Such is the life of a Christian who really loves his Lord.

We have seen that the chief attributes of the Father and the Son are love for each other and love for man. These should be the chief characteristics of the true Christian. The love of God and of Christ is poured out in his heart (see Romans 5:5) and becomes a well of living water, flowing forth as love for the Lord Jesus.

This love is not merely a blessed feeling. It is an active principle. It takes pleasure in doing the will of the beloved Lord. It is joy to keep His commandments. The love of Christ for us was shown by His death on the cross; our love must be exhibited in unselfish, self-sacrificing living. Oh, that we understood this: in the Christian life, love for Christ is everything!

Great love will beget great faith—faith in His love for us, faith in the powerful revelations of His love in our hearts, faith that He through His love will work all His good pleasure in us. The wings of faith and love will lift us up to heaven, and we will be filled with *"joy unspeakable."* The joy of the Christian is an indispensable witness to the world of the power of Christ to change hearts and to fill them with heavenly love and gladness.

Oh, you who love the Lord Jesus, take time daily in the inner chamber with Him to drink in a fresh supply of His heavenly love. It will make you strong in faith, and your joy will be full. Love, joy, faith—these will fill your life each day through the grace of the Lord Jesus.

January 15

Love for Fellow Christians

A new commandment I give unto you, That ye love one another; as I have loved you, that ye also love one another.
—John 13:34

The Lord Jesus told His disciples that He loved them just as the Father had loved Him. And now, following His example, we must love one another with the same love.

"By this shall all men know that ye are my disciples, if ye have love one to another" (v. 35). Christ later prayed, *"That they all may be one; as thou, Father, art in me, and I in thee, that they also may be one in us: that the world may believe that thou hast sent me"* (John 17:21). If we exhibit the love that was in God toward Christ, and in Christ toward us, the world will be obliged to confess that our Christianity is genuine and from above.

This is what actually happened in Bible times. The Greeks and Romans, Jews and heathen, hated each other. Among all the nations of the world, there was hardly a thought of love for each other. The very idea of self-sacrifice was a strange one. When the unsaved saw that Christians from different nations, under the powerful workings of the Holy Spirit, became one and loved one another, even to the point of self-sacrifice in time of plague or illness, they were amazed and said, "Behold how these people love one another!" (See John 13:35.)

Among professing Christians, there is a certain oneness of belief and feeling of brotherhood, but Christ's heavenly love is often lacking, and we do not bear one another's burdens or love others as heartily as we should. Pray that you will love your fellow believers with the same love with which Christ loves you. If we abide in Christ's love and let that love fill our hearts, supernatural power will be given to us to love all God's children. As the bond of love between the Father and the Son, and between Christ and His followers, is close, so must the bond of love be between all God's children.

January 16

Love for Souls

He which converteth the sinner from the error of his way shall save a soul from death.
—James 5:20

What a wonderful thought, that I may save a soul from everlasting death! How can this be? I must convert him from the error of his ways. This is the calling not only of the minister, but also of every Christian: to work for the salvation of sinners.

When Christ and His love take possession of our hearts, He gives us this love so that we might bring others to Him. In this way, Christ's kingdom is extended. Everyone who has the love of Christ in his heart is commissioned to tell others. This was the case in the early church. After the day of Pentecost, people went out and told of the love of Christ, which they had themselves experienced. Even heathen writers have told us that the rapid spread of Christianity in the first century was due to the fact that each convert, being filled with the love of Christ, tried to deliver the good news to others.

What a change has come over the church! Many Christians never try to win others to Christ. Their love is so weak and faint that they have no desire to help others. May the time soon come when Christians will feel constrained to tell of the love of Christ. In a particular revival in Korea, the converts were filled with such a burning love for Christ that they felt bound to tell others of His love. It was even taken as a test of membership that each one should have brought another to the Lord before being admitted to the church.

Reader, examine your heart. Pray that, in fellowship with Christ, you will not only think of your own soul, but having received the gift of God's love, will also pass it on to others. You will then know true happiness, the joy of bringing souls to Christ.

Let us pray earnestly to be so filled with God's love that we may wholeheartedly surrender ourselves to win others for Him.

January 17

The Spirit of Love

The love of God is shed abroad in our hearts by the Holy Ghost which is given unto us.
—Romans 5:5

The fruit of the Spirit is love.
—Galatians 5:22

When we consider Christ's love for us, our love for Christ, and our love for fellow Christians or for souls around us, the thought sometimes arises: "The demand is too great; it is unattainable; it is impossible for a Christian to live this life of love and to show it to others in the church and to needy souls." And because we deem it impossible, and because of our unbelief and lack of faith in God's promises, we make little progress in this spirit of love.

We need to remind ourselves continually that it is not in our own strength, or even by serious thought, that we can obtain the love of Christ. We must realize the truth, that the love of God is *"shed abroad in our hearts"* and will be poured out daily by the Spirit of God. Only as we are wholly surrendered to the leading of the Spirit will we be able to live according to God's will. When the inner life of love is renewed from day to day, we will feel compelled to work for souls.

Here is a prayer that you can offer: *"I bow my knees unto the father...that he would grant you...to be strengthened with might by his Spirit in the inner man; that Christ may dwell in your hearts by faith; that ye, being rooted and grounded in love, may...know the love of Christ, which passeth knowledge"* (Ephesians 3:14, 16–19).

You may be *"rooted and grounded"* in this love and may know the love *"which passeth knowledge,"* but only on one condition: you must be strengthened by the Spirit *"in the inner man,"* so that Christ may dwell in your heart. Then you will indeed be *"rooted and grounded in love."*

Christian, take this message from God's Word, and let it influence your life. Unless you wait upon God daily, on your knees, for His Spirit to be revealed in your heart, you cannot live in this love. A life of prayer will cause you to experience the blessed reality of the love of Christ, the love of fellow believers, and love for souls.

Put your confidence each day in the Holy Spirit—the Spirit of love that God will give to those who ask in faith.

Persevering Prayer

Men ought always to pray, and not to faint.
—Luke 18:1

Continuing instant in prayer.
—Romans 12:12

Pray without ceasing.
—1 Thessalonians 5:17

One of the greatest drawbacks to the life of prayer is that the answer does not come as speedily as we expect. We are discouraged by the thought, "Perhaps I do not pray correctly," and so we do not persevere in prayer. This was a lesson that our Lord taught often and urgently. If we look further into the matter, we can see that there may be a reason for the delay and that the waiting may bring a blessing to our souls. Remember Daniel, who waited twenty-one days for the answer to his prayer. (See Daniel 10:1–15.)

When we pray, our desire must grow deeper and stronger, and we must ask with our whole hearts. God puts us into the school of persevering prayer so that our weak faith may be strengthened. Believe that there is a great blessing in the delayed answer to prayer.

Above all, God wants to draw us into closer fellowship with Himself. When our prayers are not answered, we learn to realize that the fellowship, nearness, and love of God are more to us than the answers to our petitions, and we continue in prayer. What a blessing Jacob received through the delay of the answer to his prayer! He saw God face-to-face, and as a prince he had power with God and prevailed. (See Genesis 32:28.)

Christians, listen to this warning. Do not be impatient or discouraged if the answer does not come. Rather, continue in prayer. *"Pray without ceasing."* You will find it an unspeakable blessing to do so. You may ask whether your prayer agrees with God's will and His Word. You may inquire if it is in the right spirit and in the name of Christ. Keep on praying; you will learn that the delay in the answer to prayer is one of the most precious means of grace that God can bestow on you. You will also learn that those who have persevered in pleading God's promises are those who have had the greatest power with God in prayer.

January 19

The Prayer Meeting

These all continued with one accord in prayer and supplication.
—Acts 1:14

And they were all filled with the Holy Ghost.
—Acts 2:4

The value of a genuine prayer meeting is enormous. There, God's children meet together, not as in church, to listen to one speaker, but instead to lift up their hearts in unison to God. By this means, Christians are drawn closer to each other. Those who are weak are strengthened and encouraged by the testimony of the older and more experienced members, and even young Christians have the opportunity to tell of the joy of the Lord.

The prayer meeting may become a great power for good in a congregation and a spiritual help to both minister and members. By means of intercession, God's blessing is poured out at home and abroad.

But there are also dangers to be considered. Many attend and are edified but never learn to pray themselves. Others go for the sake of social and religious fervor and have *"a form of godliness"* (2 Timothy 3:5) but do not know the hidden life of prayer. Unless there is much and earnest prayer in the inner chamber, attendance at a prayer meeting may be a mere formality.

It is well to ask, "What constitutes a living prayer meeting?" There should be hearty love and fellowship between the members.

The leaders should realize how great the influence of such a meeting may be, with its roots nourished by the life of prayer in the inner chamber. Prayer should include God's people and His church all over the world. Above all, as on the day of Pentecost, there must be a waiting on God for the filling of the Holy Spirit.

Dear reader, I aim to help you in your spiritual life. But remember, you do not live for yourself alone; you are part of the body of Christ. You must include all Christians in your intercession. As the roots of the tree hidden deep in the earth are one with the branches that spread out to the sky, so the hidden prayer life is inseparably bound with united prayer.

January 20

Intercession

Praying always…in the Spirit…with all perseverance and supplication for all saints.
—Ephesians 6:18

What an unspeakable blessing there is in intercession! That one should pray down heavenly gifts on himself is a wonder of grace, but that he should bring down blessings on others is indeed an inconceivable honor. But God makes the pouring out of blessing on others dependent on our prayers. Indeed, He makes us His fellow workers. He has taken us into partnership in His work; if we fail in doing our part, others will suffer, and His work will suffer unspeakable loss.

God has appointed intercession as one of the means by which souls are saved, and by which saints and ministers of the gospel are built up in the faith. Even the ends of the earth will receive life and blessing through our prayers. Should we not expect God's children to strive joyfully and with all their powers, by means of intercession, to bring down blessing on the world?

Christian, begin to use intercession as a means of grace for yourself and for others. Pray for your neighbors. Pray for souls with the definite desire that they may be won for Christ. Pray for your minister, for all ministers and missionaries. Pray for your country and its people. Pray for all men. If you surrender yourself to the guidance of the Holy Spirit and live a life wholly for God, you will realize that the time spent in prayer is an offering well pleasing to God, bringing blessing to yourself and power into the lives of those for whom you pray.

Yes, pray *"always with all prayer and supplication in the Spirit, and watching thereunto with all perseverance and supplication for all saints"* (v. 18). In so doing, you will learn the lesson that intercession is the chief means of winning souls and of bringing glory to God.

January 21

Prayer and Fasting

Jesus said unto them, "Because of your unbelief...Howbeit this kind goeth not out but by prayer and fasting."
—Matthew 17:20–21

Our Lord here taught us that a life of faith requires both prayer and fasting. That is, prayer grasps the power of heaven, and fasting loosens the hold on earthly pleasure.

Jesus Himself fasted to get strength to resist the devil. He taught His disciples that fasting should be in secret and that the heavenly Father would reward openly. (See Matthew 6:6.) Abstinence from food, or moderation in taking it, helps to strengthen the soul for communion with God.

Let us learn this great lesson that abstinence, moderation, and self-denial in temporal things are a help to the spiritual life. After eating a hearty meal, one does not feel much desire to pray. To willingly sacrifice our own pleasure or bodily enjoyment, and to subdue the lust of the flesh and the lust of the eyes, will help to set our minds more fully on heavenly things. The very exertion needed in overcoming the desires of the flesh will give us strength to take hold of God in prayer.

The great lesson is this: our dullness in prayer comes from our fleshly desires for comfort and ease. *"And they that are Christ's have crucified the flesh with the affections and lusts"* (Galatians 5:24). Prayer is not easy work. It may easily become a mere form. For the real practice of prayer, to really take hold of God and have communion with Him, it is necessary that all that can please the flesh is sacrificed and given over to death.

Beloved Christian, it is worth any trouble we might have to endure to deny ourselves daily, in order to meet the holy God and receive heavenly blessings from Him.

January 22

The Spirit of Prayer

The Spirit...maketh intercession for the saints.
—Romans 8:27

Prayer is not our work, but God's work, which He works within us by His almighty power. As we consider this statement, our attitude should be one of silent expectation that as we pray, the Holy Spirit will help our weaknesses and will pray within us with *"groanings which cannot be uttered"* (v. 26).

What a thought! When I feel how defective my prayers are, when I have no strength of my own, I may bow in silence before God in the confidence that His Holy Spirit will teach me to pray. The Spirit is the Spirit of prayer. It is not my work, but God's work in me. My desire to pray is a sign that God will hear me.

When God moves to grant our requests, He first works the desire in our hearts, and the Spirit will perfect the work, even in our weakness. We see this in the story of Jacob. The same One who wrestled with him and seemed to withhold the blessing was in reality strengthening him to continue and to prevail in prayer. (See Genesis 32:24–30.) What a wondrous thought! Prayer is the work of the triune God: the Father, who wakens the desire and will give all we need; the Son, who through His intercession teaches us to pray in His name; and the Holy Spirit, who in secret will strengthen our feeble desires.

I have already told you about the Spirit of truth, who will glorify Christ in us, and of the Spirit of love, who will pour out this love in our hearts. Now we have the Spirit of prayer, through whom our lives may be ones of continual prayer. Thank God. The Spirit has been given from heaven to dwell in our hearts and to teach us to pray.

Christian, listen to the leading of the Spirit. Obey His voice in all things. He will make you a man or woman of prayer. You will then realize the glory of your calling as an intercessor, asking great things of God for those around you, for the church, and for the whole unsaved world.

January 23

Wholly for Christ

One died for all...that they which live should no longer live unto themselves, but unto Him who for their sakes died and rose again. —2 Corinthians 5:15–16 (RV)

Here we have a threefold life described. First is the life of the Christian who lives according to his old nature: he lives for himself alone. The second is the life of a true Christian: he lives wholly for Christ. Third is the life of Christ in heaven: He lives wholly for us.

Many Christians need to be convinced of the foolishness of living only for themselves. At conversion, they tend to think more of their own salvation and less of the glory of God and the claim that Christ, who has redeemed us with His precious blood, has upon them. Many Christians live for themselves, content with doing a little for the Master. The believer who realizes his high calling and the privilege and blessedness of consecrating His life entirely to God's service will find true happiness.

The great hindrance to such a life is unbelief, which says that complete submission to God is impossible. But when the truth takes hold of us—"Christ in heaven lives wholly for me; He will impart His life to me and will enable me to live wholly for Him"—then we will be able to say joyfully, "Dear Lord Jesus, from this moment let my prayer each day be, 'Wholly for Christ, wholly for Christ.'"

Dear brother or sister, let nothing less than this be your earnest desire, your prayer, and your firm expectation. Say, "Christ has not only died for me, but He also lives in heaven to keep and sanctify me, His purchased possession." Ponder this wonderful thought: that Christ will keep you as a member of His body, to work and live for Him. Pray for grace to live wholly for God in seeking souls and in serving His people. Take time from day to day to be so united to Christ in the inner man that you can say with all your heart, "I live wholly for Him, who gave Himself wholly for me and who now lives in heaven wholly for me."

January 24

The Cross of Christ

I am crucified with Christ.
—Galatians 2:20

The cross of Christ is His greatest glory. Because He humbled Himself to death on the cross, God has highly exalted Him. (See Philippians 2:8–9.) The cross was the power that conquered Satan and sin.

The Christian shares with Christ in the cross. The crucified Christ lives in him through the Holy Spirit, and the spirit of the cross inspires him. He lives as one who has died with Christ. As he realizes the power of Christ's crucifixion, he lives as one who has died to the world and to sin, and the power becomes a reality in his life. It is as the Crucified One that Christ lives in him.

Our Lord said to His disciples, *"Take up* [your] *cross, and follow me"* (Matthew 16:24). Did they understand this? They had seen men carrying a cross, and they knew it meant a painful death. All His life, Christ bore His cross—the death sentence that He would die for the world. Similarly, each Christian must bear his cross, acknowledge that he is worthy of death, and believe that he is crucified with Christ and that the Crucified One lives in him. *"Our old man is crucified with him"* (Romans 6:6). *"And they that are Christ's have crucified the flesh with the affections and lusts"* (Galatians 5:24). When we have accepted this life of the cross, we will be able to say with Paul, *"But God forbid that I should glory, save in the cross of our Lord Jesus Christ"* (Galatians 6:14).

This is a deep spiritual truth. Think and pray over it, and the Holy Spirit will teach you. Let the disposition of Christ on the cross, His humility, His sacrifice of all worldly honor, His spirit of self-denial, take possession of you. The power of His death will work in you, you will become like Him in His death, and you will *"know Him, and the power of his resurrection"* (Philippians 3:10). Take time, dear reader, so that Christ through His Spirit may reveal Himself as the Crucified One.

January 25

The World

Love not the world, neither the things that are in the world. If any man love the world, the love of the Father is not in him.
—1 John 2:15

John taught us clearly what he meant by *"the world."* He wrote, *"For all that is in the world, the lust of the flesh, and the lust of the eyes, and the pride of life, is not of the Father, but is of the world"* (v. 16).

The world is the disposition or power under which man has fallen through sin. And the god of this world, in order to deceive man, conceals himself under the form of what God has created. The world, with its pleasures, surrounds the Christian each day with temptations.

This was the case with Eve in the Garden of Eden. In Genesis 3:6, we find the three characteristics that John mentioned: first, the lust of the flesh: *"The woman saw that the tree was good for food"*; second, the lust of the eyes: *"It was pleasant to the eyes"*; and third, the pride of life: *"A tree to be desired to make one wise."* The world still comes to us, offering desirable food and much to please the fleshly appetites. It offers much that the eye desires, including riches, beauty, and luxury. And it offers the pride of life, which is shown when a man imagines he knows and understands everything, and prides himself on it.

Are our lives in the world not full of danger, with the allurements of the flesh, so much to occupy our eyes and our hearts, and so much worldly wisdom and knowledge?

John told us, "Do not love the world, for then the love of the Father is not in you." Our Lord calls us, as He called His disciples, to leave all and follow Him.

Christian, you live in a dangerous world; cling to the Lord Jesus. As He teaches you to shun the world and its attractions, your love will go out to Him in loyal-hearted service. But remember, there must be daily fellowship with Jesus. His love alone can expel the love of the world. Take time to be alone with your Lord.

Put On Christ

For as many of you as have been baptized into Christ have put on Christ.
—Galatians 3:27

But put ye on the Lord Jesus Christ, and make not provision for the flesh, to fulfil the lusts thereof.
—Romans 13:14

The word that is translated *"put on"* is the same that is used in regard to putting on clothes. We have *"put on the new man"* (Ephesians 4:24), and the new nature is like a garment that is worn so that all can see who we are. Paul said that the Christian, when he has confessed Christ at baptism, has *"put on Christ."* Just as a man may be recognized by the garment he wears, so the Christian is known by the fact that he has put on Christ and exhibits Him in his whole life and character.

"Put ye on the Lord Jesus Christ," not just at conversion, but also on a daily basis. As I put on my clothes each day and am seen in them, so the Christian must daily put on the Lord Jesus, so that he no longer lives to fulfill the lusts of the flesh, but shows forth the image of his Lord and the new man formed in His likeness.

Put on Christ! This work must be done each day in the inner chamber. I must put on the Lord, the heavenly Jesus. But I need time to put on Christ. Just as my garments cover me and protect me from the wind and the sun, even so Christ Jesus will be my beauty, my defense, and my joy. As I commune with Him in prayer, He imparts Himself to me and strengthens me to walk as one who is in Him and is bound to Him forever.

Reader, take time to meditate on this wonderful truth. Just as your clothing is a necessity as you go out into the world, let it be equally indispensable for you to put on Jesus Christ, to abide in Him, and to walk with Him all day long.

This cannot be done hastily and superficially. It takes time, quiet time in living fellowship with Jesus, to realize that you have put Him on. Take the time and the trouble. Your reward will be great.

January 27

The Strength of the Christian

Finally, my brethren, be strong in the Lord and in the power of his might.
—Ephesians 6:10

As the apostle reached the end of his epistle, he began the last section of it with the words, *"Finally, my brethren, be strong in the Lord."*

The Christian needs strength. This we all know. We also know the truth that the Christian has no strength of his own. Where may strength be obtained? Notice the answer: *"Be strong in the Lord and in the power of his might."*

Paul had spoken of this power in the earlier part of his epistle. He had prayed, "God, give them the Spirit, that they might know *'the exceeding greatness of his power...according to the working of his mighty power which he wrought in Christ, when he raised him from the dead'*" (Ephesians 1:19–20). This is the literal truth: *"the exceeding greatness of his power,"* which raised Christ from the dead, works in every believer—in me and in you. We hardly believe it, and we experience it even less. This is why Paul prayed, and we must pray with him, that God through His Spirit would teach us to believe in His almighty power. Pray with all your heart: "Father, grant me the Spirit of wisdom, so that I may experience this power in my life."

In Ephesians 3, Paul asked God to grant the Ephesians, *"according to the riches of his glory, to be strengthened with might by his Spirit in the inner man; that Christ may dwell in* [their] *hearts"* (vv. 16–17). And then he added, *"Now unto him that is able to do exceeding abundantly above all that we ask or think, according to the power that worketh in us, unto him be glory"* (vv. 20–21).

Read over these two passages again, and pray for God's Spirit to enlighten your eyes. Believe in the divine power working within you. Pray that the Holy Spirit will reveal it to you, and take hold of the promise that God will manifest His power in your heart, supplying all your needs.

Have you not begun to realize that much time in communion with the Father and the Son is necessary if you want to experience the power of God within you?

The Whole Heart

With my whole heart have I sought thee.
—Psalm 119:10

Notice how often the psalmist spoke about the whole heart in Psalm 119: *"They...that seek him with the whole heart"* (v. 2); *"I shall keep* [Your law] *with my whole heart"* (v. 34); *"I will keep thy precepts with my whole heart"* (v. 69); *"I cried with my whole heart"* (v. 145). In seeking God, in observing His law, in crying for His help—each time it is with the whole heart.

When we want to make anything a success in worldly affairs, we put our whole heart into it. Is this not much more necessary in the service of the holy God? Is He not worthy? Does His great holiness, and the natural aversion of our hearts from God, not demand it? The whole heart is needed in the service of God when we worship Him in secret.

And yet how little most Christians think of this! They do not remember how necessary it is in prayer, in reading God's Word, in striving to do His will, to say continually, *"With my whole heart have I sought thee."* Yes, when we pray, and when we try to understand God's Word and obey His commands, let us say, "I desire to seek God, to serve Him, and to please Him with my whole heart."

"With my whole heart have I sought thee." Dear reader, take these words into your heart. Think over them. Pray over them. Speak them out before God until you feel, "I really mean what I say, and I have the assurance that God will hear my prayer." Say them each morning as you approach God in prayer, "I seek You with my whole heart." You will soon feel the need of waiting in holy stillness upon God, so that He may take possession of your whole heart, and you will learn to love Him with your whole heart and with all your strength.

January 29

In Christ

But of [God] are ye in Christ Jesus.
—1 Corinthians 1:30

The expression *"in Christ"* is often used in the Epistles. The Christian cannot read God's Word correctly, nor experience its full power in his life, until he prayerfully and believingly accepts this truth: I am in Christ Jesus.

The Lord Jesus, on the last night with His disciples, used this expression more than once. He said that when the Spirit had been poured out, *"at that day ye shall know that I am in my Father, and ye in me, and I in you"* (John 14:20). And then follows, *"Abide in Me.... He that abideth in me, and I in him, the same bringeth forth much fruit"* (John 15:4–5); *"If ye abide in me...ye shall ask what ye will, and it shall be done unto you"* (v. 7). But the Christian cannot take hold of these promises unless he first prayerfully accepts the words, *"in Christ."*

Paul expressed the same thought in Romans: *"We are buried with him"* (Romans 6:4); we are *"dead indeed unto sin, but alive unto God through Jesus Christ our Lord"* (v. 11); *"there is therefore now no condemnation to them which are in Christ Jesus"* (Romans 8:1). In Ephesians, Paul wrote that God *"hath blessed us with all spiritual blessings...in Christ"* (Ephesians 1:3); He has *"chosen us in him"* (v. 4); and *"he hath made us accepted in the beloved. In whom we have redemption"* (vv. 6–7). And in Colossians we find: *"In him dwelleth all the fulness"* (Colossians 2:9); we are *"perfect in Christ Jesus"* (Colossians 1:28); *"walk ye in him"* (Colossians 2:6); *"and ye are complete in him"* (v. 10).

Let your faith take hold of these words: it is God who establishes us in Christ. *"He which stablisheth...you in Christ"* (2 Corinthians 1:21). The Holy Spirit will make it your experience. Pray earnestly, and follow the leading of the Spirit. The Word will take root in your heart, and you will realize something of its heavenly power. But remember that abiding in Christ is a matter of the heart. It must be cultivated in a spirit of love. Only as you take time from day to day in fellowship with Christ will the abiding in Christ become a blessed reality, and the inner man will be renewed from day to day.

January 30

Christ in Me

Know ye not…that Jesus Christ is in you?
—2 Corinthians 13:5

The apostle Paul wanted each Christian to live in the full assurance that "Christ is in me." What a difference it would make in our lives if we could take time every morning to be filled with the thought, "Christ is in me"! As surely as I am in Christ, Christ is also in me.

On His last night on earth, Christ clearly told His disciples that the Spirit would teach them: *"At that day ye shall know that I am in my Father, and ye in me, and I in you"* (John 14:20). Through the power of God, all of us who believe were crucified with Christ and raised again with Him. As a result, Christ is in us. But this knowledge does not come easily. Through faith in God's Word, we Christians accept it, and the Holy Spirit will lead us into all truth. (See John 16:13.) Take time this very day to realize and take hold of this blessing in prayer.

Paul clearly expressed this thought in the prayer of Ephesians 3:16–17: *"That* [the Father] *would grant you, according to the riches of his glory"*—notice that it is not the ordinary gift of grace, but a special revelation of the riches of His love and power—*"to be strengthened with might by his Spirit in the inner man; that Christ may dwell in your hearts by faith."* Have you grasped it? Every Christian may really have the experience of being filled with the fullness of God.

Dear Christian, Paul said, *"I bow my knees unto the Father"* (v. 14). That is the only way to obtain the blessing. Take time in the inner chamber to realize, "Christ dwells in me. Too little have I experienced this in the past, but I will cry to God and wait upon Him to perfect His work in me. Even in the midst of my daily work, I must look upon my heart as the dwelling place of the Son of God and say, 'I am crucified with Christ. I live no more; Christ lives in me.' (See Galatians 2:20.) Only in this way will Christ's words, *'Abide in me, and I in you'* (John 15:4), become my daily experience."

January 31

Christ Is All

Christ is all, and in all.
—Colossians 3:11

In the eternal counsel of God, in the redemption on the cross, and as King on the throne in heaven and on earth, *"Christ is all."* In the salvation of sinners, in their justification and sanctification, in the building up of Christ's body, and in the care for individuals, even the most sinful, *"Christ is all."* Every day and every hour, the child of God is comforted and strengthened when he accepts, in faith, that *"Christ is all."*

Perhaps you have thought, in reading these pages, that the full salvation described here is not meant for you. You feel too weak, too unworthy, too untrustworthy. My dear reader, if you will only accept the Lord Jesus in childlike faith you will have a Leader and a Guide who will supply all your needs. (See Philippians 4:19.) Believe with your whole heart in the words of our Savior—*"Lo, I am with you alway*[s]*"* (Matthew 28:20)—and you will experience His presence each day.

However cold and dull your feelings may be, however sinful you are, meet the Lord Jesus in secret, and He will reveal Himself to you. Tell Him how wretched you are, and then trust Him to help and sustain you. Wait before Him until by faith you can rejoice in Him. Read this book year after year, and read it with the thought, *"Christ is all."* You may have failed to remember this at times, but each day as you go into secret prayer, let this thought be with you: *"Christ is all."* Take it as your motto to teach you to pray, to strengthen your faith, to give you the assurance of His love and access to the Father, to make you strong for the work of the day. *"Christ is all."* Yes, Christ, your Christ, is all you need. This will teach you to abide in His love. It will give you the assurance that He dwells in your heart, and you may know *"the love…which passeth knowledge"* (Ephesians 3:19). God be praised to all eternity! Christ, your Christ, is your all in all!

February

February 1

Intercession

Pray one for another.
—James 5:16

What a mystery of glory there is in prayer! On the one hand, we see God, in His holiness and love and power, waiting, longing to bless man; on the other, we see sinful man, a worm of the dust, bringing down from God by prayer the very life and love of heaven to dwell in his heart.

But the glory of intercession is even greater! Through it a man comes boldly to God to say what he desires for others, and through it he seeks to bring down on one soul—or even on hundreds and thousands—the power of eternal life with all its blessings.

Intercession! Would you not say that this is the holiest exercise of our boldness as God's children, the highest privilege and enjoyment connected with our communion with God? It is the power of being used by God as instruments for His great work of making men His habitation and showing forth His glory. Would you not think that the church would consider this one of the chief means of grace and seek above everything to cultivate in God's children the power of an unceasing prayerfulness on behalf of the perishing world? Would you not expect that believers would feel what strength there is in unity and what assurance there is that God will certainly *"avenge his own elect, which cry day and night unto him"* (Luke 18:7)? When Christians cease from looking for help in external union and aim at being bound together to the throne of God by an unceasing devotion to Jesus Christ and by an unceasing continuance in supplication for the power of God's Spirit, the church will put on her beautiful garments and her strength (see Isaiah 52:1) and will overcome the world.

Our gracious Father, hear our prayer and teach Your church the glory, the blessing, and the all-prevailing power of intercession. Give us, we pray, the vision of what intercession means to You; how it is essential for carrying out Your blessed purpose and for bringing down the Spirit in power. Show us what it means to us as the exercise of our royal priesthood, and what it will mean to Your church and to perishing men. Amen.

February 2

The Opening of the Eyes

And Elisha prayed, and said, LORD, I pray thee, open his eyes, that he may see...LORD, open the eyes of these men, that they may see.
—2 Kings 6:17, 20

How wonderfully the prayer of Elisha for his servant was answered! The young man saw the mountain full of chariots of fire and horsemen surrounding Elisha. The heavenly host had been sent by God to protect the Lord's servant.

Then Elisha prayed a second time. The Syrian army had been stricken with blindness and was led into Samaria. There, Elisha prayed for the opening of their eyes, and they found themselves hopeless prisoners in the hand of the enemy.

We ought to use these prayers in the spiritual sphere. First of all, we ought to ask that our eyes may see the wonderful provision that God has made for His church in the baptism with the Holy Spirit and with fire. (See Matthew 3:11.) All the powers of the heavenly world are at our disposal in the service of the heavenly kingdom. How little the children of God live in the faith of that heavenly vision—the power of the Holy Spirit on them, with them, and in them, for their own spiritual life and as their strength to joyfully witness for their Lord and His work!

But we will find that we need that second prayer, too, so that God may open the eyes of those of His children who do not yet see the power that the world and sin have upon His people. They are still unaware of the feebleness that marks the church, making it powerless to do the work of winning souls for Christ and building up believers for a life of holiness and fruitfulness. Let us pray especially that God may open all eyes to see what the great and fundamental need of the church is—to bring down His blessing in intercession, so that the power of the Spirit may be known unceasingly in its divine effectiveness and blessing.

Our Father, who is in heaven, You who are so unspeakably willing to give us the Holy Spirit in power, hear our humble prayer. Open our eyes so that we may realize fully the low estate of Your church and that we may fully know what treasures of grace and power You are willing to bestow in answer to the fervent prayer of a united church. Amen.

Man's Place in God's Plan

The heaven, even the heavens, are the Lord's: but the earth hath he given to the children of men.
—Psalm 115:16

God created heaven as a dwelling for Himself—perfect, glorious, and most holy. The earth He gave to man as his dwelling—everything very good, but only as a beginning, with the need of being kept and cultivated. Man was to continue and perfect the work God had done. Think of the iron and the coal hidden away in the earth, of the steam hidden away in the water. It was left to man to discover and use all this, as we see in the network of railways that span the world and the steamers that cover the ocean. God had created everything to be thus used. But He made the discovery and the use of such things dependent on the wisdom and diligence of man. What the earth is today, with its cities and its cornfields, it owes to man. The work God had begun and prepared was to be carried out by man in fulfillment of God's purpose. And so nature teaches us the wonderful partnership to which God calls man for the carrying out of the work of creation to its destined end.

This principle is equally strong in the kingdom of grace. In His great plan of redemption, God has revealed the power of the heavenly life and the spiritual blessings of which heaven is full. But He has entrusted to His people the work of making these blessings known and of making men partakers of them.

What diligence the children of this world show in seeking the treasures that God has hidden in the earth for their use! Will the children of God not be equally faithful in seeking the treasures hidden in heaven, to bring them down in blessings on the world? It is by the unceasing intercession of God's people that His kingdom will come and His will be done on earth as it is in heaven. (See Luke 11:2.)

Ever blessed Lord, how wonderful is the place You have given man, trusting him to continue the work You have begun. Open our hearts for the great thought that, through the preaching of the gospel and the work of intercession, Your people are to work out Your purpose. Lord, open our eyes, for Jesus' sake. Amen.

Intercession in the Plan of Redemption

O thou that hearest prayer, unto thee shall all flesh come.
—Psalm 65:2

When God gave the world into the power of man, who was made in His own image and who was to rule over it as a representative under Him, it was His plan that Adam should do nothing without God, and God Himself would do all His work in the world through Adam. Adam was to be the owner, master, and ruler of the earth. When sin entered the world, Adam's power was proven to be a terrible reality, for through him the earth, with the whole race of man, was brought under the curse of sin.

When God established the plan of redemption, His objective was to restore man to the place from which he had fallen. God chose servants who, through the power of intercession, could ask what they desired, and it would be given to them. (See John 15:7.) When Christ became man, it was so that, as man, both on earth and in heaven, He might intercede for man. And before He left the world, He imparted this right of intercession to His disciples, in the sevenfold promise of the Farewell Discourse (see John 15–17), that whatever they would ask, He would do for them. God's intense longing to bless seems in some sense to be graciously limited by His dependence on the intercession that rises from the earth. He seeks to rouse the spirit of intercession so that He may be able to bestow His blessings on mankind. God regards intercession as the highest expression of His people's readiness to receive and to yield themselves wholly to the working of His almighty power.

Christians need to realize this as their true nobility and their only power with God—the right to claim and expect that God will hear prayer. Only as God's children begin to see what intercession means in regard to God's kingdom will they realize how solemn their responsibility is.

Each individual believer will be led to see that God waits for him to take his part. He will feel that the highest, the most blessed, the mightiest of all human positions for the fulfillment of the petition, *"as in heaven, so on earth"* (Luke 11:2) is the intercession that rises day and night, pleading with God for the power of heaven to be sent down into the hearts of men. Oh, that God might burn into our hearts this one thought: intercession in its omnipotent power is according to His will and is most certainly effective!

February 5

God Seeks Intercessors

And he saw that there was no man, and wondered that there was no intercessor.
—Isaiah 59:16

In Old Testament times, God had among His people intercessors to whose voices He had listened and given deliverance. In Isaiah 59, we read of a time of trouble when God sought for an intercessor but found none. And He wondered! Think of what that means—the amazement of God that there was no one who loved the people enough, or who had enough faith in His power to deliver, that he would intercede on their behalf. If there had been an intercessor, God would have given deliverance; without an intercessor, His judgments came down. (See Ezekiel 22:30–31.)

Of what infinite importance is the place the intercessor holds in the kingdom of God! Is it not indeed a matter of wonder that God should give men such power, and yet there are so few who know what it is to take hold of His strength and to pray down His blessings on the world?

Let us try to realize this position. When God had worked out the new creation through His Son and Christ had taken His place on the throne, the work of the extension of His kingdom was given into the hands of men. All that Christ was to do in heaven was to be in fellowship with His people on earth. In His divine condescension, God has willed that the working of His Spirit will follow the prayers of His people. He waits for their intercession that shows the preparation of their hearts—where and how much of His Spirit they are ready to receive.

God rules the world and His church through the prayers of His people. God calls for intercessors: in His grace He has made His work dependent on them; He waits for them.

Our Father, open our eyes to see that You invite Your children to have a part in the extension of Your kingdom by their faithfulness in prayer and intercession. Give us an insight into the glory of this holy calling, so that with our whole hearts we may yield ourselves to its blessed service. Amen.

Christ as Intercessor

Wherefore he is able also to save them to the uttermost that come unto God by him, seeing he ever liveth to make intercession for them. —Hebrews 7:25

When God had said in Isaiah that He wondered that there was no intercessor, there followed these words: *"Therefore his arm brought salvation unto him....the Redeemer shall come to Zion"* (Isaiah 59:16, 20). God Himself would provide the true Intercessor, Christ His Son, of whom it had already been said, *"He bare the sin of many, and made intercession for the transgressors"* (Isaiah 53:12).

In His life on earth, Christ began His work as Intercessor. Think of His high-priestly prayer on behalf of His disciples and all who would, through them, believe in His name. Think of His words to Peter: *"I have prayed for thee, that thy faith fail not"* (Luke 22:32)—a proof of how intensely personal His intercession is. And on the cross He spoke as Intercessor: *"Father, forgive them"* (Luke 23:34).

Now that He is seated at God's right hand, He continues, as our great High Priest, the work of intercession without ceasing. But He does so with this difference: He gives His people power to take part in it. Seven times in His Farewell Discourse (see John 15–17) He repeated the assurance that what they asked, He would do.

The power of heaven was to be at their disposal. The grace and power of God waited for man's asking. Through the leading of the Holy Spirit, they would know what the will of God was. They would learn in faith to pray in His name. He would present their petition to the Father, and through His and their united intercession, the church would be clothed with the power of the Spirit.

Blessed Redeemer, what wonderful grace it is that You call us to share in Your intercession! Awake in Your redeemed people an awareness of the glory of this calling, and of all the rich blessings that Your church in its powerlessness can, through its intercession in Your name, bring down upon this earth. May Your Holy Spirit work in Your people a deep conviction of the sin of prayerlessness, of the sloth and unbelief and selfishness that are the cause of it, and of Your loving desire to pour out the Spirit of prayer in answer to their petitions, for Your name's sake. Amen.

The Intercessors God Seeks

I have set watchmen upon thy walls, O Jerusalem, which shall never hold their peace day nor night: ye that make mention of the LORD, keep not silence. And give him no rest. —Isaiah 62:6–7

Watchmen were ordinarily placed on the walls of a city to give notice to the rulers of coming danger. Similarly, God appoints watchmen not only to warn men—often they will not hear—but also to summon Him to come to their aid whenever need or enemies may be threatening. The great mark of intercessors is that they are not to hold their peace day or night; they are to take no rest, and to give God no rest, until the deliverance comes. In faith they may be assured that God will answer their prayers.

It is concerning this that our Lord Jesus said, *"shall not God avenge his own elect, which cry day and night unto him?"* (Luke 18:7). From every land the voice is heard that the church of Christ, under the influence of the power of the world, is losing its influence over its members. There is little proof of God's presence in the conversion of sinners or in the holiness of His people. With the great majority of Christians, there is an utter neglect of Christ's call to take part in the spreading of His gospel. The power of the Holy Spirit is experienced very little.

Amid all the discussions as to what can be done to interest young and old in the study of God's Word, one seldom hears of the indispensable necessity of the power of the Holy Spirit in the membership of the church. Few people are truly convinced that it is owing to the lack of prayer that the workings of the Spirit are so feeble, and many people fail to see that only through fervent prayer can change be brought about. If ever there was a time when God's elect should cry out to Him, it is now. Will you not offer yourself to God for this blessed work of intercession and learn to consider it the highest privilege of your life to be a channel through whose prayers God's blessings can be brought down to earth?

Ever blessed Father, hear us, we pray, and raise up the intercessors that You require. Give us men and women to act as Your watchmen, taking no rest and giving You no rest, until Your church again is praised in the earth. Blessed Father, let Your Spirit teach us how to pray. Amen.

February 8

The School of Intercession

Who in the days of his flesh, when he had offered up prayers and supplications with strong crying and tears...was heard in that he feared. —Hebrews 5:7

Christ, as the Head of the church, is Intercessor in heaven; we, as the members of His body, are partners with Him on earth. Let no one imagine that it cost Christ nothing to become an intercessor. He is our example because of the enormous price He paid. What do we read about Him? *"When thou shalt make his soul an offering for sin, he shall see his seed....He shall see of the travail of his soul....Therefore will I divide him a portion with the great...because he hath poured out his soul unto death"* (Isaiah 53:10–12). Notice the repeated expression in regard to the pouring out of His soul.

The pouring out of the soul is the divine meaning of intercession—nothing less than this was needed if His sacrifice and prayer were to have power with God. This giving over of Himself to live and die so that He might save the perishing was a revelation of the spirit that has power to prevail with God.

If we, as helpers and fellow laborers with the Lord Jesus, are to share His power of intercession, we will need to have the travail of soul that He had, the same giving up of our life and its pleasures for the one supreme work of interceding for our fellowmen. Intercession must not be a passing interest; it must become an ever growing object of intense desire, for which we long and live above everything else. It is the life of consecration and self-sacrifice that will indeed give power for intercession.

The longer we study this blessed truth and think of what it means to exercise this power for the glory of God and the salvation of men, the deeper our conviction will become that it is worth giving up everything to take part with Christ in His work of intercession.

Blessed Lord Jesus, teach us how to unite with You in calling upon God for the souls You have bought. Let Your love fill us and all Your saints, so that we may learn to plead for the power of Your Holy Spirit to be made known. Amen.

The Name of Jesus, Intercession's Power

Hitherto have ye asked nothing in my name: ask, and ye shall receive, that your joy may be full....At that day ye shall ask in my name.
—John 16:24, 26

During Christ's life on earth, the disciples had known little of the power of prayer. In Gethsemane, Peter and the others utterly failed. They had no concept of what it meant to ask in the name of Jesus and to receive. The Lord promised them that, in the day that was coming, they would be able to pray with such a power in His name that they would ask what they desired and it would be given to them.

"Hitherto...nothing." "At that day ye shall ask in my name" and *"shall receive."* These two conditions are still found in the church. With the great majority of Christians, there is such a lack of knowledge of their oneness with Christ Jesus, and of the Holy Spirit as the Spirit of prayer, that they do not even attempt to claim the wonderful promises Christ gave here. But when God's children know what it means to abide in Christ in vital union with Him and to yield to the Holy Spirit's teaching, they begin to learn that their intercession is effective and that God will give the power of His Spirit in answer to their prayers.

It is faith in the power of Jesus' name and in our right to use it that will give us the courage to follow where God invites us—to the holy office of intercessors. When our Lord Jesus, in His Farewell Discourse, gave His unlimited prayer promise, He sent the disciples out into the world with this thought: "He who sits upon the throne and lives in my heart has promised that what I ask in His name I will receive. He will do it."

Oh, if Christians only knew what it means to yield themselves wholly and absolutely to Jesus Christ and His service, how their eyes would be opened to see that intense and unceasing prayerfulness is the essential mark of the healthy spiritual life! They would see that the power of all-prevailing intercession will indeed be the portion of those who live only in and for their Lord.

Blessed Savior, give us the grace of the Holy Spirit to live in You, with You, and for You to such a degree that we may boldly look to You for the assurance that our prayers are heard. Amen.

February 10

Prayer, the Work of the Spirit

God hath sent forth the Spirit of his Son into your hearts, crying, Abba, Father.
—Galatians 4:6

We know what *"Abba, Father"* meant in the mouth of Christ at Gethsemane. It was the entire surrender of Himself to death, so that the holy will of God's love in the redemption of sinners might be accomplished. In His prayer, He was ready for any sacrifice, even the yielding of His life. In that prayer, the heart of Him whose place is at the right hand of God is revealed to us, with the wonderful power of intercession that He exercises there and the power to pour down the Holy Spirit.

The Holy Spirit has been bestowed by the Father to breathe the very Spirit of His Son into our hearts. Our Lord desires us to yield ourselves as wholly to God as He did—to pray as He did, that God's will of love would be done on earth at any cost. As God's love is revealed in His desire for the salvation of souls, so also the desire of Jesus was made plain when He gave Himself for them. And He now asks that the same love would fill His people, too, so that they would give themselves wholly to the work of intercession and, at any cost, pray down God's love upon the perishing world.

Lest anyone should begin to think that this is beyond his reach, the Holy Spirit of Jesus is actually given into our hearts so that we may pray in His likeness, in His name, and in His power. The man who yields himself wholly to the leading of the Holy Spirit will feel urged, by the compulsion of a divine love, to surrender himself completely to a life of continual intercession, because he knows that it is God who is working in him.

Now we can understand how Christ could give such unlimited promises of answer to prayer to His disciples: they were first going to be filled with the Holy Spirit. Now we understand how God can give such a high place to intercession in the fulfillment of His purpose of redemption. It is the Holy Spirit who breathes God's own desire into us and enables us to intercede for souls.

"Abba, Father!" Grant, by Your Holy Spirit, that there may be maintained in us the unceasing intercession of love for the souls for whom Christ died. Give to Your children the vision of the blessedness and power that come to those who yield themselves to this high calling. Amen.

Christ, Our Example in Intercession

He shall divide the spoil with the strong; because...he bare the sin of many, and made intercession for the transgressors.
—Isaiah 53:12

Christ *"made intercession for the transgressors."* What did that mean to Him? Think of what it cost Him to pray that prayer effectively. He had to pour out His soul as an offering for sin, and He had to cry at Gethsemane, "Father, Your holy will of love be done."

Think of what moved Him thus to sacrifice Himself to the very uttermost! It was His love for the Father, so that His holiness might be manifested, and His love for souls, so that they might be partakers of His holiness.

Think of the reward He won! As Conqueror of every enemy, He is seated at the right hand of God with the power of unlimited and assured intercession. And He desires to *"see his seed"* (Isaiah 53:10), a generation of those who have the same mind as Himself, whom He can train to share in His great work of intercession.

And what does this mean for us, when we seek to pray for the transgressors? That we, too, yield ourselves wholly to the glory of the holiness and the love of the Father; that we, too, say, "God's will be done, no matter what it may cost"; that we, too, sacrifice ourselves, even to pouring out our souls unto death.

The Lord Jesus has taken us up into a partnership with Himself in carrying out the great work of intercession. He in heaven and we on earth must have one mind, one aim in life: that we, out of love for the Father and for the lost, consecrate our lives to intercession for God's blessing. The burning desire of Father and Son for the salvation of souls must be the burning desire of our hearts, too.

What an honor! What blessedness! And what a power for us to do the work because He lives and because, by His Spirit, He pours forth His love into our hearts! (See Romans 5:5.)

Everlasting God of love, open our eyes to the vision of the glory of Your Son, who always lives to pray. (See Hebrews 7:25.) Open our eyes to the glory of the grace that enables us to live in His likeness so that we may pray for the transgressors. For Jesus' sake. Amen.

February 12

God's Will and Ours

Thy will be done.
—Matthew 26:42

It is the high prerogative of God that everything in heaven and earth is to be done according to His will and as the fulfillment of His desires. When He made man in His image, man's desires were intended to be in perfect accord with the desires of God. This is the high honor of being made in the likeness of God—that we are to feel and wish just as God does. In human flesh, man was to be the embodiment and fulfillment of God's desires.

When God created man with the power of willing and choosing what he should be, He limited Himself in the exercise of His will. And when man had fallen and yielded himself to the will of God's enemy, God in His infinite love set about the great work of winning man back and of making the desires of God his own. As desire is the great motivating power in God, so it is in man. And just as man had yielded himself to a life of desire after the things of the earth and the flesh, God had to redeem him and educate him into a life of harmony with Himself. His one aim was that man's desires would be in perfect accord with His own.

The great step in this direction was when the Son of the Father came into this world. He reproduced the divine desires in His human nature and in His prayer to yield Himself up to the perfect fulfillment of all that God wished and willed. The Son, as Man, said in agony and blood, *"Thy will be done,"* and made the surrender even to being forsaken by God, so that the power that had deceived man might be conquered and deliverance might be procured. It was in the wonderful and complete harmony between the Father and the Son when the Son said, *"Thy will* [of love] *be done,"* that the great redemption was accomplished.

In taking hold of that redemption, believers have to say, first of all for themselves and then in lives devoted to intercession for others, "Your will be done in heaven as on earth." (See Matthew 6:10.) As we plead for the church, its ministers, and its missionaries, its strong Christians and its young converts, and for the unsaved, whether nominally Christian or unchurched, we have the privilege of knowing that we are pleading for what God wills, and that through our prayers His will is to be done on earth as in heaven.

February 13

The Blessedness of a Life of Intercession

Ye that make mention of the LORD, keep not silence. And give him no rest, till he establish, and till he make Jerusalem a praise in the earth. —Isaiah 62:6–7

What unspeakable grace to be allowed to deal with God in intercession for the supply of the needs of others!

What a blessing, in close union with Christ, to take part in His great work as Intercessor and to mingle my prayers with His! What an honor to have power with God in heaven over souls and to obtain for them what they do not know or think!

What a privilege, as a steward of the grace of God, to bring to Him the state of the church or of individual souls, of the ministers of the Word or His messengers working among the unsaved, and plead on their behalf until He entrusts me with the answer!

What blessedness, in union with other children of God, to strive together in prayer until the victory is gained over difficulties here on earth, or over the powers of darkness in high places!

It is indeed worth living for the knowledge that God will use me as an intercessor, to receive and dispense here on earth His heavenly blessing and, above all, the power of His Holy Spirit.

This is the life of heaven, the life of the Lord Jesus Himself, in His self-denying love, taking possession of me and urging me to yield myself wholly to bear the burden of souls before Him, and to plead that they may live.

For too long we have thought of prayer simply as a means for supplying our needs in life and service. May God help us to see the place intercession takes in His divine counsel and in His work for the kingdom. And may our hearts indeed feel that there is no honor or blessedness on earth at all equal to the unspeakable privilege of waiting upon God and of bringing down from heaven the blessings He delights to give!

O my Father, let Your life flow down to this earth and fill the hearts of Your children! As the Lord Jesus pours out His love in His unceasing intercession in heaven, let it be the same with us also upon earth—a life of overflowing love and never-ending intercession. Amen.

February 14

The Place of Prayer

These all continued with one accord in prayer and supplication. —Acts 1:14

Christ instructed His disciples to *"wait for the promise of the Father"* (v. 4). He also said, *"But ye shall receive power, after that the Holy Ghost is come upon you: and ye shall be witnesses unto me both in Jerusalem...and unto the uttermost part of the earth"* (v. 8).

United and unceasing prayer, the power of the Holy Spirit, living witnesses to the living Christ from Jerusalem to the end of the earth—such are the marks of the true gospel, the true ministry, the true church of the New Testament.

A church of united and unceasing prayerfulness, a ministry filled with the Holy Spirit, the members living witnesses to a living Christ, with a message to every creature on earth—such was the church that Christ founded, and such was the church that went out to conquer the world.

When Christ had ascended to heaven, the disciples knew at once what their work was to be: continuing *"with one accord in prayer and supplication."* They were to be bound together into one body by the love and Spirit of Christ. This gave them their wonderful power in heaven with God, and upon earth with men.

Their own duty was to wait in united and unceasing prayer for the power of the Holy Spirit, the power to be witnesses for Christ to the end of the earth. A praying church, a Spirit-filled church, a witnessing church, with the entire world as its sphere and aim—such is the church of Jesus Christ.

As long as it maintained this character, the church had power to conquer. However, as it came under the influence of the world, it lost so much of its heavenly, supernatural beauty and strength! How unfaithful in prayer, how feeble the workings of the Spirit, how formal its witness to Christ, and how unfaithful to its worldwide mission!

Blessed Lord Jesus, have mercy upon Your church and give us the Spirit of prayer and supplication the early church had, so that we may prove that Your power rests upon us and our testimony for You, to win the world to You. Amen.

Paul as an Intercessor

I bow my knees unto the Father...that he would grant you...to be strengthened with might by his Spirit.
—Ephesians 3:14, 16

We think of Paul as the great missionary, preacher, writer, and apostle *"in labours more abundant"* (2 Corinthians 11:23). We do not think of him as the intercessor that sought and obtained, by his supplication, the power that rested on the churches that he served.

Look beyond what he wrote to the Ephesians. Think of what he said to the Thessalonians: *"Night and day praying exceedingly that we might see your face, and might perfect that which is lacking in your faith...to the end he may stablish your hearts unblameable in holiness"* (1 Thessalonians 3:10, 13). To the Romans he said, *"Without ceasing I make mention of you always in my prayers"* (Romans 1:9). To the Philippians he wrote, *"Always in every prayer of mine for you all making request with joy"* (Philippians 1:4). And to the Colossians it was, "[We] *do not cease to pray for you...for I would that ye knew what great conflict I have for you"* (Colossians 1:9; 2:1).

Day and night he cried to God in his intercession for them, that the light and the power of the Holy Spirit might be in them. As earnestly as he believed in the power of his intercession for them, so did he also believe in the blessings that their prayers would bring upon him: *"I beseech you...that ye strive together with me in your prayers to God for me"* (Romans 15:30); "[God] *will yet deliver us; ye also helping together by prayer for us"* (2 Corinthians 1:10–11); *"Praying...*[also] *for me...that I may open my mouth boldly"* (Ephesians 6:18–19); *"this shall turn to my salvation through your prayer"* (Philippians 1:19).

The whole relationship between pastor and people depends on their united, continual prayerfulness. Their whole relationship to each other is a heavenly one and can only be maintained by unceasing prayer. When believers wake up to see that the power and blessing of the Holy Spirit are waiting for their unceasing prayer, the church will begin to know what Pentecostal apostolic Christianity is.

Ever blessed Father, we humbly pray that You will restore again graciously to Your church the spirit of supplication and intercession, for Jesus' sake. Amen.

Intercession for Laborers

The harvest truly is plenteous, but the labourers are few; pray ye therefore the Lord of the harvest, that he will send forth labourers into his harvest. —Matthew 9:37–38

The disciples understood little of what these words meant. Christ gave these words as seeds to be lodged in their hearts for later use. At Pentecost, as they saw how many of the new converts were ready in the power of the Spirit to testify of Christ, they must have felt that the ten days of continuous prayer had brought this blessing of laborers in the harvest as the fruit of the Spirit's power.

Christ meant to teach us that, however large the field and however few the laborers, prayer is the best, the surest, the only means for supplying the need.

What we need to understand is that prayer must be sent up not only in the time of need, but also in the time of plenty. The whole work is to be carried on in the spirit of prayer so that the prayer for laborers will be in perfect harmony with the whole of our lives and efforts.

At one time in the China Inland Mission, the number of missionaries had risen to two hundred. But there was still such a deep need for more laborers in some districts that, after much prayer, the attendees at a certain conference felt at liberty to ask God to give them one hundred additional laborers and $10,000 to meet the expenses. They agreed to continue in prayer every day throughout the year. At the end of the time, the one hundred suitable men and women had been found, along with $11,000.

To meet the need of the world, its open fields, and waiting souls, the churches all complain of the lack of laborers and of funds. Does not Christ's voice call us to the united and unceasing prayer that the first disciples had? God is faithful, by the power of His Spirit, to supply every need. Let the church take the posture of united prayer and supplication. God hears our prayer.

Blessed Lord Jesus, teach Your church what it means to live and work for You in the spirit of unceasing prayerfulness so that our faith may rise in the assurance that You will meet the dire needs of a dying world beyond all our expectations. Amen.

February 17

Intercession for Individual Souls

Ye shall be gathered one by one, O ye children of Israel.
—Isaiah 27:12

In our bodies, every member has its appointed place. The same is true in society and in the church. The work must always aim at the welfare and the highest perfection of the whole, through the cooperation of every individual member.

In the church, the thought is too prevalent that the salvation of men is the work of the minister. But the minister generally only deals with the crowd, seldom reaching the individual. This is the cause of a twofold evil. First, the individual believer does not understand that it is necessary for him to testify to those around him for the nourishment and strengthening of his own spiritual life and for the ingathering of souls. Second, unconverted souls suffer unspeakable loss because Christ is not personally brought to them by each believer they meet.

Intercession for those around us is far too rare. Its restoration to its right place in the Christian life—how much that would mean to the church and its missions! Oh, when will Christians learn the great truth that what God desires to do needs prayer on earth? As we realize this, we will see that intercession is the chief element in the conversion of souls. Only when ministers and people unite in a covenant of prayer and testimony will the church flourish, and every believer will understand the part he has to take.

And what can we do to stir up the spirit of intercession? There is a twofold answer. Every Christian, as he begins to get insight into the need and the power of intercession, must begin to intercede on behalf of other individuals. Pray for your children, for your relatives and friends, for all with whom God brings you into contact. If you find that you do not have the power to intercede, let this discovery humble you and drive you to the mercy seat. God wants every redeemed child of His to intercede for the perishing. Prayer is the vital breath of the normal Christian life, the proof that it is born from above.

Then pray intensely and persistently that God may give the power of His Holy Spirit to you and to those around you, so that the power of intercession may have the place that God will honor.

Intercession for Ministers

Praying also for us.
—Colossians 4:3

Finally, brethren, pray for us.
—2 Thessalonians 3:1

These expressions from Paul suggest his conviction that Christians had power with God and that their prayers would bring new strength to him in his work. Paul had such a sense of the unity of the body of Christ, of the interdependence of each member—even the most honorable—on the life that flowed through the whole body, that he sought to rouse Christians, for their own sakes and for his sake and for the sake of the kingdom of God, with this call: *"Continue in prayer, and watch in the same with thanksgiving; withal praying also for us"* (Colossians 4:2–3).

The church depends on the ministry to an extent that we very seldom realize. The place of the minister is so high—he is the steward of the mysteries of God, the ambassador for God to beseech men to be reconciled to Him—that any unfaithfulness or inefficiency in him must bring a terrible blight on the church that he serves. If Paul, after having preached for twenty years in the power of God, still needed the prayers of the church, how much more does the ministry in our day need them?

The minister needs the prayers of his people. He has a right to them. He is dependent on them. It is his task to train Christians for their work of intercession on behalf of the church and the world. He must begin by training them to pray for himself. He may even have to learn to pray more for himself and for them.

Let all intercessors who seek to enter more deeply into their blessed work give a larger place to the ministers, both of their own church and of other churches. Let them plead with God for individual men and for special circles. Let them continue in prayer, so that ministers may be men of power, men of prayer, and men full of the Holy Spirit. Fellow Christians, pray for the ministers!

Our Father in heaven, we humbly ask You to arouse believers to a sense of their calling to pray for the ministers of the gospel in the spirit of faith. Amen.

February 19

Prayer for All Believers

With all prayer and supplication praying at all seasons in the Spirit, and watching thereunto in all perseverance and supplication for all the saints.
—Ephesians 6:18 (RV)

Notice how Paul repeated the words in the intensity of his desire to reach the hearts of his readers: *"With all prayer and supplication praying at all seasons...watching thereunto in all perseverance and supplication."* It is *"all prayer...all seasons...all perseverance and supplication."*

Paul felt so deeply the unity of the body of Christ, and he was so sure that that unity could only be realized in the exercise of love and prayer, that he pleaded with the believers at Ephesus to pray unceasingly and fervently for all believers, not only all believers in their immediate circle, but also all believers in all the church of Christ of whom they might hear. Paul knew that unity is strength. As we exercise this power of intercession with all perseverance, we will be delivered from self with all its feeble prayers, and our hearts will be enlarged so that the love of Christ can flow freely and fully through us.

The great lack in true believers often is that, in prayer, they are occupied with themselves and with what God must do for them. Here we have a call to every believer to give himself without ceasing to the exercise of love and prayer. As we forget ourselves, in the faith that God will take charge of us, and as we yield ourselves to the great and blessed work of calling down the blessings of God on our fellowmen, the whole church will be equipped to do its work in making Christ known to every creature. This alone is the healthy and blessed life of a child of God who has yielded himself wholly to Christ Jesus.

Pray for God's children and the church around you. Pray for all the work in which they are engaged, or ought to be. Pray *"at all seasons in the Spirit"* for all believers. There is no blessedness greater than that of abiding communion with God. And there is no way that leads to the enjoyment of this more surely than the life of intercession for which these words of Paul appeal so pleadingly.

Missionary Intercession

And when they had fasted and prayed, and laid their hands on them, they sent them away.
—Acts 13:3

The supreme question of foreign missions is, How do we multiply the number of Christians who will individually and collectively wield this force of intercession for the conversion and transformation of men? Every other consideration and plan is secondary to that of wielding the forces of prayer.

We take for granted that those who love this work and who bear it in their hearts will follow the scriptural command to pray unceasingly for its triumph. With unceasing devotion and intercession, God's people need to approach Him with an attitude that refuses to let God go until He crowns His workers with victory.

Missions have their root in the love of Christ, which was proven on the cross and now lives in our hearts. As men are so earnest in seeking to carry out God's plans for the natural world, so God's children should be at least as wholehearted in seeking to bring Christ's love to all mankind. Intercession is the chief means appointed by God to bring the great redemption within the reach of all.

Pray for missionaries, that the life of Christ may be clear and strong, and that they may be people of prayer, filled with love, people in whom the power of the spiritual life is obvious.

Pray for Christians, that they may know *"the glory of this mystery among the Gentiles* [the unsaved]*: which is Christ in you, the hope of glory"* (Colossians 1:27).

Pray for the teaching of God's Word, that it may be in power. Pray especially for pastors and evangelists, that the Holy Spirit may fill them to be witnesses for Christ among their fellowmen.

Pray, above all, for the church of Christ, that it may be lifted out of its indifference, and that every believer may be brought to understand that the one purpose of his life is to help to make Christ King on the earth.

Our gracious God, our eyes are focused on You. Will You not in mercy hear our prayers, and by the Holy Spirit reveal the presence and the power of Christ in the work of Your servants? Amen.

The Grace of Intercession

Continue in prayer, and watch in the same with thanksgiving; withal praying also for us.
—Colossians 4:2–3

Nothing can give us a higher experience of the likeness of God than the power of pouring out our hearts to God in prayer for those around us. Nothing can so closely link us to Jesus Christ, the great Intercessor, and give us the experience of His power and Spirit resting on us, as the yielding of our lives to the work of bringing the great redemption into the hearts and lives of our fellowmen. There is nothing in which we will know more of the powerful working of the Holy Spirit than the prayer breathed by Him into our hearts, *"Abba, Father"* (Mark 14:36), in all the fullness of meaning that it had for Christ at Gethsemane.

Nothing can so help us to prove the power and faithfulness of God to His Word as when we reach out in intercession to the multitudes, either in the church of Christ or in the darkness of heathenism. As we pour out our souls before God with the one persistent plea that He will open the windows of heaven and send down His abundant blessings, God will be glorified, our souls will reach their highest destiny, and God's kingdom will come.

Nothing will help us to understand and experience the living unity of the body of Christ, and the irresistible power that it can exert, so much as uniting with God's children in the persistent plea that God *"shalt arise, and have mercy upon Zion"* (Psalm 102:13), and will make her a *"light to them that sit in darkness"* (Luke 1:79). My brothers and sisters in Christ, how little we realize what we are losing by not living in fervent intercession! Think of what we will gain for ourselves and for the world if we allow God's Spirit, as a Spirit of grace and of supplication, to master our whole beings!

In heaven, Christ lives to pray. (See Hebrews 7:25.) His whole fellowship with His Father is prayer—an asking and receiving of the fullness of the Spirit for His people. God delights in nothing so much as prayer. Will we not learn to believe that the highest blessings of heaven will be unfolded to us as we pray more?

Blessed Father, pour down the Spirit of supplication and intercession on Your people, for Jesus Christ's sake. Amen.

United Intercession

There is one body, and one Spirit.
—Ephesians 4:4

Our own bodies teach us how essential it is for every member to seek the welfare of the whole. It is the same in the body of Christ. There are, unfortunately, too many who look upon salvation only in connection with their own happiness. There are also those who know that they do not live for themselves, and they truly seek to bring others to share in their happiness; but they do not yet understand that, in addition to their personal circle or church, they have a calling to include the whole body of Christ Jesus in their love and their intercession.

Only when intercession for the whole church, by the whole church, ascends to God's throne, can the Spirit of unity and of power have His full influence. The desire that has been awakened for closer union among the different branches of the church of Christ is cause for thanksgiving. And yet the difficulties are so great and, in the case of different nationalities of the world, so apparently insurmountable, that the thought of a united church on earth appears beyond reach.

Let us bless God that there is unity in Christ Jesus, deeper and stronger than any visible manifestation could make it. Let us thank Him that there is a way in which, even now, amid the diversity of denominations, the unity can be practically exemplified and utilized in order to access previously unknown divine strength and blessings in the work of the kingdom. Only in the cultivation and increase of intercession can true unity be realized. As believers are taught the meaning of their calling as *"a royal priesthood"* (1 Peter 2:9), they are led to see that God's love and promises are not confined to their limited spheres of labor. Rather, He invites them to enlarge their hearts, and like Christ—and also like Paul, I might say—to pray for all who believe, or who may still be brought to believe, that this earth and the church of Christ in it will by intercession be bound to the throne of heaven, as it has never been before.

Christians and ministers must bind themselves together for this worldwide intercession. This unity will strengthen the confidence that prayer will be heard and that their prayers will become indispensable for the coming of the kingdom.

Unceasing Intercession

Pray without ceasing.
—1 Thessalonians 5:17

How different is the standard of the average Christian, with regard to a life in the service of God, from that which Scripture gives us! In the former the chief thought is personal safety—grace to pardon his sin and to live the kind of life that will secure his entrance into heaven. How high above this is the Bible standard—a Christian surrendering himself with all his powers, with his time, thoughts, and love wholly yielded to the glorious God who has redeemed him! He now delights in serving this God, in whose fellowship heaven is begun.

To the average Christian, the command, *"Pray without ceasing,"* is simply a needless and impossible life of perfection. Who can do it? We can get to heaven without it. To the true believer, on the contrary, it holds out the promise of the highest happiness, of a life crowned by all the blessings that can be brought down on other souls through his intercession. And as he perseveres, unceasing intercession becomes increasingly his highest aim upon earth, his highest joy, his highest experience of the wonderful fellowship with the holy God.

"Pray without ceasing." Let us take hold of these words with a large faith, as a promise of what God's Spirit will work in us, of how close and intimate our union to the Lord Jesus can be, and of our likeness to Him, in His ever blessed intercession at the right hand of God. Let these words become to us one of the chief elements of our heavenly calling, to be consciously the stewards and administrators of God's grace to the world around us. As we think of how Christ said, *"I in them, and thou in me"* (John 17:23), let us believe that just as the Father worked in Him, so Christ the interceding High Priest will work and pray in us. As the faith of our high calling fills our hearts, we will begin literally to feel that there is nothing on earth for one moment to be compared to the privilege of being God's priests, walking without intermission in His holy presence, bringing the burdens of the souls around us to the footstool of His throne, and receiving at His hands the power and blessing to dispense to our fellowmen.

This is indeed the fulfillment of the Scriptures that say, "Man was created in the likeness and the image of God." (See Genesis 1:26–27.)

The Link Between Heaven and Earth

Thy will be done, as in heaven, so in earth.
—Luke 11:2

When God created heaven and earth, He meant heaven to be the divine pattern to which earth was to be conformed; *"as in heaven, so in earth"* was to be the law of its existence.

This Scripture calls us to think of what constitutes the glory of heaven. God is all in all there. Everything lives in Him and for His glory. As we think of what this earth has now become—with all its sin and misery, with the great majority of people lacking any knowledge of the true God, and with the remainder living only as nominal Christians who are for the most part estranged from His holiness and love—we feel what a miracle is needed if these words are to be fulfilled: *"As in heaven, so in earth."*

How is this ever to come true? Only through the prayers of God's children. Our Lord taught us to pray for it. Intercession is the great link between heaven and earth. The intercession of the Son, begun on earth, continued in heaven, and carried on by His redeemed people on earth, will bring about the mighty change—*"in earth as it is in heaven"* (Matthew 6:10). Christ's redeemed ones make His prayer their own and unceasingly send up the cry, *"Thy will be done, as in heaven, so in earth."*

Every prayer of a parent for a child, every prayer of a believer for the saving of the lost or for more grace for those who have been saved, is part of the great unceasing cry going up day and night from this earth: *"As in heaven, so in earth."*

But when God's children not only learn to pray for their immediate circles and interests, but also enlarge their hearts to take in the whole church and the whole world, then their united supplication will have power with God and will hurry the day when it will indeed be *"as in heaven, so in earth"*—the whole earth filled with the glory of God. Child of God, will you not yield yourself, like Christ, to live with this one prayer: *"Our Father...thy will be done, as in heaven, so in earth"*?

"Our Father which art in heaven, hallowed be thy name. Thy kingdom come. Thy will be done, as in heaven, so in earth" (Luke 11:2). Amen.

February 25

The Fulfillment of God's Desire

For the LORD hath chosen Zion; he hath desired it for his habitation....here will I dwell; for I have desired it.
—Psalm 132:13–14

Here you have the one great desire of God that moved Him in the work of redemption. His heart longed for man; He desired to dwell with him and in him.

To Moses He said, *"And let them make me a sanctuary; that I may dwell among them"* (Exodus 25:8). And just as Israel had to prepare the dwelling for God, His children are now called to yield themselves to God so that He might dwell in them and they might win others to become His habitation.

What an honor! What a high calling, to count my worldly business as entirely secondary and to find my life and my delight in winning souls, in whom God finds His heart's delight! *"Here will I dwell, for I have desired it."*

And this is what I can do through intercession. I can pray for those around me, that God would give them His Holy Spirit. God's great plan is that man himself will build Him a habitation. In answer to the unceasing intercession of His children, God will give His power and blessing. As this great desire of God fills us, we will give ourselves wholly to work for its fulfillment.

When David thought of God's desire to dwell in Israel, he said, *"I will not give sleep to mine eyes, or slumber to mine eyelids, until I find out a place for the LORD, an habitation for the mighty God of Jacob"* (Psalm 132:4). And since it has been revealed to us what that indwelling of God may be, should we not give our lives for the fulfillment of His heart's desire?

Oh, let us begin, as never before, to pray for our children, for the souls around us, and for all the world—not only because we love them, but especially because God longs for them and gives us the honor of being the channels through whom His blessings are brought down upon them. Children of God, awaken to the realization that God is seeking to train you as intercessors, through whom the great desire of His loving heart can be satisfied!

O God, who has said of human hearts, *"Here will I dwell, for I have desired it,"* teach us to pray, day and night, that the desire of Your heart may be fulfilled. Amen.

The Fulfillment of Man's Desires

Delight thyself also in the LORD; and he shall give thee the desires of thine heart.
—Psalm 37:4

God is love, an ever flowing fountain out of which streams the unceasing desire to make His creatures the partakers of all the holiness (see Hebrews 12:10) and blessedness in Himself. This desire for the salvation of souls is God's perfect will, His highest glory.

To all His children who are willing to yield themselves wholly to Him, God imparts His desire to take His place in the hearts of all men. It is in this that the likeness and image of God consist: to have a heart in which His love takes complete possession and leads us to find our highest joy in loving as He does.

It is thus that our text finds its fulfillment: *"Delight thyself also in the LORD"* and in His life of love, *"and he shall give thee the desires of thine heart."* You can be sure that the intercession of love, rising up to heaven, will be met with the fulfillment of the desires of our hearts. As we delight in what God delights in, such prayer is inspired by God and will have its answer. And our prayer becomes unceasingly, "Your desires, my Father, are mine. Your holy will of love is my will, too."

In fellowship with Him, we acquire the courage to bring our concerns before the Lord in an ever-growing confidence that our prayers will be heard. As we reach out in love, we will obtain power to take hold of the will and the blessings of God. We will also begin to believe that God will work out His own blessed will in giving us the desires of our hearts, because the fulfillment of His desire has been the delight of our souls.

We then become, in the highest sense of the word, God's fellow laborers. Our prayers become part of God's divine work of reaching and saving the lost. And we learn to find our happiness in losing ourselves in the salvation of those around us.

Dear Father, teach us that nothing less than delighting in You and Your desires toward men can inspire us to pray correctly or can give us the assurance of an answer. Amen.

My Great Desire

One thing have I desired of the LORD, that will I seek after; that I may dwell in the house of the LORD all the days of my life, to behold the beauty of the LORD, and to inquire in his temple.
—Psalm 27:4

Here we have man's response to God's desire to dwell in us. When the desire of God toward us begins to rule our lives and hearts, our desire is fixed on one thing, and that is to dwell in the house of the Lord all the days of our lives, to behold the beauty of the Lord, to worship Him in the beauty of holiness, and then to inquire in His temple and to learn what He meant when He said, *"I the LORD have spoken it, and I will do it.…I will yet for this be inquired of by the house of Israel, to do it for them"* (Ezekiel 36:36–37).

The more we realize the desire of God's love to put His rest in our hearts, and the more we desire to dwell every day in His temple and to behold His beauty, the more the Spirit of intercession will grow upon us, to claim all that God has promised in His new covenant. Whether we think of our church or country, of our home or school, of people close to us or far away; whether we think of the saved and all their needs or the unsaved and their danger, the thought that God is longing to find His home in the hearts of men if we only *"inquire"* of Him will rouse us entirely. All the thoughts of our feebleness and unworthiness will be swallowed up in the wonderful assurance that He has said of human hearts, *"This is my rest for ever: here will I dwell; for I have desired it"* (Psalm 132:14).

As we see by faith how indispensable God has made fervent, intense, persistent prayer as the condition of His purpose being fulfilled, we will be drawn to give up our lives to a closer walk with God, to an unceasing waiting upon Him, and to a testimony to our fellow man of what God will do in them and in us.

Isn't this divine partnership wonderful beyond all thought, in which God commits the fulfillment of His desires to our keeping? We should be ashamed that we have largely failed to realize it!

Our Father in heaven, we ask that You would give the Spirit of grace and supplication to Your people, for Jesus' sake. Amen.

Intercession Day and Night

And shall not God avenge his own elect, which cry day and night unto him, though he bear long with them?
—Luke 18:7

When Nehemiah heard of the destruction of Jerusalem, he cried to God, *"Hear the prayer of thy servant, which I pray before thee now, day and night"* (Nehemiah 1:6). Concerning the watchman on the walls of Jerusalem, God said, *"Which shall never hold their peace day nor night"* (Isaiah 62:6). And Paul wrote, *"Night and day praying exceedingly...to the end he may stablish your hearts unblameable in holiness before God, even our Father"* (1 Thessalonians 3:10, 13).

Is such prayer really possible? Yes. It is needed when the heart is so entirely possessed by desire that it cannot rest until that desire is fulfilled. It is possible when one's life has come under the power of the heavenly blessing to such a degree that nothing can keep it from sacrificing all to obtain it.

When a child of God begins to get a real vision for the need of the church and of the world—a vision of the promised divine redemption, a vision of the power of intercession to bring down the heavenly blessing, and a vision of the honor of taking part in that work as intercessors—it naturally follows that he will regard his work of crying out, day and night, to God as the most heavenly thing upon earth.

Let us learn from David, who said, *"For the zeal of thine house hath eaten me up"* (Psalm 69:9). Let us learn from Christ our Lord, of whom these words were so true. There is nothing so much worth living for as satisfying the heart of God in His longing for human fellowship, and winning hearts to be His dwelling places. How can we rest until we have found a place for the Mighty One in our hearts and have yielded ourselves to the great work of intercession for so many after whom the desires of God are going out?

God grant that our hearts may be so brought under the influence of these divine truths that we will yield ourselves in pure devotion to Christ. May our longing to satisfy the heart of God be the chief aim of our lives.

Lord Jesus, the great Intercessor, breathe Your own Spirit into our hearts, for Your name's sake. Amen.

Intercession, a Divine Reality

And another angel came,...and there was given unto him much incense, that he should offer it with the prayers of all saints upon the golden altar which was before the throne.
—Revelation 8:3

Intercession is, by amazing grace, an essential element in God's redeeming purpose—to such a degree that, without it, the failure of its accomplishment may lie at our door. Christ's intercession in heaven is essential to His carrying out the work He began on earth, but He calls for the intercession of the saints in the attainment of His purpose. Just think of what we read: *"And all things are of God, who hath reconciled us to himself by Jesus Christ, and hath given to us the ministry of reconciliation"* (2 Corinthians 5:18). As the reconciliation was dependent on Christ's doing His part, so in the accomplishment of the work He calls on the church to do her part. Paul regarded unceasing intercession as indispensable to the fulfillment of the work that had been entrusted to him. It is just one aspect of the mighty power of God that works in the hearts of His believing people.

Intercession is indeed a divine reality. Without it, the church loses one of its chief beauties, loses the joy and the power of the Spirit life for achieving great things for God. Without it, the command to preach the gospel to every creature can never be carried out. Without it, there is no power for the church to recover from her sickly, feeble life and to conquer the world. And in the life of the believer, there can be no entrance into the abundant life and joy of daily fellowship with God unless he takes his place among God's elect—the watchmen and remembrancers of God who cry to Him *"day and night"* (Luke 18:7).

Church of Christ, awaken! Listen to the call: *"Pray without ceasing"* (1 Thessalonians 5:17). Take no rest, and give God no rest. Even though it may be with a sigh from the depths of the heart, let the answer be, *"For Zion's sake will I not hold my peace"* (Isaiah 62:1). God's Spirit will reveal to us the power of a life of intercession as a divine reality, an essential and indispensable element of the great redemption and therefore also of the true Christian life.

May God help us to know and fulfill our calling!

March

March

March 1

True Worship

Worship God.
—Revelation 22:9

Those who have read the previous section on the secret of intercession have undoubtedly asked more than once, "What is the reason that prayer and intercession are not a greater joy and delight to Christians? Is there any way in which we may be more inclined to make fellowship with God our chief joy and, as intercessors, to bring down His power and blessing on those for whom we pray?"

The chief answer is undoubtedly: we know God too little. In our prayers, our hearts are not set primarily on waiting for His presence. It should be so. We think mostly of ourselves, our needs and weaknesses, our desires and prayers. But we forget that, in every prayer, God must be first, He must be all. To seek Him, to find Him, to wait in His presence, to be assured that His presence rests upon us, that He actually listens to what we say and is working in us—this alone gives the inspiration that makes prayer as natural to us as the fellowship of a child with his father.

How is one to reach this nearness to God and fellowship with Him? The answer is simple: we must give God time to make Himself known to us. Believe with all your heart that, just as you present yourself to God in prayer, so God presents Himself to you as the Hearer of prayer. But you cannot realize this unless you give Him time and quiet. It is not the volume or the earnestness of your words in which prayer has its power, but in the living faith that God Himself is taking you and your prayer into His loving heart. He Himself will give the assurance that, in His time, your prayer will be heard.

The purpose of this month is to help you to know the way to meet God in every prayer. In it, I will give you Scriptures with which your heart can bow before God, waiting on Him to make them living and true in your experience.

Begin today with this verse: *"Unto thee, O Lord, do I lift up my soul"* (Psalm 25:1). Bow before Him in stillness, believing that He looks on you and will reveal His presence.

"My soul thirsteth for God, for the living God" (Psalm 42:2).

God Is a Spirit

God is a Spirit: and they that worship him must worship him in spirit and in truth.
—John 4:24

When God created man and breathed into him His own spirit, man became a living soul. The soul stood midway between the spirit and the body, to yield either to the spirit to be lifted up to God, or to the flesh and its lusts. When man fell in the Garden of Eden, he refused to listen to his own spirit, and so his spirit became the slave of the body. The spirit in man became utterly darkened.

In regeneration, it is this spirit that is quickened and born again from above. In the regenerated life, it is the spirit of man that must continually yield itself to the Spirit of God. Man's spirit is the deepest inward part of the human being. The Scriptures read, *"Thou desirest truth in the inward parts: and in the hidden part thou shalt make me to know wisdom."* (Psalm 51:6), and *"I will put my law in their inward parts"* (Jerermiah 31:33). Also concerning this, Isaiah said, *"With my soul have I desired thee in the night; yea, with my spirit within me will I seek thee early"* (Isaiah 26:9). The soul must sink down into the depths of the hidden spirit and must stir itself to seek God.

God is a Spirit, most holy and glorious. He gave us a spirit with the one purpose of holding fellowship with Himself. Through sin, that purpose has been darkened and nearly quenched. There is no way for it to be restored except by presenting the soul in stillness before God for the working of His Holy Spirit in our spirits. Deeper than our thoughts and feelings, God will, in our inward parts, teach us to worship Him *"in spirit and truth."*

"For the Father seeketh such to worship him" (John 4:23). He Himself, by the Holy Spirit, will teach us this if we wait upon Him. In this quiet hour, be still before God, yield yourself with your whole heart to believe in and to receive the gentle working of His Spirit, and breathe out such words as these: *"With my soul have I desired thee in the night; yea, with my spirit within me will I seek thee early"* (Isaiah 26:9); *"On thee do I wait all the day"* (Psalm 25:5).

Intercession and Adoration

O worship the LORD in the beauty of holiness.
—Psalm 96:9

The better we know God, the more wonderful our insight into the power of intercession becomes. We begin to understand that it is the great means by which man can take part in the carrying out of God's purpose. God has commissioned His people to make known and communicate to men the whole plan of redemption through Christ. In all this, intercession is the chief element, because in it His servants enter into the full fellowship with Christ, and they receive the power of the Spirit as their power for service.

It is easy to see why God has so ordered it. He desires to renew us after His image. And there is no other way to do this but by making His desires our own, so that we breathe His character; and by sacrificing ourselves in love, so that we may become to some degree like Christ, ever living to make intercession. (See Hebrews 7:25.) Such can be the life of the consecrated believer.

The clearer one's insight into this great purpose of God, the more the need will be felt to enter very truly into God's presence in the spirit of humble worship and holy adoration. The more we take time to abide in God's presence, the stronger our faith will become that God will Himself work out all the good pleasure of His will (see Philippians 2:13) through our prayers. As the glory of God shines upon us, we will become conscious of the depths of our helplessness, and so we will rise up into the faith that believes that God will do *"above all that we ask or think"* (Ephesians 3:20).

Intercession will lead us to feel the need for a deeper adoration. Adoration will give us new power for intercession. A true intercession and a deeper adoration will always be inseparable.

The secret of true adoration can only be known by the individual who spends time waiting in God's presence, yielding to God, so that He may reveal Himself. Adoration will indeed equip us for the great work of making God's glory known.

"O come, let us worship and bow down: let us kneel before the LORD *our maker. For he is our God"* (Psalm 95:6–7).

"Give unto the LORD *the glory due unto his name"* (1 Chronicles 16:29).

March 4

The Desire for God

With my soul have I desired thee in the night.
—Isaiah 26:9

What is the most glorious thing that man can see or find upon earth? Nothing less than God Himself.

And what is the most glorious thing that a man can and needs to do every day? Nothing less than to seek, to know, to love, and to praise this glorious God. As glorious as God is, so is the glory that begins to work in the heart and life of the man who gives himself to live for God.

My brother or sister in Christ, have you learned the first and greatest thing you have to do every day? Nothing less than to seek this God, to meet Him, to worship Him, and to live for Him and for His glory. It is a great step in the life of a Christian when he truly sees this truth and yields himself to consider fellowship with God every day as the chief purpose of his life.

Take time and ask whether this is not the highest wisdom, and the one thing for which a Christian is to live above all—to know his God rightly, and to love Him with his whole heart. Believe not only that it is true, but also that God's greatest desire is for you to live thus with Him. In answer to prayer, He will indeed enable you to do so.

Begin today, and take a word from God's Book to speak to Him in the stillness of your soul: *"O God, thou art my God; early will I seek thee: my soul thirsteth for thee, my flesh longeth for thee....My soul followeth hard after thee"* (Psalm 63:1, 8); *"With my whole heart have I sought thee"* (Psalm 119:10).

Repeat these words in deep reverence and childlike longing until their spirit and power enter your heart. Then wait upon God until you begin to realize the blessedness of meeting with Him in this way. As you persevere, you will learn to expect that the fear and the presence of God can abide with you throughout the day.

"I waited patiently for the LORD; and he inclined unto me, and heard my cry" (Psalm 40:1).

March 5

Silent Adoration

Truly my soul waiteth upon God....My soul, wait thou only upon God; for my expectation is from him.
—Psalm 62:1, 5

When man in his littleness and God in His glory meet, we all understand that what God says has infinitely more worth than what man says. Yet our prayers so often consist of telling God what we need that we give Him no time to speak to us. Our prayers are often so indefinite and vague. It is a great lesson to learn, that to be silent before God is the secret of true adoration. Let us remember the promise: *"In quietness and in confidence shall be your strength"* (Isaiah 30:15).

"My soul, wait thou only upon God; for my expectation is from him." "I wait for the LORD, my soul doth wait, and in his word do I hope" (Psalm 130:5).

As the soul bows before Him, to remember His greatness, His holiness, His power, and His love, and as it seeks to give Him the honor, reverence, and worship that are His due, the heart will be opened to receive the divine impression of the nearness of God and of the working of His power.

O Christian, believe that such worship of God is the sure way to give Him the glory that is His due, and will lead to the highest blessedness that can be found in prayer.

Do not imagine that such worship is time lost. Do not turn from it if at first it appears difficult. Be assured that it brings you into the right relation with God. It opens the way to fellowship with Him. It leads to the blessed assurance that He is looking upon you in tender love and is working in you with divine power. As you become more accustomed to it, it will give you the sense of His presence abiding with you all day long. It will make you strong to testify for God. Men will begin to feel that you have been with God. Someone once said, "No one is able to influence others for goodness and holiness beyond the amount of God that is in him."

"But the LORD is in his holy temple: let all the earth keep silence before him" (Habakkuk 2:20).

"Be silent, O all flesh, before the LORD: for he is raised up out of his holy habitation" (Zechariah 2:13).

The Light of God's Countenance

God is light.
—1 John 1:5

The LORD is my light.
—Psalm 27:1

Every morning the sun rises, and we walk in its light and perform our daily duties with gladness. Whether we think of it or not, the light of the sun shines on us all day. Every morning the light of God shines upon His children. But in order to enjoy the light of God's countenance, the soul must turn to God and trust Him to let His light shine upon it.

When there is a shipwreck at midnight, with what longing the sailors look for the morning! How often the sigh goes up, "When will the day break?" Similarly, the Christian must wait on God and rest patiently until His light shines upon him. *"My soul waiteth for the Lord more than they that watch for the morning"* (Psalm 130:6).

Dear reader, begin each day with one of these prayers:

"Make thy face to shine upon thy servant" (Psalm 31:16).

"LORD, lift thou up the light of thy countenance upon us" (Psalm 4:6).

"Cause thy face to shine; and we shall be saved" (Psalm 80:3).

Do not rest until you know that the light of His countenance and His blessing is resting on you. Then you will experience these words: *"They shall walk…in the light of thy countenance. In thy name shall they rejoice all the day"* (Psalm 89:15–16).

Child of God, believe that it is the ardent longing of your Father that you should dwell and rejoice in His light all day long. Just as you need the light of the sun each hour, so the heavenly light, the light of the Father, is indispensable.

If you are sure that the sun has risen, you count on its light all day. Even when there are clouds, you can rest in the knowledge that the sun is still there. In the midst of life's difficulties, the light of God will rest upon you without ceasing.

Do not rest until you have said, *"There be many that say, Who will show us any good? LORD, lift thou up the light of thy countenance upon us"* (Psalm 4:6). Take time, until that light shines in your heart and you can say, *"The LORD is my light."*

March 7

Faith in God

And Jesus answering saith unto them, Have faith in God. —Mark 11:22

As the eye is the organ by which we see the light and rejoice in it, so faith is the power by which we see the light of God and walk in it.

Man was made for God, in His likeness; his whole being was formed according to the divine pattern. Just think of man's wonderful power of discovering all the thoughts of God hidden in nature. Think of the heart, with its unlimited powers of self-sacrifice and love. Man was made for God, to seek Him, to find Him, to grow up into His likeness, and to show forth His glory—in the fullest sense, to be His dwelling. And faith is the eye that, turning away from the world and self, looks up to God and sees light in His light. To the man of faith, God reveals Himself.

How often we toil and try to waken thoughts and feelings concerning God, which are but a faint shadow, and we forget to gaze on the God who is the Incomparable Original! If only we could realize that God reveals Himself within the depths of our souls!

"Without faith it is impossible to please [God]" (Hebrews 11:6) or to know Him. In our quiet time, we have to pray to our *"Father which is in secret"* (Matthew 6:6). There He hides us *"in the secret of his tabernacle"* (Psalm 27:5). And there, as we wait and worship before Him, He will let His light shine into our hearts.

Let your one desire be to take time and be still before God, believing with faith in His longing to make Himself known to you. Feed on God's Word, to make you strong in faith. Let that faith extend itself to think of what God's glory is, of what His power is to reveal Himself to you, and of what His longing love is to get complete possession of you.

Such faith, strengthened day by day in secret fellowship with God, will become the habit of our lives, keeping us ever in the enjoyment of His presence and the experience of His saving power.

Abraham *"was strong in faith, giving glory to God; and being fully persuaded that, what he had promised, he was able also to perform"* (Romans 4:20–21).

"I believe God, that it shall be even as it was told me" (Acts 27:25).

"Wait on the Lord: be of good courage, and he shall strengthen thine heart: wait, I say, on the Lord" (Psalm 27:14).

 March 8

Alone with God

And it came to pass, as he was alone praying.
—Luke 9:18

He departed again into a mountain himself alone.
—John 6:15

Man needs to be alone with God. Man fell when, through the lust of the flesh, he was brought under the power of things visible and earthly. His restoration is meant to bring him back to the Father's house, the Father's presence and fellowship. Salvation means being brought to delight in the presence of God.

Man needs to be alone with God. Without this, God cannot have the opportunity to shine into his heart, to transform his nature, to take possession of him, and to fill him with His fullness.

Man needs to be alone with God, to yield to the presence and power of His holiness, of His life, and of His love. Christ on earth needed it; He could not live the life of a Son here in the flesh without at times separating Himself entirely from His surroundings and being alone with God. How much more must this be indispensable to us!

When Jesus gave us the command to enter our inner chamber and shut the door in order to pray to our Father in secret, He gave us the promise that the Father would hear such prayers and would mightily answer them in our lives before men. (See Matthew 6:4.)

Alone with God—that is the secret of true prayer, of true power in prayer, of real living, of face-to-face fellowship with God, and of power for service. There is no true, deep conversion; no true, deep holiness; no clothing with the Holy Spirit and with power; no abiding peace or joy, without being daily alone with God. As someone has said, "There is no path to holiness but in being much and long alone with God."

The institution of daily, secret prayer is an inestimable privilege. Let it be the one thing our hearts are set on: seeking, finding, and meeting God. Take time to be alone with God. The time will come when you will be amazed at the thought that one could suggest that five minutes was enough.

"Hearken unto the voice of my cry, my King, and my God: for unto thee will I pray. My voice shalt thou hear in the morning, O Lord; in the morning will I direct my prayer unto thee, and will look up" (Psalm 5:2–3).

Wholly for God

Whom have I in heaven but thee? and there is none upon earth that I desire beside thee.
—Psalm 73:25

Alone with God—this is a lesson of the deepest importance. May we seek grace from God to reach its depths. Then we will learn that there is another lesson of equally deep significance: wholly for God.

As we find that it is not easy to persevere in being alone with God, we begin to see that it is because the other is lacking; we are not "wholly for God." Because He is the only God, He has a right to demand to have us wholly for Himself. Without this surrender, He cannot make His power known. We read in the Old Testament that His servants Abraham, Moses, Elijah, and David gave themselves wholly and unreservedly to God, so that He could work out His plans through them. It is only the fully surrendered heart that can fully trust God for all He has promised.

This world teaches us that if anyone desires to do a great work, he must give himself wholly to it. This principle is especially true of the love of a mother for her child. She gives herself wholly to the little one whom she loves. Is it not reasonable that the great God of love should have us wholly for Himself? And will we not take the words wholly for God as the keynote for our devotions every morning when we awaken? Just as God gives Himself wholly to us, so does He desire that we give ourselves wholly to Him.

In the inner chamber, let us meditate on these things alone with God, and with earnest desire ask Him by His almighty power to work in us all that is pleasing in His sight.

Wholly for God—what a privilege! What wonderful grace prepares us for it! Wholly for God—separated from men, from work, and from all that might draw us away—what great blessedness as the soul learns what it means, and what God gives with it!

"Thou shalt love the Lord thy God with all thy heart, and with all thy soul, and with all thy mind" (Matthew 22:37). "[They] *sought him with their whole desire; and he was found of them"* (2 Chronicles 15:15). *"With my whole heart have I sought thee"* (Psalm 119:10).

The Knowledge of God

This is life eternal, that they might know thee.
—John 17:3

The knowledge of God is absolutely necessary for the spiritual life. It is eternal life. It is not the intellectual knowledge we receive from others, or through our own powers of thought, but the living, experiential knowledge in which God makes Himself known to the soul. Just as the rays of the sun on a cold winter's day warm the body, imparting its heat to us, so the living God sheds the life-giving rays of His holiness and love into the heart of one who waits on Him.

Why do we so seldom experience this life-giving power of the true knowledge of God? Because we do not give God enough time to reveal Himself to us. When we pray, we think we know well enough how to speak to God. And we forget that one of the very first things in prayer is to be silent before God, so that He may reveal Himself. By His hidden but mighty power, God will manifest His presence, resting on us and working in us. To know God in the personal experience of His presence and love is life indeed.

Brother Lawrence, author of *The Practice of the Presence of God,* had a great longing to know God, and for this purpose went into a monastery. His spiritual advisers gave him prayer books to use, but he put them aside. "It helps little to pray," he said, "if I do not know the God to whom I pray." Brother Lawrence remained in silent adoration for a long time in order to come under the presence of this great and holy Being. He continued in this practice until, later, he lived consciously and constantly in God's presence and experienced His blessed nearness and keeping power. Just as the sun rising each morning is the pledge of light throughout the day, so the quiet time of waiting upon God will be the pledge of His presence and His power abiding with us all day long.

Learn this great lesson: as the sun on a cold day shines on us and imparts its warmth, believe that the living God will work in you with His love and almighty power. God will reveal Himself as life and light and joy and strength to the soul who waits upon Him.

"Lord, lift thou up the light of thy countenance upon us" (Psalm 4:6).

"Be still, and know that I am God" (Psalm 46:10).

March 11

God the Father

Baptizing them in the name of the Father, and of the Son, and of the Holy Ghost.
—Matthew 28:19

March

We will do well to remember that the doctrine of the Holy Trinity has a deep devotional aspect. As we think of God, we remember the inconceivable distance that separates Him in His holiness from sinful men, and we bow in deep contrition and holy fear. As we think of Christ the Son, we remember the inconceivable nearness in which He came to be born of a woman, a daughter of Adam, and to die the accursed death, and so to be inseparably joined to us for all eternity. And as we think of the Holy Spirit, we remember the inconceivable blessedness of God having His abode in us, and making us His home and His temple throughout eternity.

When Christ taught us to say, *"Our Father which art in heaven"* (Matthew 6:9), He immediately added, *"Hallowed be thy name"* (v. 9). As God is holy, so we are to be holy, too. And there is no way of becoming holy but by considering His name most holy and drawing near to Him in prayer.

How often we speak His name without any sense of the unspeakable privilege of our relationship with God! If we would just take time to come into contact with God and to worship Him in His love, how the inner chamber would become to us the gate of heaven!

Child of God, if you pray to your Father in secret, bow very low before Him and seek to adore His name as most holy. Remember that this is the highest blessedness of prayer.

"Pray to thy Father which is in secret; and thy Father which seeth in secret shall reward thee openly" (Matthew 6:6).

What an unspeakable privilege, to be alone with God in secret and to say, "My Father!" How incredible to have the assurance that He has indeed seen me in secret and will reward me openly. Take time until you can say, *"I have seen God face to face, and my life is preserved"* (Genesis 32:30).

God the Son

Grace to you and peace from God our Father, and the Lord Jesus Christ.
—Romans 1:7

It is remarkable that the apostle Paul in each of his thirteen epistles wrote: *"Grace to you and peace from God our Father, and the Lord Jesus Christ."* He had such a deep sense of the inseparable oneness of the Father and the Son in the work of grace, that in each opening benediction he referred to both.

This is a lesson of the utmost importance for us. There may be times in the Christian life when we think chiefly of God the Father, and so pray only to Him. But later on, we realize that it may cause spiritual loss if we do not grasp the truth that each day and each hour it is only through faith in Christ and in being united with Him that we can enjoy a full and abiding fellowship with God.

Remember the account of the Lamb in the midst of the throne. *"The four beasts…rest not day and night, saying, Holy, holy, holy, Lord God Almighty, which was, and is, and is to come'"* (Revelation 4:8). Later, John saw *"in the midst of the throne…a Lamb as it had been slain"* (Revelation 5:6). Of the entire worshipping multitude, none could see God without first seeing Christ, the Lamb of God. And none could see Christ without seeing the glory of God, the Father and Son—inseparably One.

O Christian, if you wish to know and worship God fully, seek Him and worship Him in Christ. And if you seek Christ, seek Him and worship Him in God. Then you will understand what it means to have *"your life…hid with Christ in God"* (Colossians 3:3), and your experience will be that the adoration of Christ is indispensable to the full knowledge of the love and holiness of God.

Be still, and speak these words in deepest reverence: *"Grace…and peace"*—all I can desire—*"from God our Father, and the Lord Jesus Christ."*

Take time to meditate on this, to believe and to expect all from God the Father who sits upon the throne, and from the Lord Jesus Christ, the Lamb in the midst of the throne. Then you will learn to truly worship God. Return frequently to this sacred scene, to give *"glory…unto him that sitteth upon the throne, and unto the Lamb"* (Revelation 5:13).

March 13

God the Holy Spirit

For through him we both have access by one Spirit unto the Father. —Ephesians 2:18

In our communion with God in the inner chamber, we must guard against the danger of seeking to know God and Christ in the power of the intellect or the emotions. The Holy Spirit has been given for the sole purpose that *"through him we...have access by one Spirit unto the Father."* Let us beware, lest all our labor be in vain because we do not wait for the teaching of the Spirit.

Christ taught His disciples this truth on His last night. Speaking of the coming of the Comforter, He said, *"In that day ye shall ask...the Father in my name....Ask, and ye shall receive, that your joy may be full"* (John 16:23–24). Take hold of the truth that the Holy Spirit was given with the one great purpose of teaching us to pray. He makes fellowship with the Father and the Son a blessed reality. Be strong in the faith that He is working secretly in you. As you enter the inner chamber, give yourself wholly to His guidance as your Teacher in all your intercession and adoration.

When Christ said to the disciples on the evening of the Resurrection, *"Receive ye the Holy Ghost"* (John 20:22), it was, for one thing, to strengthen and equip them for the ten days of prayer and for their receiving the fullness of the Spirit. This suggests to us three things we ought to remember when we draw near to God in prayer:

1. **We must pray in the confidence that the Holy Spirit dwells in us.** And we must yield ourselves definitely, in stillness of soul, to His leading. Take time for this.

2. **We must believe that the *"greater works"* (John 5:20) of the Spirit will be given in answer to prayer.** Such *"works"* bring us toward the enlightening and strengthening of the spiritual life, toward the fullness of the Spirit.

3. **We must believe that through the Spirit, in unity with all God's children, we may ask and expect the mighty workings of that Spirit on His church and people.**

"He that believeth on me, as the scripture hath said, out of his belly shall flow rivers of living water" (John 7:38). *"Believest thou this?"* (John 11:26).

March 14

The Secret of the Lord

Enter into thy closet, and when thou hast shut thy door, pray to thy Father which is in secret; and thy Father which seeth in secret shall reward thee openly.
—Matthew 6:6

Christ greatly desired that His disciples would know God as their Father, and that they would have secret fellowship with Him. In His own life, He found it not only indispensable, but also the highest happiness to meet the Father in secret. He wants us to realize that it is impossible to be true, wholehearted disciples without daily fellowship with the Father in heaven, who waits for us "in secret."

God is a God who hides Himself from the world and all that is of the world. He wants to draw us away from the world and from ourselves. Instead, He offers us the blessedness of close, intimate communion with Himself. Oh, that God's children would understand this!

Believers enjoyed this experience in Old Testament times: *"Thou art my hiding place"* (Psalm 32:7); *"He that dwelleth in the secret place of the most High shall abide under the shadow of the Almighty"* (Psalm 91:1); *"The secret of the LORD is with them that fear him"* (Psalm 25:14). How much more Christians in the new covenant ought to value this secret fellowship with God! We read: *"Ye are dead, and your life is hid with Christ in God"* (Colossians 3:3). If we believe this, we will have the joyful assurance that our lives, hidden *"with Christ in God,"* are safe and beyond the reach of every enemy. We should confidently and daily seek the renewal of our spiritual lives in prayer to our Father who is *"in secret."*

Because we are dead with Christ, because we are one with Him in the likeness of His death and of His resurrection, we know that, as the roots of a tree are hidden under the earth, so the roots of our daily lives are hidden deep in God.

O soul, take time to realize: *"Thou shalt hide* [me] *in the secret of thy presence"* (Psalm 31:20).

Our first thought in prayer should be, "I must know that I am alone with God, and that God is with me."

"In the secret of his tabernacle shall he hide me" (Psalm 27:5).

Half an Hour of Silence in Heaven

There was silence in heaven about the space of half an hour....And another angel came and stood at the altar...and there was given unto him much incense, that he should offer it with the prayers of all saints upon the golden altar which was before the throne. And the smoke of the incense, which came with the prayers of the saints, ascended up before God.
—Revelation 8:1, 3–4

"There was silence in heaven about the space of half an hour," to bring the prayers of the saints before God. Tens of thousands of God's children have felt the absolute need for silence and detachment from the things of earth for half an hour, in order to present their prayers before God and, in fellowship with Him, to be strengthened for their daily work.

How often the complaint is heard that there is no time for prayer! Very often the confession is made that, even if time could be found, one feels unable to spend the time in real fellowship with God. No one needs to ask what it is that hinders growth in the spiritual life. The secret of strength can only be found in living communion with God.

O dear Christian, if you would only obey Christ when He says, *"When thou hast shut thy door, pray to thy Father which is in secret"* (Matthew 6:6)! If you would only have the courage to be alone with God for half an hour! Do not say to yourself, "I will not know how to spend the time." Just believe that if you are faithful, bowing in silence before God, He will reveal Himself to you.

If you need help, read some passage of Scripture and let God's Word speak to you. Then bow in deepest humility before God, and wait on Him. He will work within you. Read Psalm 61, 62, or 63, and speak the words out. Then begin to pray. Intercede for your own household, for the congregation, for the church and minister, for schools and missions. Continue praying though the time may seem long. God will reward you.

God desires to bless you. Is it not worth the trouble to spend half an hour alone with God? If you persevere, you may find that the half hour that seems the most difficult in the whole day may eventually become the most blessed in your whole life.

"My soul, wait thou only upon God; for my expectation is from him" (Psalm 62:5).

March 16

God's Greatness

For thou art great, and doest wondrous things: thou art God alone. —Psalm 86:10

When anyone begins an important work, he takes time and gives his attention to consider the greatness of his undertaking. Scientists, in studying nature, require years of labor to grasp the magnitude of, for instance, the sun, the stars, and the planets. Is not our glorious God worthy that we should take time to know and adore His greatness?

Yet how superficial our knowledge of God's greatness is! We do not allow ourselves time to bow before Him and to come under the deep impression of His incomprehensible majesty and glory.

Meditate on the following Scriptures until you are filled with some sense of what a glorious being God is: *"Great is the LORD, and greatly to be praised; and his greatness is unsearchable"* (Psalm 145:3); *"I will declare thy greatness. They shall abundantly utter the memory of thy great goodness"* (vv. 6–7).

Do not imagine that it is easy to grasp the meaning of these words. Take time for them to master your heart, until you bow in what may be speechless adoration before God.

"Ah Lord GOD!...There is nothing too hard for thee....The Great, the Mighty God, the LORD of hosts, is his name, great in counsel, and mighty in work" (Jeremiah 32:17–19). To this God answers, *"Behold, I am the LORD, the God of all flesh: is there any thing too hard for me?"* (v. 27).

The right understanding of God's greatness will take time. But if we give God the honor that is His due, and if our faith grows strong in the knowledge of what a great and powerful God we have, we will be led to wait in the inner chamber, to bow in humble worship before this great and mighty God. In His abundant mercy, He will teach us through the Holy Spirit to say, *"For the LORD is a great God, and a great King above all gods....O come, let us worship and bow down: let us kneel before the LORD our maker"* (Psalm 95:3, 6).

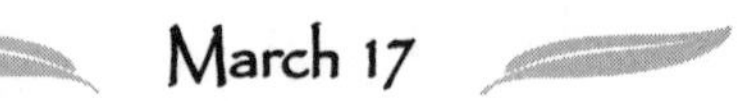

March 17

A Perfect Heart

For the eyes of the LORD run to and fro throughout the whole earth, to show himself strong in the behalf of them whose heart is perfect toward him.
—2 Chronicles 16:9

March

In worldly matters, we know how important it is that our work be done with the whole heart. In the spiritual realm, this rule still holds true. God has given the commandment, *"Thou shalt love the LORD thy God with all thine heart...and with all thy might"* (Deuteronomy 6:5). In Jeremiah we read, *"Ye shall seek me, and find me, when ye shall search for me with all your heart"* (Jeremiah 29:13).

It is amazing that earnest Christians, who attend to their earthly work with all their hearts, are so content to take things easy when it comes to the service of God. They do not realize that, if in anything, they should give themselves to God's service with all the power of their wills.

In 2 Chronicles 16:9, we are given insight into the absolute necessity of seeking God with a perfect heart: *"The eyes of the LORD run to and fro throughout the whole earth, to show himself strong in the behalf of them whose heart is perfect toward him."*

What an encouragement this should be to us—to humbly wait on God with an upright heart! We may be assured that His eye will be upon us and that He will show forth His mighty power in us and through our earthly work.

O Christian, have you learned this lesson in your worship of God, yielding yourself each morning, yielding your whole heart to do God's will? Pray each prayer with a perfect heart in true wholehearted devotion to Him. Then expect, by faith, the power of God to work in you and through you.

Remember that in order to come to this, you must begin by being silent before God, until you realize that He is indeed working in secret within your heart.

"I wait for my God" (Psalm 69:3).

"In the secret of his tabernacle shall he hide me" (Psalm 27:5).

The Omnipotence of God

I am the Almighty God.
—Genesis 17:1

When Abraham heard these words, he fell on his face. God spoke to him and filled his heart with faith in what God would do for him.

O Christian, have you bowed in deep humility before God until you felt that you were in living contact with the Almighty; until your heart had been filled with the faith that almighty God is working in you and will perfect His work in you?

Read in the Psalms how believers gloried in God and in His strength: *"I will love thee, O LORD, my strength"* (Psalm 18:1); *"God is the strength of my heart"* (Psalm 73:26); *"The LORD is the strength of my life"* (Psalm 27:1); *"It is God that girdeth me with strength"* (Psalm 18:32); *"God is our refuge and strength"* (Psalm 46:1). Take hold of these words, and take time to adore God as the Almighty One, your strength.

Christ taught us that salvation is the work of God, and impossible for man. When the disciples asked, *"Who then can be saved?"* (Matthew 19:25), His answer was, *"With men this is impossible; but with God all things are possible"* (v. 26). If we firmly believe this, we will have courage to believe that God is working in us all that is well pleasing in His sight.

Remember how Paul prayed for the Ephesians, that through the enlightening of the Spirit they might know *"the exceeding greatness of his power to us-ward who believe, according to the working of his mighty power"* (Ephesians 1:19). For the Colossians he prayed that they might be *"strengthened with all might, according to His glorious power"* (Colossians 1:11). When a person fully believes that the mighty power of God is working unceasingly within him, he can joyfully say, *"The LORD is the strength of my life"* (Psalm 27:1).

Do you wonder why many Christians complain of weakness and shortcomings? They do not understand that the almighty God must work in them every hour of the day. That is the secret of the true life of faith.

Do not rest until you can say to God, *"I will love thee, O LORD, my strength"* (Psalm 18:1). Let God have complete possession of you, and you will be able to say with all God's people, *"For thou art the glory of their strength"* (Psalm 89:17).

The Fear of the Lord

Blessed is the man that feareth the LORD, that delighteth greatly in his commandments.
—Psalm 112:1

The fear of God—these words characterize the religion of the Old Testament and the foundation that it laid for the more abundant life of the New Testament. The gift of holy fear is still the great desire of each child of God, and it is an essential part of a life that is to make a real impression on the world. It is one of the great promises of the new covenant in Jeremiah: *"And I will make an everlasting covenant with them…*[and] *I will put my fear in their hearts, that they shall not depart from me"* (Jeremiah 32:40).

We find the perfect combination of the two in Acts 9:31: *"Then had the churches rest throughout all Judaea and Galilee and Samaria, and were edified; and walking in the fear of the Lord, and in the comfort of the Holy Ghost, were multiplied."* More than once, Paul gave the fear of God a high place in the Christian life: *"Work out your own salvation with fear and trembling. For it is God which worketh in you"* (Philippians 2:12–13); *"Perfecting holiness in the fear of God"* (2 Corinthians 7:1).

It has often been said that the lack of the fear of God is one of the areas where our modern times cannot compare favorably with the times of the Puritans. It is no wonder that there is so much cause of complaint in regard to the reading of God's Word, the worship of His house, and the absence of the spirit of continuous prayer that marked the early church. We need texts like the one at the beginning of this devotion to be expounded, and new converts must be fully instructed in the need for and the blessedness of a deep fear of God, leading to an unceasing prayerfulness as one of the essential elements of the life of faith.

Let us earnestly cultivate this grace in the inner chamber. Let us hear these words coming out of the very heavens: *"Who shall not fear thee, O Lord, and glorify thy name? for thou only art holy"* (Revelation 15:4). *"Let us have grace, whereby we may serve God acceptably with reverence and godly fear"* (Hebrews 12:28).

"Blessed is the man that feareth the LORD." As we take these words into our hearts and believe that this is one of the deepest secrets of blessedness, we will seek to worship Him in holy fear.

"Serve the LORD with fear, and rejoice with trembling" (Psalm 2:11).

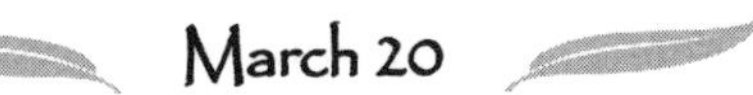

God Incomprehensible

Behold, God is great, and we know him not.
—Job 36:26

Touching the Almighty, we cannot find him out: he is excellent in power.
—Job 37:23

This attribute of God, as a Spirit whose being and glory are entirely beyond our power of comprehension, is one that we ponder all too little. And yet in the spiritual life, it is of the utmost importance to feel deeply that, as the heavens are high above the earth, so God's thoughts and ways are infinitely exalted beyond all our thoughts. (See Isaiah 55:9.)

It is only right that we look up to God with deep humility and holy reverence, and then with childlike simplicity yield ourselves to the teaching of His Holy Spirit. *"O the depth of the riches both of the wisdom and knowledge of God! how unsearchable are his judgments, and his ways past finding out!"* (Romans 11:33).

Let our hearts respond, "O Lord, O God of gods, how wonderful You are in all Your thoughts, and how deep in Your purposes!" The study of what God is should always fill us with holy awe, and the sacred longing to know and honor Him rightly.

Just think:

His greatness…	Incomprehensible
His might…	Incomprehensible
His omnipresence…	Incomprehensible
His wisdom…	Incomprehensible
His holiness…	Incomprehensible
His mercy…	Incomprehensible
His love…	Incomprehensible

As we worship, let us cry out, "What an inconceivable glory is in this great Being who is my God and Father!" Confess with shame how little you have sought to know Him fully or to wait upon Him to reveal Himself. Begin in faith to trust that, in a way passing all understanding, this incomprehensible and all-glorious God will work in your heart and life and allow you, in ever growing measure, to know Him fully.

"Mine eyes are unto thee, O God the Lord: in thee is my trust" (Psalm 141:8). *"Be still, and know that I am God"* (Psalm 46:10).

The Holiness of God in the Old Testament

Be holy, for I am holy.
—Leviticus 11:45

I am the LORD which sanctify you.
—Leviticus 20:8

These two ideas are recorded nine times in Leviticus. (See Leviticus 19:2; 20:7; 21:8, 15, 23; 22:9, 16.) Israel had to learn that, just as holiness is the highest and most glorious attribute of God, so it must be the obvious characteristic of His people. He who desires to meet God in secret must desire to be holy as He is holy.

The priests who were to have access to God had to be set apart for a life of holiness. It was the same for the prophet Isaiah who was to speak for Him: *"I saw also the Lord sitting upon a throne, high and lifted up....*[And the seraphim] *said: Holy holy, holy is the LORD of hosts"* (Isaiah 6:1, 3). This is the voice of adoration.

"Then said I: Woe is me, for I am undone!...for mine eyes have seen the King, the LORD of hosts" (v. 5). This is the voice of a broken, contrite heart.

Then one of the seraphim touched Isaiah's mouth with a live coal from the altar and said, *"Lo, this hath touched thy lips; and thine iniquity is taken away, and thy sin purged"* (v. 7). This is the voice of grace and full redemption.

Then follows the voice of God: *"Whom shall I send?"* (v. 8). And the willing answer is, *"Here am I; send me"* (v. 8). Pause with holy fear, and ask God to reveal Himself as the Holy One. *"For thus saith the high and lofty One that inhabiteth eternity, whose name is Holy; I dwell in the high and holy place, with him also that is of a contrite and humble spirit"* (Isaiah 57:15).

Be still, and take time to worship God in that deep condescension in which He longs to dwell with us and in us.

Child of God, if you wish to meet your Father in secret, bow low and worship Him in the glory of His holiness. Give Him time to make Himself known to you. It is indeed an unspeakable grace to know God as the Holy One.

"Ye shall be holy: for I the LORD your God am holy" (Leviticus 19:2). *"Holy, holy, holy is the LORD of hosts"* (Isaiah 6:3). *"Worship the LORD in the beauty of holiness"* (1 Chronicles 16:29). *"Let the beauty of the LORD our God be upon us"* (Psalm 90:17).

The Holiness of God in the New Testament

Holy Father, keep through thine own name those whom thou hast given me....Sanctify them....And for their sakes I sanctify myself, that they also might be sanctified through the truth.
—John 17:11, 17, 19

Christ always lives to pray this great prayer. Expect and take hold of God's answer.

Read the words of the apostle Paul in 1 Thessalonians: *"Night and day praying exceedingly...to the end he* [the Lord] *may stablish your hearts unblameable in holiness before God"* (1 Thessalonians 3:10, 13); *"And the very God of peace sanctify you wholly...who also will do it"* (1 Thessalonians 5:23–24).

Ponder deeply these words as you read them, and use them as a prayer to God: "Blessed Lord, strengthen my heart to be *'unblameable in holiness.'* Sanctify me wholly. I know that You are faithful, and You will do it."

What a privilege to commune with God in secret, to speak these words in prayer, and then to wait upon Him until, through the working of the Spirit, they live in our hearts and we begin to know something of the holiness of God!

God's holiness has been revealed in the Old Testament. In the New Testament, we find the holiness of God's people in Christ, through the sanctification of the Spirit. Oh, that we understood the blessedness of God's saying, *"Be holy, for I am holy"* (Leviticus 11:45)!

God is saying to us, "With you, My children, as it is with Me, holiness should be the chief thing." For this purpose, the Holy One has revealed Himself to us through the Son and the Holy Spirit. Let us use the word *holy* with great reverence of God, and then, for ourselves, with holy desire. Worship the God who says, *"I am the LORD which hallow you"* (Leviticus 22:32).

Bow before Him in holy fear and strong desire, and then, in the fullness of faith, listen to the prayer promise: *"And the very God of peace sanctify you wholly...who also will do it"* (1 Thessalonians 5:23–24).

Sin

And the grace of our Lord was exceeding abundant with faith and love which is in Christ Jesus....Christ Jesus came into the world to save sinners; of whom I am chief.
—1 Timothy 1:14–15

Never forget for a moment, as you enter the secret chamber, that your whole relationship to God depends on what you think of sin and of yourself as a redeemed sinner.

It is sin that makes God's holiness so amazing. It is sin that makes God's holiness so glorious, because He has said: *"Be holy, for I am holy"* (Leviticus 11:45); *"I am the LORD which hallow you"* (Leviticus 22:32).

It is sin that called forth the wonderful love of God in not sparing His Son. It was sin that nailed Jesus to the cross and revealed the depth and the power of the love with which He loved. Through all eternity in the glory of heaven, it is our being redeemed sinners that will give music to our praise.

Never forget for a moment that it is sin that has led to the great transaction between you and Christ Jesus. Each day in your fellowship with God, His one aim is to deliver and keep you fully from its power, and to lift you up into His likeness and His infinite love.

It is the thought of sin that will keep you low at His feet and will give the deep undertone to all your adoration. It is the thought of sin, ever seeking to tempt you, that will give fervency to your prayer and urgency to the faith that hides itself in Christ. It is the thought of sin that makes Christ so unspeakably precious that keeps you every moment dependent on His grace, and that gives you the right to be more than a conqueror *"through him that loved us"* (Romans 8:37). It is the thought of sin that calls you to thank God with *"a broken and a contrite heart...*[that] *God...wilt not despise"* (Psalm 51:17), and that works in you a contrite and humble spirit in which He delights to dwell.

It is in the inner chamber, in secret with the Father, that sin can be conquered, the holiness of Christ can be imparted, and the Spirit of holiness can take possession of our lives. It is in the inner chamber that we learn to know and experience fully the divine power of these precious words of promise: *"The blood of Jesus Christ his Son cleanseth us from all sin"* (1 John 1:7), and *"Whosoever abideth in him sinneth not"* (1 John 3:6).

The Mercy of God

O give thanks unto the LORD; for he is good: for his mercy endureth for ever.
—Psalm 136:1

This psalm is wholly devoted to the praise of God's mercy. In each of the twenty-six verses, we have the expression, *"His mercy endureth for ever."* The psalmist was full of this glad thought. Our hearts, too, should be filled with this blessed assurance. The everlasting, unchangeable mercy of God is cause for unceasing praise and thanksgiving.

Read what is said about God's mercy in the well-known Psalm 103: *"Bless the LORD, O my soul, and forget not all his benefits:...who crowneth thee with lovingkindness and tender mercies"* (vv. 2, 4). Of all God's other attributes, mercy is the crown. May it be a crown upon my head and in my life!

"The LORD is merciful and gracious...and plenteous in mercy" (v. 8). As wonderful as God's greatness is, so infinite is His mercy: *"As the heaven is high above the earth, so great is his mercy toward them that fear him"* (v. 11). What a thought! As high as heaven is above the earth, so immeasurably and inconceivably great is the mercy of God while He waits to bestow His richest blessing.

"The mercy of the LORD is from everlasting to everlasting upon them that fear him" (v. 17). Here again the psalmist spoke of God's boundless lovingkindness and mercy.

How frequently we have read these familiar words without the least thought of their immeasurable greatness! Be still, and meditate until your heart responds in the words of Psalm 36: *"Thy mercy, O LORD, is in the heavens"* (v. 5); *"How excellent is thy lovingkindness, O God! therefore the children of men put their trust under the shadow of thy wings"* (v. 7); *"O continue thy lovingkindness unto them that know thee"* (v. 10).

Take time to thank God with great joy for the wonderful mercy with which He crowns your life, and say: *"Thy lovingkindness is better than life"* (Psalm 63:3).

March 25

The Word of God

The word of God is quick, and powerful.
—Hebrews 4:12

March

Both the Word of God and prayer are indispensable for communion with God, and in the inner chamber they should not be separated. In His Word, God speaks to us; in prayer, we speak to God.

The Word teaches us to know the God to whom we pray. It teaches us how He wants us to pray. It gives us precious promises to encourage us in prayer. It often gives us wonderful answers to prayer.

The Word comes from God's heart and brings His thoughts and His love into our hearts. And then, through prayer, the Word goes back from our hearts into His great heart of love. Prayer is the means of fellowship between God's heart and ours.

The Word teaches us God's will—the will of His promises as to what He will do for us, and also the will of His commands. His promises are food for our faith, and to His commands we surrender ourselves in loving obedience.

The more we pray, the more we will feel our need for the Word and will rejoice in it. The more we read God's Word, the more we will have to pray about, and the more power we will have in prayer. One great cause of prayerlessness is that we read God's Word too little, only superficially, or in the light of human wisdom.

The Holy Spirit, through whom the Word has been spoken, is also the Spirit of prayer. He will teach us how to receive the Word and how to approach God.

When we take God's Word in deepest reverence in our hearts, on our lips, and in our lives, it will be a never failing fountain of strength and blessing to us. Let us believe that God's Word is indeed full of power that will make us strong, able to expect and receive great things from God. Above all, it will give us the daily blessed fellowship with Him as the living God.

"Blessed is the man…[whose] *delight is in the law of the LORD; and in his law doth he meditate day and night"* (Psalm 1:1–2).

March 26

The Psalms

How sweet are thy words unto my taste! yea, sweeter than honey to my mouth!
—Psalm 119:103

The book of Psalms seeks to help us to worship God. Of the sixty-six books in the Bible, this book was written especially for this purpose. The other books are historical, doctrinal, or practical. But the Psalms take us into the inner sanctuary of God's holy presence to enjoy the blessedness of fellowship with Him. It is a book of devotions inspired by the Holy Spirit.

If you desire each morning to truly meet God and worship Him in spirit and in truth, then let your heart be filled with the Word of God in the Psalms.

As you read the Psalms, underline the word *Lord* or *God* wherever it occurs, and also the pronouns referring to God—*I, You,* and *He.* This will help to connect the contents of the psalm with God, who is the object of all prayer. When you have taken the trouble to mark the different names of God, you will find that more than one difficult psalm will have light shed upon it. These underlined words will make God the central thought and will lead you to a new worship of Him. Take the psalms upon your lips, and speak them out before Him. Your faith will be strengthened anew to realize how God is your strength and help in all circumstances of life. (See Psalm 46:1.)

Just as the Holy Spirit has taught God's people to pray in years gone by, so the Psalms will, by the power of that Spirit, teach us always to abide in God's presence.

Read Psalm 119. Every time the word *Lord* or *You* or *Your* occurs, underline it. You will be surprised to find that almost every verse contains these words once or more. Meditate on the thought that the God who is found throughout the whole psalm is the same God who gives us His law and will enable us to keep it.

Psalm 119 will soon become one of your most beloved passages of Scripture, and you will find its prayers and its teachings concerning God's Word drawing you continually up to God, in the blessed consciousness of His power and love.

"O how love I thy law! It is my meditation all the day" (Psalm 119:97).

March 27

The Glory of God

Unto him be glory...throughout all ages.
—Ephesians 3:21

March

God Himself must reveal His glory to us; only then are we able to know and glorify Him rightly.

There is no more wonderful image of the glory of God in nature than we find in the starry heavens. Telescopes have long proclaimed the wonders of God's universe. And by means of photography, the wonders of that glory have been revealed. A photographic plate* fixed below the telescope will reveal millions of stars that could never have been seen by the eye through even the best telescope. Man must step aside and allow the glory of the heavens to reveal itself; and the stars, at first wholly invisible, will leave their image upon the plate.

What a lesson for the believer who longs to see the glory of God in His Word! Put aside your own efforts and thoughts. Let your heart be like a photographic plate that waits for God's glory to be revealed. As the plate must be prepared and clean, let your heart be prepared and purified by God's Spirit. *"Blessed are the pure in heart: for they shall see God"* (Matthew 5:8). As the plate must be stationary, let your heart be still before God. As the plate must be exposed up to seven or eight hours in order to obtain the full impression of the farthest stars, let your heart take time in silent waiting upon God, and He will reveal His glory.

If you are silent before God and give Him time, He will put thoughts into your heart that may be of unspeakable blessing to yourself and others. He will create within you desires and dispositions that will be as the rays of His glory shining in you.

Test this principle today. Offer your spirit to God in deep humility, and have faith that He will reveal Himself in His holy love. His glory will descend upon you. *"My soul, wait thou only upon God; for my expectation is from him"* (Psalm 62:5). *"Be still, and know that I am God"* (Psalm 46:10).

---

* Note: The photographic plates of which Murray writes are simply glass squares coated with light-sensitive emulsions. Most astronomers now use common negative film, which does not produce the positive image that can be achieved with plate technology but must be printed onto paper in order to obtain a picture of what was seen through the telescope. Slides, however, are similar to plates and allow one to get a positive image without having to print onto paper.

March 28

The Holy Trinity

Elect according to the foreknowledge of God the Father, through sanctification of the Spirit, unto obedience and sprinkling of the blood of Jesus Christ.
—1 Peter 1:2

In our daily studies, I have written much about the adoration of God the Father and about the need for enough time each day to worship Him. But we must remind ourselves that, for all our fellowship with God, the presence and power of the Son and the Spirit are absolutely necessary.

We need time to realize how all our fellowship with the Father is determined by the active and personal presence and working of the Lord Jesus. It takes time to become fully conscious of how much we need Him every time we approach Him, of what confidence we may have in the work that He is doing for us and in us, and of what the holy and intimate love is in which we may count upon His presence and all-prevailing intercession. But, oh, to learn the lesson that prayer takes time, and that that time will be most blessedly rewarded!

It is the same with the divine and almighty power of the Holy Spirit working in the depths of our hearts as the One who alone is able to reveal the Son within each of us. Through Him alone we have the power to know what and how to pray; above all, through Him we know how to plead the name of Jesus and to receive the assurance that our prayers have been accepted.

Dear reader, have you not felt more than once that it was almost a mockery to speak of spending five minutes alone with God to come under the impression of His glory? And now, does not the thought of the true worship of God in Christ through the Holy Spirit make you feel more than ever that it takes time to enter into such holy alliance with God and to keep the heart and mind in His peace and presence throughout the day?

Just pause and think: *"Elect according to the foreknowledge of God the Father, through sanctification of the Spirit, unto obedience and sprinkling of the blood of Jesus Christ."* What food for worship!

"When thou saidst, Seek ye my face; my heart said unto thee, Thy face, LORD, *will I seek"* (Psalm 27:8).

March 29

The Love of God

God is love; and he that dwelleth in love dwelleth in God, and God in him.
—1 John 4:16

March

The best and most wonderful word in heaven is *love*, for *"God is love."* And the best and most wonderful word in the inner chamber must also be *love*, for the God who meets us there is love.

What is love? It is the deep desire to give itself for the one who is loved. Love finds its joy in imparting all that it has in order to make the loved one happy. And the heavenly Father, who offers to meet us in the inner chamber—let there be no doubt of this in our minds—has no other aim than to fill our hearts with His love.

All the other attributes of God that have been mentioned find their highest glory in this. The true and full blessing of the inner chamber is nothing less than a life lived in the abundant love of God.

Because of this, our first and chief thought in the inner chamber should be faith in the love of God. As you set yourself to pray, seek to exercise great and unbounded faith in the love of God.

Take time in silence to meditate on the wonderful revelation of God's love in Christ, until you are filled with the spirit of worship and wonder and longing desire. Take time to believe the precious truth: *"The love of God is shed abroad in our hearts by the Holy Ghost which is given unto us"* (Romans 5:5).

Let us remember with shame how little we have believed in and sought this love. As we pray, let us be assured that our heavenly Father longs to manifest His love to us. We can say aloud, "I am deeply convinced of the truth. He can and will do it."

"Yea, I have loved thee with an everlasting love" (Jeremiah 31:3).

"That ye, being rooted and grounded in love, may be able to comprehend with all saints what is the breadth, and length, and depth, and height; and to know the love of Christ, which passeth knowledge" (Ephesians 3:17–19).

"Behold, what manner of love the Father hath bestowed upon us" (1 John 3:1).

March 30

Waiting on God

On thee do I wait all the day.
—Psalm 25:5

Waiting on God—in this expression we find one of the deepest truths of God's Word in regard to the attitude of the soul in its communion with God.

As we wait on God—just think—He will reveal Himself in us, He will teach us all His will, He will do to us what He has promised, and in all things He will be the Infinite God.

Such is the attitude with which each day should begin. In the inner chamber, in quiet meditation, in expressing our ardent desires through prayer, in the course of our daily work, in all our striving after obedience and holiness, in all our struggles against sin and self-will—in everything we must wait on God to receive what He will bestow, to see what He will do, and to allow Him to be the almighty God.

Meditate on these things, and they will help you to truly value the precious promises of God's Word. *"They that wait upon the LORD shall renew their strength; they shall mount up with wings as eagles"* (Isaiah 40:31). In this we have the secret of heavenly power and joy. *"Wait on the LORD: be of good courage, and he shall strengthen thine heart: wait, I say, on the LORD"* (Psalm 27:14). *"Rest in the LORD, and wait patiently for him"* (Psalm 37:7).

The deep root of all scriptural theology is absolute dependence on God. As we exercise this attitude, it will become more natural and blessedly possible to say, *"On thee do I wait all the day."* Here we have the secret of true, uninterrupted, silent adoration and worship of God.

Has this book helped to teach you the true worship of God? If so, the Lord's name be praised. Or have you only learned how little you know of it? For this, too, let us thank Him.

If you desire a fuller experience of this blessing, read this book again with a deeper insight into what is meant, and a greater knowledge of the absolute need of each day and all day waiting on God. May the God of all grace grant us this.

"I wait for the LORD, my soul doth wait, and in his word do I hope" (Psalm 130:5). *"Rest in the LORD, and wait patiently for him....and he shall give thee the desires of thine heart"* (Psalm 37:7, 4).

The Praise of God

Praise is comely for the upright.
—Psalm 33:1

Praise will always be a part of adoration. Adoration, when it has entered God's presence and has fellowshipped with Him, will always lead to the praise of His name. Let praise be a part of the incense we bring before God in our quiet time.

When the children of Israel, at their birth as the people of God at the Red Sea, had been delivered from the power of Egypt, their joy of redemption burst forth in the song of Moses, filled with praise: *"Who is like unto thee, O Lord, among the gods? who is like thee, glorious in holiness, fearful in praises, doing wonders?"* (Exodus 15:11).

In the Psalms we see what a large place praise ought to have in the spiritual life. There are more than sixty psalms of praise, becoming more frequent as the book draws to its close. (See Psalm 95–101, 103–107, 111–118, 134–138, 144–150.) The last five are Hallelujah psalms, with the words *"Praise ye the Lord"* at the beginning and the end. The very last psalm repeats, *"Praise him,"* twice in every verse, and it ends with, *"Let every thing that hath breath praise the Lord"* (Psalm 150:6).

Take time to study this until your heart and life are entirely a continual song of praise: *"I will bless the Lord at all times: his praise shall continually be in my mouth"* (Psalm 34:1); *"Every day will I bless thee"* (Psalm 145:2); *"I will sing praises unto my God while I have any being"* (Psalm 146:2).

With the coming of Christ into the world, there was a new outburst of praise in the song of the angels, the song of Mary, the song of Zechariah, and the song of Simeon. And then, in *"the song of Moses…and the song of the Lamb"* (Revelation 15:3), we find the praise of God filling creation: *"Great and marvellous are thy works, Lord God Almighty…Who shall not fear thee, O Lord, and glorify thy name? for thou only art holy"* (vv. 3–4). This song of praise ends with the fourfold *"Alleluia"* (Revelation 19:1, 3–4, 6). *"For the Lord God omnipotent reigneth"* (v. 6).

O child of God, let the inner chamber and your quiet time with God always lead your heart to unceasing praise!

April

April 1

The Image of God

**And God said, Let us make man in our image, after our likeness.
—Genesis 1:26**

Here we have the first thought of man in the mind of God; here man's origin and his destiny are shown to be entirely divine. God undertook the stupendous work of making a creature, who is not God, to be a perfect likeness of Him in His divine glory. Man was to live in entire dependence on God and to receive directly and unceasingly from Him the inflow of all that was holy and blessed in the Divine Being. God's glory, His holiness, and His love were to dwell in man and shine through him.

When sin had done its terrible work and had spoiled the image of God, the promise was given in Paradise of the woman's seed, in whom the divine purpose would be fulfilled: God's Son, *"the brightness of his glory, and the express image of his person"* (Hebrews 1:3), was to become a son of mankind. In Christ, God's plan would be carried out, His image revealed in human form. The New Testament speaks of those who are *"predestinate to be conformed to the image of his Son"* (Romans 8:29) and of *"the new man, which is renewed in knowledge after the image of him that created him"* (Colossians 3:10). We are given the promise: *"We know that, when he shall appear, we shall be like him; for we shall see him as he is"* (1 John 3:2).

Between God's eternal purpose for man and its eternal realization, we have a wonderful promise in regard to life here on earth: *"We all...beholding...the glory of the Lord, are changed into the same image from glory to glory, even as by the Spirit of the Lord"* (2 Corinthians 3:18). Let us take hold of this promise as the possible and assured experience of daily life for everyone who gives Christ His place as the Glorified One. Let us keep our hearts set on the glory of the image of God in Christ, in the assurance that the Spirit will change us into that image day by day. Dear reader, take time to believe firmly and confidently that this promise will be made true in your Christian life. God Almighty, who created man in His image, seeks now to work out His purpose in changing you into the image of Christ Jesus by the power of the Holy Spirit.

"Let this mind be in you, which was also in Christ Jesus" (Philippians 2:5). *"For I have given you an example, that ye should do as I have done to you"* (John 13:15).

April 2

The Obedience of Faith

The LORD appeared to Abram, and said unto him, I am the Almighty God; walk before me, and be thou perfect. And I will...multiply thee exceedingly.
—Genesis 17:1–2

In Abraham we see not only how God asks for and rewards faith, but also how He works faith by the gracious training that He gives. When God first called Abraham, He gave the great promise, *"In thee shall all families of the earth be blessed"* (Genesis 12:3).

God sought to strengthen Abraham's faith before the birth of Isaac, so He said, *"Walk before me, and be thou perfect. And I will...multiply thee exceedingly."* Again in the plains of Mamre, God asked, *"Is anything too hard for the* LORD*?"* (Genesis 18:14). God led Abraham step by step until his faith was perfected for full obedience in the sacrifice of Isaac. As *"by faith Abraham, when he was called to go out...went out"* (Hebrews 11:8), so by faith, at the end of forty years, he was able to obey God's will to the utmost—even when it appeared to conflict with all His promises.

Children of Abraham, the Father makes great demands on your faith. If you are to follow in Abraham's footsteps, you, too, must forsake all and live in the land of spiritual promise, separated unto God, with nothing but His Word to depend on. For this you will need a deep and clear insight that the God who is working in you is the Almighty who works according to *"the exceeding greatness of his power to us-ward who believe"* (Ephesians 1:19).

Do not think that it is easy to live the life of faith. It requires a life of abiding in His presence all day long. Bow before God in humble worship, until He speaks to you: *"I am the Almighty God; walk before me, and be thou perfect. And I will...multiply thee exceedingly."* When Abraham heard this, he *"fell on his face: and God talked with him"* (Genesis 17:3). In this lies the secret of the power to trust God for everything that He promises.

We can only go out like Abraham when we are called to a life of true consecration to God. Walk in the footsteps of Abraham. Hide deep in your heart the testimony of God's Word: *"He...was strong in faith... being fully persuaded that, what* [God] *had promised, he was able also to perform"* (Romans 4:20–21).

April 3

The Love of God

And thou shalt love the LORD thy God with all thine heart, and with all thy soul, and with all thy might. —Deuteronomy 6:5

April

God taught Abraham what it was to believe in Him with all his heart; therefore, he *"was strong in faith, giving glory to God"* (Romans 4:20). Moses taught Israel the first and great commandment: to love God with their whole hearts. This was the first commandment, the fountain out of which the others naturally proceed. It has its foundation in the relationship between God and man—God as the loving Creator, and man made in His image. It could never be otherwise.

Man finds his destiny and happiness in one thing: loving God with all his heart and strength. Moses said, *"The LORD had a delight in thy fathers to love them"* (Deuteronomy 10:15). Our entire lives are to be inspired by one thought: we are to love God with all our hearts and all our strength. The first duty of the child of God is to live out this command.

How seldom Israel was able to obey the command! But before Moses died, he was able to make known the promise: *"And the LORD thy God will circumcise thine heart...to love the LORD thy God with all thine heart, and with all thy soul"* (Deuteronomy 30:6), and He will do it *"with the circumcision made without hands"* (Colossians 2:11), by the circumcision of Christ on the cross.

This blessed promise was the first indication of the new covenant. Jeremiah foretold of the law being written in their hearts by the Holy Spirit so that they would no longer depart from God but would walk in His ways. (See Jeremiah 31:33.) But how little have Christians understood this; how easily they rest content with the thought that it is impossible!

Learn the double lesson. A perfect heart, loving God with all your might, is what God claims, is what God is infinitely worthy of, is what God will Himself give and work in you. Let your whole soul go out in faith to meet, to wait for, and to expect the fulfillment of the promise, that to love God with the whole heart is what God Himself will work in you.

"The love of God is shed abroad in our hearts by the Holy Ghost which is given unto us" (Romans 5:5). That makes the grace of loving God with all our hearts most sure and blessed.

April 4

The Joyful Sound

Blessed is the people that know the joyful sound: they shall walk, O LORD, in the light of thy countenance. In thy name shall they rejoice all the day. —Psalm 89:15–16

"Good tidings of great joy" (Luke 2:10) was what the angel called the gospel message, which is called *"the joyful sound"* in Psalm 89. Such blessedness consists of God's people walking in the light of God and rejoicing in His name all day long. Undisturbed fellowship and never ending joy are their portion. In the Old Testament, such things were at times the experience of believers. But there was no continuance; the Old Testament could not secure it. Only the New Testament can and does give it.

In every well-ordered family, one finds the father delighting in his children, and children rejoicing in their father's presence. This mark of a happy home is what the heavenly Father has promised and delights to work in His people—walking and rejoicing in His name all day long. It has been promised; it has been made possible in Christ through the Holy Spirit filling the heart with the love of God. It is the heritage of everyone who is seeking to love God with all his heart and with all his strength.

And yet, how many of God's children think it impossible and have even given up the hope and desire for a life of rejoicing in God's presence all day long! But Christ promised it so definitely: *"These things have I spoken unto you, that my joy might remain in you, and that your joy might be full"* (John 15:11); *"I will see you again, and your heart shall rejoice"* (John 16:22).

The Father wants His children to have perfect confidence in and love for Him. He knows their need for His presence every moment of the day for their happiness and strength. Christ maintains this life in us by the power of the Holy Spirit. Let us be content with nothing less than the blessedness of those who know the joyful sound: *"They shall walk…in the light of thy countenance. In thy name shall they rejoice all the day…For thou art the glory of their strength"* (Psalm 89:15–17).

The deeper we seek to enter into God's will for us, the stronger our faith will be that the Father can be content with nothing less than His child walking and rejoicing in His name all day long. We can be assured that what the Father has meant for us will be brought about in us through Christ and the Holy Spirit.

April 5

The Thoughts of God

For as the heavens are higher than the earth, so are... my thoughts than your thoughts.
—Isaiah 55:9

In giving us His promises of what He will work in us, God reminds us that, as high as the heavens are above the earth, so high are His thoughts above ours—altogether beyond our power of spiritual understanding.

When He tells us that we are made in His image, that by grace we are renewed again into that image, and that as we gaze upon God's glory in Christ we are changed into the same image, these are indeed thoughts higher than the heavens. When He told Abraham of all the mighty work He would do in him and his descendants, this again is a thought higher than the heavens. Our human minds cannot take it in. When God calls us to love Him with all our hearts and promises to renew our hearts so that we will love Him with all our strength, here again is a thought out of the very heights of heaven. And when the Father calls us to a life in the light of His countenance and rejoicing in His name all day long, this is a gift out of the very depths of God's heart of love.

We ought to have deep reverence, humility, and patience while we are waiting for God to impart to our hearts, by His Holy Spirit, the life and light that can make us feel at home with these thoughts. What great faith is needed to believe that God not only will reveal the glory of these thoughts, but also will so mightily work in us that their divine reality and blessing will fill our inmost beings!

Think of what Isaiah said, as quoted by Paul: *"Eye hath not seen, nor ear heard, neither have entered into the heart of man, the things which God hath prepared for them that love him. But God hath revealed them unto us by his Spirit"* (1 Corinthians 2:9–10). When Christ promised His disciples that the Holy Spirit would come from heaven to dwell with them, He said that the Spirit would fill us with the light and life of the heavenly world. In this way, Christ and the purposes of God—which are higher than the heavens are above the earth—were made their abiding experience. Dear reader, seek to realize that every day the Holy Spirit will fill your heart with the thoughts of God in all their heavenly power and glory.

April 6

The New Covenant in Jeremiah 31

I will make a new covenant with the house of Israel…I will put my law in their inward parts, and write it in their hearts.
—Jeremiah 31:31, 33

When God made the first covenant with Israel at Sinai, He said, *"If ye will obey my voice indeed, and keep my covenant, then ye shall be a peculiar treasure unto me above all people"* (Exodus 19:5). But Israel, unfortunately, did not have the power to obey. Their whole nature was carnal and sinful. There was no provision in the covenant for the grace that would make them obedient. The law only served to show them their sin.

April

In Jeremiah 31, God promised to make a new covenant in which provision would be made to enable men to live a life of obedience. In this new covenant, the law was to be put in their minds and written in their hearts, *"not with ink, but with the Spirit of the living God"* (2 Corinthians 3:3), so that they could say with David, *"I delight to do thy will, O my God: yea, thy law is within my heart"* (Psalm 40:8). Through the Holy Spirit, the law and the people's delight in it would take possession of their inner lives. Or, as we see in Jeremiah 32:40, God would put His fear in their hearts so that they would not depart from Him.

In contrast to the Old Testament covenant, which made it impossible to remain faithful, this promise ensures a continual, wholehearted obedience as the mark of the believer who takes God at His Word and fully claims what the promise secures.

Learn the lesson well. In the new covenant, God's mighty power is shown in the heart of everyone who believes the promise, *"They shall not depart from me"* (Jeremiah 32:40). Bow in deep stillness before God, and believe what He says. The measure of our experience of this power of God, which will keep us from departing from Him, will always be in harmony with the law: *"According to your faith be it unto you"* (Matthew 9:29).

We need to make a great effort to keep the contrast between the Old and New Testaments very clear. The Old had a wonderful measure of grace, but not enough for continually abiding in the faith of obedience. But that is the definite promise of the New Testament: the power of the Holy Spirit leading the soul and revealing the fullness of grace to keep us "*unblameable in holiness*" (1 Thessalonians 3:13).

April 7

The New Covenant in Ezekiel

Then will I sprinkle clean water upon you, and ye shall be clean: from all your filthiness....I will put my spirit within you, and cause you to walk in my statutes, and ye shall keep my judgments.
—Ezekiel 36:25, 27

Here we find the same promise as in Jeremiah, the promise of being so cleansed from sin, and so renewed in the heart, that there would be no doubt of walking in God's statutes and keeping His law. In Jeremiah God had said, *"I will put my law in their inward parts"* (Jeremiah 31:33), and *"I will put my fear in their hearts, that they shall not depart from me"* (Jeremiah 32:40). In Ezekiel He said, *"I will...cause you to walk in my statutes, and ye shall keep my judgments."* In contrast to the old covenant, in which there was no power to enable them to continue in God's law, the great mark of the new covenant would be a divine power enabling them to walk in His statutes and keep His judgments.

"Where sin abounded, grace did much more abound" (Romans 5:20), bringing about wholehearted obedience. Why is this so seldom experienced? The answer is very simple: the promise is not believed, is not preached; its fulfillment is not expected. Yet how clearly it is laid out for us in a passage like Romans 8:1–4! In this passage, the man who had complained of the power *"bringing* [him] *into captivity to the law of sin"* (Romans 7:23) thanks God that he is now "*in Christ Jesus"* (Romans 8:1) and that the *"law of the Spirit of life in Christ Jesus hath made* [him] *free from the law of sin and death"* (v. 2), so that the requirement of the law is fulfilled in all who walk after the Spirit. (See verse 4.)

Once again, why are there so few who can give such testimony, and what is to be done to attain it? Just one thing is needed: faith in an omnipotent God who will, by His wonderful power, do what He has promised. *"I the LORD have spoken it, and will do it"* (Ezekiel 22:14). Oh, let us begin to believe that the promise will come true: "*Ye shall be clean: from all your filthiness...I will...cause you to walk in my statutes, and ye shall keep my judgments."* Let us believe all that God promises here, and God will do it. Beyond all power of thought, God has made His great and glorious promises dependent on our faith. And the promises will bring about more of that faith as we believe them. *"According to your faith be it unto you"* (Matthew 9:29). Let us put this truth to the test even now.

April 8

The New Covenant and Prayer

Call unto me, and I will answer thee, and show thee great and mighty things, which thou knowest not.
—Jeremiah 33:3

I the LORD have spoken it, and I will do it....I will yet for this be inquired of by the house of Israel, to do it for them.
—Ezekiel 36:36–37

The fulfillment of the great promises of the new covenant is dependent on prayer. In answer to the prayer of Jeremiah, God had said, *"I will put my fear in their hearts, that they shall not depart from me"* (Jeremiah 32:40). And to Ezekiel He had spoken, *"I will...cause you to walk in my statutes, and ye shall keep my judgments"* (Ezekiel 36:27). Because we are unbelieving and we judge the meaning of God's Word according to human thought and experience, there is no expectation of these promises being truly fulfilled. We do not have the faith in the mighty power of God that is waiting to make His promise true in our experience.

God has said that without such faith, our lives will be partial and limited. He has graciously pointed out the way such faith can be found; it is in the path of much prayer: *"Call unto me, and I will answer thee, and show thee great and mighty things, which thou knowest not."* Moreover, *"I will yet for this be inquired of by the house of Israel, to do it for them."* When individual men and women turn to God with their whole hearts to plead these promises, He will fulfill them. It is in the exercise of intense, persevering prayer that faith will be strengthened to take hold of God and will surrender itself to His omnipotent working. Then, as one after another testifies of what God has done and will do, believers will help each other and will take their place as the church of the living God, pleading for and firmly expecting His promises to be fulfilled in larger measure. Then power will be given to them for the great work of preaching Christ in the fullness of His redemption to perishing men.

The state of the church calls for unceasing prayer. We need to pray intensely and persistently that the need for the power of the Holy Spirit may be deeply felt and that a strong faith may be roused in the hearts of many to claim and to expect His mighty working. *"I the LORD have spoken it, and will do it"* (Ezekiel 22:14).

"Lord, I believe; help thou mine unbelief" (Mark 9:24).

April 9

The New Covenant in Hebrews

For I will be merciful to their unrighteousness, and their sins and their iniquities will I remember no more.
—Hebrews 8:12

April

In the book of Hebrews, Christ is called the *"Mediator of a better covenant, which was established upon better promises"* (v. 6). In Him the two parts of the covenant find their fulfillment.

First, He came to atone for sin, so that its power over man was destroyed and free access to God's presence and favor was secured. With that came the fuller blessing: the new heart, freed from the power of sin, with God's Holy Spirit breathing into it the delight in God's law and the power to obey.

These two parts of the covenant can never be separated. And yet, unfortunately, many people put their trust in Christ for the forgiveness of sin but never think of claiming the fullness of the promise of being God's people and knowing Him as their God. They do not allow God to bring into their experience a new heart cleansed from sin, with the Holy Spirit breathing into it such love and delight in God's law, and such power to obey, that they have access to the full blessing of the new covenant.

Jesus is *"the mediator of the new testament"* (Hebrews 9:15), in which the forgiveness of sin is in the power of His blood, and in which the law is written in hearts by the power of His Spirit. Oh, if only we could understand that, just as surely as the complete pardon of sin is assured, so the complete fulfillment of the promises may be expected, too: *"I will put my fear in their hearts, that they shall not depart from me"* (Jeremiah 32:40); *"I will…cause you to walk in my statutes, and you will keep my judgments"* (Ezekiel 36:27).

But God has said, *"Behold, I am the LORD, the God of all flesh: is there any thing too hard for me?"* (Jeremiah 32:27). He spoke these words to Jeremiah in regard to the new covenant. The new covenant requires strong, wholehearted desire for a life wholly given up to God. It means we must set aside all our preconceived opinions, and in faith believe in the mighty power of God. It means a surrender to Jesus Christ, a willingness to accept our place with Him, crucified to the world, to sin, and to self. It means a readiness to follow Him at any cost. Succinctly, the new covenant means wholehearted acceptance of Christ as Lord—heart and life wholly His. *"I the LORD have spoken it, and will do it"* (Ezekiel 22:14).

April 10

The Trial of Faith

And [Naaman's] servants came near, and spake unto him, and said, My father, if the prophet had bid thee do some great thing, wouldest thou not have done it? How much rather then, when he saith to thee, Wash, and be clean?
—2 Kings 5:13

In Naaman we have a striking illustration of the place faith holds in God's dealings with man. Think first of how intense Naaman's desire was for healing. He would do anything, even appeal to the kings of Syria and Israel. He would undertake a long journey and humble himself before the prophet, who did not even come out and see him. In this intense desire for blessing, we have the first mark of a strong faith.

A second mark of faith is that it has given up all its preconceived opinions and bows before the Word of God. This was more than Naaman was willing to do, and he turned away in rage. It was well for him that a wise and faithful servant gave him better advice. Faith is often held back by the thought that such a simple thing as accepting God's Word can bring about a mighty revolution in the heart.

Third, faith submits implicitly to the Word of God: *"Wash, and be clean."* At first it might appear futile, but faith proves itself in obedience. It does not obey only once or twice, but *"seven times"* (2 Kings 5:10), in the assurance that the mighty wonder will be brought about. Taking hold of the simple word, *"Wash, and be clean,"* it finds itself renewed as with the life of a little child, *"clean every whit"* (John 13:10). The mighty deed is done.

When God's Word brings us to the promise, *"I will sprinkle clean water upon you, and ye shall be clean: from all your filthiness...will I cleanse you"* (Ezekiel 36:25), it is nothing but unbelief that holds us back. Let us believe that a determined surrender of the whole will to God's promise will indeed bring the heart-cleansing we need. *"There is a river, the streams whereof shall make glad the city of God"* (Psalm 46:4). It flows from under the throne of God and the Lamb, through the channels of a thousand precious promises, and at each step the word is heard: *"Wash, and be clean."* Christ cleanses *"with the washing of water by the word"* (Ephesians 5:26), and He says to you, *"Now ye are clean through the word which I have spoken unto you"* (John 15:3)—*"clean every whit".* (John 13:10).

April 11

Faith in Christ

Ye believe in God, believe also in me.
—John 14:1

In John, chapters 14–17, when Christ was about to leave His disciples, He taught that they were to believe in Him with the same confidence with which they had rested in God. *"Ye believe in God, believe also in me"; "Believe me that I am in the Father….He that believeth on me, the works that I do shall he do also"* (John 14:11–12). Here on earth, He had not been able to make Himself fully known to His disciples. But in heaven, the fullness of God's power would be His; and He would, through His disciples, do greater things than He had ever done on earth.

April

This faith must first of all focus itself on the person of Christ in His union with the Father. The disciples were to have perfect confidence that all the things that God had done could now be done by Jesus, too. The deity of Christ is the rock on which our faith depends. Christ as man, partaker of our nature, is indeed the true God. As the divine power has worked in Christ even to the resurrection from the dead, so Christ can also, in His divine omnipotence, work in us all that we need.

Dear Christian, do you not see of what deep importance it is that you take time to worship Jesus in His divine omnipotence as one with the Father? That will teach you to depend on Him in His sufficiency to work in you all that you can desire. This faith must so possess you that every thought of Christ will be filled with the consciousness of His presence as an almighty Redeemer, able to save, sanctify, and empower you to the uttermost.

Child of God, bow in deep humility before this blessed Lord Jesus, and worship Him—*"My Lord and my God"* (John 20:28). Take time until you become fully conscious of an assured faith that Christ, as the almighty God, will work for you, in you, and through you all that God desires and all that you need. Let Him be your confidence and your strength.

On their last night together, the Savior began by telling His disciples that everything in their lives would depend on simply believing Him. By this, they would do greater things than He had ever done. At the close of His address He repeated again, *"Be of good cheer, I have overcome the world"* (John 16:33). Our one need is a direct, definite, unceasing faith in the mighty power of Christ working in us.

April 12

Christ's Life in Us

Because I live, ye shall live also.
—John 14:19

There is a great difference between the first three gospels and that of John. John was the beloved friend of Jesus. He understood the Master better than the others. Many consider John 13–17 to be the innermost sanctuary of the New Testament. The other gospel writers spoke of repentance and of the pardon of sin as the first great gift of the New Testament. But they said little of the new life that the new covenant was to bring, with the new heart in which the law had been put as a living power. John recorded what Christ taught about His life really becoming ours and of our being united with Him just as He was with the Father. The other gospel writers spoke of Christ as the Shepherd seeking and saving the lost; John spoke of Him as the Shepherd who so gives His life for the sheep that His very life becomes theirs. *"I came that they may have life, and may have it abundantly"* (John 10:10 RV).

And so Christ said, *"Because I live, ye shall live also."* The disciples were to receive from Him, not the life He then had, but the resurrection life in the power of its victory over death and of His exaltation to the right hand of God. He would from then on always dwell in them; a new, heavenly, eternal life—the life of Jesus Himself—would fill them. And this promise is to all who will accept it in faith.

Unfortunately, so many people are content with the beginnings of the Christian life but never desire to have it in its fullness—the more abundant life. They do not believe in it; they are not ready for the sacrifice implied in being wholly filled with the life of Jesus. Child of God, the message comes again to you: *"The things which are impossible with men are possible with God"* (Luke 18:27). Take time and let Christ's wonderful promise possess your heart. Be content with nothing less than a full salvation, Christ living in you, and you living in Christ. Be assured that it is meant for everyone who will take time to listen to Christ's promises and will believe that the almighty power of God will work in him the mighty wonder of His grace—Christ dwelling in the heart by faith.

April 13

The Obedience of Love

If ye keep my commandments, ye shall abide in my love.
—John 15:10

Believers often ask, "How can I come to abide in Christ always, to live wholly for Him?" In the above verse, the Lord gave the simple but far-reaching answer: *"Keep my commandments."* This is the only sure way of abiding in Him. *"If ye keep my commandments, ye shall abide in my love; even as I have kept my Father's commandments, and abide in his love"* (v. 10).

The Lord spoke of this relationship between love and obedience on His last night. In John 14 we find it three times: *"If ye love me, keep my commandments"* (v. 15); *"He that hath my commandments, and keepeth them, he it is that loveth me: and he that loveth me shall be loved of my Father, and I will love him, and will manifest myself to him"* (v. 21); *"If a man love me, he will keep my words: and my Father will love him, and we will come unto him, and make our abode with him"* (v. 23). In chapter fifteen are three more instances: *"If…my words abide in you, ye shall ask what ye will, and it shall be done unto you"* (v. 7); *"If ye keep my commandments, ye shall abide in my love"* (v. 10); and *"Ye are my friends, if ye do whatsoever I command you"* (v. 14). All six times the Lord connected the keeping of the commandments with the blessing that accompanies obedience—the indwelling of the Father and the Son in the heart. The love that keeps His commandments is the only way to abide in His love. In our relationship with Christ, love is everything—Christ's love for us, our love for Him, proven in our love for fellow Christians.

How seldom believers have accepted this teaching! Many are content to think that it is impossible. They do not believe that, through the grace of God, we can be kept from sin. They do not believe in the promise of the new covenant: *"I will put my spirit within you, and cause you to walk in my statutes, and ye shall keep my judgments"* (Ezekiel 36:27). They have no concept how Christ will make possible what otherwise appears beyond our reach: loving Him, keeping His commandments, and abiding in His love.

The wonderful promise of the Holy Spirit as the power of Christ's life in us is the pledge that we will indeed love Him and keep His words. This is the great secret of abiding in Christ, of having the indwelling of Christ and of God, and of the effectiveness of our prayers to bring God's blessing on all our work.

April 14

The Promise of the Spirit

If I depart, I will send him [the Holy Spirit] unto you....He shall glorify me: for he shall receive of mine, and shall show it unto you.
—John 16:7, 14

The crucified Christ was to be glorified on the throne of heaven. Out of that glory, He would send down the Holy Spirit into the hearts of His disciples to glorify Him in them. The Spirit of the crucified and glorified Christ would be their life in fellowship with Him. The Spirit comes to us as the Spirit of divine glory; as such we are to welcome Him and yield ourselves absolutely to His leading.

Yes, the Spirit who *"searcheth...the deep things of God"* (1 Corinthians 2:10), who had been with Christ through His life and in His death upon the cross—this Spirit of the Father and the Son was to come and dwell in the disciples and make them the conscious possessors of the presence of the glorified Christ. It was this blessed Spirit who was to be their power for a life of loving obedience, to be their Teacher and Leader in praying down from heaven the blessing that they needed. And it was in His power that they were to conquer God's enemies and carry the gospel to the ends of the world.

It is this Spirit that the church lacks so sadly; it is this Spirit she grieves so unceasingly. It is owing to this spiritual poverty that her work is so often feeble and fruitless.

The Spirit is God. As God, He claims possession of our entire beings. We have too often thought of Him as our help in the Christian life, while we have not known that our hearts and lives are to be entirely and unceasingly under His control. Indeed, we are to be led by the Spirit every day and every hour. In His power, we are to directly and continually abide in the love and fellowship of Jesus. No wonder we do not have the courage to believe that Christ's mighty power will work in us and through us! No wonder His divine prayer-promises are beyond our reach! The Spirit who *"searcheth...the deep things of God"* claims the very depths of our beings, so that He may there reveal Christ as Lord and Ruler.

The promise waits for its fulfillment in our lives: *"He shall glorify me: for he shall receive of mine, and shall show it unto you."* Let us yield ourselves today to believe the promise at once and with our whole hearts.

April 15

In Christ

At that day ye shall know that I am in my Father, and ye in me, and I in you. —John 14:20

Our Lord spoke of His life in the Father: *"Believe me that I am in the Father, and the Father in me"* (John 14:11). He and the Father were not two individuals next to each other; They were in each other. Though Christ was on earth as a man, He lived in the Father. Everything He did was what the Father did in Him.

April

Christ in God and God in Christ is the picture of what our life in Christ is to be here on earth. It is in the very nature of the divine life that the Son is in the Father. Even so, we must ever live in the faith that we are in Christ. Then we will learn that, even as the Father worked in Christ, so Christ will also work in us if we only yield ourselves to His power.

And even as the Son waited on the Father and as the Father worked through Him, so the disciples would make known to Him in prayer what they wanted done on earth, and He would do it. As the Father worked in Him, because He lived in the Father, so Christ would work in them as they lived in Him.

But this would not be fulfilled until the Holy Spirit came. They had to wait until they were filled with the power from on high. For this they abided in Him by daily fellowship and prayer, so that He might do in them the greater works He had promised.

How little the church understands that the secret of her power is to be found in nothing less than where Christ found it, abiding in the Father and His love! Ministers, too, seldom understand that this should be their one great goal, daily and hourly to abide in Christ as the only possible way of being equipped and used by Him in the great work of winning souls to Him. If anyone asks what the lost secret of the pulpit is, we have it here: *"At that day"*—when the Spirit fills your heart—*"At that day ye shall know that I am in my Father, and ye in me, and I in you."*

Blessed Lord, teach us to surrender ourselves unreservedly to the Holy Spirit. Teach us, above everything, to wait daily for His teaching, so that we, too, may know the blessed secret, that as You are in the Father, so we are in You, and You work through us.

April 16

Abiding in Christ

Abide in me, and I in you.
—John 15:4

Using the parable of the vine and the branches, our Lord sought to enforce and illustrate what He had taught in John 14 concerning our union with Him and His union with the Father. He did this all for the sake of bringing home to the apostles and to all His servants in the gospel the absolute necessity of a life in daily, full communion with Him.

On the one hand, He pointed to Himself and to the Father and indicated, "Just as truly and fully as I am in the Father, so you are in Me." Then, pointing to the vine, He essentially said, "Just as truly as the branch is in the vine, you are in Me. Just as the Father abides in Me and works in Me; just as I work out what He works in Me; just as the branch abides in the vine, the vine gives its life and strength to the branch, and the branch receives it and puts it forth in fruit—even so do you abide in Me and receive My strength. *'Abide in me.'*"

Do you not feel that you still have much to learn in order to have Christ's almighty power working in you as He desires? The great need is to take time in waiting on the Lord Jesus in the power of His Spirit, until the two great truths get complete mastery of your being: Christ is in God, and you are in Christ.

"He that abideth in me, and I in him, the same bringeth forth much fruit" (v. 5), said our Lord. Fruit is what Christ seeks, is what He works, is what He will assuredly give to the person who trusts Him.

To the feeblest of God's children, Christ says, "You are in Me. Abide in Me, and you will bear much fruit." To the strongest of His messengers, He still says, "Abide in Me, and you will bear much fruit." To one and all the message comes: continuous, unbroken abiding in Christ Jesus is the one condition of a life of power and blessing. Take time, and let the Holy Spirit so renew in you the secret abiding in Him that you may understand the meaning of His words: *"These things have I spoken unto you, that my joy might remain in you, and that your joy might be full"* (v. 11).

The Lord says to us, "Do you believe that I can do this, that I can keep you abiding in My love?" And when we answer Him, "Yes, Lord," He tells us, *"Be not afraid; only believe"* (Mark 5:36).

April 17

The Power of Prayer

If ye abide in me, and my words abide in you, ask whatsoever ye will, and it shall be done unto you.
—John 15:7 (RV)

April

Before our Lord went up to heaven, He taught His disciples two great lessons in regard to their relationship with Him in the great work they had to do. The one was that in heaven, He would have much more power than He had upon earth, and He would use that power for the salvation of men, solely through them, their words, and their work. The other lesson was that, without Him, they could do nothing, but they could depend on Him to work in them and through them, and so carry out His purpose. Their first and chief work would therefore be to bring everything they wanted done to Him in prayer. They knew and depended on His promise: *"Ask whatsoever ye will, and it shall be done unto you."*

With these two truths written in their hearts, He sent them out into the world. The almighty, glorified Jesus was ready to do in and through them greater things than He Himself had ever done upon earth. The helpless disciples on earth unceasingly looked up to Him in prayer, with the full confidence that He would hear those prayers—but on the condition that they have an unflinching confidence in the power of His promise. The chief thing in their lives and ministry was to be the maintenance of a spirit of prayer and supplication.

But how little the church has understood and believed this! Why? Simply because believers live so little in the daily abiding in Christ that they are powerless in believing His *"great and precious promises"* (2 Peter 1:4). As the members of Christ's body, the chief thing every day must be a close abiding fellowship with Christ that is based in deep dependence and unceasing supplication. Only then can we do our work in the full assurance that He has heard our prayers and will be faithful in doing His part—in giving the power from on high as the source of strength and abundant blessing. Take time, you *"servants of the LORD"* (Psalm 113:1), and with your whole hearts believe the word Christ has spoken. Christ asks, *"Believest thou this?...Yea, Lord: I believe"* (John 11:26–27). *"If ye abide in me, and my words abide in you, ask whatsoever ye will, and it shall be done unto you."*

"Continue [abide] *ye in my love"* (John 15:9).

April 18

The Mystery of Love

That they all may be one; as thou, Father, art in me, and I in thee....that they may be one, even as we are one: I in them, and thou in me. —John 17:21–23

During His last evening on earth, Christ especially pressed the thought of the disciples being in Him and abiding in Him. He also mentioned His being in them, but He did not emphasize this as much as their being in Him. But in His prayer as High Priest, He gave greater place to the thought of His being in them, just as the Father was in Him: *"And the glory which thou gavest me I have given them; that they may be one, even as we are one: I in them, and thou in me, that they may be made perfect in one; and that the world may know that thou hast sent me, and hast loved them, as thou hast loved me"* (vv. 22–23).

The power to convince the world that God loved the disciples as He loved His Son could only come as believers lived their lives with Christ in them and proved it by loving others as Christ loved them. The feebleness of the church is owing to the fact that we have not, by our example, proven to the world that our lives are in Christ and His life is in us. What is needed? Nothing less than a complete indwelling of Christ in the heart, and a binding together of believers because they know each other as those who have Christ dwelling in them. The last words of Christ's prayer in John 17 read, *"And I have declared unto them thy name, and will declare it: that the love wherewith thou hast loved me may be in them, and I in them"* (v. 26). The divine indwelling has its chief glory in that it is the manifestation of divine love. It is the Father's love for Christ flowing out from us to all men.

Christ gave this great promise to every disciple: *"My Father will love him, and we will come unto him, and make our abode with him"* (John 14:23). The Holy Spirit, in whom the Father and the Son are one, desires to live in our hearts in order that we may live this life of love for Christ and one's fellowmen. Let nothing less than this be what you seek with your whole heart—the indwelling of the Lord Jesus in the love *"which passeth knowledge"* (Ephesians 3:19). In this way the world will be constrained by the love God's children have for each other to acknowledge that Christ's words are fulfilled: *"That the love wherewith thou hast loved me may be in them, and I in them."*

"Believest thou this?...Yea, Lord: I believe" (John 11:26–27).

April 19

Christ, Our Righteousness

Being justified freely by his grace through the redemption that is in Christ Jesus.
—Romans 3:24

The first three gospel writers spoke of redemption as a pardon of sin, or justification. John spoke of it as a life that Christ is to live in us—regeneration. In Paul's letters, however, we find both truths in beautiful harmony.

Paul first spoke of justification in Romans 3:21–5:11. Then he went on from 5:12 to 8:39 to speak of the life that is lived in union with Christ. In Romans 4 he told us that we find both these things in Abraham: *"Abraham believed God....To him that...believeth on him that justifieth the ungodly, his faith is counted for righteousness"* (v. 3, 5). Then, in verse 17, Abraham *"believed, even God, who quickeneth the dead."* Just as God considered Abraham's faith as righteousness and then led him to believe in Him as the God who can give life to the dead, so it is with every believer.

Justification comes when the eye of faith is fixed on Christ. But that is only the beginning. Gradually the believer begins to understand that he was at the same time born again, that he has Christ in him, and that his calling now is to abide in Christ and let Christ abide and live and work in him.

Most Christians strive, by holding on to their faith in justification, to stir themselves up and strengthen themselves for a life of gratitude and obedience. But they fail sadly because they do not know, do not in full faith yield themselves to Christ, to maintain His life in them. They have learned from Abraham the first lesson: to believe that God *"justifieth the ungodly."* But they have not gone on to the second great lesson: to believe in God *"who quickeneth the dead"* and daily renews that life through Christ, who lives in them and in whose life alone there is strength and fullness of blessing. The Christian life must be *"from faith to faith"* (Romans 1:17). The grace of pardon is only the beginning; growing in grace leads on to the fuller insight and experience of what it means to be in Christ, to live in Him, and to *"grow up into him in all things, which is the head, even Christ"* (Ephesians 4:15).

Christ, Our Life

**Much more they which receive abundance of grace and of the gift of righteousness shall reign in life by one, Jesus Christ.
—Romans 5:17**

**Likewise reckon ye also yourselves to be dead indeed unto sin, but alive unto God through Jesus Christ our Lord.
—Romans 6:11**

Paul taught us that our faith in Christ as our righteousness is to be followed by our faith in Him as our life from the dead. He asked, *"Know ye not, that so many of us as were baptized into Jesus Christ were baptized into his death?"* (Romans 6:3). We were buried with Him and were raised from the dead with Him. Just as all of mankind died in Adam, so all believers in Christ actually died in Him. *"Our old man is crucified with him"* (v. 6); with Him we were raised from the dead (see Colossians 2:12); and now we are to consider ourselves as *"dead indeed to sin, but alive unto God."*

Truly, just as the new life in us is an experience of the risen life of Christ, so our death to sin is also a spiritual reality. When we, by the power of the Holy Spirit, are enabled to see how we were really one with Christ in His death and in His resurrection, we will understand that in Him sin has no power over us. We present ourselves unto God as being *"alive from the dead"* (Romans 6:13).

The man who knows that he died in Christ and is now alive in Him can confidently depend on it that *"sin shall not have dominion over* [him]" (v. 14), not even for a single moment. *"Reckon ye also yourselves to be dead indeed unto sin, but alive unto God through Jesus Christ our Lord."* This is the true life of faith.

Just as we can only live in Christ and have Him live in us as we experience the power of the Holy Spirit, so it is here. Paul said, *"For the law of the Spirit of life in Christ Jesus hath made me free from the law of sin and death"* (Romans 8:2), which, he had complained, had kept him in captivity. Then he added, *"That the righteousness of the law might be fulfilled in us, who walk not after the flesh, but after the Spirit"* (v. 4). Through the Spirit we enter into the glorious liberty of the children of God.

Oh, that God might open the eyes of His children to see what the power is of Christ living in them for a life of holiness and fruitfulness, when they consider themselves *"dead indeed unto sin, but alive unto God through Jesus Christ."*

April 21

Crucified with Christ

I am crucified with Christ: nevertheless I live; yet not I, but Christ liveth in me. —Galatians 2:20

As in Adam we died and went out of the life and will of God into sin and corruption, so in Christ we are made partakers of a new spiritual death—a death out of sin and into the will and life of God. Such was the death Christ died; such is the death we are made partakers of in Him. To Paul, this was such a reality that he was able to say, *"I am crucified with Christ: nevertheless I live; yet not I, but Christ liveth in me."* Dying with Christ had had such power that he no longer lived his own life; instead, Christ lived His life in him. He had indeed died to the old nature and to sin and had been raised up into the power of the living Christ dwelling in him.

It was the crucified Christ who lived in Paul and made him a partaker of all that the cross had meant to Christ Himself. The very mind that was in Christ—who emptied Himself and took *"the form of a servant"* (Philippians 2:7) and who *"humbled himself, and became obedient unto death"* (v. 8)—was at work in him because the crucified Christ lived in him. He lived as a crucified man.

Christ's death on the cross was His highest display of holiness and victory over sin. The believer who receives Christ is made a partaker of all the power and blessing that the crucified Lord has won. As the believer learns to accept this by faith, he yields himself as crucified to the world and dead to its pleasure and pride, its lusts and self-pleasing. He learns that the mystery of the cross, as the crucified Lord reveals its power in him, opens the door into the fullest fellowship with Christ and the conformity to His sufferings. And so he learns, in the full depth of its meaning, what the Word has said: *"Christ crucified...the power of God, and the wisdom of God"* (1 Corinthians 1:23–24). He grows into a fuller understanding of the blessedness of daring to say, *"I am crucified with Christ: nevertheless I live; yet not I, but Christ liveth in me."*

Oh, the blessedness and power of the God-given faith that enables a man to live all day yielding himself to God and considering himself as *"dead indeed unto sin, but alive unto God through Jesus Christ"* (Romans 6:11).

April 22

The Faith Life

The life which I now live in the flesh I live by the faith of the Son of God, who loved me, and gave himself for me.
—Galatians 2:20

If we were able to ask Paul, "What is your part in living life, if you no longer live but Christ lives in you?" he would answer, *"The life which I now live in the flesh I live by the faith of the Son of God, who loved me, and gave himself for me."* His whole life, day by day and all day long, was one of unceasing faith in the wonderful Love that had given itself for him. Faith was the power that possessed and permeated Paul's whole being and his every action.

Here we have the simple but full statement of the secret of the true Christian life. It is not faith that rests only in certain promises of God or in certain blessings that we receive from Christ. It is a faith that sees how entirely Christ gives Himself to the soul to be his entire life and all that that implies for every moment of the day. Just as continuous breathing is essential to the support of our physical life, so is the unceasing faith in which the soul trusts Christ and depends on Him to maintain the life of the Spirit within us. Faith always rests on the infinite love in which Christ gave Himself wholly for us to be entirely ours and to live His life over again in us. By virtue of His divine omnipresence, by which He *"filleth all in all"* (Ephesians 1:23), He can be to each what He is to all—a complete and perfect Savior, an abiding Guest, taking charge and maintaining our life in us and for us—as if each of us were the only one in whom He lives. Just as truly as the Father lived in Him and worked in Him all that He was to work out, so will Christ live and work in each one of us.

When our faith is led and taught by God's Holy Spirit, we obtain such a confidence in the omnipotence and omnipresence of Christ that we carry all day in the depths of our hearts this unbroken assurance: "He who loved me and gave Himself for me, He lives in me; He is my life and my all." *"I can do all things through Christ which strengtheneth me"* (Philippians 4:13). May God reveal to us the inseparable union between Christ and us, in which the consciousness of Christ's presence may become as natural to us as the consciousness of our existence.

April 23

Full Consecration

Yea doubtless, and I count all things but loss for the excellency of the knowledge of Christ Jesus my Lord.
—Philippians 3:8

In studying the promises Jesus gave to His disciples during His last night, the question arises: what was it that made these men worthy of the high honor of being baptized with the Holy Spirit from heaven? The answer is simple. When Christ called them, they forsook all and followed Him. They denied themselves, even to the point of hating their own lives, and gave themselves to obey His commands. They followed Him to Calvary, and amid its suffering and death, their hearts clung to Him alone. It was this that prepared them for receiving a share in His resurrection life, and so they were made ready to be filled with the Spirit, even as Christ received the fullness of the Spirit from the Father in glory.

Just as Jesus had to sacrifice all to be wholly an offering to God, so all His people—from Abraham, Jacob, and Joseph to His twelve disciples to today's believers—have had to give up all to follow the divine leading, and have lived separated unto God, before the divine power could fulfill God's purposes through them.

It was this way with Paul, too. To *"count all things but loss for the excellency of the knowledge of Christ Jesus my Lord"* was the keynote of his life, as it must be in ours if we are to share fully in the power of His resurrection. But how little the church understands that we have been entirely redeemed from the world, to live wholly and only for God and His love! The law of God's kingdom is unchangeable—*"all things loss for the excellency of the knowledge of Christ Jesus my Lord."*

The disciples had to spend years with Christ in order to be prepared for Pentecost. Christ calls us to walk every day in the closest union with Himself, to abide in Him without ceasing, and so to live as those who are not their own, but wholly His. In this life of full surrender, we will find the path to the fullness of the Spirit.

In faith, boldly believe that such a life is meant for you. Let your heart's fervent desire reach out for nothing less. Love the Lord and Christ your Savior with your whole heart. You will be *"more than conquerors through him that loved us"* (Romans 8:37).

April 24

Entire Sanctification

And the very God of peace sanctify you wholly; and I pray...[you be] blameless unto the coming of our Lord Jesus Christ. Faithful is he that calleth you, who also will do it.
—1 Thessalonians 5:23–24

What a promise! One would expect to see all God's children clinging to it, claiming its fulfillment. But, unfortunately, unbelief does not know what to think of it, and only a few people consider it their treasure and joy.

"The very God of peace" alone can and will do it. This God of peace promises to *"sanctify* [us] *wholly,"* in Christ our sanctification, in the sanctification of the Spirit. It is God who is doing the work. It is in close, personal fellowship with God that we become holy.

Should not all of us rejoice at the prospect? But it is as if the promise is too great for many of us, and so it is repeated and amplified. May your spirit (the inmost part of your being, created for fellowship with God), your soul (the seat of the life and all its powers), and your body (through which sin entered and proved its power even unto death, but which has been redeemed in Christ)—may these be preserved whole, without blame, at the coming of our Lord Jesus Christ. (See 1 Thessalonians 5:23.)

To prevent the possibility of any misunderstanding, as if it is too great to be literally true, these words are added to our text verse: *"Faithful is he that calleth you, who also will do it."* Yes, God has said, *"I the LORD have spoken it, and I* [in Christ and through the Holy Spirit], *will do it"* (Ezekiel 36:36). He asks only that we come and abide in close fellowship with Him every day. As the heat of the sun shines on the body and warms it, so the fire of His holiness will burn in us and make us holy.

Child of God, beware of unbelief. It dishonors God, it robs your soul of its heritage. Take refuge in this: *"Faithful is he that calleth you, who also will do it."* Let every thought of your high and holy calling elicit the response: *"Faithful is he that calleth you, who also will do it."* Yes, He will do it, and He will give you grace to abide in His nearness so that you can always be under the cover of His perfect peace and of the holiness that He alone can give. *"All things are possible to him that believeth....Lord, I believe; help thou mine unbelief"* (Mark 9:23–24).

April 25

The Exceeding Greatness of His Power

[May] the God of our Lord Jesus Christ, the Father of glory,...give unto you the spirit of wisdom and revelation...the eyes of your understanding being enlightened; that ye may know...what is the exceeding greatness of his power to us-ward who believe, according to the working of his mighty power, which he wrought in Christ, when he raised him from the dead. —Ephesians 1:17–20

April

Here is one of the great Scriptures that will make our faith strong and bold. Paul was writing to those who had been sealed with the Holy Spirit. And yet he felt the need for unceasing prayer and for the enlightening of the Spirit, so that they might truly know the mighty power of God working in them. It was nothing less than this same power by which He raised Christ from the dead.

Christ died on the tree, weighed down by the sin of the world and its curse. When He descended into the grave, it was under the weight of all that sin and under the power of the death that had apparently mastered Him. What a mighty working of the power of God, to raise that Man out of the grave to the power and the glory of His throne! And now it is that same power, in its *"exceeding greatness...to us-ward who believe,"* that we, by the teaching of the Holy Spirit, are to know as working in us every day of our lives.

It is by that same almighty power that the risen and exalted Christ can be revealed in our hearts as our life and strength. How rarely Christians believe this! Oh, let us cry to God; let us trust God for His Holy Spirit to enable us to claim nothing less every day than the *"exceeding greatness"* of this resurrection power working in us!

Let us especially pray for all believers around us and throughout the church, that they may have their eyes opened to the wonderful vision of God's almighty resurrection power working in them. And let ministers, like Paul, make this a matter of continual intercession for those among whom they labor. What a difference it would make in their ministry—the unceasing prayer for the Spirit to reveal the power that dwells and works in them!

April 26

The Indwelling Christ

For this cause I bow my knees unto the Father of our Lord Jesus Christ...that he would grant you, according to the riches of his glory, to be strengthened with might by his Spirit in the inner man; that Christ may dwell in your hearts by faith; that ye, being rooted and grounded in love...might be filled with all the fulness of God.
—Ephesians 3:14, 16–17, 19

The great privilege that separated Israel from other nations was this: they had God dwelling in their midst; His home was in *"the Holiest of all"* (Hebrews 9:3).

The New Testament is the dispensation of the indwelling God in the hearts of His people. Christ said, *"If a man love me, he will keep my words: and my Father will love him, and we will come unto him, and make our abode with him"* (John 14:23). This is what Paul referred to as *"the riches of the glory of this mystery among the Gentiles; which is Christ in you, the hope of glory"* (Colossians 1:27). How few experience this! Let us study Paul's teaching on the way to experience this crowning blessing of the Christian life.

1. *"I bow my knees unto the Father."* The blessing must come from the Father. It is to be found in much prayer.

2. *"That he would grant you, according to the riches of his glory"*—something very special and divine—*"to be strengthened with might through his Spirit in the inner man."* God gives us the strength to be separate from sin and the world, to yield to Christ as Lord and Master, and to live the life of love for Christ and keeping His commandments to which the promise has been given: *"We will come unto him, and make our abode with him."*

3. *"That Christ may dwell in your hearts through faith."* Christ longs for hearts to dwell in. As a believer sees this by faith, bows his knee, and asks God for this great blessing, he receives grace to believe that the prayer is answered. And through that faith, he accepts the wonderful gift—Christ dwelling in the heart by faith.

4. *"That you, being rooted and grounded in love...might be filled with all the fulness of God,"* as far as it is possible for man to experience it.

Feed on the words the Holy Spirit has given here, and hold fast to the assurance that God will do *"abundantly above all that we ask or think"* (Ephesians 3:20).

April 27

Christian Perfection

Now the God of peace...make you perfect in every good work to do his will, working in you that which is wellpleasing in his sight, through Jesus Christ.
—Hebrews 13:20–21

April

Prepare your heart, my reader, for a large and strong faith—a faith that takes hold of one of God's promises that are as high above all our thoughts as the heaven is above the earth. (See Isaiah 55:9.)

In the epistle to the Hebrews, we have a wonderful presentation of the eternal redemption that Christ our great High Priest, *"the mediator of the new testament"* (Hebrews 9:15), worked out for us through the shedding of His precious blood. The writer of the epistle closed his whole argument and all its deep spiritual teaching with the benediction, *"Now the God of peace...make you perfect in every good work to do his will."* Does that not include everything? Can we desire more? Yes, *"working in you that which is wellpleasing in his sight,"* and that through Jesus Christ.

The great thought here is that all that Christ had accomplished for our redemption, and all that God had done in raising Him from the dead, was done just with the one aim that He might have more room to work in us the everlasting redemption that Christ brought in. He Himself, as God the Omnipotent, will make us *"perfect in every good work."* And if we want to know in what way, we have the answer: by His working within us *"that which is wellpleasing in his sight, through Jesus Christ."*

All that we have been taught about the completeness of the salvation in Christ here finds its consummation: we may be assured that God Himself takes such an entire charge of the man who really trusts Him that He Himself will, through Jesus Christ, work all that *"is wellpleasing in his sight."*

The thought is too high; the promise is too large; we cannot attain it. And yet there it is, claiming, stimulating our faith. It calls us to take hold of the one truth that the everlasting God works in us every hour of the day *"through Jesus Christ."* We have just one thing to do: yield ourselves into God's hands for Him to work—not to hinder Him by our working, but in a silent adoring faith to be assured that He Himself through Jesus Christ will work in us all that *"is wellpleasing in his sight."*

Lord, *"Increase our faith"* (Luke 17:5)!

April 28

The God of All Grace

But the God of all grace, who hath called us unto his eternal glory by Christ Jesus, after that ye have suffered a while, make you perfect, stablish, strengthen, settle you.
—1 Peter 5:10

The book of Hebrews gathers up all its teaching in the wonderful promise, *"The God of peace…make you perfect in every good work"* (Hebrews 13:20–21). Peter did the same thing here: *"The God of all grace… perfect, stablish, strengthen,* [and] *settle you."* God Himself is to be the one object of our trust every day. As we think of our work, our needs, our lives, and all our hearts' desires, God Himself must be the one object of our hope and trust.

Just as God is the center of the universe, the one source of its strength, the one Guide who orders and controls its movements, so God must have the same place in the life of the believer. With every new day, the first and chief thought ought to be, "God, God alone, can help me to live today as He wants me to live."

And what is to be our position toward this God? Should not our first thought every day be to humbly place ourselves in His hands, to confess our absolute helplessness, and to yield ourselves in childlike surrender to receive from Him the fulfillment of His promises—promises such as *"the God of peace…make you perfect in every good work"*; *"the God of all grace…perfect, stablish, strengthen,* [and] *settle you"*?

In an earlier devotion of this book, you saw how indispensable it is to meet God every morning, to give Him time to reveal Himself and take charge of your life for the day. Do we not have to do the same with these wonderful words of Peter? Yes, it must be understood between God and ourselves that our hearts are resting on Him, that our hope is in His Word: *"The God of peace…make you perfect in every good work"*; *"The God of all grace…perfect, establish, strengthen,* [and] *settle you."*

By His grace, may this henceforth be the spirit in which we awake every morning to go out to our work, humbly trusting in the promise that God Himself will perfect us: *"The LORD will perfect that which concerneth me"* (Psalm 138:8).

April 29

Not Sinning

And ye know that he was manifested to take away our sins; and in him is no sin. Whosoever abideth in him sinneth not.
—1 John 3:5–6

John had taken deep into his heart and life the words that Christ had spoken on the last night—words about abiding in Him. He always remembered how the Lord had spoken six times of loving Him and keeping His commandments as the way to abide in His love and to receive the indwelling of the Father and the Son. Abiding in Christ is one of the key promises in this epistle that he wrote in his old age. (See 1 John 2:6, 24, 28; 3:6, 24; 4:13, 16.)

In the text verse above, John taught how we can be kept from sinning. *"Whosoever abideth in him sinneth not."* Though there is sin in our nature, the abiding in Christ, in whom there is no sin, does indeed free us from the power of sin and enable us to live daily so as to please God. The Scriptures record that Christ had said of the Father, *"I do always those things that please him"* (John 8:29). And so John wrote later in his epistle, *"Beloved, if our heart condemn us not, then have we confidence toward God. And whatsoever we ask, we receive of him, because we keep his commandments, and do those things that are pleasing in his sight"* (1 John 3:21–22).

Let the soul who longs to be free from the power of sin take hold of these simple but far-reaching words: *"In him is no sin"* (1 John 3:5), and *"He which stablisheth us...in Christ...is God"* (2 Corinthians 1:21). As you seek to abide in Him in whom there is no sin, Christ will indeed live out His own life in you in the power of the Holy Spirit and will equip you for a life in which you always do the things that are pleasing in His sight.

Dear child of God, you are called to a life in which faith—great faith, strong, continuous, and unbroken—in the almighty power of God is your one hope. As you daily take time and yield yourself to the God of peace, who perfects you *"in every good work"* (Hebrews 13:21) to do His will, you will experience that God indeed works in those who wait for Him. (See Lamentations 3:25.)

"Whosoever abideth in him sinneth not." The promise is sure: God Almighty has pledged that He will work in you what is well pleasing in His sight, through Christ Jesus. (See Hebrews 13:20–21.) In that faith, abide in Him.

April 30

Overcoming the World

Who is he that overcometh the world, but he that believeth that Jesus is the Son of God?
—1 John 5:5

Christ spoke strongly about the world hating Him. His kingdom and the kingdom of this world were in deadly hostility. John summed it up: *"And we know that we are of God, and the whole world lieth in wickedness"* (1 John 5:19); *"Love not the world, neither the things that are in the world. If any man love the world, the love of the Father is not in him"* (1 John 2:15).

John also taught us what the real nature and power of the world is: *"the lust of the flesh* [with its self-pleasing], *and the lust of the eyes* [which sees and seeks the glory of the world], *and the pride of life* [with its self-exaltation]" (v. 16). Eve, in Paradise, had these three marks of the world. She *"saw that the tree was good for food, and that it was pleasant to the eyes, and a tree to be desired to make one wise"* (Genesis 3:6). Through her body, eyes, and pride, the world acquired mastery over her and over us.

The world still exerts a terrible influence over the Christian who does not know that, in Christ, he has been crucified to the world. (See Galatians 6:14.) The power of this world proves itself in all that constitutes the pride of life. Most Christians are either utterly ignorant of the danger of a worldly spirit, or they feel themselves utterly powerless to conquer it.

Christ left us with a far-reaching promise: *"Be of good cheer; I have overcome the world"* (John 16:33). As the child of God abides in Christ and seeks to live life in the power of the Holy Spirit, he may confidently depend on the power given him to overcome the world. *"Who is he that overcometh the world, but he that believeth that Jesus is the Son of God?"* This is the secret of daily, hourly victory over the world and all its secret, subtle temptations: *"I live by the faith of the Son of God, who loved me, and gave himself for me"* (Galatians 2:20). But it needs a heart and a life entirely possessed by the faith of Jesus Christ to maintain the victor's attitude at all times. My fellow believer, take time to ask whether you believe with your whole heart in the victory that faith gives over the world. Put your trust in the mighty power of God, in the abiding presence of Jesus, as the only pledge of certain, continual victory.

"Believest thou this?...Yea, Lord: I believe" (John 11:26–27).

May

May 1

The Lost Secret

Wait for the promise of the Father. . .ye shall be baptized with the Holy Ghost not many days hence.
—Acts 1:4–5

After our Lord had given the great command, *"Go ye into all the world, and preach the gospel to every creature"* (Mark 16:15), He added His very last command: *"Tarry ye in the city of Jerusalem, until ye be endued with power from on high"* (Luke 24:49); *"Wait for the promise of the Father. . .ye shall be baptized with the Holy Ghost not many days hence."*

All Christians agree that the great command to preach the gospel to every creature was not only for the disciples, but is our obligation as well. But not everyone appears to believe that Christ's very last command—not to preach until they had received the power from on high—is as binding on us as it was on the disciples. The church seems to have lost possession of what ought to be her secret of secrets—the daily, abiding consciousness that only as she lives in the power of the Holy Spirit can she preach the gospel with Spirit and power. Therefore, there is much preaching and working with little spiritual result. It is owing to nothing but this that the universal complaint is heard that there is too little prayer, especially that much-availing prayer that brings down the power from on high. Without the baptism of the Holy Spirit, prayer is not likely to produce results.

In this section, I desire to study the secret of Pentecost as it is revealed in the words and deeds of our blessed Master, and in the words and deeds of His disciples as they took Him at His word and continued with one accord in prayer and supplication until the promise was fulfilled. As the disciples were filled with the Holy Spirit, they proved what the mighty power of their God could do through them.

Let us seek earnestly the grace of the Holy Spirit, who alone can reveal to us what *"eye hath not seen, nor ear heard, neither have entered into the heart of man,"* that is, *"the things which God hath prepared for them that love him"* (1 Corinthians 2:9). Let us pray that the lost secret may be found—the sure promise that in answer to fervent prayer, the power of the Holy Spirit will indeed be given.

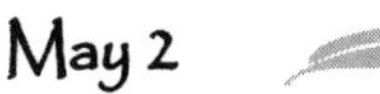

May 2

The Kingdom of God

[Jesus] showed himself alive [to His disciples]...being seen of them forty days, and speaking of the things pertaining to the kingdom of God.
—Acts 1:3

When Jesus began to preach, He took up the message of John the Baptist: *"The kingdom of heaven is at hand"* (Matthew 4:17). Later He said, *"That there be some of them that stand here, which shall not taste of death, till they have seen the kingdom of God come with power"* (Mark 9:1). This could not be until the King had ascended His throne. Then He and His disciples would be ready to receive the Holy Spirit, bringing the kingdom of God into their hearts.

Acts 1:3 tells us that all the teaching of Jesus during the forty days after the Resurrection dealt with the kingdom of God. It is remarkable how Luke, in the last verses of Acts, summed up all the teaching of Paul at Rome, who *"testified the kingdom of God"* (Acts 28:23) and was *"preaching the kingdom of God"* (v. 31).

Christ, seated upon the throne of God, was now King and Lord of all. To His disciples He had entrusted the announcement of the kingdom, which is *"righteousness, and peace, and joy in the Holy Ghost"* (Romans 14:17). The prayer He had taught them—*"Our Father which art in heaven....Thy kingdom come"* (Luke 11:2)—now had new meaning for them. The reign of God in heaven came down in the power of the Spirit, and the disciples were full of this one thought: to preach the coming of the Spirit into the hearts of men.

When Jesus spoke about the kingdom of God in Acts 1, He implied all the characteristics of a kingdom. The first two characteristics of every kingdom are the king and his subjects. We know the King of God's government to be the crucified Christ, and the disciples His faithful followers. Acts 1:8 tells us of a power that enabled the disciples to serve their King, and that was the Holy Spirit, the third mark of a kingdom. Their work was to testify of Christ as His witnesses, and their aim was to reach the ends of the earth—the fourth and fifth marks of a kingdom. But before they could begin, their first duty was to wait on God in united, unceasing prayer, and so we have the sixth mark of a kingdom.

If we are to take up the prayer of the disciples, it is essential to have a clear impression of all that Christ spoke to them in that last moment, and what it meant for their inner lives and service.

May 3

Christ as King

And he said unto them, Verily I say unto you, That there be some of them that stand here, which shall not taste of death, till they have seen the kingdom of God come with power.
—Mark 9:1

The first mark of the kingdom of God, the church, is that Christ is King. Christ and John had both preached that the kingdom of God was *"at hand"* (Matthrew 3:2; 4:17). In Mark 9:1 Christ said that the kingdom would come in power during the lifetimes of some who heard Him. That could mean nothing else but that when He, as King, had ascended the throne of the Father, the kingdom would be revealed in the hearts of His disciples by the power of the Holy Spirit. In the kingdom of heaven, God's will was always being done; in the power of the Holy Spirit, Christ's disciples would do His will on earth as it was done in heaven.

The characteristics of a kingdom can be seen in its king. Christ now reigns on the throne of the Father. There is no external manifestation of the kingdom on earth; rather, its power is seen in the lives of those in whom it rules. It is only in the church, the members of Christ, that the united body can be seen and known. Christ lives and dwells and rules in their hearts. Our Lord Himself taught how close the relationship would be: *"At that day ye shall know that I am in my Father, and ye in me, and I in you"* (John 14:20). The faith of His oneness with God and His omnipotent power would be next to the knowledge that they lived in Him and He in them.

This must be our first lesson if we are to follow in the steps of the disciples and share their blessing. We must know that Christ, as King, dwells and rules in our hearts. We must know that we live in Him and by His power are able to accomplish all that He wants us to do. Our lives are to be entirely devoted to our King and the service of His kingdom.

This blessed relationship to Christ means, above all, a daily fellowship with Him in prayer. The prayer life is to be a continuous and unbroken exercise. It is in this way that His people can rejoice in their King and can be *"more than conquerors"* (Romans 8:37) in Him.

May 4

The Crucified Jesus

God hath made that same Jesus, whom ye have crucified, both Lord and Christ.
—Acts 2:36

The King of the kingdom of heaven is none other than the crucified Jesus. All that we have to say of Him, of His divine power, His abiding presence, and His wonderful love, does not teach us to know Him fully unless we maintain the deep awareness that our King is the crucified Jesus. God has placed Him *"in the midst of* [His] *throne"* as a Lamb, *"as it had been slain"* (Revelation 5:6), and it is thus that the hosts of heaven adore Him. It is thus that we worship Him as a King.

Christ's cross is His highest glory. It is through this that He has conquered every enemy and gained His place on the throne of God. And it is this that He will impart to us, too, if we are to know fully the meaning of victory over sin. When Paul wrote, *"I am crucified with Christ…Christ liveth in me"* (Galatians 2:20), he taught us that Christ ruled on the throne of his heart as the Crucified One, and that the spirit of the cross would triumph over us as it did in Him.

This was true of the disciples. This was their deepest preparation for receiving the Holy Spirit. With their Lord, they had been crucified to the world. The *"old man"* (Romans 6:6) had been crucified; in Him they were *"dead indeed to sin"* (v. 11), and their lives were *"hid with Christ in God"* (Colossians 3:3). Each one of us needs to experience this fellowship with Christ in His cross if the Spirit of Pentecost is really to take possession of us. It was through the eternal Spirit that Christ gave Himself as a sacrifice and became the King on the throne of God. As we become *"conformable unto his death"* (Philippians 3:10) in the entire surrender of our wills, in the entire self-denial of our old natures, and in the entire separation from the spirit of this world, we can become the worthy servants of a crucified King, and our hearts the worthy temples of His glory.

May 5

The Apostles

Being assembled together with them, he charged them not to depart from Jerusalem, but to wait for the promise of the Father.
—Acts 1:4 (RV)

The second mark of the church is found in the disciples whom the Lord had prepared to receive His Spirit and to be His witnesses. If we want to understand fully the outpouring of the Spirit in answer to the prayer of the disciples, we must above all ask, "What was in these men that enabled them to speak forth such powerful, effective prayer, and to receive the wonderful fulfillment of the promise that came to them?" They were simple, uneducated men with many faults whom the Lord had called to forsake all and follow Him. They had done this as far as they could; they followed Him in the life He led and the work He did. Though there was much sin in them and they had as yet no power to deny themselves fully, their hearts clung to Him in deep sincerity. In the midst of much stumbling, they followed Him to the cross. They shared with Him His death; unconsciously, but in truth, they died with Him to sin and were raised with Him in the power of a new life. It was this that prepared them for power in prayer and for being clothed with the *"power from on high"* (Luke 24:49).

Let this be the test by which we examine ourselves: have we indeed surrendered to the fellowship of Christ's sufferings and death? Have we hated our own lives and crucified them? And have we received the power of Christ's life in us? It is this that will give us liberty to believe that God will hear our prayers. It is this that will assure us that God will give us His Holy Spirit to work in us what we and He desire. Let us indeed with one accord take up the disciples' prayer and share in the answer. We must, like them, be willing learners in the school of Jesus, and we must seek, above everything, the intimate fellowship with Him that will prepare us for praying the prayer of Pentecost and receiving its answer.

May 6

Not of This World

They are not of the world, even as I am not of the world.
—John 17:14

During His last night, our Lord took great effort to make clear to His disciples the impassable gulf between Him and the world, and between them and the world. He had said of the Spirit, *"whom the world cannot receive, because it seeth him not, neither knoweth him"* (John 14:17). *"Because ye are not of the world...therefore the world hateth you"* (John 15:19).

One great characteristic of the disciples was that they were to be as separated from the world as Christ had been. They and Christ had become united in the Cross and the Resurrection; they both belonged to another world, the kingdom of heaven. This separation from the world is to be the mark of all believers who long to be filled with the Spirit.

Why is faith in the Holy Spirit so seldom preached and practiced in Christendom? The world rules too much in the lives of Christians. Christians rarely live the heavenly life to which they are called in Christ Jesus. The love of the world—*"the lust of the flesh* [pleasure in eating, drinking, ease, and comfort], *the lust of the eyes* [delight in all that the world offers of beauty and possession], *and the pride of life* [the self-exaltation in what the wisdom and power of man has accomplished]*"* (1 John 2:16) robs the heart of its desire for the true self-denial that enables a man to receive the Holy Spirit.

If you wish to pray the Pentecostal prayer for the power of the Holy Spirit, examine yourself. Is the spirit of the world the reason that you do not love to pray the prayer that is absolutely necessary to receive the promise of the Father? May the Lord write this thought deep in every heart: the world cannot receive the Holy Spirit!

"[You] *are not of the world, even as I am not of the world."*

May 7

Obedience

If ye love me, keep my commandments. And I will pray the Father, and he shall give you another Comforter.
—John 14:15–16

We have learned to know the disciples in their preparation for the baptism of the Spirit, and we have seen what was needed for their continuing *"with one accord"* (Acts 1:14) in prayer for the power of the Spirit. Christ was everything to them. Even before the cross, He was literally their life, their one thought, their only desire. But He was much more so after the cross, and with the resurrection.

Was such devotion to Christ something particular to the disciples, not to be expected of everyone? Or was it indeed something that the Lord asked from all who desired to be filled with the Spirit? God expects it of all His children. The Lord needs such individuals now, as much as He did then, to receive His Spirit and His power, to show them forth here on earth, and, as intercessors, to link the world to the throne of God.

Is Christ nothing, something, or everything to us? For the unconverted, Christ is nothing. For the half-converted, the average Christian, Christ is something. But for the true Christian, Christ is everything. Each one who prays for the power of the Spirit must be ready to say, "Today I yield myself with my whole heart to the leading of the Spirit." A full surrender is the question of life or death, an absolute necessity.

My brother or sister in Christ, you have read the words of John 14:15: *"If ye love me, keep my commandments."* The surrender to live every day, all day long, abiding in Christ and keeping His commandments, is to be the one sign of your discipleship. Only when the heart longs in everything to do God's will can the Father's love and Spirit rest upon the child of God. This was the disposition in which the disciples continued with one accord in prayer, and this will be the secret of power in our intercession as we plead for the church and the world.

May 8

The Holy Spirit

Ye shall be baptized with the Holy Ghost....Ye shall receive power, after that the Holy Ghost is come upon you.
—Acts 1:5, 8

The third mark of the church is the power for service through the Holy Spirit. Since the time of Adam's fall, when he lost the spirit that God had breathed into him, God's Spirit had striven with men and had worked in some with power, but He had never been able to find His permanent home in them. Only when Christ had come, had broken the power of sin by His death, and had won, through resurrection, a new life for men to live in Himself, could the Spirit of God come and take possession of the whole heart and make it a dwelling place for Christ and for God.

Nothing less than this is the power in us by which sin can be overcome and the prisoners be set free. This power is the Holy Spirit. In the Old Testament He was called *"the Spirit of God"* (Genesis 1:2). But now that the holiness of God has been magnified in the cross of Christ, and now that Christ has sanctified us so that we might be like Him, the Spirit of God's holiness descends to dwell in men and take possession of them as God's holy temple.

He is also the Spirit of the Son. On earth He led the Son first into the desert to be tempted by Satan, then to the synagogue in Nazareth to proclaim Himself as the fulfillment of what the prophet had spoken in Isaiah 61:1. (See Luke 4:18.) And later on the cross, Christ yielded Himself implicitly to the leading of the Spirit.

The Spirit now reveals Christ in us as our Life, our Strength for a perfect obedience, and the Word that is preached in the power of God.

Amazing mystery—the Spirit of God, our Life; the Spirit of Christ, our Light and Strength! As we become men and women who are led by this Spirit of the first disciples, we will have the power to pray *"the effectual fervent prayer of a righteous man* [that] *availeth much"* (James 5:16).

May 9

The Power from On High

Tarry ye in the city of Jerusalem, until ye be endued with power from on high.
—Luke 24:49

The Lord had said to the disciples, *"Without me ye can do nothing"* (John 15:5). Why, then, did He choose these powerless, helpless men to go out to conquer the world for Him? So that in their feebleness they might yield themselves and give Him, as Lord on His throne, the opportunity to show His power working through them. As the Father had done all the work in Christ when He was on earth, so Christ in heaven would now be the Great Worker, proving in them that all power had been given to Him *"in heaven and in earth"* (Matthew 28:18). Their place would be to pray, to believe, and to yield themselves to the mighty power of Christ.

The Holy Spirit would not live in them as a power of which they could have possession. But He would possess them, and their work would indeed be the work of the almighty Christ. Their whole attitude each day would be that of unceasing dependence and prayer, and of confident expectation.

The apostles had learned to know Christ intimately. They had seen all His mighty works; they had received His teaching; they had gone with Him through all His sufferings, even to His death on the cross. They had not only seen Him, but they had also known Him in the power of His resurrection and the experience of that resurrection life in their own hearts. Yet they were not capable of fully making Him known, until He Himself, from the throne of heaven, had taken possession of them by His Spirit dwelling in them.

Every minister of the gospel is called to rest content with nothing less than the indwelling life and power of the Holy Spirit. This is to be his only preparation for preaching the gospel in power. Nothing less than having Christ speaking through us in the power of His omnipotence will make us able ministers of the New Testament, bringing salvation to all who hear us.

My Witnesses

Ye shall be witnesses unto me.
—Acts 1:8

The fourth mark of Christ's church is that His servants are to be witnesses for Him, continually testifying of His wonderful love, His power to redeem, His continual abiding presence, and His wonderful power to work in them.

This is the only weapon that the King allows His redeemed ones to use. Without claiming authority or power, without wisdom or eloquence, without influence or position, each one is called, not only by his words, but also by his life and actions, to be a living proof and witness of what Jesus can do.

This is the only weapon they are to use in conquering men and bringing them to the feet of Christ. This is what the first disciples did. When they were filled with the Spirit, they began to speak of the mighty things that Christ had done.

It was in this power that those who were scattered abroad by persecution went forth, even as far as Antioch, preaching in the name of Jesus, so that a multitude of the unsaved believed. They had no commission from the apostles; they had no special gifts or training, but out of the fullness of their hearts they spoke of Jesus Christ. They could not be silent; they were filled with the life and love of Christ and could not help but witness for Him. It was this that gave the gospel its power to increase; every new convert became a witness for Christ.

One non-Christian writer wrote, in regard to the persecutions, that if the Christians had only been content to keep the worship of Jesus to themselves, they would not have had to suffer. But in their zeal, they had wanted Christ to rule over all.

This is the secret of a flourishing church: every believer is a witness for Jesus. And here we see that the cause of the weakness of the church is that so few are willing in daily life to testify that Jesus is Lord.

What a call to prayer! Lord, teach Your disciples the blessedness of knowing Jesus and the power of His love in such a way that they may find their highest joy in testifying of what He is doing and what He has done for them.

May 11

The Gospel Ministry

Ye shall be witnesses unto me.
—Acts 1:8

The Spirit of truth...shall testify of me: and ye also shall bear witness, because ye have been with me from the beginning.
—John 15:26–27

When Christ said the words, "*witnesses unto me,*" He not only referred to all believers, but especially to all ministers of the gospel. This is the high calling and the only power of the preacher of the gospel—in everything to be a witness for Jesus.

This gives us two great truths. The first is that the preacher must place the preaching of Christ Himself above everything he teaches from the Word of God. This is what the first disciples did: *"In every house, they ceased not to teach and preach Jesus Christ"* (Acts 5:42). This was what Philip did at Samaria: he *"preached Christ unto them"* (Acts 8:5). And so Paul wrote, *"For I determined not to know any thing among you, save Jesus Christ, and him crucified"* (1 Corinthians 2:2).

Ministers of the gospel must never forget that it is especially for this that they have been set apart: to be, along with the Holy Spirit, witnesses for Christ. As they do this, sinners will find salvation, and God's children will be sanctified and equipped for His service. Only in this way can Christ have His place in the hearts of His people and in the world around.

But there is a second thought of equal importance: the preacher's teaching must always be a personal testimony from his own experience of what Christ is doing now and can do in the future. As this note is sounded, the Holy Spirit carries the message as a living reality to the listeners' hearts. This is what will build up believers so that they can walk in such fellowship with Jesus Christ that He can reveal Himself through them. And this is what will lead them to the knowledge of the indispensable secret of spiritual health—the prayer life in daily fellowship, in childlike love, and true consecration with the Father and the Son.

Such thoughts will bring much unity in prayer and will cultivate among believers and ministers the joy of the Holy Spirit, in which the mouth speaks out of the abundance of the heart (see Matthew 12:34), to the praise and glory of our ever blessed Redeemer, Jesus Christ our Lord.

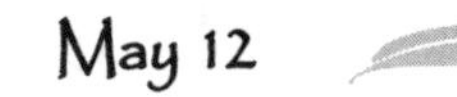

May 12

The Whole World

Witnesses...unto the uttermost part of the earth.
—Acts 1:8

Here we have the fifth mark of Christ's church: reaching the whole world. These must have seemed remarkable words from the Man who, in what appeared to be absolute powerlessness, had been crucified by His enemies. How could He speak of the ends of the earth as His dominion? How could it have entered the mind of any writer to venture the prophecy that a Jew who had been crucified—whose whole life had seemingly been proven by that cross to be an utter failure and whose disciples had utterly forsaken Him in the end—would conquer the world through the very disciples who had abandoned Him?

But what foolishness it is on the part of those who speak of Christ as being nothing but a man! No human mind could have formed such an idea. It is the thought of God; He alone could plan and execute such a purpose.

The words that Jesus spoke to His disciples, *"Ye shall receive power, after that the Holy Ghost is come upon you"* (Acts 1:8), gave them the assurance that the Holy Spirit would maintain Christ's divine power in them. As Christ did His works only because the Father worked in Him, so Christ assured His disciples that He Himself from the throne of heaven would work all their works in them. They might ask what they desired and it would be done for them. (See John 15:7.) In the strength of that promise, the church of Christ can make the ends of the earth its one aim.

Oh, that Christian people might understand that the extension of God's kingdom can only be brought about by the united, continued prayer of men and women who give their hearts wholly to wait on Christ in the assurance that what they desire He will do for them!

Oh, that God would grant that His children prove their faith in Christ by making His aim their aim, and by yielding themselves to be His witnesses in united, persevering prayer, waiting upon Him in the full assurance that He will most surely and most gloriously give all that they can ask.

My reader, become one of those intercessors who really believes that in answer to their prayers the crucified Jesus will do far more than they can ask or think. (See Ephesians 3:20.)

May 13

The Whole Earth Filled with His Glory

And blessed be his glorious name for ever: and let the whole earth be filled with his glory; Amen, and Amen.
—Psalm 72:19

What a prospect—this earth, now under the power of the Evil One, renewed and filled with the glory of God's new earth in which righteousness will dwell! Though we believe it so little, it will surely come to pass; God's Word is the pledge of it. God's Son conquered the power of sin by His blood and death, and through the eternal Spirit, the power of God is working out His purpose. What a vision—the whole earth *"filled with his glory"*!

But what a great and difficult work. It has been two thousand years since Christ gave the promise and ascended the throne, and yet more than half of the human race has never learned to know even the name of Jesus. And in the other half, millions are called by His name yet do not know Him. This great work of bringing the knowledge of Christ to every creature has been entrusted to a church that hardly thinks of her responsibility and of what the consequence of her neglect will be. We may indeed ask, "Will the work ever be done?" Blessed be His name, His power and His faithfulness are pledges that one day we will see it—the whole earth filled with the glory of God.

What a wonderful prayer our text contains: *"Let the whole earth be filled with his glory; Amen, and Amen."* It is to this prayer that every believer is called, and he can depend on the Holy Spirit to inspire and strengthen him. It is to this prayer that we desire to strengthen each other, so that every day of our lives, with all the power there is in us, we desire with one accord to pray continually in the faith of the name of Jesus and the power of His Spirit.

What blessedness to know that true prayer will indeed help and be answered! What blessedness every day of our lives to seek God's face, and with confidence to lay hold of Him and give Him no rest until the earth is full of His glory! Once again, what blessedness to unite with all God's willing children who are seeking to prepare the way for our King in this the day of His power!

May 14

The First Prayer Meeting

These all continued with one accord in prayer and supplication, with the women.
—Acts 1:14

The sixth mark of the early church is that they waited on the promise of the Father in united prayer. It is difficult to form a correct idea of the unspeakable importance of this first prayer meeting in the history of the kingdom—a prayer meeting that was the simple fulfillment of the command of Christ. It was to be for all time the indication of the one condition on which His presence and Spirit would be known in power. In it we have the secret key that opens the storehouse of heaven with all its blessings.

Christ had prayed that the disciples might be one, just as He and the Father were one. (See John 17:22.) He prayed *"that they may be made perfect in one; and that the world may know that thou hast sent me, and hast loved them, as thou hast loved me"* (v. 23). We see, in the strife that was among them at the Lord's Table as to who would be chief, how far the disciples were from such a state when Christ prayed the prayer. It was only after the resurrection and after Christ had gone to heaven that they were brought, in the ten days of united supplication, to that holy unity of love and purpose that would make them the one body of Christ prepared to receive the Spirit in all His power.

What a prayer meeting! It was the fruit of Christ's training during His three years of fellowship with them. Adam's body was created before God breathed His Spirit into him; likewise, the body of Christ had to be formed before the Spirit could take possession.

This prayer meeting gave us the law of the kingdom for all time. Where Christ's disciples are linked to each other in love and yield themselves wholly to Him in undivided consecration, the Spirit will be given from heaven as the seal of God's approval, and Christ will show His mighty power. One of the great marks of the new dispensation is the united, unceasing prayer that *"availeth much"* (James 5:16) and is crowned with the power of the Holy Spirit. Do we not have here the reason why, if our prayers are confined in great measure to our own church or interests, the answer cannot come in such power as we expected?

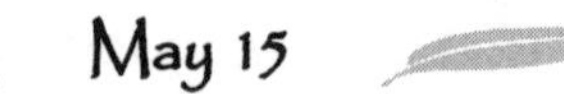

May 15

The Unity of the Spirit

Endeavouring to keep the unity of the Spirit...
There is one body, and one Spirit.
—Ephesians 4:3–4

From Paul we learn how the Christian communities in different places ought to remember each other in the fellowship of prayer. He pointed out how God is glorified in such prayer. So he wrote more than once about how the ministry of intercession abounds to the glory of God. (See 2 Corinthians 1:11; 9:14.)

In today's church, there is a great need for the children of God throughout the world to be drawn close together in the knowledge of having been chosen by God to be a holy priesthood (see 1 Peter 2:9), ministering continually the *"sacrifice of praise"* (Jeremiah 33:11) and prayer. There is too little distinction between the world and the body of Christ; in the lives of many of God's children there is little difference from what the world is.

Nothing will help so much as the separation to a life of more prayer, interceding that God's people may prove their unity in a life of holiness and love. When Paul wrote, *"Praying always with all prayer and supplication in the Spirit, and watching thereunto with all perseverance and supplication for all saints"* (Ephesians 6:18), he named one of the essential differences between God's people and the world.

You say you desire to bear this mark of the children of God, and to be able to pray for them so that you may prove to yourself and to others that you are indeed not of the world. Resolve in your life to carry with you this one great distinctive feature of the true Christian—a life of prayer and intercession. Join with God's children who are unceasingly seeking God with one accord to maintain the *"unity of the Spirit"* and the body of Christ, to *"be strong in the Lord, and in the power of His might"* (Ephesians 6:10), and to pray a blessing upon His church. Let none of us think it too much to give fifteen minutes every day for meditation on some word of God connected with His promises to His church, and then to plead with Him for its fulfillment. Slowly yet surely, you will taste the blessedness of being one, heart and soul, with God's people, and you will receive the power to pray *"the effectual fervent prayer...*[that] *availeth much"* (James 5:16).

May 16

Union Is Strength

And when they had prayed...they were all filled with the Holy Ghost, and they spake the word of God with boldness. And the multitude of them that believed were of one heart and of one soul.
—Acts 4:31–32

We see the power of union everywhere in nature. How feeble is a drop of rain as it falls to earth! But when the many drops are united in one stream and become one body, the power is soon irresistible. Such is the power of true union in prayer. Some translations of Psalm 34:5, rather than saying, *"They looked unto him,"* read instead, "They flowed to Him," or even, "They rushed toward Him like a stream of water." Such was the prayer in the upper room. And so can our prayer be if we unite all our forces in pleading the promise of the Father. Then, when the world *"come*[s] *in like a flood"* (Isaiah 59:19), it can be overcome in the power of united prayer.

In Natal, South Africa, owing to the many mountains, the streams often flow down with great force. The Zulus, who live there, are accustomed to joining hands when they wish to pass through a stream. The leader will have a strong stick in his right hand, and he will give his left hand to the man who comes behind him. And so they form a chain of men and help each other to cross the current. Let us believe that when God's people reach out their hands to each other in spirit, there will be power to resist the terrible influence that the world can exert. And in that unity, God's children, when they have overcome the power of the world and the flesh, will have power to prevail with God.

It was in the upper room that the disciples spent the ten days until they had truly become one heart and one soul. When the Spirit of God descended, He not only filled each individual, but He also took possession of the whole company as the body of Christ.

Dear reader, in this century the prayer of our Lord Jesus is still being offered: *"Father,...that they may be one, even as we are one"* (John 17:21–22). In the fellowship of loving and believing prayer, our hearts can be melted into one, and we will become strong in faith to believe and accept what God has promised us.

May 17

Prayer in the Name of Christ

And whatsoever ye shall ask in my name, that will I do, that the Father may be glorified in the Son.
—John 14:13

How wonderful is the link between our prayers and Christ's glorifying the Father in heaven! Much prayer on earth brings Him much glory in heaven. What an incentive to pray much, to intercede incessantly! Our prayer is indispensable to the glorifying of the Father.

During His last night on earth, Christ's desire was so deep for His disciples to learn to believe in the power of His name, and to take hold of His promise of a sure and abundant answer, that we find the promise repeated seven times. He knew how slow men are to believe in the wonderful promise of answer to prayer in His name. He desires to rouse a large and confident faith, to free our prayers from every shadow of doubt, and to teach us to look upon intercession as the most certain and most blessed way of bringing glory to God, joy to our own souls, and blessing to the perishing world around us.

If the thought comes to us that such prayer is not easy to attain, we only need to remember what Christ told His disciples. It was when the Holy Spirit came that they would have power to pray in power. In order to draw us on to yield ourselves fully to the control of the blessed Spirit, He holds out to us the precious promise: *"Ask, and ye shall receive, that your joy may be full"* (John 16:24). As we believe in the power of the Spirit working in us in full measure, intercession will become to us the joy and the strength of all our service.

When Paul wrote, *"And whatsoever ye do in word or deed, do all in the name of the Lord Jesus"* (Colossians 3:17), he reminded us how, in daily life, everything is to bear the signature of the name of Jesus. As we learn to do this, we will have the confidence to say to the Father, "As we live in Your name before men, we come to You with the full confidence that our prayers in Your name will be answered." Our lives lived among men are to be lived in communion with God. When the name of Jesus rules everything in our lives, it will give power to our prayers, too.

May 18

Our Heavenly Father

Our Father which art in heaven…
—Luke 11:2

How simple, how beautiful, is this invocation that Christ puts on our lips! And yet how inconceivably rich is its meaning, in the fullness of the love and blessing it contains!

Just think of the book that could be written of all the memories that there have been on earth of wise and loving fathers. Just think of what this world owes to the fathers who have made their children strong and happy to give their lives for the welfare of their fellowmen. Then think how all this is only a shadow of exquisite beauty, and only a shadow of what the Father in heaven is to His children on earth.

Christ bestowed a great gift on us when He gave us the right to say "Father" to the God of the universe. We have the privilege of calling upon Him as "The Father of Christ," "Our Father," and "My Father."

We call Him *"our Father which art in heaven,"* our heavenly Father. We consider it a great privilege as we bow in worship to know that the Father comes near to us where we are upon earth. But we soon begin to feel the need to rise up to enter into His holy presence in heaven, to breathe its atmosphere, to drink in its spirit, and to become truly heavenly minded. And as our thoughts leave earth behind, and in the power of the Holy Spirit we enter the Holiest of All, where the seraphim worship, the words heavenly Father take on a new meaning, and our hearts come under an influence that can abide all day long.

As we then gather up our thoughts of what fatherhood on earth has meant, and as we hear the voice of Christ saying, *"How much more"* (Luke 11:13), we feel the distance between the earthly picture and the heavenly reality. And we can only bow in lowly, loving adoration, saying, "Father, our Father, my Father." Only in this way can full joy and power come to us as we rest rejoicingly in this Scripture: *"How much more shall your heavenly Father give the Holy Spirit to them that ask him?"* (v. 13).

Oh, for grace to cultivate a heavenly spirit, to prove daily that we are children who have a Father in heaven and who love to dwell in His holy presence every day!

May 19

The Power of Prayer

The effectual fervent prayer of a righteous man availeth much.
—James 5:16

Prayer *"availeth much."* It *"availeth much"* with God. It *"availeth much"* in the history of His church and people. Prayer is the one great power that the church can exercise in securing the working of God's omnipotence in the world.

The *"prayer of a righteous man availeth much."* That is, a man who has the righteousness of Christ, not only as a garment covering him, but also as a life-power inspiring him, is a *"new man, which after God is created in righteousness and true holiness"* (Ephesians 4:24), a man who lives *"as* [a slave] *to righteousness"* (Romans 6:19). These are the righteous whom the Lord loves and whose prayers have power. (See Psalm 66:18–19; 1 John 3:22.)

When Christ gave His great prayer promises during His last night, it was to those who keep His commandments: *"If ye love me, keep my commandments. And I will pray the Father, and he shall give you another Comforter"* (John 14:15–16); *"If ye keep my commandments, ye shall abide in my love...*[and] *ye shall ask what ye will, and it shall be done unto you"* (John 15:10, 7).

"The effectual fervent prayer of a righteous man availeth much." It is only when the righteous man stirs up himself and rouses his whole being to take hold of God that the prayer *"availeth much."* As Jacob said, *"I will not let thee go"* (Genesis 32:26); as the importunate widow gave the just judge no rest, so does the *"effectual fervent prayer"* bring about great things.

And then comes the *"effectual fervent prayer"* of many righteous people. When two or three agree, there is the promise of an answer. (See Matthew 18:19.) How much more when hundreds and thousands unite with one accord to cry to God to display His mighty power on behalf of His people!

Let us join those who have united themselves to call upon God for the mighty power of His Holy Spirit in His church. What a great and blessed work, and what a sure prospect, in God's time, of an abundant answer! Let us ask God individually and unitedly for the grace of the *"effectual fervent prayer* [that] *availeth much."*

May 20

Prayer and Sacrifice

I would that ye knew what great conflict I have for you.
—Colossians 2:1

Just as men who are undertaking a great thing in the world have to prepare themselves and use all their natural abilities to succeed, so Christians need to prepare themselves to pray with their whole hearts and strength. This is the law of the kingdom. Prayer requires the Christian to sacrifice his ease, his time, and his self. The secret of powerful prayer is sacrifice. It was the same with Christ Jesus, the Great Intercessor. It is written of Him, *"When thou shalt make his soul an offering for sin, he shall see his seed....He shall see of the travail of his soul....He shall divide the spoil with the strong; because he hath poured out his soul unto death"* (Isaiah 53:10–12). In Gethsemane, *"He had offered up prayers and supplications with strong crying and tears"* (Hebrews 5:7). The psalmist said, *"Let my prayer be set forth before thee as incense; and the lifting up of my hands as the evening sacrifice"* (Psalm 141:2).

Prayer is sacrifice. Our prayers have worth only from being rooted in the sacrifice of Jesus Christ. Just as He gave up everything in His prayer, *"Thy will be done"* (Matthew 6:10), so our posture and disposition must ever be the offering up of everything to God and His service.

A pious miner had a relative whom the doctor ordered to go to a nearby state in order to get well. But there was no money. The miner resolved to take the little money that he had and ventured to use it all. He procured a comfortable lodging at a few dollars per day for the invalid. He was content with a small shack for himself and lived on only a few pennies a day for an entire month. He spent much time in prayer until he got the assurance that the invalid would recover. On the last day of the month, the sick one was well. When the miner reached home, he said that he had now learned more than ever that the secret law and hidden power of prayer lay in self-sacrifice.

Do we need to ask why we lack power in our prayers when there is so much reluctance to make the necessary sacrifice in waiting upon God? Christ, the Christ we trust in, the Christ who lives in us, offered Himself as a sacrifice to God. As this attitude lives and rules in us, we will receive power from Him as intercessors to pray the *"effectual fervent prayer* [that] *availeth much"* (James 5:16).

May 21

The Spirit's Intercession for Believers

And he that searcheth the hearts knoweth what is the mind of the Spirit, because he maketh intercession for the saints according to the will of God. —Romans 8:27

What a light these words cast upon the prayer life in the hearts of the saints! *"For we know not what we should pray for as we ought"* (v. 26). How often this hinders our prayer or hinders the faith that is essential to its success! But here we are told for our encouragement that the Holy Spirit *"maketh intercession for us with groanings which cannot be uttered"* (v. 26). *"He maketh intercession for the saints according to the will of God."*

What a prospect is opened up to us here! Where and how does the Spirit make intercession for all believers? In the heart that does not know what to pray, He secretly and effectively prays what is according to the will of God. This of course implies that we trust Him to do His work in us, and that we wait before God even when we know what to pray, in the assurance that the Holy Spirit is praying in us. This further implies that we take time to wait in God's presence, that we exercise an unbounded dependence on the Holy Spirit who has been given to cry *"Abba Father"* (v. 15) within us, even when we have nothing to offer but *"groanings which cannot be uttered"* (v. 26).

What a difference it would make in the lives of many of God's children if they realized this! They have not only Jesus the Son of God, the great High Priest, *"ever liv*[ing] *to make intercession for them"* (Hebrews 7:25); they have not only the liberty of asking in faith what they desire, and the promise that it will be given them; but they have actually the Holy Spirit, *"the spirit of grace and of supplications"* (Zechariah 12:10), to carry on, in the depths of their beings, His work of interceding for them according to the will of God.

What a call to separate ourselves from the world, to yield ourselves wholeheartedly to the leading and praying of the Spirit within us, deeper than all our thoughts or expectations! What a call to surrender ourselves in stillness of soul, resting in the Lord and waiting patiently for Him, as the Holy Spirit prays within us not only for ourselves, but especially for all believers according to the will of God!

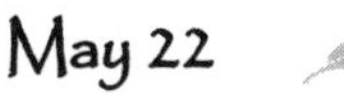

May 22

That They May Be One

Holy Father, keep through thine own name those whom thou hast given me, that they may be one, as we are….Neither pray I for these alone, but for them also which shall believe on me through their word; that they all may be one; as thou, Father, art in me, and I in thee, that they also may be one in us….And the glory which thou gavest me I have given them; that they may be one, even as we are one: I in them, and thou in me, that they may be made perfect in one; and that the world may know that thou hast sent me. —John 17:11, 20–23

Notice carefully how the Lord used the expression, *"that they may be one,"* five times. It is as if He felt the need of strongly placing the emphasis on these words if we are going to realize the chief thought of His prayer. He desires that the words will indeed have the same place in our hearts that they have in His.

As He was on the way to go to the Father through the cross, He wanted us to understand that He took the thought and the desire with Him to heaven, to make it the object of His unceasing intercession there. And He entrusted the words to us, so that we would take them into the world with us and make them the object of our unceasing intercession, too. This alone would enable us to fulfill the new commandment to love our fellowmen as He loves us, so that our joy might be full. (See John 15:11–12.)

How little the church has understood this! How little its different branches are marked by a fervent love toward believers of whatever name or denomination. Will we not heartily welcome the invitation to make this prayer, *"That they may be one,"* a chief part of our daily fellowship with God? How simple it would be once we connected the words *our Father* with all the children of God throughout the world. Each time we used these sacred words, we would only have to expand the little word *our* into all the largeness and riches of God's fatherly love, and our hearts would soon learn to say our with a childlike affection for all the saints of God, whoever and wherever they may be. We would do this as naturally as we say "Father" with the thought of His infinite love and our love for Him. The prayer *"that they may be one"* would then become a joy and a strength, a deeper bond of fellowship with Christ Jesus and all His saints.

May 23

The Disciples' Prayer

These all continued with one accord in prayer and supplication.
—Acts 1:14

And they continued stedfastly in...fellowship...and in prayers.
—Acts 2:42

What a lesson it would be to us in the school of prayer to have a clear understanding of what this continuing *"with one accord in prayer"* meant to the disciples!

Just think of the object of their desire. However defective the thoughts were that they had of the Blessed Spirit, this they knew from the words of Jesus: *"It is expedient for you that I go away"* (John 16:7), so that the Spirit would give the glorified Christ into their very hearts in a way they had never known Him before. And it would be He Himself, in the mighty power of God's Spirit, who would be their strength for the work to which He had called them.

With what confidence they expected the fulfillment of the promise! Had not the Master, who had loved them so well, given them the assurance of what He would send to them from the throne of the Father in heaven?

And with what intensity and persistency they pleaded! In the midst of the praise and thanksgiving that filled their hearts as they worshipped their Lord in heaven, remembering all He had taught them about importunity, they had the full assurance that He would fulfill their desires, however long the answer might be delayed. Let us nourish our hearts with thoughts such as these, until we see that the very same promise that was given to the disciples is given to us, and that we, too, even though we have to cry day and night to God, can count upon the Father to answer our prayers.

Lastly—and this is not the least—let us believe that as they continued *"with one accord in prayer,"* we also may unite in presenting our petitions even though we cannot be together in one place. In the love with which His Spirit makes us one, and in the experience of our Lord's presence with each one who joins with his fellow believers in pleading the blessed name, we can claim the promise that we, too, will be filled with the Holy Spirit.

May 24

Paul's Call to Prayer

With all prayer and supplication praying at all seasons in the Spirit, and watching thereunto in all perseverance and supplication for all the saints, and on my behalf.
—Ephesians 6:18–19 (RV)

Paul had a deep sense of the divine unity of the whole body of Christ and of the need for unceasing prayer for all the members of the body by all who belong to it. It is evident from the words he used that he did not mean this to be an occasional thing, but the unceasing exercise of the life union in which they were bound together. *"With all prayer and supplication praying at all seasons in the Spirit, and watching thereunto in all perseverance and supplication for all the saints."*

Paul expected believers to be so filled with the consciousness of living in Christ, and through Him being united so consciously to the whole body, that in their daily lives and activities, their highest aim would always be the welfare of the body of Christ of which they had become members. He counted on their being filled with the Spirit, so that it would be perfectly natural to them—not ever a burden or constraint to them—to pray for all who belong to the body of Jesus Christ. As natural as it is for each member of my body to be ready every moment to do what is necessary for the welfare of the whole, even so, where the Holy Spirit has entire possession, the consciousness of union with Christ will always be accompanied by consciousness of the union, joy, and love of all the members.

Is this not what we need in our daily lives, that every believer who has yielded himself undividedly to Christ Jesus will daily and continually live in the consciousness that he is one with Christ and His body? Just as a war will bring to light the intensity and the readiness with which millions of the subjects of the king sacrifice their all for the king and his service, so the saints of God will live for Christ their King, and also for all the members of the body of which He is the Head. May God's people be willing for this sacrifice of prayer and intercession at all times and for all believers!

May 25

Paul's Request for Prayer

And for me, that utterance may be given unto me, that I may open my mouth boldly, to make known the mystery of the gospel...that therein I may speak boldly, as I ought to speak.
—Ephesians 6:19–20

"A*nd for me"*—what light these words cast on the deep reality of Paul's faith in the absolute necessity and the wonderful power of prayer! What did he ask the Ephesians to pray for? *"That utterance may be given unto me, that I may open my mouth boldly...that therein I may speak boldly, as I ought to speak."* By this time, Paul had been a minister of the gospel for more than twenty years. One might think that he had such experience in preaching that it would come naturally to him to *"speak boldly, as* [he] *ought to speak."* But so deep was his conviction of his own insufficiency and weakness, so absolute was his dependence on divine teaching and power, that he felt that he could not do the work as it should have been done without the direct help of God. The sense of his total and unalterable dependence on God, who was with him, teaching him what and how to speak, was the basis for all his confidence and the keynote of his whole life.

But there is more. In his twenty years of ministry, there were innumerable times when his circumstances were so bad that he was left to throw himself upon God alone, with no one to help him in prayer. And yet, such was his deep spiritual insight into the unity of the body of Christ, and into his own actual dependence on the prayers of others, that he pleaded with them to pray *"with all prayer and supplication in the Spirit, and watching thereunto with all perseverance and supplication"* (v. 18), and he asked them not to forget to pray for him. Just as a wrestler cannot afford to dispense with the help of the weakest members of his body in the struggle in which he is engaged, so Paul could not do without the prayers of the believers.

What a call to us in this century, to awake to the consciousness that Christ our Intercessor in heaven, and all believers here upon earth, are engaged in one mighty battle! It is our duty to call out and cultivate the gift for the power of God's Spirit in all His servants, so that all may be given divine utterance and all *"may speak boldly, as* [they] *ought to speak."*

May 26

Prayer for All Believers

To the saints and faithful brethren in Christ which are at Colosse....We give thanks to God...praying always for you, since we heard of...the love which ye have to all the saints.
—Colossians 1:2–4

Continue in prayer,...withal praying also for us.
—Colossians 4:2–3

Prayer for all believers—it will take much time, thought, and love to see all that is included in this simple expression. Think of your own neighborhood and the believers you know. Think of your whole country, and praise God for all who are His children. Think of all the Christian nations of the world, and the believers to be found in each of these. Think of all the unsaved nations and the children of God to be found among them in ever increasing numbers.

Think of all the different circumstances and conditions in which these are to be found, and all the varying needs that call for God's grace and help. Think of many—oh, so many—who are God's children, and yet through ignorance or sloth, through worldly-mindedness or an evil heart of unbelief, are walking in the dark and are bringing no honor to God. Think of so many who are in earnest and yet are conscious of a life of failure, with little or no power to please God or to bless man. Then think again of those who are to be found everywhere, in solitary places or among company, whose one aim is to serve the Lord who bought them and to be the light of those around them. Think of them especially as joining, often unaware of their relationship to the whole body of Christ, in pleading for the great promise of the Holy Spirit and the love and oneness of heart that He alone can give.

This is not the work of one day or one night. It needs a heart that will set itself to do serious thinking in regard to the condition of the body of Christ to which we belong. But once we begin, we will find what abundant reason there is for our persevering and yielding to God's Spirit, so that He may prepare us for the great and blessed work of daily praying the twofold prayer: for the love of God and Christ to fill the hearts of His people, and for the power of the Holy Spirit to come down and accomplish God's work in this sinful world.

May 27

Prayer by All Believers

We trust that he will yet deliver us; ye also helping together by prayer for us.
—2 Corinthians 1:10–11

[Some] preach Christ of contention...supposing to add affliction to my bonds....For I know that this shall turn to my salvation through your prayer, and the supply of the Spirit of Jesus Christ.
—Philippians 1:16, 19

This subject calls us once again to think of all believers throughout the world, but leads us to view them from a different standpoint. If we ask God to increase the number and the power of those who do pray, we will be led to form some impression of the hope that our circle of intercessors may gradually increase in number and power.

Our first thoughts will naturally turn to the multitude of believers who know very little about the duty or the blessedness of pleading for the body of Christ, or for all the work that has to be done to perfect its members. We then have to remember how many people do intercede for the power of His Spirit but whose thoughts are chiefly limited to spheres of work with which they are acquainted or in which they are directly interested.

That leaves us with what is, comparatively speaking, a very limited number of people who will be ready to take part in the prayer that ought to be sent up by the whole church for the unity of the body and the power of the Spirit. And even then, the number may be small who really feel drawn to take part in this daily prayer for the outpouring of the Spirit on all God's people.

And yet many may be feeling that the proposal meets a longfelt need, and that it is an unspeakable privilege, whether with few or many, to make Christ's last prayer, *"That they may be one"* (John 17:11), the daily supplication of our faith and love. In time, believers might join together in small circles or throughout wider districts, helping to rouse those around them to take part in the great work of making prayer for all believers become one prayer prayed by all believers.

This message is sent out to all who desire to be in touch with it and who seek to prove their consecration to their Lord in the unceasing, daily supplication for the power of His love and Spirit to be revealed to all His people.

Prayer for All the Fullness of the Spirit

Bring ye all the tithes into the storehouse…and prove me now herewith, saith the LORD of hosts, if I will not open you the windows of heaven, and pour you out a blessing, that there shall not be room enough to receive it. —Malachi 3:10

This last promise in the Old Testament tells us how abundant the blessing is to be. Pentecost was only the beginning of what God is willing to do. The promise of the Father, as Christ presented it, still waits for its perfect fulfillment. Let us try to realize the liberty that we possess to ask and expect great things.

Just as the great command to *"go…and preach the gospel"* (Mark 16:15) was meant not only for the disciples, but also for us, so the very last command—*"Tarry…until ye be endued with power from on high"* (Luke 24:49); *"Wait for the promise of the Father.…Ye shall be baptized with the Holy Ghost"* (Acts 1:4–5)—is also for us and is the basis for the confident assurance that our prayers prayed in one accord will be heard.

Take time to think of the cry of need that can be heard throughout the whole church and throughout all our mission fields. Let us realize that the only remedy that can be found for ineffectiveness or powerlessness, to enable us to gain the victory over the powers of this world and of darkness, is in the manifested presence of our Lord in the midst of His hosts and in the power of His Spirit. Let us take time to think of the state of all the churches throughout Christendom, until we are brought deeper than ever to believe that nothing except the supernatural, almighty intervention of our Lord Himself will rouse His hosts for the great battle against evil. Can anyone imagine or suggest any other matter for prayer that can compete with this: for the power of God on the ministers of the gospel, and on all His people, to fill them *"with power from on high"* (Luke 24:49) that will make the gospel the power of God unto salvation?

As we connect the prayer for the whole church on earth with the prayer for the whole power of God in heaven, we will feel that the greatest truths of the heavenly world and the kingdom of God have possession of us, and that we are indeed asking what God is longing to give, as soon as He finds hearts utterly yielded to Him in faith and obedience.

May 29

Every Day

Give us day by day our daily bread.
—Luke 11:3

Some Christians are afraid that a promise to pray every day is altogether beyond them. They could not undertake it, and yet they pray to God to give them their bread *"day by day."* Surely if a child of God has once yielded himself with his whole life to God's love and service, he should consider it a privilege to take advantage of any invitation that would help him every day to come into God's presence with the great need of His church and kingdom.

Many confess that they desire to live wholly for God. They acknowledge that Christ gave Himself for them and that His love now watches over them and works in them without ceasing. They acknowledge the claim that nothing less than the measure of Christ's love for us is to be the measure of our love for Him. They feel that if this is indeed to be the standard of their lives, they surely ought to welcome every opportunity for proving each day that they are devoting their hearts' strength to the interests of Christ's kingdom and to the prayer that can bring down God's blessings.

Our invitation to daily, united prayer may come to some as a new and perhaps unexpected opportunity of becoming God's remembrancers who *"cry day and night"* (Luke 18:7) for His power and blessing on His people and on this needy world. Think of the privilege of being allowed to plead every day with God on behalf of His children, for the outpouring of His Spirit, and for the coming of His kingdom that His will may indeed be done on earth as it is in heaven. (See Matthew 6:10.) To those who have to confess that they have scarcely understood the high privilege and the solemn duty of waiting on God in prayer for His blessing on the world, the invitation ought to be most welcome. And even to those who already have their special circles for which to pray, the thought that their vision and their hearts can be enlarged to include all God's children, all the work of His kingdom, and all the promise of an abundant outpouring of His Spirit, should urge them to take part in a ministry by which their other work will not suffer, but their hearts will be strengthened with a joy, a love, and a faith that they have never known before.

May 30

With One Accord

They were all with one accord in one place....And they were all filled with the Holy Ghost.
—Acts 2:1, 4

Several of the previous chapters have opened to us wonderful thoughts of the unity of the whole body of Christ, and the need for deliberately cultivating the slumbering or buried talents of intercession. We may indeed thank God, for we know of the tens of thousands of His children who in daily prayer are pleading for some portion of the work of God's kingdom in which they are personally interested. But in many cases in which they take an interest, there is a lack of the large-hearted and universal love that embraces all the children of God and their service. The people do not have the boldness and strength that come from the consciousness of being part of a large and conquering army under the leadership of our conquering King.

A wrestler must gather up all his strength and depend on every member of his body to do its very utmost. In an army with millions of soldiers at war, each detachment not only throws its whole heart into the work that it has to do, but it is also ready to rejoice and take new courage from every report of bravery and enthusiasm of the far-distant members of the same army. Is this not what we need in the church of Christ—such an enthusiasm for the King and His kingdom that His name will be made known to every human being? Do we not need such a faith in His purpose that our prayers will rise up every day with a large-hearted love that grasps the whole body of Christ and pleads daily for the power of the Holy Spirit on all its members, even to the very weakest?

The strength that unity gives is something inconceivable. The power of each individual member is increased greatly by the inspiration of fellowshipping with a large and conquering multitude. Nothing can so help believers to an ever larger faith as the consciousness of being one body and one spirit in Christ Jesus. Only as the disciples were all *"with one accord in one place"* on the day of Pentecost *"were* [they] *all filled with the Holy Ghost."* United prayer brings the answer to prayer.

A Personal Call

We should not trust in ourselves, but in God…who delivered us…and…will yet deliver us.
—2 Corinthians 1:9–10

For I know that this shall turn to my salvation through your prayer, and the supply of the Spirit of Jesus Christ.
—Philippians 1:19

Scriptures like these prove that there were still Christians in the churches under the full power of the Holy Spirit, on whom Paul could depend for *"effectual fervent prayer"* (James 5:16). When we plead with Christians to *"pray without ceasing"* (1 Thessalonians 5:17), there are many who quietly decide that such a life is not possible for them. They do not have any special gift for prayer; they do not have that intense desire for glorifying Christ in the salvation of souls; they have not yet learned what it is, under the power of the love of Christ, to live not for themselves, but for Him who died for them and rose again. (See 2 Corinthians 5:15.)

And yet we bring to them the call to offer themselves in wholehearted surrender to live entirely for Christ. We ask them whether they are not ashamed of the selfish life that simply uses Christ as a convenience to escape from hell and to secure a place in heaven. We come to them with the assurance that God can change their lives and fill their hearts with Christ and His Holy Spirit. We plead with them to believe that *"with God all things are possible"* (Matthew 19:26).

In order to attain this, they must listen to the call for men and women who will daily and continually, in the power of Christ's abiding presence, live in the spirit of unceasing intercession for all believers. They must receive the power of the Holy Spirit and acknowledge that this is nothing less than a duty, a sacrifice that Christ's love has a right to claim, and that He by His Spirit will indeed work in them. The person who accepts the call as coming from Christ and draws near to God in humble prayer for the needed grace, however far he may have come short, will have taken the first step on the path that leads to fellowship with God, to a new faith and life in Christ Jesus, and to the surrender of his whole being to the intercession of the Spirit that will help to bring Pentecost again into the hearts of God's people.

June

June 1

The Redemption of the Cross

Christ hath redeemed us from the curse of the law, being made a curse for us. —Galatians 3:13

Scripture teaches us that there are two points of view from which we may regard Christ's death upon the cross. The one is the redemption of the cross: Christ dying for us as our complete deliverance from the curse of sin. The other is the fellowship of the cross: Christ taking us up to die with Him and making us partakers of the fellowship of His death.

In the above verse, we find three great unsearchable thoughts. First, the law of God has pronounced a curse on all sin and on all that is sinful. Second, Christ took our curse upon Him and even became a curse, thereby destroying its power. Third, in the cross we now have the everlasting redemption from sin and all its power. The cross reveals to us that man's sin is under the curse, that Christ became a curse and overcame it, and that He is our full and everlasting deliverance from the curse.

In these thoughts, the most lost and hopeless sinner may find a sure ground of confidence and hope. In Paradise, God had indeed pronounced a curse on this earth and all that belongs to it. (See Genesis 3:17–19.) On Mount Ebal, in connection with giving the law, half of the people of Israel were to pronounce a curse on all sin. (See Deuteronomy 27:11–26.) And there was to be in their midst a continual reminder of it: *"He that is hanged is accursed of God"* (Deuteronomy 21:23). And yet, who could ever have thought that the Son of God Himself would die on the accursed tree and become a curse for us? But such is the gospel of God's love, and the penitent sinner can now rejoice in the confident assurance that the curse is forever put away from all who believe in Christ Jesus.

The preaching of the redemption of the cross is the foundation and center of the salvation the gospel brings us. To those who believe its full truth, it is a cause of unceasing thanksgiving. It gives us boldness to rejoice in God. There is nothing else that will keep the heart more tender toward God, enabling us to live in His love and to make Him known to those who have never yet found Him. God be praised for the redemption of the cross!

June 2

The Fellowship of the Cross

Let this mind be in you, which was also in Christ Jesus.
—Philippians 2:5

Paul told us here of the mind that was in Christ: He emptied Himself; He took the form of a servant; He humbled Himself, *"even* [to] *the death of the cross"* (v. 8). It is this mind that was in Christ—the deep humility that gave up His life to the very death—that is to be the spirit that animates us. In this way, we will prove and enjoy the blessed fellowship of His cross.

Paul had said to the Philippians, *"If there be therefore any consolation in Christ"* (v. 1)—the Comforter had come to reveal His real presence in them—*"if any fellowship of the Spirit"* (v. 1)—it was in this power of the Spirit that they were to breathe the Spirit of the crucified Christ and manifest His disposition in the fellowship of the cross in their lives.

As they strove to do this, they would feel the need of a deeper insight into their real oneness with Christ. They would learn to appreciate the truth that they had been crucified with Christ, that their *"old man"* (Romans 6:6) had been crucified, and that they had died to sin in Christ's death and were now living to God in His life. They would learn to know what it meant that the crucified Christ lived in them, and that they had *"crucified the flesh with the affections and lusts"* (Galatians 5:24). Because the crucified Jesus lived in them, they could live crucified to the world.

And so they would gradually enter more deeply into the meaning and power of their high calling to live as those who were dead to sin, the world, and self. Each in his own measure would bear the marks of the cross, with its sentence of death on the flesh, with its hating of the self-life and its entire denial of self, and with its growing conformity to the crucified Redeemer in His deep humility and entire surrender of His will to the life of God.

This is a difficult thing to learn; there is no quick lesson in this school of the cross. But the personal experience of the fellowship of the cross will lead to a deeper understanding and a higher appreciation of the redemption of the cross.

June 3

Crucified with Christ

I am crucified with Christ: nevertheless I live; yet not I, but Christ liveth in me. —Galatians 2:20

The thought of fellowship with Christ in bearing His cross has often led to the futile attempt to follow Him and bear His image in our own power. But this is impossible for man until he first learns to know what it means to say, *"I am crucified with Christ."*

Let us try to understand this. When Adam died, all his descendants died with him and in him. In his sin in Paradise, and in the spiritual death into which he fell, you and I had a share; we died in him. And the power of that sin and death, in which all his descendants share, works in every child of Adam every day.

Christ came as the Second Adam. All who believe in Him have a share in His death on the cross. Each one may say in truth, *"I am crucified with Christ."* As the Representative of His people, He took them up with Him on the cross. This includes you and me. The life that He gives is the crucified life in which He entered heaven and was exalted to the throne, standing as *"a Lamb as it had been slain"* (Revelation 5:6). The power of His death and life does its work in us. As we hold fast the truth that we have been crucified with Him, and that now we no longer live, but Christ lives in us, we receive power to conquer sin. The life that we have received from Him is a life that has been crucified and made free from the power of sin.

This is a deep and very precious truth. Most Christians have little knowledge of it. This knowledge is not gained easily or speedily. It requires a great desire to be dead to all sin. It requires a strong faith, given by the Holy Spirit, so that the union with the crucified Christ and the fellowship of His cross can each day become our life. The life that He lives in heaven has its strength and its glory in the fact that it is a crucified life. And the life that He imparts to the believing disciple is a crucified life with its victory over sin and its power of access into God's presence.

It is indeed true that *"nevertheless I live; yet not I, but Christ liveth in me."* As we realize this by faith and hold fast the fact that the crucified Christ lives in us, life in the fellowship of the cross becomes a possibility and a blessed experience.

 June 4

Crucified to the World

But God forbid that I should glory, save in the cross of our Lord Jesus Christ, by whom the world is crucified unto me, and I unto the world. —Galatians 6:14

What Paul had written in Galatians 2 is here confirmed at the end of the epistle and is expressed even more strongly. He insisted that his only glory was that, in Christ, he had been crucified to the world and entirely delivered from its power. When he said, *"I am crucified with Christ"* (Galatians 2:20), it was not only an inner spiritual truth, but also an actual, practical experience in relation to the world and its temptations.

Christ had spoken about the world hating Him and about His having overcome the world. Paul knew that the world that had nailed Christ to the cross had in that deed done the same to him. He boasted that he lived as one who had been crucified to the world, and that the world as a powerless enemy was now crucified to him. It was this that made him glory in the cross of Christ. It had brought him complete deliverance from the world.

How very different is the relationship of Christians to the world today! They acknowledge that they must not commit the sins that the world allows. But still they are good friends with the world, and they feel free to enjoy as much of it as they can, if they only stay away from "open sin." They do not know that the most dangerous source of sin is the love of the world with its lusts and pleasures.

Dear Christian, when the world crucified Christ, it crucified you with Him. When Christ overcame the world on the cross, He made you an overcomer, too. He calls you now, at whatever cost of self-denial, to regard the world, in its hostility to God and His kingdom, as a crucified enemy over whom the cross can ever keep you a conqueror.

The Christian who has learned to say by the Holy Spirit, *"I am crucified with Christ*...[the crucified] *Christ liveth in me"* (Galatians 2:20), has a very different relationship to the pleasures and attractions of the world. Let us ask God fervently that the Holy Spirit, through whom Christ offered Himself on the cross, may reveal to us in power what it means to *"glory... in the cross of our Lord Jesus Christ, by whom the world is crucified unto me."*

June 5

The Flesh Crucified

And they that are Christ's have crucified the flesh with the affections and lusts. —Galatians 5:24

Concerning the flesh Paul taught us, *"In me (that is, in my flesh) dwelleth no good thing"* (Romans 7:18). And again he said, *"The carnal mind* [the mind of the flesh] *is enmity against God: for it is not subject to the law of God, neither indeed can be"* (Romans 8:7). When Adam lost the Spirit of God, he became ruled by the flesh. *"The flesh"* is the expression for the evil, corrupt nature that we inherit from Adam. Of this flesh it is written, *"Our old man is crucified with him"* (Romans 6:6). And here Paul put it even more strongly: *"And they that are Christ's have crucified the flesh."*

When the disciples heard and obeyed the call of Jesus to follow Him, they honestly meant to do so; but, as He later taught them what that would imply, they were far from being ready to yield immediate obedience. Likewise, those who are Christ's and have accepted Him as the Crucified One scarcely understand what that includes. By their act of surrender, they actually have crucified the flesh and consented to regard it as an accursed thing, nailed to the cross of Christ.

But unfortunately, many Christians have never for a moment thought of such a thing! It may be that the preaching of Christ crucified has been defective. It may be that the truth of our being crucified with Christ has not been taught. They shrink back from the self-denial that it implies, and as a result, where the flesh is allowed in any measure to have its way, the Spirit of Christ cannot exert His power.

Paul taught the Galatians, *"Walk in the Spirit, and ye shall not fulfil the lust of the flesh"* (Galatians 5:16); *"For as many as are led by the Spirit of God, they are the sons of God"* (Romans 8:14). The Spirit alone can guide us as the flesh, in living faith and fellowship with Christ Jesus, is kept in the place of crucifixion.

Blessed Lord, how little I understood when I accepted You in faith that I once and for all *"crucified the flesh with the affections and lusts"*! I humbly ask You, teach me to believe and to live in You, the Crucified One, in such a way that, like Paul, I may always glory in the cross on which the world and the flesh are crucified.

June 6

Bearing the Cross

And he that taketh not his cross, and followeth after me, is not worthy of me....he that loseth his life for my sake shall find it.
—Matthew 10:38–39

Thus far we have looked at some of Paul's words to the Galatians about the cross and our being crucified with Christ. Let us now turn to the Master Himself to see what He has to teach us. We find that what Paul could teach openly and fully after the crucifixion was given by the Master in words that could at first hardly be understood and yet contained the seed of the full truth.

It was when Christ sent forth His disciples that He first used the expression that the disciple must take up his cross and follow Him. The only meaning the disciples could attach to these words was from what they had often seen, when an evildoer who had been sentenced to death by the cross was led out, bearing his cross, to the place of execution. In bearing the cross, the criminal acknowledged the sentence of death that was on him.

Christ wanted His disciples to understand that their natures were so evil and corrupt that only by losing their natural lives could they find true life. Of Himself it was true: all His life He bore His cross, the sentence of death that He knew was resting upon Him on account of our sins. And so He wants each of His disciples to bear his own cross, the sentence of death that is on himself and on his evil, carnal nature.

The disciples could not understand all this right away. But Christ gave them words that, like seeds, would germinate in their hearts and later begin to reveal their full meaning. Each disciple of Christ was not only to carry the sentence of death in himself, but also to learn that in following the Master to His cross, he would find the power to lose his life and to receive instead of it the life that would come through the cross of Christ.

Christ asks His disciples to forsake all and take up their crosses, to give up their whole wills and lives, and to follow Him. The call comes to us, too, to give up the self-life with its self-pleasing and self-exaltation, and to bear the cross in fellowship with Him. In this way, we will be made partakers of His victory.

June 7

Self-denial

If any man will come after me, let him deny himself, and take up his cross, and follow me.
—Matthew 16:24

For the first time, Christ had definitely announced that He would have to suffer much and be killed and be raised again. *"Then Peter took him, and began to rebuke him, saying, Be it far from thee, Lord: this shall not be unto thee"* (v. 22). Christ's answer was, *"Get thee behind me, Satan"* (v. 23). The spirit of Peter, seeking to turn Him away from the cross and its suffering, was nothing but Satan tempting Him to turn aside from the path that God had appointed as our way of salvation.

Christ then added the words of our next verse, in which He used for the second time the words *"take up his cross."* But with these words, He used a very significant expression revealing what is implied: *"If any man will come after me, let him deny himself."* When Adam sinned, he fell out of the life of heaven and of God into the life of the world and of self. Self-pleasing, self-sufficiency, and self-exaltation became the laws of his life. When Jesus Christ came to restore man to his original place, *"He humbled himself, and became obedient unto death, even the death of the cross"* (Philippians 2:8). What He has done Himself He asks of all who desire to follow Him: *"If any man will come after me, let him deny himself."*

Instead of denying himself, Peter denied his Lord: *"I do not know the man"* (Matthew 26:72)! When a man learns to obey Christ's commands, he says of himself, *"I do not know the man."* The secret of true discipleship is to bear the cross, to acknowledge the death sentence that has been passed on self, and to deny any right that self has to rule over us.

Death to self—such is to be the Christian's watchword. The surrender to Christ is to be so entire, the surrender to live for those around us so complete, that self is never allowed to come down from the cross to which it has been nailed, but is always kept in the place of death.

Listen to the voice of Jesus: "Deny self." Let us ask God that we, as the disciples of Christ, who denied Himself for us, may by the grace of the Holy Spirit always live as those in whom self has been crucified with Christ, and in whom the crucified Christ now lives as Lord and Master.

He Cannot Be My Disciple

If any man come to me, and hate not...his own life...he cannot be my disciple. And whosoever doth not bear his cross, and come after me, cannot be my disciple....So likewise, whosoever he be of you that forsaketh not all that he hath, he cannot be my disciple.
—Luke 14:26–27, 33

For the third time, Christ spoke here about bearing the cross. He gave new meaning to it when He said that a man must hate his own life and forsake all that he has. Three times He solemnly repeated the words that without this a man cannot be His disciple.

If a man *"hate not...his own life"*—why does Christ make such an exacting demand the condition of discipleship? Because the sinful nature we have inherited from Adam is indeed so vile and full of sin that if our eyes were only opened to see it in its true nature, we would flee from it as loathsome and incurably evil. The flesh is *"enmity against God"* (Romans 8:7); the soul that seeks to love God cannot help hating the *"old man"* (Romans 6:6) that is corrupt through its whole being. Nothing less than this, the hating of our own lives, will make us willing to bear the cross and carry within us the sentence of death on our evil natures. Not until we hate this life with a deadly hatred will we be ready to give up the old nature to die the death that is its due.

Christ added one more thing: *"whosoever he be of you that forsaketh not all that he hath"*—whether in property or character—*"cannot be my disciple."* Christ claims all. Christ undertakes to satisfy every need and to give a hundredfold more than we give up. When we by faith become conscious of what it means to know Christ, to love Him, and to receive from Him what can enrich and satisfy our immortal spirits, then we will regard as our highest privilege the surrender that at first appeared so difficult. As we learn what it means that Christ is our life, we will *"count all things but loss for the excellency of the knowledge of Christ Jesus* [our] *Lord"* (Philippians 3:8). In the path of following Him and always learning to know and love Him better, we will willingly sacrifice all—including self with all its life—to make room for Him who is more than all.

Follow Me

Then Jesus beholding him loved him, and said unto him, One thing thou lackest: go thy way, sell whatsoever thou hast, and give to the poor, and thou shalt have treasure in heaven: and come, take up the cross, and follow me.
—Mark 10:21

When Christ spoke these words to the young ruler, he went away grieved. Jesus said, *"How hardly shall they that have riches enter into the kingdom of God!"* (v. 23). The disciples were astonished at His words. When Christ repeated once again what He had said, they were astonished beyond measure. *"Who then can be saved? And Jesus looking upon them saith, With men it is impossible, but not with God: for with God all things are possible"* (vv. 26–27).

Christ had spoken about bearing the cross as the one condition of discipleship. This is the human side. Here with the rich young ruler, He revealed from the side of God what is needed to give men the will and the power to sacrifice all in order to enter the kingdom. He said to Peter, when he had confessed Him as Christ, the Son of God, that *"flesh and blood"* (Matthew 16:17) had not revealed it to him, but his Father in heaven. This was to remind Peter and the other disciples that it was only by divine teaching that he could make the confession. With the young ruler, likewise, He unveiled the great mystery that it is only by divine power that a man can take up his cross, can lose his life, can deny himself, and can hate the life to which he is by nature so attached.

Multitudes have sought to follow Christ and obey His command yet have found that they have utterly failed. Multitudes have felt that Christ's claims were beyond their reach and have sought to be Christians without any attempt at the wholehearted devotion and the entire self-denial that Christ asks for.

In our study of what the fellowship of the cross means, let us take today's lesson to heart. Let us believe that only by putting our trust in the living God and the mighty power in which He is willing to work in the heart can we attempt to be disciples who forsake all and follow Christ in the fellowship of His cross.

June 10

A Grain of Wheat

Verily, verily, I say unto you, Except a grain of wheat fall into the earth and die, it abideth by itself alone; but if it die, it beareth much fruit. He that loveth his life loseth it; and he that hateth his life in this world shall keep it unto life eternal.
—John 12:24–25 (RV)

All nature is the parable of how the losing of a life can be the way of securing a truer and a higher life. Every grain of wheat, every seed throughout the world, teaches the lesson that through death lies the path to beautiful and fruitful life.

It was so with the Son of God. He had to pass through death in all its bitterness and suffering before He could rise to heaven and impart His life to His redeemed people. And here, under the shadow of the approaching cross, He called His disciples: "If any man will serve me, let him follow me." (See Matthew 16:24.) He repeated the words: *"He that hateth his life in this world shall keep it unto life eternal."*

One might have thought that Christ did not need to lose His holy life before He could find it again. But so it was: God had *"laid on him the iniquity of us all"* (Isaiah 53:6), and He yielded to the inexorable law that through death comes life and fruit.

How much more should we, in the consciousness of that evil nature and the death that we inherited in Adam, be most grateful that there is a way open to us by which, in the fellowship of Christ and His cross, we can die to this accursed self! With what gratitude we should listen to the call to bear our cross, to yield our *"old man"* (Romans 6:6) as crucified with Christ daily to the death that he deserves! Surely the thought that the power of eternal life is working in us ought to make us willing and glad to die the death that brings us into the fellowship and the power of life in a risen Christ.

Unfortunately, this is rarely understood. Let us believe that what is impossible to man is possible to God. (See Matthew 19:26.) Let us believe that the law of the Spirit of Christ Jesus, the Risen Lord, can indeed make His death and His life the daily experience of our souls.

June 11

Your Will Be Done

O my Father, if it be possible, let this cup pass away from me: nevertheless, not as I will, but as thou wilt.
—Matthew 26:39 (RV)

The death of Christ on the cross is the highest and holiest thing that can be known of Him even in the glory of heaven. And the highest and holiest thing that the Holy Spirit can work in us is to take us up and keep us in the fellowship of the cross of Christ. We need to enter deeply into the truth that Christ, the beloved Son of the Father, could not return to the glory of heaven until He had first given Himself over to death. As this great truth opens up to us, it will help us to understand how, in our lives and in our fellowship with Christ, it is impossible for us to share His life until we have first surrendered ourselves every day to die to sin and the world, and so to abide in unbroken fellowship with our crucified Lord.

From Christ alone we can learn what it means to have fellowship with His sufferings and to be *"made conformable unto his death"* (Philippians 3:10). In the agony of Gethsemane, when He looked toward what a death on the cross would be, He got such a vision of what it meant to die the accursed death under the power of sin, with God's face turned from Him so that not a single ray of its light could penetrate the darkness, that He prayed that the cup might pass from Him. But when no answer came and He understood that the Father could not allow the cup to pass by, He yielded up His whole will and life: *"Thy will be done"* (Matthew 26:42).

Dear Christian, in these words of your Lord in His agony, you can enter into fellowship with Him. In His strength, your heart will be made strong to believe most confidently that God in His omnipotence will enable you to yield up everything, because you have been crucified with Him.

"Thy will be done." Let this be the deepest and highest word in your life. In the power of Christ, with whom you have been crucified, and in the power of His Spirit, the definite daily surrender to the ever blessed will of God will become the joy and strength of your life.

The Love of the Cross

Then said Jesus, Father, forgive them; for they know not what they do. —Luke 23:34

The seven words on the cross, *"For they know not what they do,"* reveal the mind of Christ and show what the minds of His disciples should be. Three words express Christ's wonderful love: *"Father, forgive them."* Christ prayed for His enemies. In the hour of their triumph over Him, in the hour of shame and suffering that they delighted in showering on Him, He poured out His love in prayer for them. The call to everyone who believes in a crucified Christ is to go and do likewise, even as He said, *"Love your enemies, bless them that curse you, do good to them that hate you, and pray for them which…persecute you"* (Matthew 5:44).

The love that cared for His enemies also cared for His friends. Jesus felt what the anguish must be in the heart of His widowed mother and so committed her to the care of the beloved disciple: *"Woman, behold your son!…Behold your mother!"* (John 19:26–27). Jesus knew that for John there could be no higher privilege and no more blessed service than that of taking His place in the care of Mary. Similarly, we who are the disciples of Christ must not only pray for His enemies, but must also prove our love to Him and to all who belong to Him by making sure that every person is comforted and that every loving heart has some work to do in caring for those who belong to the blessed Master.

"Verily I say unto thee, To day shalt thou be with me in paradise" (Luke 23:43). The penitent thief had appealed to Christ's mercy to remember him. With what readiness of joy and love Christ gave the immediate answer to his prayer! Whether it was the love that prayed for His enemies, the love that cared for His friends, or the love that rejoiced over the penitent sinner who was being cast out by man—in all these Christ proved that the cross is a cross of love, that the Crucified One is the embodiment of a love that *"passeth knowledge"* (Ephesians 3:19).

With every thought of what we owe to that love, with every act of faith in which we rejoice in its redemption, let us prove that the mind of the crucified Christ is our mind, and that His love is not only what we trust in for ourselves, but also what guides us in our loving fellowship with the world around us.

June 13

The Sacrifice of the Cross

My God, my God, why hast thou forsaken me?
—Matthew 27:46

I thirst....It is finished!
—John 19:28, 30

These words spoken on the cross reveal love in its outflow to men, and in the tremendous sacrifice that it brought to deliver us and give the victory over every foe. They reveal the mind that was in Christ, which is to be the disposition of our whole lives.

"My God, my God, why hast thou forsaken me?" How deep must have been the darkness that overshadowed Him, when not one ray of light from the Father shone upon Him and He could not say, "My Father"! It was this awful desertion, breaking in upon that life of childlike fellowship with the Father in which He had always walked, that caused Him the agony and the bloody sweat in Gethsemane. *"O my Father...let this cup pass from me"* (Matthew 26:39). But He knew it could not pass away, and He bowed His head in submission: *"Thy will be done"* (v. 42). As we learn to believe and to worship that love, we, too, will learn to say, *"Thy will be done."*

"I thirst." The body of Christ here gave expression to the terrible experience of what it passed through when the fire of God's wrath against sin came upon Him in the hour of His desertion. He had spoken of the rich man crying out, *"I am tormented in this flame"* (Luke 16:24). Likewise, Christ uttered His complaint of what He had suffered. Physicians tell us that in crucifixion the whole body is in agony with terrible fever and pain. Our Lord endured it all and cried, *"I thirst."* He sacrificed both soul and body to the Father.

And now comes the great word: *"It is finished!"* All that there was to suffer and endure had been suffered and endured. His love held nothing back. He gave Himself as an offering and a sacrifice. Such was the mind of Christ, and such must be the attitude of everyone who owes himself and his life to that sacrifice. The mind that was in Christ must be in us, ready to say, "I have come *'to do the will of him that sent me, and to finish his work'* (John 4:34)." And every day that our confidence grows fuller in Christ's finished work, our hearts must more entirely yield themselves as burnt offerings in the service of God and His love.

June 14

The Death of the Cross

**Father, into thy hands I commend my spirit: and having said thus, he gave up the ghost.
—Luke 23:46**

Like David, Christ had often committed His spirit into the hands of the Father for His daily life and needs. (See Psalm 31:5.) But here is something new and very special. He gave up His spirit into the power of death, gave up all control over it, and sank down into the darkness and death of the grave, where He could neither think, pray, nor will. He surrendered Himself completely into the Father's hands, trusting Him to care for Him in the dark, and in due time to raise Him up again.

If we have indeed died in Christ and are now to carry with us the death of our Lord Jesus in faith every day (see 2 Corinthians 4:10), this word is the one that we need. Just think once again what Christ meant when He said that we must hate and lose our lives. (See John 12:24–25.)

We died in Adam. The life we receive from him is death; there is nothing good or heavenly in us by nature. It is to this inward evil nature, to all the life that we have from this world, that we must die. There cannot be any thought of any real holiness without totally dying to this self, this *"old man"* (Romans 6:6). Many people deceive themselves because they seek to be alive in God before they are dead to their own natures—something as impossible as a grain of wheat producing a crop without dying first. This dying to self lies at the root of true piety. Spiritual life must grow out of death.

And if you ask how you can do this, you will find the answer in the mind in which Christ died. Like Him, you may cast yourself upon God, without knowing how the new life is to be attained. But as you say in fellowship with Jesus, *"Father, into thy hands I commend my spirit,"'* and as you depend simply and absolutely on God to raise you up into the new life, the wonderful promise of God's Word will be fulfilled in you. You will know *"what is the exceeding greatness of his power to us-ward who believe, according to the working of his mighty power, which he wrought in Christ, when he raised him from the dead"* (Ephesians 1:19–20).

This is indeed the true rest of faith: living every day and every hour in absolute dependence on the continual and immediate quickening of the divine life in us by God Himself through the Holy Spirit.

June

June 15

It Is Finished

When Jesus therefore had received the vinegar, he said, It is finished. —John 19:30

Once again, these words of our Lord on the cross reveal to us His mind and disposition. At the beginning of His ministry, He said, *"My meat is to do the will of him that sent me, and to finish his work"* (John 4:34). In all things, the small as well as the great, He would accomplish God's work. In His high-priestly prayer at the end of His three years of earthly ministry, He could say, *"I have glorified thee on the earth: I have finished the work which thou gavest me to do"* (John 17:4). He sacrificed all, and in dying on the cross could in truth say, *"It is finished"*!

With these words to the Father, Christ laid down His life. With these words, He was strengthened, after the terrible agony on the cross, in the knowledge that all was now fulfilled. And with these words, He uttered the truth of the gospel of our redemption, that all that was needed for man's salvation had been accomplished on the cross.

June

This disposition should characterize every follower of Christ. The mind that was in Him must be in us (see Philippians 2:5)—it must be our food, the strength of our lives, to do the will of God in all things and to finish His work. There may be small things about which we are not aware that bring harm to ourselves and to God's work. Or we might draw back before some great thing that demands too much sacrifice. No matter what happens, however, we may find strength to perform our duty in Christ's words: *"It is finished"*! His finished work secured the victory over every foe. By faith we may take hold of these dying words of Christ on the cross and may find the power for daily living and daily dying in the fellowship of the crucified Christ.

Child of God, study the inexhaustible treasure contained in this Scripture: *"It is finished"*! Faith in what Christ accomplished on the cross will enable you to manifest in daily life the spirit of the cross.

June 16

Dead to Sin

How shall we, that are dead to sin, live any longer therein?
—Romans 6:2

In the first section of the epistle to the Romans, Paul had expounded the great doctrine of justification by faith. (See Romans 1:16–5:11.) After having done this, Paul proceeded in the second section to unfold the related doctrine of the new life by faith in Christ. (See Romans 5:12–8:39.) Using Adam as an illustration of Christ, Paul taught that, just as we all died in Adam and his death reigns in our natures, so those who believe in Christ actually died to sin in Him, were set free from it, and became partakers of the new holy life of Christ.

Paul asked, *"How shall we, that are dead to sin, live any longer therein?"* In these words we have the deep spiritual truth that our death to sin in Christ delivers us from its power, so that we no longer can or need to live in it. The secret of true and full holiness is to live, by faith and in the power of the Holy Spirit, with the knowledge that you are dead to sin.

In expounding this truth, Paul reminded the Romans that they were baptized into the death of Christ. *"Therefore we are buried with him by baptism into death....We have been planted together in the likeness of his death....Our old man is crucified with him, that the body of sin might be destroyed"* (Romans 6:4–6)—rendered void and powerless. Take time to quietly ask for the teaching of the Holy Spirit. Ponder these words until this truth masters you: you are indeed dead to sin in Christ Jesus. As you grow in the consciousness of your union with the crucified Christ, you will experience that the power of His life in you has made you free from the power of sin.

Romans 6 is one of the most blessed portions of the New Testament of our Lord Jesus, teaching us that our *"old man"* (v. 6)—the old nature that is in us—was actually crucified with Him, so that we no longer need to be in bondage to sin. But remember, only as the Holy Spirit makes Christ's death a reality within us will we know—not by force of argument or conviction, but in the reality of the power of a divine life—that we are indeed dead to sin. It only requires the continual living in Christ Jesus.

The Righteousness of God

Abraham believed God, and it was counted unto him for righteousness.... he believed...God, who quickeneth the dead.
—Romans 4:3, 17

Now that we have studied the words of our Lord Jesus about our fellowship with Him in the cross, let us turn to Paul to see how, through the Holy Spirit, he gave deeper insight into what our death in Christ means.

As I said before, the first section of Romans is devoted to the doctrine of justification by faith in Christ. After writing about the awful sin of the heathen (see Romans 1:18–32) and then about the sins of the Jews (see Romans 2:1–29), he pointed out how both Jew and Gentile are *"guilty before God"* (Romans 3:19). *"All have sinned, and come short"* (v. 23). And then Paul set forth the free grace that gave the redemption that is in Christ Jesus (vv. 21–31). In chapter 4, he pointed to Abraham, who, when he believed, understood that God justified him freely by His grace, and not for anything that he had done.

Abraham had believed not only this, but also something more. He *"believed...God, who quickeneth the dead, and calleth those things which be not as though they were"* (Romans 4:3, 17). This is significant because it indicates the two essential needs in the redemption of man in Christ Jesus. There is the need for justification by faith, to restore man to the favor of God. But something more is needed. Man must also be quickened to a new life. Just as justification is by faith alone, so is regeneration. Christ died for our sins; He was raised again out of, or through, our justification.

In the first section of Romans (see Romans 1:1–5:11), Paul dealt exclusively with the great thought of our justification. But in the second section (see Romans 5:12–8:39), he expounded the wonderful union with Christ through faith, by which we died with Him, by which we live in Him, and by which we are made free through the Holy Spirit. We are free not only from the punishment, but also from the power of sin, and we are enabled to live the life of righteousness, obedience, and sanctification.

Dead with Christ

Now if we be dead with Christ, we believe that we shall also live with him.
—Romans 6:8

The reason God's children live so little in the power of the resurrection life of Christ is that they have so little understanding of or faith in their death with Christ. How clearly this appears from what Paul said: *"Now if we be dead with Christ, we believe that we shall also live with him."* Such is the knowledge and experience that give us the assurance of His resurrection power in us. *"He died unto sin once: but in that he liveth, he liveth unto God"* (v. 10). Only as we know that we are dead with Him can we live with Him.

On the strength of this, Paul pleaded earnestly with his readers: *"Likewise reckon ye also yourselves to be dead indeed unto sin, but alive unto God through Jesus Christ"* (v. 11). The words *"likewise reckon ye also yourselves"* are a call to bold and confident faith. *"Reckon ye also yourselves to be dead indeed unto sin"* as much as Christ is, *"but alive unto God through Jesus Christ."* These words give us a divine assurance of what we actually are and have in Christ—not as a truth that our minds can master and take hold of, but as a reality that the Holy Spirit will reveal within us. In His power, we accept our death with Christ on the cross as the power of our daily lives.

Then we are able to accept and obey the command: *"Let not sin therefore reign in your mortal body...but yield yourselves unto God, as those that are alive from the dead...for sin shall not have dominion over you"* (vv. 12–14). *"Being then made free from sin, ye became the servants of righteousness...so now yield your members servants to righteousness unto holiness...But now being made free from sin...ye have your fruit unto holiness"* (vv. 18–19, 22).

All of Romans 6 is a wonderful revelation of the deep meaning of its opening words: *"How shall we, that are dead to sin, live any longer therein?"* (v. 2). Everything depends on our acceptance of the divine assurance that if we died with Christ, we have the power to live for God, just as Christ who died now lives for God.

June 19

Dead to the Law

Ye also are become dead to the law by the body of Christ....that being dead wherein we were held; that we should serve in newness of spirit.
—Romans 7:4, 6

The believer is not only dead to sin, but also dead to the law. This is a deeper truth, giving us deliverance from the thought of a life of effort and failure, and opening the way to life in the power of the Holy Spirit. *"Thou shalt"* is done away with; the power of the Spirit takes its place.

In the remainder of Romans 7, we find a description of the Christian as he still tries to obey the law but utterly fails. His experience is such that he says, *"In me (that is, in my flesh,) dwelleth no good thing"* (v. 18). He discovers that the law of sin, notwithstanding his greatest efforts, continually brings him into captivity and causes him to cry out, *"O wretched man that I am! who shall deliver me from the body of this death?"* (v. 24). In the whole passage, "I" is everywhere, without any thought of the Spirit's help. Only when he has cried out in despair is he brought to see that he is no longer under the law, but under the rule of the Holy Spirit. *"There is therefore now no condemnation"*—such as he had experienced in his attempt to obey the law—*"to them which are in Christ Jesus....For the law of the Spirit of life in Christ Jesus hath made me free from the law of sin and death"* (Romans 8:1–2).

As chapter 7 gives us the experience that leads to being a captive under the power of sin, chapter 8 reveals the experience of a man in Christ Jesus who has now been made free from the law of sin and death. In the former, we have the life of the ordinary Christian doing his utmost to keep the commandments of the law and to walk in God's ways, but always ending in failure and shortcoming. In the latter, we have the man who knows that he is in Christ Jesus, dead to sin and alive to God, and by the Spirit has been made free and is kept free from the bondage of sin and of death.

Oh, that men understood the deep meaning of Romans 7, where a man learns that in him, in his flesh, there is no good thing, and that there is no deliverance from this condition except by yielding to the power of the Spirit! Only in this way can men be free from the bondage of the flesh and can fulfill the righteousness of the law in the power of Christ.

June 20

The Flesh Condemned on the Cross

For what the law could not do, in that it was weak through the flesh, God sending his own Son in the likeness of sinful flesh, and for sin, condemned sin in the flesh.
—Romans 8:3

In Romans 8:7 Paul wrote, *"The carnal mind* [the mind of the flesh] *is enmity against God: for it is not subject to the law of God, neither indeed can be."* Here Paul opened up the depth of sin that is in the flesh. In Romans 7:18, he had said that *"in my flesh, dwelleth no good thing"* (v. 18). Here he went deeper and told us that the flesh is *"enmity against God"* (Romans 8:7); it hates God and His law. It was on this account that God condemned sin in the flesh on the cross; all the curse that is on sin is on the flesh in which sin dwells. As the believer understands this, he will cease from any attempt at seeking to perfect in the flesh what is begun in the Spirit. (See Galatians 3:3.) The two are at deadly, irreconcilable enmity.

This lies at the very root of the true Christian life: *"God...condemned sin in the flesh: that the righteousness of the law might be fulfilled in us, who walk not after the flesh, but after the Spirit"* (Romans 8:3–4). All the requirements of God's law will be fulfilled, not in those who strive to keep and fulfill that law (a thing that is utterly impossible), but in those who walk by the Spirit and, in His power, live out the life that Christ won for us on the cross and imparted to us in the resurrection.

May God's children learn the double lesson here. In me, that is in my flesh, in the old nature that I have from Adam, there dwells literally no good thing that can satisfy the eye of a holy God. And that flesh can never by any process of discipline, struggling, or prayer be made better than it is. But the Son of God, in the likeness of sinful flesh and in the form of a man, condemned sin on the cross. *"There is therefore now no condemnation to them which are in Christ Jesus, who walk not after the flesh, but after the Spirit"* (v. 1).

June 21

Jesus Christ and Him Crucified

For I determined not to know any thing among you, save Jesus Christ, and him crucified....And my speech and my preaching was...in demonstration of the Spirit and of power.
—1 Corinthians 2:2, 4

This passage of Scripture is very often understood to mean that Paul's purpose in his preaching was to know nothing but Jesus Christ and Him crucified. But it contains a far deeper meaning. Paul spoke of his purpose, not only in the matter of his preaching, but also in his whole spirit and life, in order to prove how he in everything sought to act in conformity to the crucified Christ. Thus he wrote, "[Christ] *was crucified through weakness, yet he liveth by the power of God. For we also are weak in him, but we shall live with him by the power of God toward you"* (2 Corinthians 13:4).

June

His whole ministry and all his actions bore the mark of Christ's likeness; he was crucified through weakness, yet he lived by the power of God. Just before the words of our text, Paul had written, *"For the preaching of the cross is to them that perish foolishness; but unto us which are saved it is the power of God"* (1 Corinthians 1:18). Not only in his preaching, but also in all his activities and behavior, he sought to act in harmony with the weakness in which Christ was crucified. He had so identified himself with the weakness of the cross and its shame that, in his whole life and conduct, he proved that he sought to show forth the likeness and the spirit of the crucified Jesus in everything. Hence he said, *"And I was with you in weakness, and in fear, and in much trembling"* (1 Corinthians 2:3).

It is on this account that he spoke so strongly and said, *"Christ sent me...to preach the gospel: not with wisdom of words, lest the cross of Christ should be made of none effect"* (1 Corinthians 1:17); *"And my speech and my preaching was not with enticing words of man's wisdom, but in demonstration of the Spirit and of power"* (1 Corinthians 2:4). Is this not the great reason why the power of God is so little manifested in the preaching of the gospel? Christ the Crucified One may be the subject of the preaching, and yet, because of men's confidence in human learning and eloquence, there may be none of the likeness of the crucified Jesus that alone gives preaching its supernatural, divine power.

God help us to understand how the life of every believer must bear the stamp of the sanctuary—nothing but Jesus Christ and Him crucified.

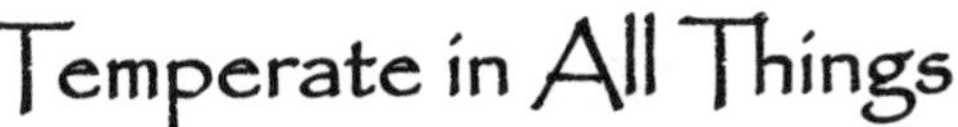

June 22

Temperate in All Things

Every man that striveth for the mastery is temperate in all things....I keep under my body, and bring it into subjection.
—1 Corinthians 9:25, 27

Here Paul reminded us of the well-known principle that anyone competing for a prize is *"temperate in all things."* Everything, however attractive, that might be a hindrance in the race is given up or set aside. And this is done in order to obtain an earthly prize. We who strive for an *"incorruptible* [crown]" (v. 25) and strive so that Christ may be Lord of all—will we not be *"temperate in all things"* that could in the very least prevent our following the Lord Jesus with an undivided heart?

Paul said, *"I keep under my body, and bring it into subjection."* He would allow nothing to hinder him. He told us, *"One thing I do...I press toward the mark for the prize"* (Philippians 3:13–14). No self-pleasing in eating and drinking, no comfort or ease, would for a moment have kept him from showing the spirit of the cross in his daily life, or from sacrificing all, like his Master. Read the following four passages that comprise Paul's life history: 1 Corinthians 4:11–13; 2 Corinthians 4:8–12; 2 Corinthians 6:4–10; and 2 Corinthians 11:23–27. The cross was not only the theme of his preaching, but also the rule of his life in all its details.

We need to ask God that this disposition may be found in all Christians and preachers of the gospel, through the power of the Holy Spirit. When the death of Christ works with power in the preacher, then Christ's life will be known among the people. Let us pray that the fellowship of the cross may regain its old place, and that God's children may obey the command: *"Let this mind be in you, which was also in Christ Jesus"* (Philippians 2:5). *"He humbled himself, and became obedient unto death, even the death of the cross"* (v. 8). *"For if we have been planted together in the likeness of his death, we shall be also in the likeness of his resurrection"* (Romans 6:5).

June 23

The Dying of the Lord Jesus

Always bearing about in the body the dying of the Lord Jesus, that the life also of Jesus might be made manifest in our body.... So then death worketh in us, but life in you.
—2 Corinthians 4:10, 12

Paul was very bold in speaking of the intimate union that was between the life of Christ in him and the life he lived in the flesh with all its suffering. In Galatians 2:20, he had spoken of being crucified with Christ and of Christ living in him. Here he talked about how he was *"bearing about in the body the dying of the Lord Jesus"*; it was through this that the life of Jesus was also manifested in his body. And he told the Corinthians that because the death of Christ was thus working in and through him, Christ's life could work in them.

June

We often speak of abiding in Christ, but we forget that this means abiding in a crucified Christ. Many believers seem to think that, once they have claimed Christ's death in the fellowship of the cross and have considered themselves as crucified with Him, they may now consider it as over and done with. They do not understand that it is in the crucified Christ, and in the fellowship of His death, that they are to abide daily and unceasingly. The fellowship of the cross is to be a daily experience. The self-emptying of our Lord, His taking the form of a servant, His humbling Himself and becoming *"obedient unto death, even the death of the cross"* (Philippians 2:8)—this mind that was in Christ is to be the disposition that marks our daily lives.

"Always bearing about in the body the dying of the Lord Jesus." This is what we are called to as much as Paul was. If we are indeed to live for the welfare of others around us, if we are to sacrifice our ease and pleasure to win souls for our Lord, it will be true of us as of Paul, that we are able to say, *"Death worketh in us, but life in* [those for whom we pray and labor]." It is in *"the fellowship of* [Christ's] *sufferings"* (Philippians 3:10) that the crucified Lord can live and work out His life in us and through us.

Let us learn the lesson that the abiding in Christ Jesus, for which we have so often prayed and worked, is nothing less than the abiding of the crucified Lord in us, and we in Him.

June 24

The Cross and the Spirit

How much more shall the blood of Christ, who through the eternal Spirit offered himself without blemish unto God, cleanse your conscience? —Hebrews 9:14 (RV)

The cross is Christ's highest glory. The glory that He received from the Father was entirely owing to His having humbled Himself to the death of the cross. *"Wherefore God also hath highly exalted him"* (Philippians 2:9). The greatest work that the Holy Spirit could ever do in the Son of God was when He enabled Him to yield Himself as a sacrifice and an offering. And the Holy Spirit can now do nothing greater or more glorious for us than to lead us into the fellowship and likeness of that crucified life of our Lord.

Do we not have here the reason that our prayers for the mighty working of the Holy Spirit are not more abundantly answered? We have prayed too little that the Holy Spirit might glorify Christ in us in the fellowship of and the conformity to His sufferings. (See Philippians 3:10.) The Spirit who led Christ to the cross desires and is able to maintain in us the life of abiding in our crucified Lord.

The Spirit and the cross are inseparable. The Spirit led Christ to the cross; the cross brought Christ to the throne to receive the fullness of the Spirit to impart to His people. The Spirit taught Peter to preach Christ crucified; it was through this preaching that the three thousand received the Spirit. (See Acts 2:14–41.) In the preaching of the gospel, in the Christian life, the Spirit and the cross are inseparable; as it was in Christ, so it must be in us. The sad lack of the mind and disposition of the crucified Christ—sacrificing self and the world to win life for the dying—is one great cause of the feebleness of the church. Let us ask God fervently to teach us to say, "We have been crucified with Christ; in Him we have died to sin." Let us always carry *"about in the body the dying of the Lord Jesus"* (2 Corinthians 4:10). In this way we will be prepared for the fullness of the Spirit that the Father desires to bestow.

June 25

The Veil of the Flesh

Having therefore, brethren, boldness to enter into the holiest by the blood of Jesus, by a new and living way, which he hath consecrated for us, through the veil, that is to say, his flesh.
—Hebrews 10:19–20

In the temple there was a veil between the Holy Place and the Holiest of All. At the altar in the court, the blood of the sacrifice was sprinkled for forgiveness of sins. This gave the priest entrance into the Holy Place to offer incense to God as part of a holy worship. But into the Holiest of All, behind the veil, the high priest alone might enter once a year. This veil was the symbol of sinful human nature; even though it had received the forgiveness of sin, full access and fellowship with God was impossible.

When Christ died, the veil was torn in two. Christ dedicated *"a new and living way"* to God through the torn veil of His flesh. This new way, by which we now can enter into the Holiest of All, always passes through the torn veil of the flesh. Every believer has *"crucified the flesh with the affections and lusts"* (Galatians 5:24). Every step on the *"new and living way"* for entering into God's holy presence maintains the fellowship with the cross of Christ. The torn veil of the flesh refers not only to Christ and His sufferings, but also to our experience in the likeness of His sufferings.

Is this not the reason why many Christians can never attain close fellowship with God? They have never yielded the flesh as an accursed thing to the condemnation of the cross. They desire to enter into the Holiest of All, yet they allow *"the flesh with the affections and lusts"* to rule over them. God grant that we may rightly understand, in the power of the Holy Spirit, that Christ has called us to hate our lives, to lose our lives, and to be dead with Him to sin so that we may live to God with Him.

There is no way to a full, abiding fellowship with God except through the torn veil of the flesh, through a life with the flesh crucified in Christ Jesus. God be praised that the Holy Spirit always dwells in us to keep the flesh in its place of crucifixion and condemnation, and to give us the abiding victory over all temptations.

Looking to Jesus

Let us run with patience the race that is set before us, looking unto Jesus the author and perfecter of our faith, who for the joy that was set before him endured the cross, despising shame.
—Hebrews 12:1–2 (RV)

In running a race, a person's eyes and heart are always set upon the goal and the prize. In Hebrews 12, the Christian is called to keep his eyes focused on Jesus, who endured the cross, as the one object of imitation and desire. In our whole lives, we are always to be animated by His Spirit as He bore the cross. This was the way that led to the throne and the glory of God. This is the *"new and living way"* (Hebrews 10:20) that He opened for us through the veil of the flesh. As we study and realize that God so highly exalted Him because He bore the cross (see Philippians 2:8–9), we will walk in His footsteps, bearing our own crosses as He did, with our flesh condemned and crucified.

The powerlessness of the church is greatly owing to the fact that this cross-bearing mind of Jesus is so little preached and practiced. Most Christians think that as long as they do not commit obvious sins, they are at liberty to possess and enjoy as much of the world as they please. There is so little insight into the deep truth that the world, and the flesh that loves the world, is *"enmity against God"* (Romans 8:7). Because of this, many Christians seek and pray for conformity to the image of Jesus for years, and yet they fail so entirely. They do not know, they do not seek with the whole heart to know, what it is to die to self and the world.

It was for *"the joy that was set before him,"* the joy of pleasing and glorifying the Father, the joy of loving and winning souls for Himself, that Christ endured the cross. We have a great need for a new crusade with the proclamation, "This is the will of God: just as Christ, through His endurance of the cross, found His highest happiness and received from the Father the fullness of the Spirit to pour down on His people, so it is only in our fellowship of the cross that we can really become *'conformed to the image of his Son'* (Romans 8:29)." As believers awake to this blessed truth, and as they always look to the crucified Jesus while running the race, they will receive power to win for Christ the souls He purchased on the cross.

Outside the Gate

For the bodies of those beasts, whose blood is brought into the sanctuary by the high priest for sin, are burned without the camp. Wherefore Jesus also, that he might sanctify the people with his own blood, suffered without the gate. Let us go forth therefore unto him without the camp, bearing his reproach.
—Hebrews 13:11–13

The body of the sacrifice was *"burned without the camp,"* and the blood of the sin offering was brought into the Holy Place. Similarly, Christ's body was cast out as an accursed thing, *"without the camp,"* but His blood was presented to the Father.

And so we read in Hebrews 13, *"Let us go forth therefore unto him without the camp, bearing his reproach."* Let us enter into the Holy Place by the blood of Jesus. The deeper my insight is into the boldness that His blood gives me in God's presence, so much greater will be the joy with which I enter the Holy Place. And the deeper my insight is into the shame of the cross that He bore *"without* [outside] *the gate"* on my behalf, the more willing I will be to follow Him *"without the camp, bearing his reproach."*

Christians love to hear of the boldness in which we can enter into the Holy Place through His blood, but have little desire for the fellowship of *"his reproach"* and are unwilling to separate themselves from the world with the same boldness. The Christian suffers inconceivable loss when he thinks of entering into the Holy Place and then feels free to enjoy the friendship of the world, as long as he does nothing too sinful. But the Word has said, *"Know ye not that the friendship of the world is enmity with God?"* (James 4:4); *"Love not the world, neither the things that are in the world. If any man love the world, the love of the Father is not in him"* (1 John 2:15); *"Be not conformed to this world"* (Romans 12:2).

To be a follower of Christ implies a heart given up to testify for Him in the midst of the world, if by any means some may be won. To be a follower of Christ means to be like Him in His love of the cross and in His willingness to sacrifice self so that the Father may be glorified and men may be saved.

Alive unto Righteousness

Who his own self bare our sins in his body upon the tree, that we, having died unto sins, might live unto righteousness.
—1 Peter 2:24 (RV)

Here in the epistle of Peter we have the same lessons that Paul taught us. First is the atonement of the cross: *"Who his own self bare our sins in his body upon the tree."* And then comes the fellowship of the cross: *"That we, having died unto sins, might live unto righteousness."*

In this last expression, we have the great thought that a Christian cannot live to righteousness unless he knows that he has died to sin. We need the Holy Spirit to make our death to sin such a reality that we know we are forever free from its power and will therefore yield our *"members as instruments of righteousness unto God"* (Romans 6:13).

Dear Christian, it cost Christ much to bear the cross and then to yield Himself so that it could bear Him. It cost Him much when He cried, *"Now is my soul troubled; and what shall I say? Father, save me from this hour: but for this cause came I unto this hour"* (John 12:27).

Let us not imagine that the fellowship of the cross—concerning which Peter wrote the words, *"That we, having died unto sins, might live unto righteousness"*—is easily understood or experienced. It means that the Holy Spirit will teach us what it is to be identified with Christ in His cross. It means that we realize by faith how we truly shared with Christ in His death, and now, as He lives in us, we abide in unceasing fellowship with Him, the Crucified One. This costs self-sacrifice; it costs earnest prayer; it costs a wholehearted surrender to God, to His will, and to the cross of Jesus; it costs abiding in Christ and having unceasing fellowship with Him.

Blessed Lord, reveal to us each day through the Holy Spirit the secret of our lives in You. Let Your Spirit reveal to us that as truly as we died in You, You now live in us the life that was crucified and now is glorified in heaven. Having died to sin, and being forever set free from its dominion, let us know that sin can no more reign over us or have dominion. (See Romans 6:14.) In the power of Your redemption, let us yield ourselves to God as those who are alive from the dead, ready and prepared for all His will.

June 29

Followers of the Cross

Hereby know we love, because he laid down his life for us: and we ought to lay down our lives for the brethren.
—1 John 3:16 (RV)

"Greater love hath no man than this, that a man lay down his life for his friends" (John 15:13). Here our Lord revealed to us the inconceivable love that moved Him to die for us. And now, under the influence and in the power of that love dwelling in us, comes the message: *"We ought to lay down our lives for the brethren."* Nothing less is expected of us than a Christlike life and a Christlike love, proving itself in all our fellowship with our fellow believers.

The cross of Christ is the measure by which we know how much Christ loves us. That cross is also the measure of the love that we owe to the believers around us. Only as the love of Christ on the cross possesses our hearts will we be able to love others. Our fellowship in the cross of Christ is to manifest itself in our sacrifice of love.

Only the faith of Christ Himself living in us can enable us to accept this great command in the assurance that Christ Himself will work it out in us. It is He who calls us: *"If any man will come after me, let him deny himself, and take up his cross, and follow me"* (Matthew 16:24). Nothing less than this—a faith that our *"old man"* (Romans 6:6), our flesh, has been crucified with Christ, so that we no longer need to sin—nothing less than this can enable us to say, "We love his commandments; this commandment, too, is not grievous." (See 1 John 5:3.)

But for such fellowship and conformity to the death of Christ, nothing will be effective except the daily, unbroken abiding in Christ Jesus that He has promised us. By the Holy Spirit revealing and glorifying Christ in us, we may trust Christ Himself to live out His life in us. He who proved His love on the cross of Calvary, He alone can enable us to say in truth, *"He laid down his life for us: and we ought to lay down our lives for the brethren."* Only as the great truth of the indwelling Christ obtains a place in the faith of the church that it does not have now, will the Christlike love for other believers become the mark of true Christianity, by which all men will know that we are Christ's disciples. (See John 13:35.) This is what will bring the world to believe that God has loved us even as He loved Christ. (See John 17:23.)

June 30

To Him Be the Glory

Unto him that loved us, and washed us from our sins in his own blood, and hath made us kings and priests unto God and his Father; to him be glory and dominion for ever and ever. Amen.
—Revelation 1:5–6

Some of my readers may feel that it is not easy to understand the lesson of the cross or to carry it out in their lives. Do not think of it as a heavy burden or yoke that you have to bear. Christ has said, *"My yoke is easy, and my burden is light"* (Matthew 11:30). Love makes everything easy. Do not think of your love for Him, but of His great love for you, given through the Holy Spirit. Meditate on this day and night, until you have the assurance that He loves you unspeakably. It is through the love of Christ on the cross that souls are drawn to Him.

We have here the answer as to what will enable us to love the fellowship of the crucified Jesus. It is nothing less than His love poured out through the continual inspiration of the Holy Spirit into the heart of every child of God.

"Unto him that loved us." Be still, dear soul, and think what this everlasting love is that seeks to take possession of you and fill you with unspeakable joy.

"And washed us from our sins in his own blood." Is this not proof enough that He will never reject you, that you are precious in His sight, and that through the power of His blood you are well pleasing to God?

"And hath made us kings and priests unto God and his Father." He now preserves us by His power. He will strengthen us through His Spirit to reign as kings over sin and the world and to appear as priests before God in intercession for others. O Christian, learn this wonderful song, and repeat it until your heart is filled with love and joy and courage, and it turns to Him in glad surrender every day. *"To him be glory and dominion for ever and ever. Amen."*

Yes, to Him who has loved me, has washed me from my sins in His blood, and has made me a king and a priest—to Him be the glory in all ages. Amen.

July

July 1

The Abiding Presence

Lo, I am with you alway[s], even unto the end of the world.
—Matthew 28:20

When the Lord chose His twelve disciples, it was so *"that they should be with him, and that he might send them forth to preach"* (Mark 3:14). A life in fellowship with Him was to be their preparation for the work of preaching.

The disciples were so deeply conscious of having this great privilege that when Christ spoke of leaving them, their hearts were filled with great sorrow. The presence of Christ had become indispensable to them; they could not think of living without Him. To comfort them, Christ gave them the promise of the Holy Spirit, with the assurance that they then would have Himself in His heavenly presence in a far deeper and more intimate sense than they ever had known while He was on earth.

When Christ gave them the Great Commission to *"go ye therefore, and teach all nations, baptizing them in the name of the Father, and of the Son, and of the Holy Ghost: teaching them to observe all things whatsoever I have commanded you"* (Matthew 28:19–20), He added the words, *"Lo, I am with you alway*[s], *even unto the end of the world."*

This principle holds true for all of Christ's servants, as it did for the twelve disciples: without the experience of His presence always abiding with them, their preaching would have no power. The secret of their strength would be the living testimony that Jesus Christ was with them every moment, inspiring, directing, and strengthening them. It was this reality that made them so bold in preaching Him as the Crucified One in the midst of His enemies. They never for a moment regretted His bodily absence; they had Him with them and in them, in the divine power of the Holy Spirit.

In all the work of the minister and the missionary, everything depends on an awareness, through a living faith, of the abiding presence of the Lord with His servant. The living experience of the presence of Jesus is an essential element in preaching the gospel. If this is clouded, our work becomes a human effort, without the freshness and the power of the heavenly life. And nothing can bring back the power and the blessing besides a return to the Master's feet, so that He may breathe into the heart, in divine power, His blessed words: *"Lo, I am with you alway*[s]*."*

The Omnipotence of Christ

All power is given unto me in heaven and in earth.
—Matthew 28:18

Before Christ gave His disciples their Great Commission to begin the great world conquest that aimed to bring His gospel to every creature, He first revealed Himself in His divine power as a partner with God Himself, the Almighty One. It was their faith in this that enabled the disciples to undertake the work in all simplicity and boldness. They had begun to know Him in the mighty resurrection power that had conquered sin and death; there was nothing too great for Him to command or for them to undertake.

Every disciple of Jesus Christ who desires to take part in *"the victory that overcometh the world"* (1 John 5:4) needs time, faith, and the Holy Spirit. These things are needed so that he may come under the full conviction that he is to take his part in the work as a servant of the omnipotent Lord Jesus. He is to depend on the daily experience of being *"strong in the Lord, and in the power of his might"* (Ephesians 6:10). God's promises give us the courage to unquestioningly obey His commands.

Just think of what the disciples had learned of the power of Christ Jesus here on earth. And yet that was such a little thing compared with the greater works that He was now to do in and through them. (See John 14:12.) He has the power to work even in the feeblest of His servants with the strength of the almighty God. He has power even to use their apparent powerlessness to carry out His purposes. He has the power over every enemy and every human heart, over every difficulty and danger.

But let us remember that this power is never meant to be experienced as if it were our own. Only as Jesus Christ lives, dwells, and works with His divine energy in our own hearts can there be any power in our preaching as a personal testimony. It was when Christ had said to Paul, *"My strength is made perfect in weakness"* (2 Corinthians 12:9), that Paul could say what he never learned to say before: *"When I am weak, then am I strong"* (v. 10).

The disciple of Christ who fully understands that all power has been entrusted to Christ, to be received from Him hour by hour, is the disciple who will feel the need and experience the power of these precious words: *"Lo, I* [the Almighty One] *am with you alway*[s]" (Matthew 28:20).

July 3

The Omnipresence of Christ

Certainly I will be with thee.
—Exodus 3:12

When a man imagines a god, he often thinks first of power, however limited. The first thought of the true God, in contrast, is omnipotence: *"I am God Almighty"* (Genesis 35:11). The second thought is omnipresence—God's promise of His unseen presence with them always. To His *"I am with thee"* (Genesis 26:24), faith responds, *"Thou art with me"* (Psalm 23:4). When Christ said to His disciples, *"All power is given unto me in heaven and in earth"* (Matthew 28:18), the promise immediately followed: *"I am with you alway*[s]*"* (v. 20). The Omnipotent One is surely the Omnipresent One.

The psalmist spoke of God's omnipresence as something beyond his comprehension: *"Such knowledge is too wonderful for me; it is high, I cannot attain unto it"* (Psalm 139:6).

The revelation of God's omnipresence in the Man, Christ Jesus, makes the mystery still deeper. It also makes the grace that enables us to claim this presence as our strength and our joy something inexpressibly blessed. Yet how many servants of Christ find it difficult to understand all that is implied in it and how it can become the experience of their daily lives!

Here, as elsewhere in the spiritual life, everything depends on faith, on accepting Christ's words as divine reality, and on trusting the Holy Spirit to make it true to us from moment to moment.

When Christ said *"alway*[s]*"* (Matthew 28:20), He meant to assure us that there is not a day of our lives in which that blessed presence is not with us. It is ours every day. There does not need to be a moment in which that presence cannot be our experience. This does not depend on what we can do, but on what He undertakes to do. The omnipotent Christ is the omnipresent Christ; the ever present is the everlasting. As surely as He is the Unchangeable One, His presence, as the power of an endless life, will be with each of His servants who trusts Him for it.

"Rest in the LORD, and wait patiently for him" (Psalm 37:7). *"Lo, I am with you alway*[s]*"* (Matthew 28:20). Let your faith in Christ, the Omnipresent One, be in the quiet confidence that He will every day and every moment keep you as the apple of His eye (see Psalm 17:8), in perfect peace and in the sure experience of all the light and strength you need in His service.

Christ, the Savior of the World

This is indeed the Christ, the Saviour of the world.
—John 4:42

Omnipotence and omnipresence are considered natural attributes of God. They have their true worth only when linked to and inspired by His moral attributes of holiness and love. When Jesus spoke of the omnipotence and omnipresence that had been given to Him—*"All power…in heaven and on earth"* (Matthew 28:18); *"Lo, I am with you alway*[s]*"* (v. 20)—His words pointed to what lies at the root of all: His divine glory as the Savior and Redeemer of men. Because *"he humbled himself, and became obedient unto death, even the death of the cross…God…highly exalted him"* (Philippians 2:8–9). While He was on earth, His share in the attributes of God was owing to the work He had done in His perfect obedience to the will of God and the finished redemption He had worked out for the salvation of men.

It is this that gives meaning and worth to what He said of Himself as the Omnipotent and Omnipresent One. Between His mention of these two attributes, He gave His command that His disciples should go out into the world and preach the gospel: *"Go ye therefore, and teach all nations, baptizing them in the name of the Father, and of the Son, and of the Holy Ghost: teaching them to observe all things whatsoever I have commanded you"* (Matthew 28:19–20). As the Redeemer who saves and keeps us from sin, as the Lord who requires obedience to all that He has commanded, He promises His divine presence to be with His servants.

Only when His servants show that they obey Him in all His commands can they expect the fullness of His power and presence to be with them. Only when they are living witnesses to the reality of His power to save and to keep from sin can they expect the full experience of His abiding presence and will they have power to demonstrate to others the life of obedience that He asks.

The abiding presence of the Savior is promised to all who have accepted Him in the fullness of His redeeming power from sin and who preach by their lives as well as by their words what a wonderful Savior He is.

July 5

Christ Crucified

But God forbid that I should glory, save in the cross of our Lord Jesus Christ, by whom the world is crucified unto me, and I unto the world. —Galatians 6:14

Christ's highest glory is His cross. It was in this that He glorified the Father, and the Father glorified Him. In the fifth chapter of Revelation, Christ, as the slain Lamb, receives the worship of the ransomed, the angels, and all creation in the midst of the throne. And it is because He is the Crucified One that His servants have learned to say, *"But God forbid that I should glory, save in the cross of our Lord Jesus Christ, by whom the world is crucified unto me, and I unto the world."* Is it not reasonable that Christ's highest glory should be our only glory, too?

When the Lord Jesus said to His disciples, *"Lo, I am with you alway*[s]*"* (Matthew 28:20), He gave the promise as the Crucified One, who had shown them His pierced hands and feet. And each one who seeks to claim the promise must realize that it is the crucified Jesus who promises, who offers, to be with him every day.

We do not glory in the cross by which we are crucified to the world. Is this not one of the reasons why we find it so difficult to expect and enjoy the abiding presence of Christ? We have been *"crucified with Christ"* (Galatians 2:20); our *"old man is crucified with him"* (Romans 6:6); *"they that are Christ's have crucified the flesh with the affections and lusts"* (Galatians 5:24); and yet how little we have learned that the world has been crucified to us, and that we are free from its power. How little we have learned, as those who are crucified with Christ, to deny ourselves, and to have the mind that was in Christ when He took *"the form of a servant, and…humbled himself and became obedient unto…the death of the cross"* (Philippians 2:7–8).

Oh, let us learn the lesson: it is the crucified Christ who comes to walk with us every day and in whose power we, too, are to live the life that can say, *"I am crucified with Christ…Christ* [crucified] *liveth in me"* (Galatians 2:20).

July 6

Christ Glorified

The Lamb which is in the midst of the throne shall feed them. —Revelation 7:17

These are they which follow the Lamb whithersoever he goeth. —Revelation 14:4

"*Lo, I am with you alway*[s]" (Matthew 28:20). Who spoke these words? We must take time to know Him well if we are to understand what we may expect from Him as He offers to be with us all day long. Who is He? None other than the Lamb standing *"in the midst of the throne…as it had been slain"* (Revelation 5:6). He is the Lamb in His deepest humiliation, enthroned in the glory of God. This is He who speaks and invites us to the closest fellowship and likeness to Himself.

It takes time, deep reverence, and adoring worship to fully understand what it means that He who dwells in the glory of the Father, before whom all heaven bows in prostrate adoration, is none other than He who offers to be your companion, to lead you like a shepherd who cares for each individual sheep, and so makes you one of those *"which follow the Lamb whithersoever he goeth."*

Read and reread the fifth chapter of Revelation, until your heart is filled with the thought of how all heaven falls prostrate, how the elders *"cast their crowns before the throne"* (Revelation 4:10), and how the Lamb reigns amid the praises and the love of His ransomed ones and all creation. If this is He who comes to you in your daily life and offers to walk with you, to be your strength, your joy, and your almighty Keeper, surely you cannot expect Him to abide with you unless your heart bows in a still deeper reverence and in a surrender to a life of praise and service that may be worthy of the love that has redeemed you.

O Christian, the Lamb in the midst of the throne is indeed the embodiment of the omnipotent glory of the everlasting God and of His love. To have this Lamb of God as your almighty Shepherd and your faithful Keeper does indeed make it possible that the thoughts and cares of earth will not separate you from His love for a single moment. (See Romans 8:38–39.)

The Great Question

Believe ye that I am able to do this? They said unto him, Yea, Lord.
—Matthew 9:28

If thou canst believe, all things are possible to him that believeth. And straightway the father of the child cried out, and said with tears, Lord, I believe; help thou mine unbelief.
—Mark 9:23–24

Jesus said unto her,...He that believeth in me, though he were dead, yet shall he live....Believest thou this? She saith unto him, Yea, Lord: I believe.
—John 11:25–27

To what we have seen and heard of Christ Jesus, our hearts are ready to say with Martha, *"Yea, Lord: I believe that thou art the Christ, the Son of God"* (John 11:27). But when it comes to believing in Christ's promises of the power of the resurrection life and of His abiding presence with us, we do not find it so easy to say, "I believe that this omnipotent, omnipresent, unchangeable Christ, our Redeemer God, will actually walk with me all day long and will give me the unceasing awareness of His holy presence." It almost looks too good to be true. And yet it is just this faith that Christ asks for and is waiting to work within us.

It is well that we understand clearly the conditions on which Christ offers to reveal to us in our daily lives the secret of His abiding presence. God cannot force His blessings on us against our will. He seeks in every possible way to stir our desire and to help us to realize that He is able and most willing to make His promises true. The resurrection of Christ from the dead is His great plea, His all-prevailing argument. If He could raise that dead Christ, who had died under the burden of all our sin and curse, surely now that Christ has conquered death and is to us the Resurrection and the Life, He can fulfill in our hearts His promise that Christ can be so with us and in us that He will be our life all day long.

And now, in view of what we have said and seen about Christ as our Lord, as our Redeeming God, the great question is whether we are willing to take His word in its fullness of meaning and to rest in the promise: *"Lo, I am with you alway*[s]*"* (Matthew 28:20). Christ's question comes to us: *"Believe ye that I am able to do this?"* Let us not rest until we have bowed before Him and said, *"Yea, Lord: I believe."*

July 8

Christ Manifesting Himself

He that hath my commandments, and keepeth them, he it is that loveth me: and he that loveth me shall be loved of my Father, and I will love him, and will manifest myself to him.
—John 14:21

Christ had promised the disciples that the Holy Spirit would come to reveal His presence and would always be with them. When the Spirit came, Christ through the Spirit would manifest Himself to them. They would know Him in a new, divine, spiritual way; in the power of the Spirit they would know Him, and He would be far more intimately and unceasingly with them than ever He had been on earth.

The condition of this revelation of Himself is comprised in the word love: *"He that hath my commandments, and keepeth them, he it is that loveth me: and he that loveth me shall be loved of my Father, and I will love him."* This is to be the meeting of divine and human love. The love with which Christ had loved them had taken possession of their hearts and would show itself in the love for a full and absolute obedience. The Father would see this, and His love would rest upon the soul; Christ would love him with the special love drawn out by the loving heart and would manifest Himself. The love of heaven poured out in the heart (see Romans 5:5) would be met by the new and blessed revelation of Christ Himself.

But this is not all. When the question was asked, "What is it?" the answer came in the words, *"If a man love me, he will keep my words: and my Father will love him, and we will come unto him, and make our abode with him"* (John 14:23). In the heart thus prepared by the Holy Spirit, showing itself in loving obedience in a fully surrendered heart, the Father and the Son will make their residence.

And now, Christ promised them nothing less: *"Lo, I am with you alway*[s]*"* (Matthew 28:20). That word *"with"* implies "in"—Christ with the Father, dwelling in the heart by faith. Oh, that everyone who wishes to enter into the secret of the abiding presence would study, believe, and claim in childlike simplicity the blessed promise: *"I will…manifest myself to him."*

July 9

Mary: The Morning Watch

Jesus saith unto her, Mary. She turned herself, and saith unto him, Rabboni; which is to say, Master.
—John 20:16

Here we have the first manifestation of the risen Savior, to Mary Magdalene, the woman who *"loved much"* (Luke 7:47). Think of what the morning watch meant to Mary. Is it not evidence of the intense longing of a love that would not rest until it had found the Lord it sought? It meant a separation from all else, even from the chief of the apostles, in her longing to find Christ. It meant the struggle of fear against a faith that refused to let go its hold of a wonderful promise. It meant Christ's coming and fulfilling the promise: *"If a man love me, he will keep my words...and I will love him, and will manifest myself to him"* (John 14:23, 21). It meant that her love was met by the love of Jesus, and she found Him, the living Lord, in all the power of His resurrection life. It meant that she now understood what He had said about ascending to the Father, to the life of divine and omnipotent glory. It meant, too, that she received her commission from her Lord to go and tell His disciples of what she had heard from Him.

That first morning watch, waiting for the risen Lord to reveal Himself, became a prophecy and a pledge of what the morning watch has been to thousands of souls since! In fear and doubt, and yet with a burning love and strong hope, they waited until He breathed on them the power of His resurrection life and manifested Himself as the Lord of Glory. They had scarcely known Him because of their feeble human understanding; but when He breathed on them, they learned—not in words or thought, but in the reality of a divine experience—that He to whom had been given *"all power...in heaven and in earth"* (Matthew 28:18) had now taken them into the keeping of His abiding presence.

And what are we now to learn? That there is nothing that can prove a greater attraction to our Lord than the love that sacrifices everything to Him and rests satisfied with nothing less than Himself. It is to such a love that Christ manifests Himself. He *"loved us, and* [has] *given himself for us"* (Ephesians 5:2). Christ's love needs our love in which to reveal itself. It is to our love that He speaks the words, *"Lo, I am with you alway*[s]*"* (Matthew 28:20). It is love that accepts, rejoices in, and lives in that word.

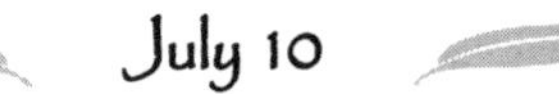

Emmaus: The Evening Prayer

They constrained him, saying, Abide with us….and he went in to tarry with them….as he sat at meat with them…their eyes were opened, and they knew him.
—Luke 24:29–31

Mary taught us what the morning watch can be for the revelation of Jesus to the soul. Emmaus reminds us of the place the evening prayer may have in preparing for the full manifestation of Christ in the soul.

To the two disciples on the way to Emmaus, the day had begun in thick darkness. When they finally heard about the angel who had said that Jesus was alive, they did not know what to think. When *"Jesus himself drew near"* (v. 15), their eyes were blinded, and they did not recognize Him. (See verse 16.) How often Jesus comes near to us with the purpose of manifesting Himself but is hindered because we are slow to believe what the Word has spoken! But as the Lord talked with the two disciples, their hearts began to burn within them, yet they never once thought it might be Him.

It is often the same with us today. The Word becomes precious to us; our hearts are stirred with the new vision of what Christ's presence may be; yet our eyes are blinded, and we do not see Him.

When the Lord acted as though He would have gone farther, their request, *"Abide with us,"* constrained Him. On His last night, Christ had given a new meaning to the word *abide.* They did not yet understand this, but by using the word they received far more than they expected—a foretaste of the life of abiding, which the resurrection had now made possible. Let us learn the lesson of how necessary it is that, toward the close of each day, there should be a pause, perhaps in fellowship with others, when the whole heart takes up anew the promise of the abiding presence of Christ and prays with the urgency that constrains Him: *"Abide with us."*

And what is the chief lesson of the story? There may be much ignorance and unbelief, but if there is a burning desire for Him above everything else—a desire that is always fostered as the Word is heard or spoken—we may be assured that He will make Himself known to us. To such intense devotion and constraining prayer, the Lord's message will be given in power: *"Lo, I am with you alway*[s]*"* (Matthew 28:20). Our eyes will be opened, and we will know Him.

The Disciples: Their Divine Mission

Then the same day at evening...when the doors were shut where the disciples were assembled for fear of the Jews, came Jesus and stood in the midst, and saith unto them, Peace be unto you.
—John 20:19

The disciples had received the message of Mary. Peter had told them that he had seen the Lord. Late in the evening, the men from Emmaus told how He had been made known to them. The disciples' hearts were prepared for what now came, when Jesus stood in the midst of them and said, *"Peace be unto you,"* and showed them His hands and His feet. This was to be not only a sign of recognition, but also the deep eternal mystery of what would be seen in heaven when He was standing *"in the midst of the throne...*[as] *a Lamb as it had been slain"* (Revelation 5:6).

"Then were the disciples glad, when they saw the Lord" (John 20:20). And He spoke again: "*Peace be unto you: as my Father hath sent me, even so send I you"* (v. 21). With Mary He revealed Himself to the fervent love that could not rest without Him. With the men at Emmaus, it was their constraining request that received the revelation. Here He met the willing servants whom He had trained for His service, and He handed over to them the work He had done on earth. The divine mission was now theirs.

For this divine work, they needed nothing less than divine power. He breathed upon them the resurrection life He had won by His death. He fulfilled the promise He gave: *"Because I live, ye shall live also"* (John 14:19). The *"exceeding greatness of...power"* (Ephesians 1:19) by which God raised Christ from the dead was the same spirit of holiness by which Christ was raised from the dead and would work in them. And all that was bound or loosed in that power would be bound or loosed in heaven. (See Matthew 16:19.)

The story comes to every messenger of the gospel with wonderful power. Christ says the same words to us: *"As my Father hath sent me, even so send I you....Receive ye the Holy Ghost"* (John 20:21–22). We can have the same manifestation of Jesus as the Living One, with His pierced hands and feet. If our hearts are set on the presence of the living Lord, we may be assured that it will be given to us. Jesus never sends His servants out without the promise of His abiding presence and His almighty power.

July 12

Thomas: The Blessedness of Believing

Jesus saith unto him, Thomas, because thou hast seen me, thou hast believed: blessed are they that have not seen, and yet have believed. —John 20:29

We all consider the blessedness of Thomas as something very wonderful—Christ manifesting Himself and allowing Thomas to touch His hands and His side. It is no wonder that this blessedness could find no words except those of holy adoration: *"My Lord and my God"* (v. 28). Has there ever been a higher expression of the overwhelming nearness and glory of God?

And yet Christ said, *"Because thou hast seen me, thou hast believed: blessed are they that have not seen, and yet have believed."* True and living faith gives a sense of Christ's divine nearness far deeper and more intimate than even the joy that filled the heart of Thomas. Here, even now, after the lapse of all these centuries, we may experience the presence and power of Christ in a far deeper reality than Thomas did. *"They that have not seen, and yet have believed"*—those who believe simply, truly, and fully in what Christ is and can be to them every moment—to these He has promised that He will manifest Himself and that the Father and He will come and dwell in them. (See John 14:21, 23.)

Let us turn to take hold of Christ's word: *"Blessed are they that have not seen, and yet have believed."* This is indeed the heavenly blessing, filling the whole heart and life—the faith that receives the love and the presence of the living Lord.

You ask how you may obtain this childlike faith. The answer is very simple. Where Jesus Christ is the one object of our desire and our confidence, He will manifest Himself in divine power. Thomas had established his intense devotion to Christ when he said, *"Let us also go, that we may die with him"* (John 11:16). To such a love, even when it is struggling with unbelief, Jesus Christ will manifest Himself. He will make His holy promise an actual reality in our conscious experience: *"Lo, I am with you alway*[s]*"* (Matthew 28:20). Let us see to it that our faith in His blessed Word, in His divine power, and in His holy abiding presence, is the one thing that masters our whole beings. Then Christ will indeed manifest Himself, abide with us, and dwell in our hearts as His home.

July 13

Peter: The Greatness of Love

Peter was grieved because he said unto him the third time, Lovest thou me? And he said unto him, Lord, thou knowest all things; thou knowest that I love thee. Jesus saith unto him, Feed my sheep.
—John 21:17

It was to Mary who *"loved much"* (Luke 7:47) that Christ first revealed Himself. He also revealed Himself in Peter's first vision (see John 21:1–14), to the two disciples on the road to Emmaus (see Luke 24:13–31), in His appearance to the ten (see John 20:19–23), and in His revelation to Thomas. (See verses 24–28.) It was always to devotion of a prepared heart that Christ manifested Himself. And here in His manifestation to Peter, love is again the keynote.

We can easily understand why Christ asked the question three times, *"Lovest thou me?"* It was to remind Peter of the terrible self-confidence in which he had said, *"Though I should die with thee, yet will I not deny thee"* (Matthew 26:35); of the need for deep heart searching before he could be sure that his love was true; of the need for deep penitence in the consciousness of how little he could trust himself; and then of love being the one thing needed for the full restoration to his place in the heart of Jesus, the first condition for feeding His sheep and caring for His lambs.

"God is love" (1 John 4:8). Christ is the Son of His love. *"Having loved his own which were in the world, he loved them unto the end"* (John 13:1) and said, *"As the Father hath loved me, so have I loved you"* (John 15:9). He asked them to prove their love to Him by keeping His commandments and by loving each other with the love with which He loved them. (See verses 10, 12.)

To everyone who desires to have Jesus manifest Himself, the prerequisite is love. Peter taught us that such love is not in our power to offer. But such love came to him through the power of Christ's death to sin—the power of His resurrection life. In his first epistle, Peter said, *"Whom having not seen, ye love; in whom, though now ye see him not, yet believing, ye rejoice with joy unspeakable and full of glory"* (1 Peter 1:8). If Peter could be so changed, Christ will certainly work change in us, too, and will manifest Himself in all the fullness of His precious word: *"Lo, I am with you alway*[s]*"* (Matthew 28:20).

July 14

John: Life from the Dead

And when I saw him, I fell at his feet as dead. And he laid his right hand upon me, saying unto me, Fear not; I am the first and the last: I am he that liveth, and was dead; and, behold, I am alive for evermore.
—Revelation 1:17–18

Here we have Christ manifesting Himself, sixty or more years after the resurrection, to the beloved disciple. John *"fell at his feet as dead."* In answer to Moses' prayer to *"show me thy glory"* (Exodus 33:18), God had said to him, *"Thou canst not see my face: for there shall no man see me, and live"* (v. 20). Man's sinful nature cannot receive the vision of the divine glory, and live; it needs the death of the natural life for the life of God in glory to enter in.

When Christ laid His right hand upon John, He said, *"Fear not.... I am he that liveth, and was dead; and, behold, I am alive for evermore."* He reminded John that He Himself had passed through death before He could rise to the life and glory of God. For the Master Himself and for every disciple, there is only one way to the glory of God. That way consists of death to all the nature that has been in contact with sin and cannot enter heaven.

This lesson is a deep and necessary one for all who desire Jesus to manifest Himself to them. The knowledge of Jesus, fellowship with Him, and the experience of His power are not possible without the sacrifice of all that is worldly in us. The disciples experienced this. When Christ spoke about forsaking one's father and mother, about taking up the cross, about losing one's life for His sake—in everything He said, down to the days before His death, when He said, *"Except a corn of wheat fall into the ground and die, it abideth alone: but if it die, it bringeth forth much fruit. He that loveth his life shall lose it"* (John 12:24–25)—He made this the one great charge: deny self, bear the cross, and follow Me.

Let us accept the lesson—through death to life. In the power of Christ Jesus, with whom we have been crucified and whose death now works in us, if we will yield ourselves to it, death to sin and to the world is to be the deepest law of our spiritual lives. The disciples had followed Christ to the cross. That was what prepared them to receive the Master's words: *"Lo, I am with you alway*[s]*"* (Matthew 28:20).

July

July 15

Paul: Christ Revealed in Him

It pleased God…to reveal his Son in me.
—Galatians 1:15–16

In all our study and worship of Christ, we find our thoughts gathering round these five points: the incarnate Christ, the crucified Christ, the enthroned Christ, the indwelling Christ, and Christ coming in glory. If the first is the seed, the second is the seed cast into the ground, and the third is the seed growing up to heaven. Then follows the fruit through the Holy Spirit, which is Christ dwelling in the heart, and then the gathering of the fruit when Christ appears.

Paul told us that it pleased God to reveal His Son in him. And he gave his testimony of the result of that revelation: *"Christ liveth in me"* (Galatians 2:20). Of that life, he said that its chief mark was that he was *"crucified with Christ"* (v. 20). It was this that enabled him to say, *"nevertheless I live; yet not I"* (v. 20); in Christ he had found the death of self. Just as the cross is the chief characteristic of Christ Himself—*"in the midst of the throne…stood a Lamb as it had been slain"* (Revelation 5:6)—so the life of Christ in Paul made him inseparably one with his crucified Lord. So completely was this the case that he could say, *"But God forbid that I should glory, save in the cross of our Lord Jesus Christ, by whom the world is crucified unto me, and I unto the world"* (Galatians 6:14).

If you had asked Paul, "If Christ so actually lives in you that you no longer live, what responsibility do you have in living your life?" the answer was ready and clear: *"I live by the faith of the Son of God, who loved me, and gave himself for me"* (Galatians 2:20). His life was every moment a life of faith in Him who had loved him and given Himself completely. Christ had undertaken at all times to be the life of His willing disciple.

This was the sum and substance of all Paul's teaching. He asked for intercession so that he might speak *"the mystery of Christ"* (Colossians 4:3), *"the riches of the glory of this mystery among the Gentiles; which is Christ in you, the hope of glory"* (Colossians 1:27). The indwelling Christ was the secret of his life of faith, the one power, the one aim of all his life and work, *"the hope of glory."* Let us believe in the abiding presence of Christ as the sure gift to each one who trusts Him fully.

July 16

Why Could We Not?

Then came the disciples to Jesus apart, and said, Why could not we cast him out? And Jesus said unto them, Because of your unbelief....Howbeit this kind goeth not out but by prayer and fasting.
—Matthew 17:19–21

The disciples had often cast out devils, but here they had been powerless. They asked the Lord what the reason might be. His answer was very simple: *"Because of your unbelief."*

We have here the reply to the question that is so often asked, "Why can we not live the life of unbroken fellowship with Christ that the Scriptures promise?" Simply because of our unbelief. We do not realize that faith must accept and expect that God will, by His almighty power, fulfill every promise He has made. We do not live in the utter helplessness and dependence on God alone that is the very essence of faith. We are not *"strong in faith...fully persuaded that, what he* [God] *had promised, he was able also to perform"* (Romans 4:20–21). We do not give ourselves with our whole hearts to believe that God, by His almighty power, will work wonders in our hearts.

But what can be the reason that this faith is so often lacking? *"Howbeit this kind goeth not out but by prayer and fasting."* A strong faith in God needs a life in close touch with Him by persistent prayer. We cannot call up faith at our bidding; it requires close fellowship with God. It requires not only prayer, but also fasting, in the larger and deeper meaning of that word. It requires the denial of self, the sacrifice of pleasing of *"the lust of the flesh, and the lust of the eyes, and the pride of life"* (1 John 2:16), which are the essence of a worldly spirit. To gain the prizes of the heavenly life here on earth, one needs to sacrifice all that earth can offer. Just as one needs God to satisfy the human heart and work His mighty miracles in it, the whole man must be utterly given up to God in order to have the power of the faith that can cast out every evil spirit. *"Prayer and fasting"* are essential.

July 17

The Power of Obedience

And he that sent me is with me: the Father hath not left me alone; for I do always those things that please him.
—John 8:29

In these words, Christ not only tells what His life with the Father was, but He also reveals the law of all communion with God—simple obedience.

In John 14 Christ said, *"If ye love me, keep my commandments. And I will pray the Father, and he shall give you another Comforter* [the Holy Spirit]*"* (vv. 15–16). He stressed this point twice more: *"And he that loveth me shall be loved of my Father, and I will love him, and will manifest myself to him"* (v. 21); *"And we will come unto him, and make our abode with him"* (v. 23). Christ also mentioned obedience three times in chapter 15: *"If...my words abide in you, ye shall ask what ye will, and it shall be done unto you"* (v. 7); *"If ye keep my commandments, ye shall abide in my love; even as I have kept my Father's commandments, and abide in his love"* (v. 10); *"Ye are my friends, if ye do whatsoever I command you"* (v. 14).

Obedience is the proof and the exercise of the love of God that has been *"shed abroad in our hearts by the Holy Ghost"* (Romans 5:5). It comes from love and leads to love. It assures us that what we ask will be given to us. It assures us that we are abiding in the love of Christ. It seals our claim to be called the friends of Christ. And so it is not only a proof of love, but also of faith, as assuring us that *"whatsoever we ask, we receive of him, because we keep his commandments, and do those things that are pleasing in his sight"* (1 John 3:22).

For the abiding enjoyment of the holy presence, simple, full obedience is necessary. The new covenant has made full provision for this: *"I will put my law in their inward parts, and write it in their hearts"* (Jeremiah 31:33); *"I will put my fear in their hearts, that they shall not depart from me"* (Jeremiah 32:40); *"I will...cause you to walk in my statutes, and ye shall keep...them"* (Ezekiel 36:27).

Obedience enables us to abide in His love and gives us the full experience of His unbroken presence. Remember, it is to the obedient disciple that Christ says, *"Lo, I am with you alway*[s]*"* (Matthew 28:20), and to whom all the fullness of its meaning will be revealed.

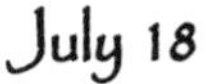

July 18

The Power of Intercession

We will give ourselves continually to prayer.
—Acts 6:4

Prayer was made without ceasing of the church unto God for him.
—Acts 12:5

Dr. John Mott, an American Methodist leader, urged us to believe in the unlimited power of united intercession. While travelling in Asia, he was charged to press upon the missionary societies the need for united intercession. He wrote:

> We can in no way better serve the deepest interest of the churches than by multiplying the number of real intercessors and by focusing the prayers of Christendom upon those great situations that demand the almighty working of the Spirit of God. Far more important and vital than any service we can render to missions is that of helping to release the superhuman energy of prayer, and, through uniting in this holy ministry true intercessors of all lands, to help the ushering in of a new era abounding in signs and wonders characteristic of the working of the living Christ. The Christian world has a right to expect mission leaders to set forth not only the facts and methods of the work, but also a larger discovery of superhuman resources and a greater irradiation of spiritual power.

And where is there a greater need of focusing the united intercession of Christendom than on the great army of missionaries, of whom I wrote in the introduction to this section? They confess the need for the presence and the power of God's Spirit in their lives and work. They long for the experience of the abiding presence and power of Christ every day. They need it; they have a right to it. Will you, my dear reader, be a part of the great army that pleads with God for that infilling of power that is so absolutely necessary for effective work? Will you, like the early apostles, *"continue in prayer"* (Colossians 4:2) until God sends an abundant answer? As we *"give ourselves continually to prayer"* (Acts 6:4), the power of the promise, *"Lo, I am with you alway*[s]*"* (Matthew 28:20), will be proven in our lives.

July 19

The Power of Time

My times are in thy hand.
—Psalm 31:15

The plural in this Scripture verse implies the singular: "All my time is in Your hands, O God. It belongs to You; You alone have the right to command it. I yield it wholly and gladly to Your disposal." What mighty power time can exert if wholly given up to God!

Time affects all things. What is all the history of the world if not proof of how, slowly but surely, time has made man what he is today? All around us we see the evidence. In the success of every pursuit, in all our efforts and accomplishments, it is under the law of time and its inconceivable power that we spend our lives.

This is especially true in religion and in our fellowship with God. Time is master here, too. Our communion with God, our likeness to His image, and our power in His service all depend on one condition: that we have sufficient time with God for His holiness to shine on us with its light and to make us partakers of His Spirit and His life. The very essence of religion lies in how much time we spend with God. Yet so many of God's servants, while giving their lives to His service, frankly confess that the feebleness of their spiritual lives and the inadequate results of their mission work as a whole are due to the failure to make the time—and to use it wisely—for daily communion with God.

What can be the cause of this sad confession? Nothing but a lack of faith in the God-given assurance that time spent alone with Him will indeed bring into the lives of His servants the power to enable them to use all their time in His fellowship. Then His abiding presence will be with them all day long.

O my fellow Christian, you complain that you are overworked, or that your zeal hinders your spiritual effectiveness. Do you not see that if you would only submit your time to the inspection of Christ and His Holy Spirit, you would find that a new life would be yours if you fully believed and put into practice this Scripture: *"My times are in thy hand"*?

The Power of Faith

All things are possible to him that believeth.
—Mark 9:23

Scripture teaches us that there is not one truth on which Christ insisted more frequently, both with His disciples and with those who came seeking His help, than the absolute necessity of faith and its unlimited possibilities. And experience has taught us that there is nothing in which we come so short as the simple and absolute trust in God to literally fulfill in us all that He has promised. A life in the abiding presence must be a life of unceasing faith.

Think for a moment of the marks of a true faith. First of all, faith depends on God to do all that He has promised. A person with true faith does not rest content with taking some of the promises; he seeks nothing less than to claim every promise that God has made in its largest and fullest meaning. Under a sense of the nothingness and utter powerlessness of his faith, he trusts the power of an almighty God to work wonders in the heart in which He dwells.

The person of faith does this with his whole heart and all his strength. His faith yields to the promise that God will take full possession, and throughout the day and night will inspire his hope and expectation. By faith, he recognizes the inseparable link that unites God's promises and His commands, and he yields to do the one as fully as he trusts the other.

In the pursuit of the power that such a life of faith can give, there is often a faith that seeks and strives but cannot grasp. This is followed by a faith that begins to see that waiting on God is needed, and quietly rests in the hope of what God will do. This should lead to an act of decision, in which the soul takes God at His word and claims the fulfillment of the promise and then looks to Him, even in utter darkness, to perform what He has spoken.

The life of faith to which the abiding presence will be granted must have complete mastery of the whole being. It is such a wonderful privilege—Christ's presence actually keeping us all day long in its blessedness—that it needs a parting with much that was formerly thought lawful, if He is indeed to be the Lord of all, the blessed Friend who is our companion, the joy and light of our lives. By such faith, we will be able to claim and experience the words of the Master: *"Lo, I am with you alway*[s]*"* (Matthew 28:20).

July 21

John's Missionary Message

That which we have seen and heard declare we unto you, that ye also may have fellowship with us: and truly our fellowship is with the Father, and with his Son Jesus Christ.
—1 John 1:3

What a revelation of the calling placed on every preacher of the gospel! His message is nothing less than to proclaim that Christ has opened the way for us to have daily, living, loving fellowship with the holy God. He is to preach this as a witness to the life he himself lives in all its blessed experience. In the power of that testimony, he is to prove its reality and show how a sinful man upon earth can indeed live in fellowship with the Father and the Son.

The message suggests to us that the very first duty of the missionary, every day of his life, is to maintain such close communion with God that he can preach the truth in the fullness of joy, with the knowledge that his life and conversation are the proof that his preaching is true, so that his words appeal with power to the heart: *"And these things write we unto you, that your joy may be full"* (v. 4).

The October 1914 issue of the *International Review of Missions* contained an article on the influence of the Keswick Convention on mission work. Keswick is well known as the English town in which a great revival began. The article provides the substance of Keswick teaching in these words: "A life of communion with God through Christ is a reality to be entered upon, and constantly maintained, by the unconditional and habitual surrender of the whole personality to Christ's control and government, in the assurance that the living Christ will take possession of the life thus yielded to Him." It is such teaching, revealing the infinite claim and power of Christ's love as maintained by the power of the Holy Spirit, that will compel men to make the measure of Christ's surrender for them the only measure of their surrender to Him and His service.

It is this intimate fellowship with Christ as the secret of daily service and testimony that has power to make Christ known as the Deliverer from sin and the Inspiration of a life of wholehearted devotion to His service. It is this intimate and abiding fellowship with Christ that the promise, *"Lo, I am with you alway*[s]*"* (Matthew 28:20), secures for us.

July 22

Paul's Missionary Message

Continue in prayer...Withal praying also for us, that God would open unto us a door of utterance, to speak the mystery of Christ...that I may make it manifest, as I ought to speak.
—Colossians 4:2–4

The mystery which...now is made manifest to his saints: to whom God would make known what is the riches of the glory of this mystery among the Gentiles; which is Christ in you, the hope of glory.
—Colossians 1:26–27

To Paul, the very substance of his gospel was the indwelling Christ. He spoke of the *"riches of the glory of this mystery...Christ in you, the hope of glory."* Though he had been a preacher of this gospel for many years, he still asked for prayer, so that he might correctly make known the mystery of it.

I often hear complaints that, after a time, there appears to be no further growth in many churches, and very little of the joy and power for bearing witness to Christ Jesus. The question arises whether the home church is living in the experience of the indwelling Christ, so that the missionaries whom she sends out know the secret and make it the substance of their message.

Years ago, I knew a minister who went to the mission field. Before he left, there was a little gathering at which he asked what his message should be. The thought was expressed that it was desirable to present a message of a full salvation, so that people would be roused to believe in and accept an indwelling Christ. On his return, he told with what deep interest the presentation of this truth had been received, many saying that they had never before understood this.

We speak of Paul's methods, but is there not a greater need for Paul's message, culminating in the words, *"Christ in you, the hope of glory"*? Are not all intercessors and missionaries called to make it a matter of first importance to lead Christians into the enjoyment of their rightful heritage? *"If a man love me, he will keep my words: and my Father will love him, and we will come unto him, and make our abode with him"* (John 14:23). And it may be the home church that will also share in the restoration of this truth to its rightful place: *"Christ in you, the hope of glory."*

July 23

The Missionary's Life

Ye are witnesses, and God also, how holily and justly and unblameably we behaved ourselves among you that believe.
—1 Thessalonians 2:10

Paul more than once appealed to what his converts had seen of his own life. He said, *"Our rejoicing is this, the testimony of our conscience, that in simplicity and godly sincerity, not with fleshly wisdom, but by the grace of God, we have had our conversation in the world, and more abundantly to you-ward"* (2 Corinthians 1:12). Christ had taught His disciples as much by His life as by His teaching. Paul had sought to be a living witness to the truth of all that he had preached about Christ—that He is able to save and to keep from sin, that He renews the whole nature by the power of His Holy Spirit, and that He Himself becomes the life of those who believe in Him.

One writer, expressing his ideas about world missions, has said, "It has come to pass that our representatives on the field, just because they are what we have made them, have far too often hidden the Christ whom they are giving their lives to reveal. Only to the degree that the missionary manifests the character of Christ in and through his own life can he gain an audience for the gospel. Only as far as he can live Christ before their eyes can he help them to understand his message."

Paul referred to his life as holy, righteous, and blameless; this gave him courage to put a high standard before his converts. In the same epistle, he called them to trust God, to *"stablish* [their] *hearts unblameable in holiness before God"* (1 Thessalonians 3:13). And later in the epistle he wrote, *"The very God of peace sanctify you wholly...who also will do it"* (1 Thessalonians 5:23–24). In Philippians 4:9 he wrote, *"Those things, which ye have both learned, and received, and heard, and seen in me, do: and the God of peace shall be with you."* And in 1 Timothy 1:14–16 we find, *"The grace of our Lord was exceeding abundant with faith and love which is in Christ Jesus. This is...a pattern to them which should hereafter believe on him to life everlasting."* Let us believe that when Paul said, *"Nevertheless I live; yet not I, but Christ liveth in me"* (Galatians 2:20), he spoke of an actual, divine, unceasing abiding of Christ in him, working in him from hour to hour all that was well pleasing to the Father. And let us not rest until we can say, "The Christ of Paul is my Christ! All that filled his soul from heaven is mine, too."

July 24

The Holy Spirit

He [the Holy Spirit] shall glorify me, for he shall receive of mine, and shall show it unto you.
—John 16:14

When our Lord said to the disciples, *"Lo, I am with you alway*[s]*"* (Matthew 28:20), they did not at first understand or experience the full meaning of His words. It was at Pentecost, when they were filled with the Holy Spirit, that they began the new life in the joy of the abiding presence.

All our attempts to live this life of continuous, unbroken communion will be in vain unless we, too, yield ourselves wholly to the power and the indwelling of the ever blessed Spirit. Throughout the church of Christ, there is an apparent lack of faith in what the Spirit is as God, in what He can enable us to be, and in how completely He demands full and undisturbed possession of our whole beings. All our faith in the fulfillment of Christ's glorious promises, especially that of the Father and Son making their abode in us (see John 14:23), is subject to one essential and indispensable condition: a life utterly and unceasingly yielded to the rule and leading of the Spirit of Christ.

Christ meant His words to be a simple and eternal reality. He meant the promises to be accepted as absolute truth: *"He it is that loveth me: and he that loveth me shall be loved of my Father, and I will love him, and will manifest myself to him"* (v. 21); *"We will come unto him, and make our abode with him"* (v. 23). But such truth can only be experienced where the Spirit, in His power as God, is known, believed in, and obeyed. What Christ spoke of in John 14 is what Paul testified of when he said, *"Christ liveth in me"* (Galatians 2:20), or, as John expressed it, *"And hereby we know that he abideth in us, by the Spirit which he hath given us"* (1 John 3:24).

We need to understand that the Spirit, as God, claims absolute surrender and is willing to take possession of our whole beings and enable us to fulfill all that Christ asks of us. It is the Spirit who can deliver us from all the power of the flesh, who can conquer the power of the world in us. It is the Spirit through whom Christ Jesus will manifest Himself to us in nothing less than His abiding presence: *"Lo, I am with you alway*[s]*"* (Matthew 28:20).

July 25

Filled with the Spirit

Be filled with the Spirit; speaking to yourselves in psalms and hymns and spiritual songs, singing and making melody in your heart to the Lord; giving thanks always for all things.
—Ephesians 5:18–20

If the expression, *"filled with the Spirit,"* could be applied only to the story of Pentecost, we might think that it was something special, and not meant for ordinary life. But the above Scripture teaches us that it is meant for every Christian and for everyday life.

To realize this more fully, think of what the Holy Spirit was in Christ Jesus and what the conditions were under which He, as man, was filled with the Spirit. He received the Spirit when He was praying and had yielded Himself as a sacrifice to God—when He was baptized in the sinner's baptism. Full of the Holy Spirit, Jesus was led to the forty days' fasting, sacrificing the needs of the body to be free for fellowship with the Father and the victory over Satan. He even refused, when He was extremely hungry, to listen to the temptation of the Evil One to use His power to make bread to supply His hunger. And so He was led by the Spirit all through life until He, by the eternal Spirit, offered Himself without blemish to God.

Likewise, if we are to follow Christ, we must seek to regard the fullness of the Spirit as a daily supply, a daily provision. There may be occasions when that fullness of the Spirit will become especially manifested, but only as we are led by the Spirit every day and all day long can we abide in Christ Jesus, conquer the flesh and the world, and live the life with God in prayer and with our fellowmen in humble, holy, fruitful service.

Above all, it is only as we are filled with the Spirit that the words of Jesus can be fully understood and experienced: *"Lo, I am with you alway*[s]*"* (Matthew 28:20). Let no one think this is impossible. *"The things which are impossible with men are possible with God"* (Luke 18:27). And if we cannot attain it immediately, let us at least make it our definite aim, our unceasing prayer, our childlike expectation. *"Lo, I am with you alway*[s]*"* was meant for daily life, with the all-sufficient aid of the blessed Spirit. Our faith in Christ will be the measure of our fullness of the Spirit. The measure of the power of the Spirit in us will be the measure of our experience of the presence of Christ.

The Christ Life

Christ...is our life.
—Colossians 3:4

Christ's life was more than His teaching, more than His work, more than even His death. It was His life in the sight of God and man that gave value to what He said, did, and suffered. And it is this life, glorified in the resurrection, that He imparts to His people and enables them to live out before men.

"By this shall all men know that ye are my disciples, if ye have love one to another" (John 13:35). It was the life in the new brotherhood of the Holy Spirit that made both Jews and Greeks feel that there was some superhuman power about Christ's disciples; they gave living proof of the truth of what they said, that God's love had come down and taken possession of them.

It has often been said that, unless the missionary lives out the Christ life on an entirely different level from that on which other men live, he misses the deepest secret of power and success in his work. When Christ sent His disciples forth, it was with the command, *"Tarry...until ye be endued with power from on high"* (Luke 24:49); *"But ye shall receive power, after that the Holy Ghost is come upon you: and ye shall be witnesses unto me...unto the uttermost part of the earth"* (Acts 1:8). Many missionaries have felt that it is not learning, zeal, or the willingness for self-sacrifice in Christ's service, but the secret experience of the life *"hid with Christ in God"* (Colossians 3:3), that enables them to meet and overcome every difficulty.

Everything depends on the life with God in Christ being right. It was so with Christ, with the disciples, and with Paul. The simplicity and intensity of our lives in Christ Jesus, and of the life of Christ Jesus in us, sustains us in the daily drudgery of work, makes us conquer self and everything that could hinder the Christ life, and gives victory over the powers of evil and over the hearts from which the evil spirits have to be cast out.

The life is everything. It was so in Christ Jesus. It must be so in His servants, too. It can be so, because Christ Himself will live in us. When He said, *"Lo, I am with you alway*[s]*"* (Matthew 28:20), He meant nothing less than this: "Every day and all day long, I am with you, the secret of your life, your joy, and your strength." Oh, to learn what hidden treasures are contained in the blessed words we love to repeat: "Lo, I am with you all the days!"

The Christlike Life

Let this mind be in you, which was also in Christ Jesus. —Philippians 2:5

What was the mind that was in Christ Jesus? He *"took upon him the form of a servant, and was made in the likeness of men....He humbled himself, and became obedient unto death, even the death of the cross"* (vv. 7–8). Self-emptying and self-sacrifice, obedience to God's will, and love for men, even to the death of the cross—such was the character of Christ for which God so *"highly exalted him"* (v. 9). Such is the character of Christ that we are to imitate. He was made in the likeness of men, so that we might be conformed into the likeness of God.

Self-sacrifice that God's will might be done and man might be saved—such was Christ's life. This was His life, to please God and to bless men.

Let no one say that this is an impossibility. *"The things which are impossible with men are possible with God"* (Luke 18:27). We are called to *"work out"* (Philippians 2:12) this salvation of a Christlike character *"with fear and trembling. For it is God which worketh in you both to will and to do of his good pleasure"* (vv. 12–13). He of whom Christ said, *"the Father that dwelleth in me, he doeth the works"* (John 14:10), is He who works in us *"to will and to do."*

It has been said that the "missionary who is to commend the gospel must first embody it in a character fully conformed to the likeness of Jesus Christ. Only as far as he can live Christ before the eyes of the converts can he help them to understand his message. At times our representatives on the field, just because they are what we have made them, have far too often hidden the Christ whom they are giving their lives to reveal."

As the church aims to make some degree of likeness to Christ's character the standard for Christian teachers, our missionaries will be able to pass this on to their converts and say to them, *"Be ye followers of me, even as I also am of Christ"* (1 Corinthians 11:1).

Let us not rest until our faith lays hold of the promise, *"It is God which worketh in you"* (Philippians 2:13). The confidence will be aroused that, as the character of Christ is the revelation with which every missionary has been entrusted, so the power will be given to fulfill this high and holy calling. Let ministers and missionaries and all intercessors make this their one great plea and aim to have this mind *"which was also in Christ Jesus."*

Christ, the Nearness of God

Draw nigh to God, and he will draw nigh to you.
—James 4:8

It has been said that the holiness of God is the union of God's infinite distance from sinful man with His infinite nearness to man in His redeeming grace. Faith must always seek to realize both the distance and the nearness.

In Christ, God has come near, so very near to man, and now the command comes: if you want to have God come still nearer, you must draw near to Him. The promised nearness of Christ Jesus expressed in the promise, *"Lo, I am with you alway*[s]*"* (Matthew 28:20), can only be experienced as we draw near to Him.

This means, first of all, that we must yield ourselves afresh at the beginning of each day for His holy presence to rest upon us. It means a voluntary, intentional, and wholehearted turning away from the world to wait on God to make Himself known to our souls. It means giving time, and all our hearts and strength, to allow Him to reveal Himself. It is impossible to expect the abiding presence of Christ with us throughout the day unless there is a definite daily exercise of strong desire and child-like trust in His word: *"Draw nigh to God, and he will draw nigh to you."*

Furthermore, this means the simple, childlike offering of ourselves and our lives in everything, in order to do His will alone and to seek above everything to please Him. His promise is sure: *"If a man love me, he will keep my words: and my Father will love him, and we will come unto him, and make our abode with him"* (John 14:23).

Then comes the quiet assurance of faith, even if there is not much feeling or sense of His presence, that God is with us and that He will watch over us and keep us as we go out to do His will. Moreover, He will strengthen us *"in the inner man"* (Ephesians 3:16) with divine strength for the work we have to do for Him.

Child of God, let these words come to you with a new meaning each morning: *"Draw nigh to God, and he will draw nigh to you."* Wait patiently, and He will speak in divine power: *"Lo, I am with you alway*[s]*."*

July 29

Love

Having loved his own which were in the world, [Jesus] loved them unto the end.
—John 13:1

These are the opening words of the confidential talk Christ had with His disciples. (See John 13–17.) They are the revelation and full display of the divine love that was manifested in His death on the cross.

He began with the new commandment: *"That ye love one another; as I have loved you"* (John 13:34). Later, He told His disciples, *"If ye love me, keep my commandments.…He that loveth me shall be loved of my Father, and I will love him, and will manifest myself to him.…And we will come unto him, and make our abode with him"* (John 14:15, 21, 23). The new life, the heavenly life in Christ Jesus, is to be the unfolding of God's love in Christ. Then, farther on, we read, *"As the Father hath loved me, so have I loved you: continue ye in my love. If ye keep my commandments, ye shall abide in my love.…This is my commandment, That ye love one another, as I have loved you. Greater love hath no man than this, that a man lay down his life for his friends"* (John 15:9–10, 12–13). *"That the world may know that thou hast sent me, and hast loved them, as thou hast loved me.…I have declared unto them thy name, and will declare it: that the love wherewith thou hast loved me may be in them, and I in them"* (John 17:23, 26).

Can words make it plainer that God's love for Christ is meant to pass into us and to become our life, so that the love with which the Father loved the Son can be in us? If the Lord Jesus is to manifest Himself to us, it can only be to the loving heart. If we are to claim His daily presence with us, it can only be as a relationship of infinite, tender love is formed between Him and us—love rooted in the faith of God's love for Christ coming into our hearts and showing itself in obedience to His commandments and in love for one another.

In the early church, the *"first love"* (Revelation 2:4) was forsaken after a time, and Christians put confidence in all the activities of service instead of in God. It is only in the atmosphere of a holy, living love that the abiding presence of the loving Christ can be known, and the depth of divine love expressed in Christ's promise, *"Lo, I am with you alway*[s]*"* (Matthew 28:20), will be realized.

July 30

The Trial and Triumph of Faith

Jesus said unto him, If thou canst believe, all things are possible to him that believeth. And straightway the father of the child cried out, and said with tears, Lord, I believe; help thou mine unbelief. —Mark 9:23–24

What a glorious promise: *"All things are possible to him that believeth"*! And yet it is just the greatness of this promise that constitutes the trial of faith. At first we do not believe its truth. But when we have grasped it, then comes the real trial in the false idea that such a wonder-working faith is utterly beyond our reach.

But what constitutes the trial of faith soon becomes its triumph. How can this be? When the father of the child heard Christ say to him, *"If thou canst believe, all things are possible to him that believeth,"* he felt that this was only casting him into deeper despair. How could his faith be able to work the miracle? But as he looked into the face of Christ, he felt sure that this blessed Man had not only the power to heal his child, but also the power to inspire him with the needed faith. The impression Christ produced upon him made possible not only the one miracle of the healing, but also the second miracle that he should have so great a faith. And with tears he cried, *"Lord, I believe; help thou mine unbelief."* The greatness of faith's trial was the greatness of faith's triumph.

What a lesson! Of all things that are possible to faith, we think the most impossible is that we should be able to exercise such faith. But the abiding presence of Christ is possible to faith, and this faith is possible to the soul that clings to Christ and trusts Him. As surely as He will lead us into His abiding presence all day long, so surely will He strengthen us with divine power for the faith that claims and receives the promise. Blessed is the hour when the believer sees how entirely dependent he is on Christ for the faith as well as the blessing. In the consciousness of the unbelief that is still struggling within, he casts himself on the power and the love of Jesus, saying, "Lord, I believe! Lord, I believe!"

Through such trial and through such triumph—sometimes the triumph of despair—we enter into our inheritance, which is the abiding presence of Him who speaks to us now: *"Lo, I am with you alway*[s]*"* (Matthew 28:20). Let us wait at His feet until we know that He has blessed us.

July 31

Exceedingly Abundantly

Now unto him that is able to do exceeding abundantly above all that we ask or think, according to the power that worketh in us, unto him be glory in the church by Christ Jesus throughout all ages, world without end. Amen. —Ephesians 3:20–21

In the above prayer, Paul had apparently reached the highest expression possible of the life to which God's power could bring the believer. But Paul was not content. In this doxology, he rose still higher and lifted us up to give glory to God as *"able to do exceeding abundantly above all that we ask or think."* Pause a moment to think what that *"exceeding abundantly"* means.

Think of *"the exceeding greatness of his power to us-ward who believe, according to the working of his mighty power, which he wrought in Christ, when he raised him from the dead"* (Ephesians 1:19–20). Think of the grace of our Lord as *"exceeding abundant with faith and love which is in Christ Jesus"* (1 Timothy 1:14), so that *"where sin abounded, grace did much more abound"* (Romans 5:20). He lifts our hearts to give glory to God as able to *"do exceeding abundantly above all that we ask or think, according to the* [greatness of the] *power that worketh in us"*—nothing less than the power that raised Christ from the dead. And as our hearts begin to feel that God will work in us beyond all imagination, He lifts our hearts to join in the chorus: *"Unto him be glory in the church by Christ Jesus throughout all ages, world without end. Amen."*

As we worship and adore, the call comes to believe in this almighty God who is working in our hearts according to His mighty power, able and willing to fulfill every one of His *"exceeding great and precious promises"* (2 Peter 1:4), and, where sin abounds, to prove that grace abounds more exceedingly. (See Romans 5:20.)

Paul began his great prayer, *"I bow my knees unto the Father"* (Ephesians 3:14). He ended it by bringing us to our knees, to give glory to Him as able to fulfill every promise, to reveal Christ dwelling in our hearts, and to keep us in the life of love that leads to being *"filled with all the fullness of God"* (v. 19).

Let us bow in adoration, giving glory to God, until the prayer is fulfilled and Jesus dwells in your heart by faith. Faith in this almighty God, and the exceeding abundance of His grace and power, will teach you that the indwelling of Christ is the secret of the abiding presence.

August

August 1

A New Spirit and God's Spirit

A new heart also will I give you, and a new spirit will I put within you….And I will put my spirit within you.
—Ezekiel 36:26–27

God has revealed Himself in two great covenants. In the old covenant, we have the promise and preparation; in the new covenant, we have fulfillment and possession. In both there is a twofold working of God's Spirit. In the Old Testament, we have the Spirit of God coming upon men and working on them in special times and ways. In the New Testament, we have the Holy Spirit entering men and women, dwelling within them, and working from within them. In the former, we have the Spirit of God as the Almighty and Holy One. In the latter, we have the Spirit of the Father of Jesus Christ.

The indwelling Spirit has indeed been given to every child of God. Yet you may experience little beyond the first half of the promise (the new spirit given to us in regeneration) and know almost nothing of God's own Spirit. The Spirit's work in the convicting of sin, and His leading to repentance and the new life, serve as the preparatory work. The distinctive glory of the gift of the Spirit is His divine personal indwelling in the heart of the believer to reveal the Father and the Son. If Christians understand, they will be able to claim the full blessing prepared for them in Christ Jesus.

In the words of Ezekiel, we find this twofold blessing of God's Spirit presented very strikingly. *"A new spirit will I put within you"*; that is, man's own spirit is to be renewed and quickened by the work of God's Spirit. When this has been done, there is a second blessing, *"I will put my spirit within you"*—to dwell in that new spirit. Where God is to dwell, He must have a habitation. So a new heart is given to us, and a new spirit put within us, as the prerequisite of God's own Spirit being given to dwell within us.

God created man's heart for His dwelling. Sin entered and defiled it. God's Spirit worked to regain possession for four thousand years. Finally the redemption was accomplished, and the kingdom of God was established through Christ. Jesus could then say, *"The kingdom of God is come unto you"* (Matthew 12:28), and *"The kingdom of God is within you"* (Luke 17:21).

August 2

God's Spirit and Your Obedience

If ye love me, keep my commandments. And I will pray the Father, and he shall give you another Comforter,...even the Spirit of truth.
—John 14:15–17

The Holy Ghost, whom God hath given to them that obey him.
—Acts 5:32

We need the Spirit to make us obedient. We long for the Spirit's power because we are disobedient, and we desire to be otherwise. Why then does the Savior claim obedience as the condition for the Father's giving and our receiving the Spirit? This difficulty will be resolved if we remember that we have a twofold manifestation of the Spirit of God, corresponding to the Old and New Testament.

In the Old Testament, He worked as the Spirit of God preparing the way for the higher revelation of God as the Father of Jesus Christ. In the New Testament, He worked in Christ's disciples as the Spirit of conversion and faith. What they were about to receive was something higher—the Spirit of the glorified Jesus, the power from on high, the experience of His full salvation.

Where there is not much knowledge of the Spirit's work, or where His power in a church or an individual is not evident, believers will not get beyond the experience of His preparatory workings in them. Even though He is in them, they do not know Him in His power as the Spirit of the glorified Lord.

When believers obey Christ's commandments, they will be promoted to the higher experience of the Spirit's indwelling as the representative and revealer of Jesus in His glory. *"If ye love me, keep my commandments. And I will pray the Father, and he shall give you another Comforter."*

The church has not given this word obedience the prominence Christ gave it. While the freedom of grace and the simplicity of faith have been preached, the absolute necessity of obedience and holiness has not been equally insisted on. It has been thought that only those who had fullness of the Spirit could be obedient. It was not seen that obedience is the lower platform. The baptism of the Spirit is something higher—the Presence that the obedient should inherit. Complete allegiance to every precept of the Word is the passport to that full life in the Spirit.

August 3

How to Wait for the Spirit

[He] commanded them that they should...wait for the promise of the Father, which, saith he, ye have heard of me.
—Acts 1:4

In the lives of the Old Testament saints, *waiting* was one of the words in which they expressed the posture of their souls toward God. They waited for God and waited upon God. Sometimes we find it in Holy Scripture as an experience: *"Truly my soul waiteth upon God"* (Psalm 62:1). At other times it is a plea: *"Be gracious unto us; we have waited for thee"* (Isaiah 33:2). Frequently, waiting encourages a person to persevere in a work that is difficult: *"Rest in the LORD, and wait patiently for him"* (Psalm 37:7).

Our Lord used the word *waiting* in regard to the promise of the coming of the Holy Spirit. What had been so deeply woven into the very substance of the religious life and language of God's people was now to receive a new and a higher application.

As they waited for the manifestation of God to come, so we must wait. We wait on the Father and the Son for ever-increasing inflowings and workings of the Spirit. We wait for His moving, leading, and strengthening, to reveal the Father and the Son within us.

Begin in simple faith in God's Word to cultivate the quiet assurance: the Holy Spirit is dwelling within me.

Acknowledge in faith and thanksgiving that the Holy Spirit is in you. Each time you enter your closet to speak to God, sit quietly to remember and believe that the Spirit is within you. Appear before God and confess to Him until you become fully conscious that you are a temple of the Spirit.

Now you are in the right posture for taking the second step: asking God very simply and quietly to grant you the power of His Holy Spirit. Ask the Father who is in heaven that His almighty Spirit may come forth from Him in greater life and power as the indwelling Spirit. Ask this on the ground of the promises. Believe that He hears and that He does it. You do not have to feel anything in your heart at once. You are to believe, that is, to rest in what God is going to do even though you do not feel it.

Then comes the waiting. Wait on the Lord. Wait for the Spirit. Quiet your soul and give the Holy Spirit time to give the assurance that God will grant Him to work mightily.

August 4

Be Filled with the Spirit

Be filled with the Spirit; speaking to yourselves.
—Ephesians 5:18–19

These words are a command. They make us realize what the ordinary, consistent experience of every true believer should be. This commandment to *"be filled with the Spirit"* has often been misunderstood. On the day of Pentecost, being filled with the Spirit was accompanied with the manifest enthusiasm of a supernatural joy and power. Such a state has been looked on as one of excitement and strain, quite inconsistent with the quiet course of ordinary life.

The suddenness of the outward manifestation has been linked with the idea of being filled with the Spirit. Many believers thought it was a blessing only possible to a very few. And if the blessing were given to them, they felt it would be impossible in their circumstances to maintain or to manifest it. However, this commandment is indeed for every believer today. The promise and the power are also for every believer.

The first condition of all filling is emptiness. A reservoir is a hole, an empty place waiting, thirsting for the water to come. Any true, abiding fullness of the Spirit is preceded by emptying.

There is one more aspect in which this fullness comes to our faith. God loves to appear in lowly and unlikely ways to clothe Himself in the garment of humility that He wants His children to wear. The kingdom of heaven is like a seed. *"The kingdom of heaven is like to a grain of mustard seed, which a man took, and sowed in his field"* (Matthew 13:31). Only faith can know the glory there is in its smallness.

It was this way in the earthly dwelling of the Son. It is this way in the indwelling of the Spirit in the heart. The Spirit asks to be believed in, even when nothing is seen or felt. Believe the fountain that springs up and flows forth in living streams is within you. Believe even when all appears dry.

Take time to retire into the inner chamber of the heart, and then send up praise and offer worship to God with the assurance of the Holy Spirit within. Take time to be still and let the Spirit Himself fill your spirit with this most spiritual and heavenly of all truths—that He dwells within you. His temple, His hidden dwelling place, is in our lives, deeper than we can see and feel. It is not in the thoughts or feelings first.

August 5

The Baptism of the Spirit

John bare record, saying,...He that sent me to baptize with water, the same said unto me, Upon whom thou shalt see the Spirit descending, and remaining on him, the same is he which baptizeth with the Holy Ghost. —John 1:32–33

There were two things that John the Baptist preached concerning the person of Christ. First, Christ was the *"Lamb of God, which taketh away the sin of the world"* (John 1:29). Second, Christ would baptize His disciples *"with the Holy* [Spirit], *and with fire"* (Matthew 3:11). The blood of the Lamb and the baptism of the Spirit were the two central truths of his preaching.

The Holy Spirit came upon the disciples in the second chapter of Acts, on the Samaritans in chapter eight, on the Gentile converts in the house of Cornelius in chapter ten, and on the twelve disciples at Ephesus in chapter nineteen. These incidents must also be regarded as separate fulfillments of the words, *"He shall baptize you with the Holy Ghost"* (Matthew 3:11).

This baptism of the Holy Spirit is the crown and glory of Jesus' work. Jesus needed it. Christ's loving, obedient disciples needed it. We need it also. It is the personal Spirit of Christ making Himself present within us, always living in the heart in the power of His glorified nature. It is the Spirit of Christ making us free from the law of sin and death.

Be very faithful to what you already know of the Spirit's working. Wait for and listen to the gentlest whispering of God's Spirit within you. Listen especially to the conscience, which has been cleansed in the blood. There may be much involuntary sin in your heart that makes you feel powerless. Deeply humble yourself and, when the sin occurs, be cleansed in the blood.

As far as your voluntary actions are concerned, tell the Lord Jesus every day that you will do all that you know is pleasing to Him. Yield to the warnings of your conscience when you fail. Then come again, have hope in God, humbly ask and wait for guidance every morning. Soon the Spirit's voice will become better known, and His strength will be felt.

Jesus taught the disciples for three years, and then the blessing came. Be His loving, obedient disciple, and believe in Him who is full of the Spirit. Then you will also be prepared for the fullness of the blessing of the baptism of the Spirit.

August 6

A Divine Outpouring

And when the day of Pentecost was fully come...they were all filled with the Holy Ghost, and began to speak with other tongues, as the Spirit gave them utterance.
—Acts 2:1, 4

The Holy Spirit is now sent forth in a new character and a new power, such as He never had come before. This new power is the very Spirit of the glorified Jesus. The work of the Son and the longing of the Father received its fulfillment. Man's heart has become the home of his God.

The entrance of the Son of God into our flesh in Bethlehem, His entrance into the curse and death of sin, His entrance into the very glory of the Father—these were but preparatory steps so that the word could be fulfilled: *"Behold, the tabernacle of God is with men, and he will dwell with them"* (Revelation 21:3).

It is no wonder that, as the Holy Spirit came down from the Father through the glorified Son, the disciples' whole nature was filled to overflowing with the joy and power of heaven. They were filled with the presence of Jesus, and their lips overflowed with the praise of the wonderful works of God.

Such was the birth of the church. Such must be its growth and strength. The most essential element of the true church after Pentecost is a membership *baptized* with the Holy Spirit and with fire. Every heart was filled with the experience of the presence of the glorified Lord. Every tongue and life witnessed to the wonderful work God had done in raising Jesus to glory and then filling His disciples with that glory.

The baptism of power is not just for preachers, but for every individual member of Christ's body. The Spirit of God cannot take possession of believers beyond their capacity to receive Him. Pentecost comes when believers continue with one accord in praise and love and prayer. The Holy Spirit comes when faith holds fast the promise and gazes upon the exalted Lord in the confidence that He will make Himself known in power in the midst of His people.

Let us yield ourselves in strong, expectant faith to be filled with the Holy Spirit and to testify for Jesus. Let the indwelling Christ be our life, our strength, and our testimony.

August 7

Power for Your Life

Ye shall be baptized with the Holy Ghost not many days hence....But ye shall receive power, after that the Holy Ghost is come upon you: and ye shall be witnesses unto me.
—Acts 1:5, 8

Tarry ye in the city of Jerusalem, until ye be endued with power from on high.
—Luke 24:49

The disciples had heard from John about the baptism of the Spirit. Jesus had spoken to them of the Father's giving of the Spirit to those who ask Him. And on the last night He had spoken of the Spirit dwelling in them. This coming of the Holy Spirit was connected in their minds with the work they would have to do and the power for it.

Our Lord summed up all His teaching in the promise, *"Ye shall receive power, after that the Holy Ghost is come upon you: and ye shall be witnesses unto me."* This must have been what the disciples were looking for: a divine power for the new work of being the witnesses of a crucified and risen Jesus.

All prayers for the guiding influence of the Holy Spirit in God's people are to have this as their aim: power to witness for Christ and do effective service in conquering the world for Him.

August

We want to get possession of the power and use it. God wants the power to get possession of us and use us. If we give up ourselves to the power to rule in us, the power will give itself to us, to rule through us. Unconditional submission and obedience to the power in our inner life is the one condition of our being clothed with it.

God gives the Spirit to the obedient. Power belongs to God and remains His forever. If you want His power to work in you, surrender to His guidance even in the least things.

Let us not be content with praying for God to visit and to bless the unsaved or with our own efforts to do the best we can for them. Rather, let each believer give himself completely to live as a witness for Jesus. Let us plead with God to show His people what it means to be Christ's representatives just as He was the Father's representative. Let us believe that the Spirit of power is within us. The Father will, as we wait on Him, fill us with the power of the Spirit.

August 8

How to Worship in the Spirit

The hour cometh, and now is, when the true worshippers shall worship the Father in spirit and in truth: for the Father seeketh such to worship him. God is a Spirit: and they that worship him must worship him in spirit and in truth.
—John 4:23–24

We are the circumcision, which worship God in the spirit, and rejoice in Christ Jesus, and have no confidence in the flesh.
—Philippians 3:3

Man's highest glory is to worship. He was created for fellowship with God. All the exercises of the Christian life—meditation and prayer, love and faith, surrender and obedience—culminate in worship. The truest and fullest and nearest approach to God is worship. Worship is man's highest destiny because in it God is all.

All that the heathen or the Samaritans called worship, even all that the Jews knew of worship in God's law, would make way for something new—the worship in Spirit and in truth.

We have received the Holy Spirit especially for this worship. The great purpose for which the Holy Spirit is within us is to make us able to worship in Spirit and in truth. *"The Father seeketh such to worship him"*—for this He sent forth His Son and His Spirit.

If we strive to become true worshippers, the first thing we need is a sense of the danger that comes from the flesh and its worship. As believers we have in us a double nature—flesh and spirit. We need the Holy Spirit's indwelling for life and worship alike. To receive this we need first of all to have the flesh silenced. *"Be silent,...all flesh, before the LORD"* (Zechariah 2:13). *"No flesh should glory in his presence"* (1 Corinthians 1:29).

Much worship is, even among believers, not in the Spirit! In private, family, and public worship, many hastily enter into God's presence in the power of the flesh, with little or no waiting for the Spirit to lift us heavenward! It is only the presence and power of the Holy Spirit that equips us for acceptable worship.

The great hindrance to the Spirit is the flesh. The secret of spiritual worship is the death of the flesh. Give it up and in great fear humbly and trustfully wait for the Spirit's life and power to take the place of the life and strength of self.

August 9

The Spirit Gives Life

It is the spirit that quickeneth; the flesh profiteth nothing: the words that I speak unto you, they are spirit, and they are life....Lord, to whom shall we go? thou hast the words of eternal life.
—John 6:63, 68

[God] hath made us able ministers of the new testament; not of the letter, but of the spirit: for the letter killeth, but the spirit giveth life.
—2 Corinthians 3:6

"It is the spirit that quickeneth." In these words and the corresponding ones of Paul, *"the spirit giveth life,"* we have the nearest approach to what may be called a definition of the Spirit. (Also see 1 Corinthians 16:4–5.) The Spirit always acts as a life-giving principle. Our Lord placed the flesh in opposition with the Spirit. He said, *"The flesh profiteth nothing."* He means the *flesh* as the power in which the natural man or the unyielded believer seeks to serve God or to understand spiritual truths. Our Lord indicates the futile efforts of the flesh in the words, *"profiteth nothing."*

This is also the reason for the weakness in the lives of many believers who read and know a great deal of Scripture. They do not know that it is the Spirit that quickens. The human understanding, however intelligent, however earnest, profits nothing. They think that in the Scriptures they have eternal life, but they know little of the living Christ as their life in the power of the Spirit.

The solution is very simple: we must refuse to deal with the written Word without the quickening Spirit. First, in a quiet act of worship, look to God to give and renew the workings of His Spirit within you. Then, in a quiet act of faith, yield yourself to the power that dwells in you. Then wait on Him so that not only the mind, but also the life in you, may be opened to receive the Word.

We must wait on the Holy Spirit within us to receive and reveal the words in His quickening power and work them into the very life of our life. Then we will know in truth that *"it is the spirit that quickeneth."* We will see how divinely right it is that the words that are Spirit and life should be met in us by the Spirit and the life dwelling within. They alone will unfold their meaning, impart their substance, and give their divine strength and fullness to the Spirit and the life already within us.

The Spirit of the Glorified Jesus

He that believeth on me, as the scripture hath said, out of his belly shall flow rivers of living water. (But this spake he of the Spirit, which they that believe on him should receive: for the Holy Ghost was not yet given; because that Jesus was not yet glorified.)
—John 7:38–39

Our Lord promises that those who come unto Him and drink, who believe in Him, not only will never thirst, but also will themselves become fountains from which streams of living water will flow forth. The apostle John explained that at the time Jesus spoke these words, the promise was a prospective one that would have to wait for its fulfillment until the Spirit would be poured out. He also gave the reason for this delay: the Holy Spirit was not yet because Jesus was not yet glorified.

The expression *the Spirit was not yet,* which is in the original Greek, seems awkward, and so the word *given* has been inserted by Bible translators. But the expression, if accepted as it stands, may guide us into the true understanding of the real significance of the Holy Spirit not coming until Jesus was glorified.

As this Spirit dwelt in Jesus in the flesh, and can also dwell in us in the flesh, it is literally true that the Holy Spirit *"was not yet."* The Spirit of the glorified Jesus—the Son of Man become the Son of God—could not be until Jesus was glorified. Having become flesh, He had to sanctify the flesh and make it a suitable receptacle for the indwelling of the Spirit of God. Having done this, He had to bear the curse of sin and to give Himself as the seed to bring forth fruit in us. His nature was glorified in the resurrection, glorified into the union with the divine. By this He made us partakers of all that He had personally acquired.

In virtue of His having perfected in Himself a new holy human nature on our behalf, He could now communicate what previously had no existence—a life at once human and divine.

According to the riches of His glory, God can now work in us. We have the personal presence of the Spirit on earth within us. By faith, the glory of Jesus in heaven and the power of the Spirit in our hearts are inseparably linked. When we are in fellowship with Jesus, the stream will flow ever stronger, into us and out of us.

August 11

The Indwelling Comforter

And I will pray the Father, and he shall give you another Comforter, that he may abide with you for ever; even the Spirit of truth; whom the world cannot receive, because it seeth him not, neither knoweth him: but ye know him; for he dwelleth with you, and shall be in you.
—John 14:16–17

He *"shall be in you."* In these simple words, our Lord announced that wonderful mystery of the Spirit's indwelling that was to be the crown of His redeeming work. For this, man was created. Throughout the ages, the Spirit struggled in vain to achieve God's mastery within the hearts of men. It was for this that Jesus lived and died. Without this mastery, the Father's purpose and the Spirit's work would fail to accomplish their task.

In writing to the Corinthians, Paul had to reprove them for their terrible sins. Yet he said to all, including the weakest and most unfaithful believer, *"Know ye not that ye are the temple of God, and that the Spirit of God dwelleth in you?"* (1 Corinthians 3:16). Paul knew that if this truth were given the place God meant it to have, it would be the motive and the power to live a new and holy life.

August

To the backsliding Galatians, Paul asserted that they had already *received* the Spirit by the preaching of faith. God had sent forth the Spirit of His Son *into their hearts.* They had life by the Spirit in them. If they could only understand and believe this, they would also walk in the Spirit.

It is this teaching the church of Christ needs in our day. I am deeply persuaded that many believers are ignorant of this aspect of the truth concerning the Holy Spirit. This is the cause of their failure to have a holy walk with the Lord. Many Christians pray for the Holy Spirit's power and confess their entire and absolute dependence on Him. However, unless His personal, continual, divine indwelling is acknowledged and experienced, failure will continue.

The Holy Spirit wants His resting place free from all intrusion and disturbance. God wants entire possession of His temple. Jesus wants His home all to Himself. He cannot do His work there, He cannot rule and reveal Himself, unless the home, the inner being, is possessed and filled by the Holy Spirit.

August 12

How to Know the Spirit

Even the Spirit of truth; whom the world cannot receive, because it seeth him not, neither knoweth him: but ye know him; for he dwelleth with you, and shall be in you.
—John 14:17

Know ye not that ye are the temple of God, and that the Spirit of God dwelleth in you?
—1 Corinthians 3:16

True spiritual knowledge is very important in the Christian life. A man whose inheritance comes to him is no richer if he does not know how to take possession of it. In the same way, the gifts of God's grace cannot bring their full blessing until we truly understand and possess them.

In Christ *"are hid all the treasures of wisdom and knowledge"* (Colossians 2:3). It is the *"knowledge of Christ Jesus"* for which the believer is willing to *"count all things but loss"* (Philippians 3:8). It is because of the lack of true knowledge of what God in Christ has prepared for us that the lives of believers are so weak.

How do we know when it is the Spirit who is teaching us? If our knowledge of spiritual things is to be to us a certainty and a comfort, we must know the Teacher Himself. Knowing Him will be to us the evidence that our spiritual knowledge is no deception. Our blessed Lord assures us that we will *know* the Spirit. Messengers and witnesses do not speak of themselves.

The Holy Spirit, when He testifies of Christ and glorifies Him, must be known and acknowledged. In this way we can have the assurance that the knowledge we receive is indeed of God and not what our human reason has gathered from the Word of God. To know the King's seal is the only safeguard against a counterfeit image. To know the Spirit is the divine foundation of certainty.

How can the Spirit be known? Jesus said, *"Ye know him; for he dwelleth with you, and shall be in you."* The indwelling of the Spirit is the condition of knowing Him. As we allow Him to dwell in us, and allow Him to testify of Jesus as Lord, He will prove Himself to be the Spirit of God. *"It is the Spirit that beareth witness, because the Spirit is truth"* (1 John 5:6).

August 13

The Evidence of the Spirit

If ye through the Spirit do mortify the deeds of the body, ye shall live. For as many as are led by the Spirit of God, they are the sons of God.
—Romans 8:13–14

If we live in the Spirit, let us also walk in the Spirit.
—Galatians 5:25

We...are changed into the same image...even as by the Spirit of the Lord.
—2 Corinthians 3:18

Words like these define the operations of the Spirit. Obedience is the evidence of the Spirit's presence in your life. Jesus gave Him as our Teacher and Guide. All Scripture speaks of His work as demanding the surrender of the whole life.

God is first known by His works, and so is the Spirit. He reveals God's will and calls us to follow Him in it. As the believer surrenders himself to a life in the Spirit and consents to the rule of Christ, he will find and know the Spirit working in him. It is as we simply make the aim of the Holy Spirit our aim that we are prepared to know Him as dwelling in us. The Spirit Himself will lead us to obey God even as Christ did. We will know the Spirit intimately as we yield ourselves to an obedient life.

There is no way of knowing a fruit except by tasting it. There is no way of knowing the light except by being in it and using it. There is no way of knowing a person except by conversation with him. There is no way of knowing the Holy Spirit except by possessing Him and being possessed by Him. To live in the Spirit is the only way to know the Spirit. To have Him in us, doing His work and giving us His fellowship, is the path the Master opens when He says, *"Ye know him; for he...shall be in you"* (John 14:17).

The Father has sent the Spirit so that we may fully share in the glorified Christ! Let us yield ourselves completely to the indwelling and teaching of the blessed Spirit whom the Son has given us from the Father.

August 14

Truth to Live By

But when the Comforter is come, whom I will send unto you from the Father, even the Spirit of truth, which proceedeth from the Father, he shall testify of me.
—John 15:26

When he, the Spirit of truth, is come, he will guide you into all truth: for he shall not speak of himself; but whatsoever he shall hear, that shall he speak.
—John 16:13

God created man in His image—to become like Himself, capable of holding fellowship with Him in His glory. In the garden, two ways were presented to man for attaining this likeness to God. These were typified by the two trees—that of life and that of knowledge. God's way was the former—through life, the knowledge and likeness of God would come.

By abiding in God's will and partaking of God's life, man would be perfected. In recommending the other, Satan assured man that knowledge was the one thing to be desired to make us like God. When man chose the light of knowledge above the life of obedience, he entered the path that leads to death. The desire to know became his greatest temptation.

Under the power of this deceit that promises happiness in knowledge, the human race is still led astray. This lie shows its power most terribly in God's own revelation of Himself. Even when the Word of God is accepted, the wisdom of the world and of the flesh always enters in. Even spiritual truth is robbed of its power when held, not in the Spirit, but in the wisdom of man.

When truth enters into our heart, it may reach only the outer parts of the soul, the intellect, and the reason. It pleases our minds and satisfies us with the imagination that it will exercise its influence. However, its power is nothing more than that of human argument and wisdom that never reach to the true life of the spirit.

There is a truth of the understanding and feelings that is only the human image, the shadow of divine truth. There is a truth that is substance and reality, communicating the life of the things that others only think and speak. The truth in shadow, in form and in thought, was all the Jewish law could give. The truth of substance, of divine life, was what Jesus brought as the only begotten Son, *"full of grace and truth"* (John 1:14). He is the Truth.

August 15

The Teachable Spirit

When he, the Spirit of truth, is come, he will guide you into all truth: for he shall not speak of himself; but whatsoever he shall hear, that shall he speak.
—John 16:13

The mark of this Spirit of Truth is a divine teachableness. In the mystery of the Holy Trinity, there is nothing more beautiful than this. With a divine equality on the part of the Son and the Spirit, there is also a perfect subordination.

The Son could demand that men honor Him even as they honored the Father (see John 5:23), and yet He said, *"The Son can do nothing of himself"* (v. 19). We would think He would surely speak His own thoughts, but He speaks only what He hears. He does only what He sees the Father do. *"For what things soever he doeth, these also doeth the Son likewise"* (v. 19). In the same way, the Holy Spirit never speaks from Himself. The Spirit who fears to speak His own words, and only speaks when God speaks, is the Spirit of Truth.

This is the kind of attitude He creates and the life He breathes in those who truly receive Him. It is that gentle teachableness that marks the poor in spirit, the broken in heart, who have become conscious that their wisdom is as worthless as their righteousness. Thus they need Christ and the Spirit within them to be the Spirit of Truth. He shows us how lacking we are in that waiting, submissive spirit to which alone spiritual meaning can be revealed.

The Spirit opens our eyes to the reason why so much Bible reading, Bible knowledge, and Bible preaching has little fruit unto true holiness. It is because the Bible is studied with a wisdom that is not from above. God was not waited upon nor was wisdom asked for. The Spirit of Truth is silent. He does not speak unless and until He hears from God in heaven.

These thoughts suggest to us the great danger of the Christian life—seeking to know the truth of God in His Word without the distinct waiting on the Spirit of Truth in the heart. Satan still moves among men. Knowledge is still his great temptation. There are many Christians who would confess that their knowledge of divine truth does little for them. It leaves them powerless against the world and sin.

August 16

The Gift of the Spirit

I tell you the truth; it is expedient for you that I go away: for if I go not away, the Comforter will not come unto you; but if I depart, I will send him unto you.
—John 16:7

As the Lord left this world, He promised the disciples that His departure would be their gain. The Comforter would take His place and be to them far better than Jesus ever had been in His bodily presence. The Lord's conversation with them had never been broken, but could be interrupted. Now it would even be broken off by death, and they would see Him no more. However, the Spirit would *abide* with them forever. The Spirit would be *in them*. His coming would be as an indwelling presence in which they would have Jesus in them as their life and their strength.

During the life of our Lord on earth, He dealt with each of His disciples according to their individual characters and the special circumstances in which they were placed. The conversation was an intensely personal one—in everything He proved that He knew His sheep by name. For each person there was a thoughtful word of wisdom that met each need. Would the Spirit supply this need, too, and provide that tender personal interest and attention that made the guidance of Jesus so precious?

All that Christ had been to His disciples, the Spirit was to restore in greater power in a relationship that would not be interrupted. They were to be happier, safer, and stronger with Jesus in heaven than they ever could have been with Him on earth. Jesus had been wise and patient to give each disciple what he needed, to make each one feel that Jesus was his best friend. The indwelling of the Spirit was given to restore Christ's very personal friendship and guidance with His disciples and all believers.

The will and wisdom of man hinders the Holy Spirit. In the service of God, self is always putting itself forward and exerting its own strength. Every thought, however good, must be brought into captivity.

Our own wisdom must be laid captive at the feet of Jesus. As we bring our fleshly activity into subjection and wait on Him, He will not put us to shame. Rather, He will do His work within us. We will learn that the presence and personal guidance of Jesus is ours just as sweetly and mightily as if He were with us on earth.

August 17

How to Glorify Christ

It is expedient for you that I go away: for if I go not away, the Comforter will not come unto you; but if I depart, I will send him unto you....He shall glorify me: for he shall receive of mine, and shall show it unto you.
—John 16:7, 14

Scripture speaks of a twofold glorifying of the Son. The one is by the Father, the other by the Spirit. The one takes place in heaven, the other here on earth. By the one He is glorified in God Himself; by the other, in us. (See John 13:32; 17:10.) Of the former Jesus spoke, *"If God be glorified in him* [the Son of Man], *God shall also glorify him in himself, and shall straightway glorify him"* (John 13:32). Of the latter He said, "[The Spirit] *shall glorify me"* (John 16:14).

To glorify is to manifest the hidden excellence and worth of an object. Jesus, the Son of Man, was to be glorified when His human nature was admitted to the full participation of the power and glory in which God dwells. He entered into the perfect spirit-life of the heavenly world. All the angels worshipped Him as the Lamb on the throne. The human mind cannot conceive or understand this heavenly, spiritual glory of Christ.

It can be truly known only by being experienced and shared in the inner life. This is the work of the Holy Spirit. He reveals the glory of Christ in us by dwelling and working in us. The Holy Spirit makes Christ glorious to us and in us. The Son does not seek His own glory. The Father glorifies Him in heaven. The Spirit glorifies Him in our hearts.

When the Holy Spirit glorifies Jesus in us, He reveals Him to us in His glory. He takes of the things of Christ and declares them to us. He does not give us just a thought or an image or a vision of that glory in heaven. Instead, He shows it to us as a personal experience and possession. He makes us partake of it in our innermost life. He shows Christ as present in us. All the true, living knowledge we have of Christ is through the Spirit of God.

Throughout our renewed nature there rises the song, "Glory to Him who sits on the throne." (See Revelation 5:13.) The holy presence of Christ as Ruler and Governor so fills the heart and life that His dominion rules over all. Sin has no dominion. The law of the Spirit of the life in Christ Jesus has made us free from the law of sin and death.

Saving the World from Sin

If I depart, I will send him [the Comforter] unto you. And when he is come, he will reprove the world of sin.
—John 16:7–8

The close connection between the two statements in these words of our Lord is not always noticed. Before the Holy Spirit was to reprove or convince the world of sin, He was first to come into the disciples. He was to dwell within them, and then, through them, He was to do His work of convicting the world of sin. *"He shall testify of me: and ye also shall bear witness"* (John 15:26–27).

The disciples were to realize that the great work of the Holy Spirit, striving with man, convincing *the world* of sin, could be done only as He had a dwelling place *in them.* They were to receive the power from on high with the one purpose of being the instruments through whom the Holy Spirit could reach the world.

The Holy Spirit comes to us so that through us He may reach others. When He enters us, He does not change His nature or lose His divine character. Wherever He is not hindered by ignorance or selfishness, He makes the heart willing and bold to testify against sin. He does this as the Spirit of the crucified Christ.

For what purpose was it that He received the Spirit without measure? *"The spirit of the Lord GOD is upon me; because the LORD hath anointed me to preach good tidings unto the meek; he hath sent me...to proclaim liberty to the captives"* (Isaiah 61:1). It was this same Spirit of Jesus whom He sent down on His church. The Spirit would pursue His divine work in them as He had in Christ, as a light shining in, revealing and condemning, conquering the darkness, as *"by the spirit of judgment, and by the spirit of burning"* (Isaiah 4:4).

The Spirit can reach others through us only by first bringing us into perfect sympathy with Himself. He enters into us to become one with us. He becomes an attitude and a life within us. His work in us and through us becomes identical with our work.

Complete surrender is needed if, by my life, He is to convince the world of the sin of unbelief. One thing is needed to do this. There must be intense, continued, united, believing prayer that the Father would strengthen us all with might by His Spirit.

August 19

Evangelism—You Can Participate

Now there were in the church that was at Antioch certain prophets and teachers....As they ministered to the Lord, and fasted, the Holy Ghost said, Separate me Barnabas and Saul for the work whereunto I have called them. And when they had fasted and prayed, and laid their hands on them, they sent them away. So they, being sent forth by the Holy Ghost, departed unto Seleucia.

—Acts 13:1–4

Christ gave this parting promise: *"Ye shall receive power, after that the Holy Ghost is come upon you: and ye shall be witnesses unto me both in Jerusalem, and in all Judaea, and in Samaria, and unto the uttermost part of the earth"* (Acts 1:8). This was one of those divine seed-words that contained the power of growth and the prophecy of its final perfection.

The book of Acts reveals that the one aim of the descent of the Spirit was to reveal the Lord's presence, guidance, and power in the disciples. The Spirit equipped them to be His witnesses even to the uttermost parts of the earth. Sending missionaries to unbelievers is one purpose of the coming of the Spirit.

It has often been remarked that true mission work has always been born out of a revival in the church. The Holy Spirit's quickening work stirs up new devotion to the blessed Lord whom He reveals, and to the lost to whom He belongs.

It is still the Holy Spirit who has charge of all mission work. But it is not enough that Christians be stirred and urged to pray and give more. There is a more urgent need. We must learn to wait more earnestly for the Holy Spirit's guidance in the selection of men and fields of labor. In the seeking of support, the Spirit's power must be expected to help the mission that has originated in much prayer and waiting on the Spirit.

However, dependence upon the Holy Spirit does not mean He has designed the work without us. There is much that needs to be done and cannot be done without our diligent labor. But it will be done as a service pleasing to the Master, as long as it is done in the power of the Holy Spirit.

Oh, that the church might learn this lesson! The Spirit has come down from heaven to be the Spirit of missions, to inspire and empower Christ's disciples to witness for Him to the uttermost parts of the earth.

August 20

Set Free!

The law of the Spirit of life in Christ Jesus hath made me free from the law of sin and death....If ye through the Spirit do mortify the deeds of the body, ye shall live.
—Romans 8:2, 13

But now we are delivered from the law, that being dead wherein we were held; that we should serve in newness of spirit, and not in the oldness of the letter.
—Romans 7:6

In the sixth chapter of Romans, Paul spoke of our having been *"made free from sin"* in Christ Jesus (vv. 18 and 22). We were made free from sin as a power, as a master. When we accepted Christ in faith, we became servants to righteousness and to God.

In the seventh chapter (vv. 1–6) Paul spoke of our being made free from the law. *"The strength of sin is the law"* (1 Corinthians 15:56). Deliverance from sin and the law go together. Being made free from the law, we were united to the living Christ so that, in union with Him, we might now serve in newness of the Spirit (Romans 7:4–6). In these two passages (Romans 6 and 7:1–6), Paul presented being made free from sin and the law as a life to be accepted and maintained by faith.

In the account of the Christian life in the epistle of Romans, the eighth chapter teaches us that when the Spirit empowers our life and walk, we can fully possess and enjoy the riches of grace that are ours in Christ.

The second verse of the eighth chapter is the key verse. It reveals the wonderful secret of how our freedom from sin and the law may become a living and abiding experience. A believer may know that he is free and yet have to mourn that his experience is that of a wretched captive. The freedom is entirely *in* Christ Jesus, and the maintenance of the living union with Him is distinctly and entirely a work of divine power.

The believer who wants to live fully in this freedom of the life in Christ will understand the path in which he must learn to walk. The eighth chapter of Romans is the goal to which the sixth and seventh chapters lead. In faith the believer will first have to study and accept all that is taught in these two earlier chapters of his being in Christ Jesus—dead to sin and alive to God, free from sin and the law, and married to Christ.

August 21

How to Be a Child of God

For as many as are led by the Spirit of God, they are the sons of God.
—Romans 8:14

Many Christians think the leading of the Spirit is just the suggestion of thoughts in the mind for our guidance. In their daily lives, they would like to have some indication from the Spirit of the right choice when making a decision or when in need of direction. However, they long and ask for such guidance in vain. When they think they have attained it, there is no assurance that they thought should be the seal from the Spirit. And so the precious truth of the Spirit's leading, instead of being a source of comfort and of strength, becomes cause for perplexity.

The error in this matter comes from not accepting that the teaching and the leading of the Spirit are first given in the life, not in the mind. The life is stirred and strengthened. As conformity to the world is crucified and dies, as we deliberately deny the will of the flesh, we are renewed in the spirit of our mind. In this way the mind becomes able to prove and know the good and perfect and acceptable will of God. (See Romans 12:2.)

This connection between the practical sanctifying work of the Spirit in our inner life, and His leading, comes out very clearly in Scripture. *"If ye through the Spirit do mortify the deeds of the body, ye shall live,"* we read in Romans 8:13. Then follows immediately, *"For as many as are led by the Spirit of God, they are the sons of God"* (v. 14). As many as allow themselves to be led by Him in this denying of the flesh, these are the sons of God.

To be led of the Spirit implies the surrender to His work as He convicts of sin and cleanses soul and body for His temple. It is the indwelling Spirit filling, sanctifying, and ruling the heart and life that enlightens and leads.

The leading of the Spirit is inseparable from the sanctifying of the Spirit. Let each one who would be led of the Spirit begin by giving himself to be led of the Word as far as he knows it. Begin at the beginning. Obey the commandments. Give up every sin. Give up everything to the voice of conscience. Give up everything to God and let Him have His way. As a son or daughter of God, place yourself at the entire disposal of the Spirit to follow where He leads. And the Spirit Himself will bear witness with your spirit that you are indeed a child of God, enjoying all a child's privileges in his Father's love and guidance.

August 22

Revitalizing Your Prayer Life

Likewise the Spirit also helpeth our infirmities: for we know not what we should pray for as we ought: but the Spirit itself maketh intercession for us with groanings which cannot be uttered. And he that searcheth the hearts knoweth what is the mind of the Spirit, because he maketh intercession for the saints according to the will of God.
—Romans 8:26–27

The ministry of the Holy Spirit that leads us most deeply into the understanding of the Holy Trinity is the work He does as the Spirit of prayer. We have the Father to whom we pray and who hears prayer. We have the Son through whom we pray and through whom we receive and appropriate the answer. And we have the Holy Spirit who prays in us with unutterable sighs according to the will of God.

In each part of that work there is a special place assigned to each of the three persons of the Holy Trinity. This is true not only in the individual, but also in the church as a whole. What the Father has purposed, and the Son has procured, can be appropriated in the body of Christ only through the operation of the Holy Spirit.

In the life of faith and prayer there are operations of the Spirit in which the Word of God is made clear to our understanding, and our faith knows to express what it asks. But there are also operations of the Spirit where He works desires and yearnings in our spirits that only God can discover and understand. The real thirst is for God Himself, to know the love that passes all knowledge. When these aspirations take possession of us, we begin to pray for what cannot be expressed, and the Spirit prays with His unutterable yearnings in a language that God alone understands.

"We know not what we should pray for as we ought." How often this has been a burden and a sorrow! Let it from now on be a comfort. When we do not know, we may stand aside and give place to One who does know. We may believe that in our stammering utterances the mighty Intercessor is pleading. Let us not be afraid to believe that within our ignorance and feebleness the Holy Spirit is hidden, doing His work.

August 23

The Holy Spirit and Your Conscience

I say the truth in Christ, I lie not, my conscience also bearing me witness in the Holy Ghost.
—Romans 9:1

God's highest glory is His holiness. He hates and destroys the evil, and loves and works the good. In man, conscience has the same work. It condemns sin and approves the right. Conscience is the remains of God's image in man. It is the guardian of God's honor amid the ruin of the Fall. As a consequence, God's work of redemption must always begin with conscience. Harmony between the work of the Holy Spirit and the work of conscience is most essential.

Conscience can be compared to the window of a room, into which the light of heaven shines and out of which we can look and see all that heaven shines on. The heart is the chamber in which our life dwells—our soul with its abilities and affections. On the walls of that chamber, the law of God is written. Even in unbelievers it is still partly legible, though sadly darkened and defaced. In the believer the law is written anew by the Holy Spirit, in letters of light. They are often dim at first, but grow clearer and brighter as they are freely exposed to the action of the light without.

The light that shines in makes every sin I commit manifest and condemns it. If the sin is not confessed and forsaken, the stain remains. Conscience becomes defiled because the mind refused the teaching of the light. (See Titus 1:15.) And so, one sin after another, the window gets darker and darker, until the light can hardly shine through at all. Then the Christian can continue sinning undisturbed, his conscience to a large extent blinded and without feeling.

In His work of renewal, the Holy Spirit does not create new faculties. Instead, He renews and sanctifies those already existing. Conscience is the work of the Spirit of God the Creator. As the redeeming Spirit of God, His first concern is to restore what sin has defiled. By restoring the conscience to healthy action and revealing in it the wonderful grace of Christ, He enables the believer to live a life in the full light of God's favor. We can walk in the light as long as the window of the heart that looks heavenward is cleansed and kept clean.

August 24

Dealing with Sin

And herein do I exercise myself, to have always a conscience void of offence toward God, and toward men.
—Acts 24:16

How is this blessed life to be attained in which we daily appeal to God and men? *"I say the truth in Christ,...my conscience also bearing me witness in the Holy Ghost"* (Romans 9:1). First, we must bow low under the reproofs of conscience. Do not be content with the general confession that there is a great deal wrong. Beware of confusing actual sinning with the involuntary workings of the sinful nature. If the latter are to be conquered and made dead by the indwelling Spirit (see Romans 8:13), you must first deal with the former.

Begin with some single sin and give your conscience time, in silent submission and humiliation, to reprove you. Say to your Father that in this one thing you are, by His grace, going to obey. Accept anew Christ's wonderful offer to take possession of your heart, to dwell in you as Lord and Keeper. And vow that by God's grace you will exercise yourself *"to have always a conscience void of offence toward God, and toward men."*

When you have begun this practice with one sin, proceed with others, step by step. As you are faithful in keeping your conscience pure, the light will shine more brightly from heaven into your heart, discovering sin you had not noticed before. God's light will bring out distinctly the law written by the Spirit you had not been able to read. Be willing to be taught. Be trustfully sure that the Spirit will teach. Every honest effort to keep your conscience clean in God's light will be met with the aid of the Spirit. Only yield yourself entirely to God's will and to the power of His Holy Spirit.

As you listen to the reproofs of conscience and give yourself completely to do God's will, your courage will grow so strong that it is possible to have *"a conscience void of offence."* The witness of conscience, as to what you are doing and will do by grace, will be met by the witness of the Spirit as to what Christ is doing and will do. In childlike simplicity, you will seek to begin each day with the simple prayer, "Father, there is nothing between You and me. My conscience has been cleansed in the blood and bears me witness. In everything I would do Your will. Your Spirit dwells in me and leads me and makes me strong in Christ."

August 25

How to Acquire Wisdom

My preaching was not with enticing words of man's wisdom, but in demonstration of the Spirit and of power: that your faith should not stand in the wisdom of men, but in the power of God. Howbeit we speak wisdom among them that are perfect: yet not the wisdom of this world, nor of the princes of this world,...but we speak the wisdom of God in a mystery, even the hidden wisdom....But God hath revealed them unto us by his Spirit.... Now we have received, not the spirit of the world, but the spirit which is of God; that we might know the things that are freely given to us of God. Which things also we speak, not in the words which man's wisdom teacheth, but which the Holy Ghost teacheth....But the natural man receiveth not the things of the Spirit of God....But he that is spiritual judgeth all things.
—1 Corinthians 2:4–7, 10, 12–15

In this passage Paul contrasted the spirit of the world and the Spirit of God. It was in seeking knowledge that man fell. It was in the pride of knowledge that heathenism had its origin: *"Professing themselves to be wise, they became fools"* (Romans 1:22).

Man's wisdom is incapable of understanding God or His wisdom. Because his heart is alienated from God his mind is darkened. Even when in Christ the light of God in its divine love shone upon men, they knew it not and saw no beauty in it.

Divine revelation, as Paul discussed it in this chapter, means three things. God must make known in His Word what He thinks and does. Every preacher who is to communicate the message must continually be taught by the Spirit how to speak it. And every hearer needs the inward illumination. As we have the mind and attitudes of Christ, we can discern the truth as it is in Christ Jesus.

Reject the spirit of the world still in you with its wisdom and self-confidence. Come, in poverty of spirit, to be led by the Spirit. *"Be not conformed to this world: but be ye transformed by the renewing of your mind, that ye may prove what is that good, and acceptable, and perfect, will of God"* (Romans 12:2). The Spirit will teach a transformed, renewed life that wants only to know God's perfect will. You will increasingly be able to testify of the things that have not entered into the hearts of men and will understand that *"God hath revealed them unto us by his Spirit."*

August 26

The Spirit and the Flesh

Are ye so foolish? having begun in the Spirit, are ye now made perfect by the flesh?
—Galatians 3:3

For we are the circumcision, which worship God in the spirit, and rejoice in Christ Jesus, and have no confidence in the flesh. Though I might also have confidence in the flesh.
—Philippians 3:3–4

The flesh is the name by which Scripture designates our fallen nature—soul and body. The soul at creation was placed between the spiritual and the worldly to guide them into that perfect union that would result in man attaining his destiny, a spiritual body.

When the soul yielded to the temptation of the senses, it broke away from the rule of the Spirit and came under the power of the body—it became flesh. And now the flesh is not only without the Spirit, but even hostile to it: *"The flesh lusteth against the Spirit"* (Galatians 5:17).

In this antagonism of the flesh to the Spirit, there are two sides. On the one hand, the flesh lusts against the Spirit. On the other hand, its hostility to the Spirit is shown no less in its seeking to serve God and do His will. In yielding to the flesh, the soul sought itself instead of seeking God. Selfishness prevailed over God's will.

This spirit of self is so subtle and mighty in sinning against God, that, even when the soul yearns to serve God, it still refuses to let the Spirit lead alone. In its efforts to be religious, it is still the great enemy that hinders the Spirit. This deceitfulness of the flesh often causes the same problem Paul found among the Galatians: *"Having begun in the Spirit, are ye now made perfect by the flesh?"* The surrender to the Spirit must be complete and maintained by waiting on Him in humility. If this is not done, then what the Spirit has begun very quickly passes over into confidence in the flesh.

Having begun in the Spirit, continue, go on, and persevere in the Spirit. Beware of continuing the work of the Spirit in the flesh. Let *"no confidence in the flesh"* be your battle cry. Let a deep distrust of the flesh and fear of grieving the Spirit keep you humble before God. The Holy Spirit will indeed take the place of your life, and Jesus will be enthroned as the Keeper, Guide, and Life of your soul.

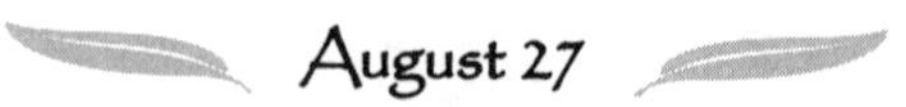

August 27

Are You Spiritual or Carnal?

And I, brethren, could not speak unto you as unto spiritual, but as unto carnal, even as unto babes in Christ. I have fed you with milk, and not with meat: for hitherto ye were not able to bear it, neither yet now are ye able....For whereas there is among you envying, and strife, and divisions, are ye not carnal, and walk as men?
—1 Corinthians 3:1–3

If we live in the Spirit, let us also walk in the Spirit.
—Galatians 5:25

In 1 Corinthians 2, Paul contrasted the believer as spiritual with the unregenerate as the natural (or physical) man. He supplemented that teaching by telling the Corinthians that though they had the Spirit, he could not call them spiritual. The word *spiritual* belongs to those who have not only received the Spirit, but have also yielded themselves to Him to possess and rule their whole life. Those who have not done this, in whom the power of the flesh is still more manifest than that of the Spirit, must not be called spiritual, but fleshly or carnal.

There are thus three states in which a man may be found. The unregenerate is still *the natural man,* not having the Spirit of God. The regenerate, who is still a babe in Christ, is *the carnal man,* giving way to the power of the flesh. The believer in whom the Spirit has obtained full supremacy is *the spiritual man.* This whole passage from Corinthians is suggestive of rich instruction in regard to the life of the Spirit within us.

All that is carnal and sinful, the works of the flesh, must be cast out. Also, all that is carnal (however religious it appears), all confidence in the flesh, and all self-effort must be rooted out. The soul must be brought into the subjection of Jesus Christ. In daily dependence on God, the Holy Spirit must be accepted, waited for, and followed.

By walking in faith and obedience, we may count on the Holy Spirit to do a divine work within us. *"If we live in the Spirit"*—this is the faith that is needed. If we believe that God's Spirit dwells in us, *"let us also walk in the Spirit."* This is the obedience that God requires. By faith in the Holy Spirit within us, we have sufficient strength to walk by the Spirit and yield ourselves to His mighty power. Then He can work in us to will and to do all that is pleasing in God's sight.

You Are the Temple of the Holy Spirit

Know ye not that ye are the temple of God, and that the Spirit of God dwelleth in you?
—1 Corinthians 3:16

The temple was made in all things according to a pattern seen by Moses. Because man was created in the image of God, the temple represented the mystery of man's approach into the presence of God. It also represented God's way of entering into man, to take up His abode with him.

The temple was divided into three parts. There was its exterior with the *Outer Court,* into which every Israelite could enter. All the external religious services were performed there. Next, there was the *Holy Place,* into which the priests alone might enter, to present to God the blood or the incense, the bread or the oil.

But God dwelt in the *Holy of Holies* where none might venture. The momentary entering of the high priest once a year brought into full consciousness the truth that there was no place for man there, until the veil would be torn and taken away.

Man is God's temple. In him, too, there are the three parts. In the *body* you have the Outer Court, the external visible life. Then there is the *soul,* with its inner life, its power of mind and feeling and will. There, the soul's thoughts and desires move to and fro as the priests of the sanctuary, rendering God their service. Then comes, within the veil, hidden from all human sight and light, the hidden, innermost sanctuary, *"the secret place of the most High"* (Psalm 91:1). This is where God dwells and where man may not enter until the veil is torn at God's own bidding.

Man does not have only body and soul, but also *spirit.* In the believer it is the inner chamber of the heart that the Spirit has taken possession of. He waits to do His glorious work, making soul and body holy to the Lord.

This indwelling, unless it is recognized, yielded to, and humbly maintained in love, often brings comparatively little blessing. The one great lesson, which the truth that we are God's temple must teach us, is this: to acknowledge the Holy Presence that dwells within us. This alone will enable us to regard the whole temple, even the Outer Court, as sacred to His service and to yield every power of our nature to His leading and will.

Receive the Spirit Through Faith

Christ hath redeemed us from the curse of the law…that the blessing of Abraham might come on the Gentiles through Jesus Christ; that we might receive the promise of the Spirit through faith.
—Galatians 3:13–14

In Scripture, the word *faith* is first used in connection with Abraham. The secret of his strength for obedience, and what made him so pleasing to God, was that he believed God. He became the father of all who believe. He also became the great example of the blessing that divine favor bestows and the path in which it comes. God proved Himself to Abraham as the God who quickens the dead. He does this in fuller measure for us, too, by giving us the Spirit of His own divine life to dwell in us. Just as this quickening power came to Abraham through faith, so the blessing of Abraham, and the promise of the Spirit, is made ours by faith.

Paul spoke of *"trust in the living God"* (1 Timothy 4:10). It is only as God draws close and touches the soul that living faith will be activated. Faith is not an independent act by which we take what God says in our own strength. Nor is it an entirely passive state in which we believe that God will do with us what He will. Rather, it is the receptive soul that causes us to yield ourselves and accept His Word and His working in and through us.

It is very evident that faith has two things to deal with: *the presence* and *the Word* of the Lord. Only the living Presence makes the Word come alive in power. There is much reading and preaching of the Word that bears little fruit, so much straining and praying for faith with little result. Men deal with the Word more than with the living God.

Faith is the spiritual vehicle of the soul through which it waits on the living God, listens to Him, takes His words from Himself, and has communion with Him. As this habit of soul is cultivated, as the whole life we live is by faith, the Spirit can enter freely and flow fully.

If you long for the power of the Holy Spirit to reveal Jesus as the ever-present Savior from sin, all you need to do is believe. Begin each day with a quiet act of meditation and faith. In quiet reflection, turn inward, not to see the work the Holy Spirit does, but to yield your spirit to Him who dwells there in secret.

August 30

The Spirit of Love

The fruit of the Spirit is love.
—Galatians 5:22

I beseech you...for the love of the Spirit.
—Romans 15:30

Who also declared unto us your love in the Spirit.
—Colossians 1:8

These verses lead us up into the very center of the inner sanctuary. We will have to learn that love is not only one of the fruits of the Spirit, but it is also the most important of all. The Spirit is nothing less than divine love, come down to dwell in us. We have only as much of the Spirit as we have of love.

God is *Spirit.* All life is owing to the Spirit of God. This is so because God is also *love.* He is love as seen in the Father giving all He has to the Son and the Son seeking all He has in the Father. In this life of love between the Father and the Son, the Spirit is the bond of fellowship. The Father is the loving One, the fountain. The Son is the beloved One, the great reservoir of love, always receiving and giving back. The Spirit is the living love that makes them one. In Him the divine life of love has its ceaseless flow and overflowing.

The outpouring of the Spirit is the inpouring of love. This love now possesses the heart. That same love with which God loves Jesus, ourselves, and all His children overflows from us to all the world. If we trust and yield to this love, it will also be power for us to live. The Spirit is the life of the love of God. The Spirit in us is the love of God taking up abode within us.

Live in the love of Jesus, and you will be a messenger of His love to everyone you meet. The more intimate your communion with Jesus through the Holy Spirit, the more accurate your translation of that life will be into the relationships of daily life.

The compensation for our not being able to see God is that *we have one another to love!* (See 1 John 3:14–24.) If we do this, God lives in us! We do not have to ask if our brother is worthy: God's love for us and for him is love for the unworthy. It is with this divine love that the Holy Spirit fills us and teaches us to love our brothers.

August 31

The Unity of the Spirit

That ye walk...with all lowliness and meekness, with longsuffering, forbearing one another in love; endeavouring to keep the unity of the Spirit in the bond of peace. There is one body, and one Spirit.
—Ephesians 4:1–4

Now there are diversities of gifts, but the same Spirit....But all these worketh that one and the selfsame Spirit, dividing to every man severally as he will....For by one Spirit are we all baptized into one body...and have been all made to drink into one Spirit.
—1 Corinthians 12:4, 11, 13

In the first three chapters of Ephesians, Paul set forth the glory of Christ Jesus as the Head of the church and the glory of God's grace in the church as the body of Christ. The body of Christ is indwelt by the Holy Spirit, growing up into a habitation of God through the Spirit.

In the second half of the epistle, Paul taught how the believer is to walk worthy of his calling. The very first lesson he had to give in regard to this life and walk on earth (Ephesians 4:1–4) rests on the truth that the Holy Spirit has united us not only to Christ in heaven, but also to Christ's body on earth. The Spirit dwells in Christ in heaven, in the believer on earth, and most especially in Christ's body, with all its members.

The full, healthy action of the Spirit can be found only where the right relationship exists between the individual and the whole body. The believer's first concern in his Christian walk must be to see that the unity of the Spirit is maintained. If this unity of the one Spirit and one body were fully acknowledged, the main virtue of the Christian life would be lowliness and meekness. (See Ephesians 4:2–3.)

Each person would give up self for others. Everyone would be patient with one another in love amid all differences and shortcomings. In this way, the new commandment would be kept, and the Spirit of love would sacrifice itself completely for others.

To keep the unity of the Spirit by living in fellowship with believers around me is life in the Spirit. It has taken time, prayer, and faith to know the Spirit of God within you. It will take time, prayer, faith, and much love to know the Spirit of God in your brother.

September

September 1

Pardon and Healing

But that ye may know that the Son of man hath power on earth to forgive sins, (then saith he to the sick of the palsy,) Arise, take up thy bed, and go unto thine house.
—Matthew 9:6

Man is a mixture of opposing natures; he is spirit and matter, soul and body. On one side he is the son of God, on the other he is doomed to destruction because of the fall. Sin in his soul and sickness in his body bear witness to the hold that death has over him. It is this twofold nature that has been redeemed by grace. It was the psalmist who cried, *"Bless the LORD, O my soul....Who forgiveth all thine iniquities; who healeth all thy diseases"* (Psalm 103:2–3). When Isaiah foresaw the deliverance of his people, he added, *"And the inhabitant shall not say, I am sick: the people that dwell therein shall be forgiven their iniquity"* (Isaiah 33:24).

This prediction was accomplished when Jesus the Redeemer came down to this earth. He showed us that the preaching of the gospel and the healing of the sick went together in the salvation that He came to bring. *"The blind receive their sight, and the lame walk...and the poor have the gospel preached to them"* (Matthew 11:5).

This truth is nowhere more evident than in the healing of the paralytic. The Lord Jesus began by saying to him, *"Thy sins be forgiven thee"* (Matthew 9:5), after which He added, *"Arise, take up thy bed, and go"* (v. 6). In the eyes of God sin and sickness are as closely united as the body and the soul.

We see, in the accounts given in the Gospels, that it was more difficult for Jews at that time to believe in the pardon of their sins than in healing. Now, it is the opposite. The Christian church has heard so much about the forgiveness of sins that the soul easily receives the message of grace. But divine healing is rarely mentioned. In order to receive healing, it is usually necessary to begin by confessing sin and desiring to live a holy life. Unbelief may attempt to separate these two gifts, healing and forgiveness, but they are always united in Christ. He is always the same Savior both of the soul and of the body, equally ready to grant pardon and healing. The redeemed may always cry, *"Bless the LORD, O my soul.... Who forgiveth all thine iniquities; who healeth all thy diseases."*

Because of Your Unbelief

Then came the disciples to Jesus apart, and said, Why could not we cast him out? And Jesus said unto them, Because of your unbelief: for verily I say unto you, If ye have faith as a grain of mustard seed, ye shall say unto this mountain, Remove hence to yonder place; and it shall remove; and nothing shall be impossible unto you.
—Matthew 17:19–20

When the Lord Jesus sent His disciples into parts of Palestine, He endued them with a double power, to cast out spirits and to heal all sickness and infirmity. (See Matthew 10:1.) He did the same for the seventy who came back to Him with joy, saying, *"Lord, even the devils are subject unto us through thy name"* (Luke 10:17).

On the day of the transfiguration, a father brought his son who was possessed with a demon to the disciples, beseeching them to cast out the evil spirit, but they could not. After Jesus had cured the child, the disciples asked why they had been unable to do it themselves. He answered, *"Because of your unbelief."* Unbelief, not the will of God, was the cause of their defeat.

Today, divine healing has almost entirely disappeared from the church. Two reasons are usually offered. The greater number think that miracles were limited to the early church in order to establish Christianity.

Other believers say that if the church has lost these gifts, it is because she has become worldly. If men and women would live the life of faith and of the Holy Spirit, the church would again see the manifestation of the same gifts as in former times.

The Bible does not grant us to believe that the gifts of healing were granted only to the early church. On the contrary, the promise that Jesus made shortly before His ascension appears to be applicable to all times. (See Mark 16:15–18.) Jesus still heals both soul and body, and the Holy Spirit is always ready to give us some manifestations of His power. When we ask why this divine power is not seen more often, He answers us, *"Because of your unbelief."* The more the Spirit of God lives in the souls of believers, the more miracles He will work in the body. By this, the world will recognize what redemption means.

September 3

Jesus and the Doctors

And a certain woman, which had an issue of blood twelve years, and had suffered many things of many physicians, and had spent all that she had, and was nothing bettered, but rather grew worse, when she had heard of Jesus, came in the press behind, and touched his garment. For she said, If I may touch but his clothes, I shall be whole. And straightway the fountain of her blood was dried up; and she felt in her body that she was healed of that plague. And Jesus, immediately knowing in himself that virtue had gone out of him, turned him about in the press, and said, Who touched my clothes?...Daughter, thy faith hath made thee whole; go in peace, and be whole of thy plague.
—Mark 5:25–30, 34

We may be thankful to God for giving us doctors, for a large number of them truly seek to do all they can do to alleviate suffering. Some are zealous servants of Jesus Christ. Nevertheless, it is Jesus Himself who is the first and the greatest Physician.

Jesus, in taking our human body upon Himself, delivered it from the dominion of sin. He has made our bodies temples of the Holy Spirit, and members of His own body. (See 1 Corinthians 6:15, 19.) Even in our day, how many have been given up by the doctors as incurable? How many cases of cancer, infection, paralysis, heart disease, blindness, and deafness have been healed by Him? Is it not then astonishing that so small a number of the sick come to Him?

Jesus' method is quite different from that of earthly physicians. They seek to make use of remedies that are found in the natural world, while the healing that proceeds from Jesus is by divine power—that of the Holy Spirit. The difference between these two ways of healing is very striking.

Healing is granted after confession of sin; therefore, it brings the sufferer nearer to Jesus. It causes him to experience His love and power; it begins within him a new life of faith and holiness.

If no "elder" is at hand to pray the prayer of faith, do not be afraid to go to the Lord yourself in solitude. Commit the care of your body to Him. Get quiet before Him, and say, "I will be healed." It may take some time to break the chains of your unbelief, but assuredly none who wait on Him will be ashamed. (See Psalm 25:3.)

Health and Salvation by Jesus' Name

Be it known unto you all, and to all the people of Israel, that by the name of Jesus Christ of Nazareth, whom ye crucified, whom God raised from the dead, even by him doth this man stand here before you whole...Neither is there salvation in any other: for there is none other name under heaven given among men, whereby we must be saved.
—Acts 4:10, 12

After Pentecost, the paralytic was healed through Peter and John at the gate of the temple. It was *"in the name of Jesus Christ of Nazareth"* that they said to him, *"Rise up and walk"* (Acts 3:6).

As a result of this miracle, many people who had heard the Word believed. (See Acts 4:4.) The next day, Peter repeated these words before the Sanhedrin: *"By the name of Jesus Christ of Nazareth...doth this man stand here before you whole"*; and then he added, *"There is none other name under heaven...whereby we must be saved."* This statement of Peter declares to us that the name of Jesus both heals and saves.

Peter clearly stated this to the Sanhedrin where, having spoken of healing, he went on to speak of salvation by Christ. (See Acts 4:10, 12.) Salvation will not be complete for us until our bodies enjoy the full redemption of Christ. Even here on earth, the health of our bodies is a fruit of the salvation that Jesus has acquired for us.

The tendency of man is to bring about his own salvation by his works, and it is only with difficulty that he comes to receive it by faith. But when it is a question of healing, he has more difficulty in seizing it. It is much easier for him to accept well-known, earthly remedies for his body. Why, then, should he seek divine healing?

God grants healing to glorify the name of Jesus. Let us seek to be healed by Jesus, so that His name may be glorified. It is the will of God to glorify His Son in the church, and He will do it wherever He finds faith. God is ready to manifest the power of His Son, and to do it in striking ways in bodies as well as in souls. Let us believe it for ourselves; let us believe it for others. Let us give ourselves to believe with firm faith in the power of the name of Jesus. Let us ask great things in His name, counting on His promise, and we will see that God still does wonders by the name of His holy Son.

September 5

Not by Our Own Power

And when Peter saw it, he answered unto the people, ye men of Israel, why marvel ye at this? or why look ye so earnestly on us, as though by our own power or holiness we had made this man to walk?
—Acts 3:12

As soon as the crippled man had been healed at the gate of the temple, the people ran to Peter and John. Peter, seeing this miracle was attributed to their power and holiness, lost no time in setting them right by telling them that all the glory of this miracle belonged to Jesus, that it is He in whom we must believe.

Peter and John were undoubtedly full of faith and of holiness; but they knew that their holiness was not of themselves, that it was of God through the Holy Spirit. They hastened, then, to declare that in this act of healing, their efforts counted for nothing; it was the work of the Lord alone! This is the purpose of divine healing: to be a proof of the power of Jesus, to be a witness in the eyes of men of what He is, proclaiming His divine intervention and attracting hearts to Him. Those whom the Lord uses in helping others should remember Peter's words: "[Not] *by our own power or holiness.*"

It is necessary to insist on this because of the tendency of believers to think the contrary. Those who have recovered their health in answer to *"the prayer of faith"* (James 5:15) and *"the effectual fervent prayer of a righteous man"* (v. 16) are in danger of being too much occupied with the human instrument that God is pleased to employ, and to think that the power lies in man's piety.

Remember this: it is not by our own power or holiness that we obtain grace, but by a faith quite simple—a childlike faith—that knows that it has no power or holiness of its own, and that commits itself completely to Him. He is faithful, and He can fulfill His promise through His almighty power. Oh, let us not seek to do or to be anything of ourselves! It is only as we feel our own powerlessness, and expect everything from God and His Word, that we realize the glorious way in which the Lord heals sickness by faith in His name.

According to the Measure of Faith

And Jesus said unto the centurion, Go thy way; and as thou hast believed, so be it done unto thee. And his servant was healed in the selfsame hour.
—Matthew 8:13

This passage of Scripture demonstrates one of the principal laws of the kingdom. Not only does God give or withhold His grace according to the faith or unbelief of each, but also it is granted in greater or lesser measure in proportion to the faith that receives it. Faith in God is nothing less than the full opening of the heart to receive everything from God. Therefore, man can receive divine grace only according to his faith. This applies as much to divine healing as to any other grace of God.

Two questions are often asked. First, is it not God's will that His children should, at times, remain in a state of sickness? Second, since it is recognized that divine healing brings with it greater spiritual blessing than the sickness itself, why does God allow some of His children to remain sick for many years and still bless them in communion with Himself? The answer to these two questions is that God gives to His children according to their faith.

We have already remarked that the church's faith in divine healing has diminished until it has almost disappeared. Believers do not seem to be aware that they may ask God for healing. They have come to seek only submission to His will. In such conditions, the Lord gives them what they ask. He would have been willing to give them much more—to grant them healing in answer to the prayer of faith—but they lacked the faith to receive it.

God always meets His children where they are. The sick ones who have desired to be submissive to His will enjoy a deep inner communion with Him. But they might have been able to receive healing, in addition, as a proof that God accepted their submission. If this has not happened, it is because faith has failed to ask for it.

We commend, then, to every suffering one who is seeking to know Jesus as his divine Healer, not to let himself be hindered by his unbelief and to doubt the promises of God. Be strong in faith, giving glory to God. If with all your heart you trust in God, you will be abundantly blessed. Do not doubt it. Persevere in believing in Him with the firm assurance that His healing power will glorify Him in you even as it heals you.

September 7

The Way of Faith

And straightway the father of the child cried out, and said with tears, Lord, I believe; help thou mine unbelief.
—Mark 9:24

These words have been a help to thousands of souls in their pursuit of salvation and the gifts of God. Notice that it is in relation to an afflicted child that they were said, as the child's father sought healing from the Lord Jesus. In them, we see that in one and the same soul a struggle between faith and unbelief can occur. It is not without a struggle that we come to believe in Jesus and in His power to heal.

I speak here especially to sufferers who do not doubt the power or the will of the Lord Jesus to heal in this day, but who lack the boldness to accept healing for themselves. They believe in the divine power of Christ; but they shrink back from accepting healing.

Take notice, first, that without faith no one can be healed. When the father of the afflicted child said to Jesus, *"If thou canst do any thing, have compassion on us, and help us"* (Mark 9:22), Jesus replied, *"If thou canst believe"* (v. 23). Jesus had the power to heal, and He was ready to do it, but He cast responsibility on the man. *"If thou canst believe, all things are possible to him that believeth"* (v. 23).

Prayer without faith is powerless. It is *"the prayer of faith"* (James 5:15) that saves the sick. You must be able to surrender your body absolutely into the Lord's hands. Faith receives healing as a spiritual grace that proceeds from the Lord, even while there is no change in the body. Faith can glorify God and say, *"Bless the Lord, O my soul…who healeth all thy diseases"* (Psalm 103:1, 3). The Lord requires this faith so that He may heal.

Confess to the Lord the difficulty you have in believing Him. Tell Him you want to be rid of unbelief. He calls on you to trust in Him and, by His grace, faith will triumph in you. Say to Him, "Lord, I am aware of the unbelief that is in me. I want to conquer this unbelief. You, Lord, will give me the victory. I desire to believe, and by Your grace, I will believe. Yes, Lord, I believe, for You help me with my unbelief." It is when we are in intimate communion with the Lord that unbelief is conquered.

It is necessary to testify to faith. Believe what the Lord says to you and believe what He is. Lean completely on His promises.

Your Body Is the Temple of the Spirit

Know ye not that your bodies are the members of Christ? shall I then take the members of Christ, and make them the members of an harlot? God forbid....Know ye not that your body is the temple of the Holy Ghost which is in you, which ye have of God, and ye are not your own? For ye are bought with a price: therefore glorify God in your body.
—1 Corinthians 6:15, 19–20

When the Bible speaks of the indwelling of the Holy Spirit, we often limit His presence to the spiritual part of our being. But, the Bible says expressly, *"Know ye not that your body is the temple of the Holy Ghost?"* The church needs to understand that the body has a part in redemption by which it becomes the dwelling place of the Spirit. The church must also recognize the place that healing has in the Bible and in the counsels of God.

The account of creation tells us that man is composed of three parts. God first breathed life into the body, *"the breath of life"* (Genesis 2:7). By this union of Spirit with matter, man became *"a living soul"* (v. 7). The soul finds its place between the body and the spirit: the link that binds them together. By the body, the soul relates to the external world; by the spirit, it relates with the spiritual world. By means of the soul, the spirit can subject the body to heavenly powers; by means of the soul, the body can act on the spirit and attract it earthward. The soul must choose between the voice of God, speaking to the spirit, or the voice of the world, speaking through the senses.

We know what sin and Satan have done with this arrangement. By means of the body, the spirit was tempted and seduced; it became a slave of the senses. We know also what God has done to destroy the work of Satan and to accomplish the purpose of creation.

The Holy Spirit brings to our souls the life of Jesus—His holiness, joy, and strength—He comes also to impart to the sick body all the vitality of Christ as soon as the hand of faith is willing to receive it. When the body is fully subjected to Christ, crucified with Him, renouncing all self-will, desiring nothing but to be the Lord's temple, it is then that the Holy Spirit manifests the power of the risen Savior in the body. Only then can He manifest His power in us, to show that He knows how to set His temple free from the domination of sickness, sin, and Satan.

The Body for the Lord

Meats for the belly, and the belly for meats: but God shall destroy both it and them. Now the body is not for fornication, but for the Lord; and the Lord for the body.
—1 Corinthians 6:13

One theologian has said that the redemption and glorification of the body is the end of the ways of God. It is this that makes the inhabitants of heaven awestruck when they contemplate the glory of the Son. Clothed with a glorified human body, Jesus has taken His place on the throne of God. It shall be recognized in that day when regenerated humanity, forming the body of Christ, shall be truly and visibly the temple of the living God. (See 1 Corinthians 6:19.)

In anticipation of this new condition of things, the Lord attaches great importance to the indwelling of our bodies here on earth by His Spirit. This truth is so little understood by believers. Many of them, believing that this body belongs to them, use it as it pleases them. Not understanding how much the sanctification of the soul and spirit depends on the body, they do not grasp the meaning of the words, *"The body is...for the Lord."*

What does this mean? The apostle had just said, *"Meats for the belly, and the belly for meats: but God shall destroy both it and them."* Eating and drinking afford the Christian an opportunity of carrying out this truth. By eating, sin and the fall came about. It was also through eating that the Devil tempted our Lord. Thus Jesus sanctified His body in eating only according to the will of His Father. (See Matthew 4:4.) Many believers fail to watch over their bodies, to observe a holy sobriety through the fear of rendering it unfit for the service of God.

The apostle spoke also of fornication, this sin that defiles the body, in opposition to the words, *"The body is...for the Lord."* It is not simply sexual promiscuity outside the married state, but all lack of sobriety regarding sensual pleasure is condemned in these words: *"Your body is the temple of the Holy Ghost"* (1 Corinthians 6:19). In the same way, all that goes to maintain the body—to clothe it, strengthen it, give it rest or enjoyment—should be under the control of the Holy Spirit. Just as the temple was constructed solely for God and for His service, even so our bodies have been created for the Lord and for Him alone.

The Lord for the Body

Meats for the belly, and the belly for meats: but God shall destroy both it and them. Now the body is not for fornication, but for the Lord; and the Lord for the body.
—1 Corinthians 6:13

There is reciprocity in God's relationship with man. What God has been for me, I should, in turn, be for Him. And what I am for Him, He desires to be for me. If, in His love, He gives Himself fully to me, it is in order that I may lovingly give myself fully to Him.

In saying, *"The body is…for the Lord,"* we express the desire to regard our bodies as wholly consecrated, offered in sacrifice to the Lord, and sanctified by Him. In saying, *"The Lord for the body,"* we express the precious certainty that our offering has been accepted. We show we believe that the Lord will impart to our bodies His own strength and holiness, and that He will strengthen and keep us.

But it is especially in divine healing that we see the truth of these words, *"The Lord for the body."* Yes, Jesus, the sovereign and merciful Healer, is always ready to save and cure.

In Switzerland some years ago, there was a young girl near death from tuberculosis. The doctor had advised a milder climate, but she was too weak to take the journey. She learned that Jesus is the Healer of the sick and believed the good news. One night, it seemed to her that the body of the Lord drew near to her, and that she ought to take these words literally, "His body for our body." From this moment, she began to improve. Some time after, she became a zealous worker for the Lord among women. She had learned to understand that the Lord is for the body.

Dear sick one, the Lord has shown you, by sickness, what power sin has over the body. By your healing, He would like to show you the power of redemption of the body. He calls to show you what you have not understood until now, that "the body is for the Lord." Give Him your body. Give it to Him with your sickness and your sin, the original source of sickness. Always believe that the Lord has taken charge of this body, and will manifest with power that He is the Lord. The Lord sends us His divine strength from heaven, where He is now clothed in His glorified body. He is willing thus to manifest His power in our bodies.

Do Not Consider Your Body

I speak after the manner of men because of the infirmity of your flesh: for as ye have yielded your members servants to uncleanness and to iniquity unto iniquity; even so now yield your members servants to righteousness unto holiness. For when ye were the servants of sin, ye were free from righteousness. What fruit had ye then in those things whereof ye are now ashamed? for the end of those things is death.
—Romans 6:19–21

When God promised to give Abraham a son, the patriarch would never have been able to believe this promise if he had considered his own body already aged and worn out. But Abraham saw only God and His promise.

This kind of faith enables us to lay hold of the difference between the healing that is expected from earthly remedies alone and the healing that is looked for from God. When we use earthly remedies alone for healing, all the attention of the sick one is on the body. Divine healing, however, calls us to turn our attention away from the body, abandoning ourselves to the Lord's care.

In order for the child of God to receive divine healing, the following must take place: sin must be confessed and renounced, one must completely surrender to the Lord, self must be yielded up to be wholly in His hands, and one must firmly believe that Jesus desires to take charge of the body. Then, the healing becomes the beginning of a new life of intimate communion with the Lord.

What a contrast this is from the greater number of sick people who look for healing from earthly remedies alone. What infinite care they exercise in observing the least symptom and what they eat and drink. How much they are taken up with whether they are thought of and visited by others. How much time is devoted to considering the body and what it needs, rather than to the Lord and the relationship that He seeks with their souls.

All this is totally different when healing is sought for in faith from the loving God. Then the first thing to learn is to cease to be anxious about the state of your body. You have trusted it to the Lord, and He has taken the responsibility. The commandment of Christ, *"Take no thought for...your body"* (Matthew 6:25), appears here in a new light.

Discipline and Sanctification

God...chasteneth...us...for our profit, that we might be partakers of his holiness.
—Hebrews 12:7, 10

If a man therefore purge himself from these, he shall be a vessel unto honour, sanctified, and meet for the master's use, and prepared unto every good work.
—2 Timothy 2:21

To sanctify anything is to set it apart—to consecrate it—to God and to His service. The temple at Jerusalem was holy; that is to say, it was dedicated to God, to serve Him as a dwelling place. The priests were holy, chosen to serve God and ready to work for Him. In the same way, the Christian ought also to be sanctified, at the Lord's disposal, ready to do every good work.

When the people of Israel went out of Egypt, the Lord reclaimed them for His service as a holy people. He said to Pharaoh, *"Let my people go, that they may serve me"* (Exodus 7:16). Set free from their hard bondage, the children of Israel immediately entered the service of God. Their deliverance led to their sanctification.

Again in this day, God is forming a holy people for Himself, and Jesus sets us free so that we may join them. He *"gave himself for us, that he might redeem us from all iniquity, and purify unto himself a peculiar people, zealous of good works"* (Titus 2:14). It is the Lord who breaks the chains by which Satan tries to hold us in bondage. He wants us to be wholly free to serve Him.

Because believers still cannot understand that sanctification means an entire consecration to God, they cannot really believe that healing will quickly follow the sanctification of the sick one. Good health is too often for them only a matter of personal comfort and enjoyment that they may dispose of at their will. God cannot minister to this kind of selfishness. If they understood better that God requires His children to be *"sanctified, and meet for the master's use,"* they would not be surprised to see Him giving healing and renewed strength to those who have learned to place their entire bodies at His disposal, willing to be sanctified and employed in His service by the Holy Spirit. The Spirit of healing is also the Spirit of sanctification.

Sickness and Death

Surely he shall deliver thee from the snare of the fowler, and from the noisome pestilence...Thou shalt not be afraid for the terror by night; nor for the arrow that flieth by day; nor for the pestilence that walketh in darkness; nor for the destruction that wasteth at noonday....With long life will I satisfy him, and show him my salvation.
—Psalm 91:3, 5–6, 16

They shall still bring forth fruit in old age; they shall be fat and flourishing.
—Psalm 92:14

An objection is often made to the words of the apostle James, *"The prayer of faith shall save the sick"* (James 5:15), in this form: If we have the promise of being healed in answer to prayer, how can it be possible to die? And some add, How can a sick person know whether God has not decided that we will die by such a sickness? In such a case, would not prayer be useless, and would it not be a sin to ask for healing?

According to the Word of God, our heavenly Father wills to see His children in good health so that they may labor in His service. For the same reason, He wills to set them free from sickness as soon as they have made a confession of sin and prayed with faith for healing. For the believer who has walked with his Savior and under the influence of the Holy Spirit, it is not necessary that he should die of sickness. The death of the believer is to fall asleep in Jesus Christ. (See 1 Corinthians 15:18.) For him, death is only sleep after fatigue, the entering into rest.

It is God's will to heal His children after the confession of their sins, and in answer to the prayer of faith. They are healed of it because it attacks the body, the dwelling place of the Holy Spirit. The sick one should then desire healing, so that the power of God may be made manifest in him, and that he may serve Him in accomplishing His will. In this, he clings to the revealed will of God.

Remember that faith is the confident attitude of a child who honors his Father and counts on His love. He knows His Father fulfills His promises and is faithful to communicate the new strength that flows from redemption to the body as well as to the soul, until the moment of departure comes.

The Holy Spirit, the Spirit of Healing

Now there are diversities of gifts, but the same Spirit....to another faith by the same Spirit; to another the gifts of healing by the same Spirit....But all these worketh that one and the selfsame Spirit, dividing to every man severally as he will.
—1 Corinthians 12:4, 9, 11

What is it that distinguishes the children of God? It is that God dwells in the midst of them and reveals Himself to them in power. God sends the Holy Spirit to His church to act in her with power. In every age, the church may look for manifestations of the Spirit, for they form our indissoluble unity: *"one body, and one Spirit"* (Ephesians 4:4).

The Spirit operates in various members of the church at different times. It is possible to be filled with the Spirit for one special work and not for another. There are also times in the history of the church when certain gifts of the Spirit are given with power, while at the same time unbelief may hinder other gifts. Wherever the more abundant life of the Spirit is to be found, we may expect Him to manifest all His gifts.

The gift of healing is one of the most beautiful manifestations of the Spirit. It is recorded of Jesus, *"God anointed Jesus of Nazareth with the Holy Ghost and with power: who went about doing good, and healing all that were oppressed of the devil"* (Acts 10:38). The Holy Spirit in Him was a healing Spirit, and He was the same in the disciples after Pentecost. The abundant outpouring of the Spirit produced abundant healings in the early churches. (See Acts 3:7; 4:30; 5:12, 15–16; 9:41; 14:9–10; 16:18–19; 19:12; 28:8–9.)

Christ's redemption extends its powerful working to the body, and the Holy Spirit is in charge of transmitting and maintaining it in us. It is Jesus who heals, Jesus who baptizes with the Holy Spirit, and Jesus who baptized His disciples with the same Spirit. It is He who sends us the Holy Spirit here on earth to take sickness away from us and to restore us to health.

Divine healing takes place wherever the Spirit of God works in power. Examples of this are to be found in the lives of the Reformers, and in other men of God called to His service over the centuries. But there are even more promises accompanying the outpouring of the Holy Spirit that have not been fulfilled up to this time. Let us live in a holy expectation, praying for the Lord to accomplish them in us.

Persevering Prayer

And he spake a parable unto them to this end, that men ought always to pray, and not to faint; saying, There was in a city a judge, which feared not God, neither regarded man: and there was a widow in that city; and she came unto him, saying, Avenge me of mine adversary. And he would not for a while: but afterward he said within himself, Though I fear not God, nor regard man; yet because this widow troubleth me, I will avenge her, lest by her continual coming she weary me. And the Lord said, Hear what the unjust judge saith. And shall not God avenge his own elect, which cry day and night unto him, though he bear long with them? I tell you that he will avenge them speedily. Nevertheless when the Son of man cometh, shall he find faith on the earth?
—Luke 18:1–8

The necessity of praying with perseverance is the secret of all spiritual life. What a blessing to be able to ask the Lord for a particular answer, knowing with certainty that it is His will to answer prayer! That our prayers can obtain from the Lord something He would not otherwise give should prove that man has been created in the image of God, that he is His friend and fellow worker. It is to Christ's intercession that the Father responds, and to which He grants His divine favors.

Jesus teaches us in these words: *"All things whatsoever ye shall ask in prayer, believing, ye shall receive"* (Matthew 21:22). Sometimes, healing is immediate and complete. But it may happen that we have to wait. That which God appears at first to refuse, He grants later in response to the prayer of the woman from Canaan, to the prayer of the widow, and to that of the friend who knocks at midnight. (See Matthew 15:22–28; Luke 18:3–8; 11:5–8.) Without regarding either change or answer, faith that is grounded on the Word of God, and that continues to pray, ends by gaining the victory. *"Shall not God avenge his own elect which cry day and night unto him, though he bear long with them? I tell you that he will avenge them speedily."*

God's timing is perfect. He can delay anything as He sees necessary, and then speedily bring the answer at just the right moment. The same two abilities should belong to our faith. Let us grasp the grace that is promised to us, as if we had already received it, but wait with untiring patience for the answer that is slow to come. Such faith belongs to living in Him.

Let Him Who Is Healed Glorify God

And immediately he received his sight, and followed him, glorifying God: and all the people, when they saw it, gave praise unto God.
—Luke 18:43

And he leaping up stood, and walked, and entered with them into the temple, walking, and leaping, and praising God.
—Acts 3:8

It is a prevalent idea that silent suffering inclines the soul to seek the Lord more than the distractions of active life. For this reason, sick people sometimes hesitate to ask for healing from the Lord. They believe the sickness may be more of a spiritual blessing than health. To think in this way is to ignore that healing is divine. Divine healing binds us more closely to Him. Thus, the believer who has been healed by Him can glorify Him far better than the one who remains sick. Sickness can glorify God only insofar as it manifests His power. (See John 9:3; 11:4.)

Healing by means of remedies shows us the power of God in nature, but it does not bring us into direct contact with Him. Divine healing, however, is an act proceeding directly from God, relying on nothing but the Holy Spirit.

In divine healing, contact with God is essential, and it is for this reason that an examination of the conscience and the confession of sins should be the preparation for it. (See 1 Corinthians 11:30–32; James 5:15–16.) One who is healed by divine intervention alone is called to consecrate himself entirely to the Lord. (See 1 Corinthians 6:13, 19.) All this depends on the act of faith that takes the Lord's promise, yields to Him, and never doubts that the Lord takes immediate possession of what is consecrated to Him.

Health obtained under such conditions ensures spiritual blessings much greater than the mere restoration to health by ordinary means. When the Lord heals the body, it is so that He may take possession of it and dwell within it. The joy that then fills the soul is indescribable. In this exuberance, the healed one exalts the Lord and consecrates all his life to God.

When every sick person *expects* a manifestation of the Lord's presence, then healings will be multiplied. Each will produce a witness of the power of God, all ready to cry with the psalmist, *"Bless the Lord, O my soul…who healeth all thy diseases"* (Psalm 103:2–3).

Needing a Manifestation of God's Power

And now, Lord, behold their threatenings: and grant unto thy servants, that with all boldness they may speak thy word, by stretching forth thine hand to heal; and that signs and wonders may be done by the name of thy holy child Jesus. And when they had prayed, the place was shaken where they were assembled together; and they were all filled with the Holy Ghost, and they spake the word of God with boldness.
—Acts 4:29–31

Is it permissible to ask the Lord, *"Grant unto thy servants, that with all boldness they may speak thy word, by stretching forth thine hand to heal"*?

Imagine the apostles in the midst of Jerusalem and her unbelief. The rulers of the people were making threats, while the blinded multitude were refusing to accept Jesus. Today's world is no longer as openly hostile to the church because it has lost its fear of her. But a Christianity of mere form, in the sleep of indifference, is just as inaccessible as an openly resisting Judaism. Even in the present day, God's servants need His power to be clearly evident among them so that the Word can be preached with all boldness

The apostles knew well that it was not the eloquence of their preaching that caused the truth to triumph. It was necessary for God to stretch forth His hand, so that there might be healings and miracles, in the name of Jesus. Then could His servants, strengthened by His presence, speak with boldness.

The apostles counted on these words of the Lord before He ascended: *"Go ye into all the world, and preach the gospel to every creature....And these signs shall follow them that believe;...they shall lay hands on the sick, and they shall recover"* (Mark 16:15, 17–18). This charge indicates the divine vocation of the church. The promise that follows proves to us that the Lord acts in agreement with her. The apostles counted on this promise and prayed for the Lord to grant them this proof of His presence.

What new strength God's people would receive today if the Lord would thus stretch forth His hand! Many who are indifferent would be led to reflect and more than one doubter would regain confidence. The poor sinner would be forced to acknowledge that the Christian's God is the living God who does wonders, the God of love who blesses!

Sin and Sickness

And the prayer of faith shall save the sick, and the Lord shall raise him up; and if he have committed sins, they shall be forgiven him. Confess your faults one to another, and pray one for another, that ye may be healed. —James 5:15–16

Here, as in other Scriptures, the pardon of sins and the healing of sickness are closely united. James declared that a pardon of sins would be granted with the healing. For this reason, he desired to see confession of sin accompanying the prayer that claims healing. Unconfessed sin presents an obstacle to the prayer of faith. When called to treat a patient, a physician should first diagnose the cause of the disease. Our God also goes back to the primary cause of sickness—sin. It is the patient's part to confess the sin; it is God's part to grant the pardon that removes this first cause, so that healing can take place.

Sickness can be a consequence of sin. Often God permits sickness in order to show us our faults and purify us from them. The one who is sick is not necessarily a greater sinner than another who is in health. On the contrary, it is often the holiest whom God chastens, as we see from the example of Job. Sickness is also not always intended to check some fault that we can easily determine. Its main purpose is to draw the attention of the sick one to that which remains in him of the *"old man"* (Romans 6:6) and of all that hinders him from a life consecrated to his God.

The first step that the sick one has to take is to let the Holy Spirit of God probe his heart and convict him of sin. This will be followed by humiliation, a decision to break with sin, and confession. To confess our sins is to lay them down before God and to subject them to His judgment, with the full intention of falling into them no more. When we have confessed our sins, we must receive the promised pardon, believing that God gives it.

Once the soul has made a confession and obtained pardon, it is ready to grasp God's healing. It is when we keep far away from God that it is difficult to believe; confession and pardon bring us quite near to Him. It now becomes easy for the sick one to believe that he should be healed. A ray of life—His divine life—quickens the body; and the sick one proves that as soon as he is no longer separated from the Lord, the prayer of faith does save the sick.

September 19

Jesus Bore Our Sickness

Surely he hath borne our griefs, and carried our sorrows: yet we did esteem him stricken, smitten of God, and afflicted....He shall see of the travail of his soul, and shall be satisfied: by his knowledge shall my righteous servant justify many; for he shall bear their iniquities. Therefore will I divide him a portion with the great, and he shall divide the spoil with the strong; because...he bare the sin of many. —Isaiah 53:4, 11–12

Are you familiar with the beautiful fifty-third chapter of Isaiah? Enlightened by the Spirit of God, Isaiah predicted the sufferings of the Lamb of God and described the divine grace that would result from them.

The words *to bear* had to appear in this prophecy. These words must accompany the mention of sin, whether committed directly by the sinner or as transmitted to a substitute. The transgressor, the priest, and the atoning victim must all bear the sin. In the same way, it is because the Lamb of God has borne our sins that God smote Him for the iniquity of us all. Sin was not found in Him, but it was put on Him; He took it voluntarily. It is because He bore it that He has the power to save us. *"My righteous servant* [shall] *justify many, for he shall bear their iniquities....He shall divide the spoil with the strong; because...he bare the sin of many."* It is because our sins have been borne by Christ that we are delivered from them as soon as we believe this truth; consequently, we no longer have to bear them ourselves.

It is said not only that the Lord's righteous Servant bore our sins (v. 12), but also that He bore our griefs, or sicknesses (v. 4). Sin had attacked and ruined the soul and body equally. Having taken sickness as well as sin on Himself, He is in a position to set us free from the one as well as the other. In order for Him to accomplish this double deliverance, He expects only one thing from us: our faith.

As soon as a sick believer understands the meaning of the words, "Jesus has borne my sins," he is not afraid to say, "I no longer need to bear my sins." As soon as he fully believes that Jesus has borne our sicknesses, he is not afraid to say, "I no longer need to bear my sickness." Jesus, in bearing sin, bore sickness also. He has made payment for both, and He delivers us from both.

Is Sickness a Chastisement?

**For if we would judge ourselves, we should not be judged. But when we are judged, we are chastened of the Lord, that we should not be condemned with the world.
—1 Corinthians 11:31–32**

In writing to the Corinthians, the apostle Paul had to reprove them for the manner in which they observed the Lord's Supper, which had caused them to be chastised by God. Here we see sickness as a judgment of God, a chastisement for sin. Paul saw it as such, and added that it was in order to prevent them from falling more deeply into sin that they were thus afflicted. He warned them that if they would rather not be judged nor chastened by the Lord, they should examine themselves to discover the cause of their sickness and condemn their own sins.

Sickness is (more often than we know) a chastisement for sin. God *"doth not afflict willingly nor grieve the children of men"* (Lamentations 3:33). It is not without cause that He allows us to be deprived of health. Perhaps it is to make us more aware of a particular sin from which we can repent. *"Sin no more, lest a worse thing come unto thee"* (John 5:14). Perhaps we have become entangled in pride and worldliness. Or it may be that self-confidence or caprice has entered our service for God.

In any case, sickness is always a discipline that ought to awaken our attention and turn us from sin. Therefore, a sick person should begin by judging himself (see 1 Corinthians 11:31), by placing himself before his heavenly Father with a sincere desire to see anything that could have grieved Him. In so doing, he may count on the Holy Spirit's light to clearly show him his failure.

One may recognize vaguely that he commits sins, without attempting to define them. Even if he does, he may not believe it is possible to give them up. And if he goes so far as to renounce them, he may fail to count on God to put an end to the chastisement, despite the glorious assurance that Paul's words give us.

Scripture assures us that if we thus examine ourselves, the Lord will not judge us. Our Father chastens His children only as far as it is necessary. God seeks to deliver us from sin and self. As soon as we understand Him and break with these, sickness may cease; it has done its work.

God's Prescription for the Sick

Is any sick among you? let him call for the elders of the church; and let them pray over him, anointing him with oil in the name of the Lord: and the prayer of faith shall save the sick, and the Lord shall raise him up; and if he have committed sins, they shall be forgiven him.
—James 5:14–15

James 5:14–15, above all other Scriptures, most clearly declares to the sick what they have to do in order to be healed. The Bible teaches us that it is the will of God to see His children in good health. The apostle James had no hesitation in saying that *"the prayer of faith shall save the sick, and the Lord shall raise him up."*

Notice, first, that James made a distinction between affliction, or suffering, and sickness. In the previous verse, he said, *"Is any among you afflicted? let him pray"* (v. 13). He definitely did not say to ask for deliverance from suffering. No, suffering that may arise from various exterior causes is the portion of every Christian.

But in dealing with the words, *"Is any sick among you?"* James replied in quite another manner. He said with assurance that the sick one may ask for healing with confidence that he will obtain it. There is, therefore, a great difference between suffering and sickness. Suffering comes to us from without, and will cease only when Jesus triumphs over the world. Sickness is an evil that is in this body saved by Christ, that it may become the temple of the Holy Spirit. This body should be healed as soon as the sick believer receives the working of the Holy Spirit, the life of Jesus in him.

What course did James instruct the sick to follow? Let him call for the elders of the church to pray for him. He did not tell the sick believer to turn to physicians. The elders were the pastors and leaders of the churches, called to the ministry because they were filled with the Holy Spirit. Couldn't he pray for himself? Couldn't his friends have prayed? Yes, but it is not so easy for everybody to exercise the faith that obtains healing.

Finally, there is a promise of healing. The apostle spoke of it as the consequence of the prayer of faith. *"The prayer of faith shall save the sick, and the Lord shall raise him up."* Shouldn't we see in these words an unlimited promise that offers healing to whoever will pray in faith? May the Lord teach us to study His Word with the faith of a truly believing heart!

The Lord Who Heals You

I will put none of these diseases upon thee, which I have brought upon the Egyptians: for I am the LORD that healeth thee.
—Exodus 15:26

How often have we read these words without expectation that the Lord would fulfill them in us! That the people of God ought to be exempt from the diseases inflicted upon the Egyptians. But we believed that this promise applied only to the Old Testament, and that we who live under the New Testament cannot expect to be healed of sickness. Because we were obliged to recognize the superiority of the new covenant, we came, in our ignorance, to assert that sickness often brings great blessings. Consequently, we believed God had done well to withdraw what He had formerly promised, and to be no longer for us what He was for Israel, *"the LORD that healeth thee."*

Today, we see the church awakening and acknowledging her mistake. She sees that it was under the new covenant that the Lord Jesus acquired the title of Healer by all His miraculous healings. She is beginning to see that in charging His church to preach the gospel to every creature, He has promised to be with her *"alway*[s]*, even unto the end of the world"* (Matthew 28:20).

As the proof of His presence, His disciples should have the power to lay hands on the sick, who should then be healed. (See Mark 16:15–18.) There is nothing in the Bible to make the church believe that the promise made to Israel has since been retracted, and she hears, from the apostle James, this new promise: *"The prayer of faith shall save* [or heal] *the sick"* (James 5:15).

The church knows that unbelief has always limited (or set boundaries around) the Holy One of Israel (see Psalm 78:41), and she asks herself if it is not this same unbelief that is hindering the manifestation of God's power to heal today. Who can doubt it?

Healing and health are of little value if they do not glorify God and unite us more closely with Him. Thus, in the matter of healing, our faith must always be put to the test. He who counts on the name of his God will have the joy of receiving from God Himself the healing of the body, and of seeing it take place in a manner worthy of God, conformable to His promises. When we read these words, *"I am the LORD that healeth thee,"* let us not fear to answer eagerly, "Yes, Lord, You are the Lord who heals me."

Jesus Heals the Sick

He...healed all that were sick: that it might be fulfilled which was spoken by Esaias [Isaiah] the prophet, saying, Himself took our infirmities, and bare our sicknesses.
—Matthew 8:16–17

In a preceding chapter, we studied the words of the prophet Isaiah. If you still have any doubt as to the interpretation that has been given, I remind you of what the Holy Spirit caused the evangelist Matthew to write. It is expressly said, regarding all the sick ones whom Jesus healed, *"That it might be fulfilled which was spoken by Esaias* [Isaiah] *the prophet."* It was because Jesus had taken our sickness on Himself that He could, that He ought to, heal them. If He had not done so, one part of His work of redemption would have remained powerless and fruitless.

It is the generally accepted view that the miraculous healings done by the Lord Jesus are to be considered only as the symbol of spiritual graces. They are not seen to be a necessary consequence of redemption, although that is what the Bible declares. The body and the soul have been created to serve together as a habitation of God. The sickly condition of the body, as well as the soul, is a consequence of sin, and that is what Jesus came to bear.

When the Lord Jesus was on earth, it was not in the character of the Son of God that He cured the sick, but as the Mediator who bore our sickness. This enables us to understand why Jesus gave so much time to His healing work, and why, also, the Bible evangelists speak of it in a manner so detailed.

These healings give us not only the proof of His power during His life here on earth, but also the continual result of His work of mercy and of love, the manifestation of His power of redemption, which delivers the soul and body from the dominion of sin.

Yes, that was in very deed the purpose of God. If, then, Jesus bore our sicknesses as an integral part of the redemption, if He has healed the sick *"that it might be fulfilled which was spoken by Esaias,"* and if His Savior-heart is always full of mercy and of love, we can believe with certainty that to this very day it is the will of Jesus to heal the sick in answer to the prayer of faith.

Fervent and Effectual Prayer

Pray one for another, that ye may be healed. The effectual fervent prayer of a righteous man availeth much. [Elijah] was a man subject to like passions as we are, and he prayed earnestly that it might not rain: and it rained not on the earth by the space of three years and six months. And he prayed again, and the heaven gave rain, and the earth brought forth her fruit.
—James 5:16–18

James knew that a faith that obtains healing is not the fruit of human nature; therefore, he added that the prayer must be *"fervent."* In this James stood on the example of Elijah, a man of the same nature as we are, drawing the inference that our prayer ought to be of the same nature as his. How, then, did Elijah pray?

Elijah received from God the promise that rain was about to fall on the earth. (See 1 Kings 18:1.) Strong in the promise of his God, he went atop Mount Carmel to pray. (See verse 42; James 5:18.) God willed that it would rain, but the rain would come only at Elijah's request repeated with faith and perseverance until the appearance of the first cloud in the sky.

This is how prayer must be made for the sick. The promise of God, *"The Lord will raise him up"* (James 5:15), must be rested on, and His will to heal recognized. Jesus Himself teaches us to pray with faith that counts on the answer of God, *"What things soever ye desire, when ye pray, believe that ye receive them, and ye shall have them"* (Mark 11:24). After the prayer of faith, which receives what God has promised before it manifests itself, comes the prayer of perseverance, which does not lose sight of what has been asked until God has fulfilled His promise. (See 1 Kings 18:43.)

Where healing is delayed, let us remember that obstacles may exist over which only perseverance in prayer can triumph. Faith that ceases to pray cannot take hold of what God has nevertheless given. Do not let your faith be shaken by those things that are as yet beyond your reach. God's promise remains the same: *"The prayer of faith shall save the sick"* (James 5:15).

September 25

The Will of God

Thy will be done.
—Matthew 6:10

If the Lord will.
—James 4:15

In days of sickness, when doctors fail, recourse is taken to such Scriptures as, *"Thy will be done"* and *"If the Lord will."* They may become a stumbling block in the way of divine healing. How can I know, it is asked, whether or not it is God's will that I remain ill?

It is, indeed, impossible to pray with faith when we are not sure that we are asking according to the will of God. "I can," one may say, "pray fervently in asking God to cure me if it is possible." As long as one prays thus, one is praying with submission, but it is not the prayer of faith. That is possible only when we are certain that we are asking according to the will of God. The question then is, How can we know what the will of God is?

To know His divine will, we must be guided by the Word of God. It is His Word that promises us healing. The promise of James 5 is so absolute that it is impossible to deny it. This promise only confirms other passages, equally strong, that tell us that Jesus Christ has obtained for us the healing of our diseases, because He has borne our sicknesses. According to this promise, we have the right to healing, because it is a part of the salvation that we have in Christ. The Scriptures tell us that sickness is, in God's hands, the means of chastening His children for their sins, but that this discipline ceases to be exercised as soon as His suffering child acknowledges and turns from the sin.

Sick Christian, if you really seek to know what the will of God is in this, do not let yourself be influenced by the opinions of others, nor by your own prejudices, but listen to and study the Word of God. Examine whether it does indeed promise you that divine healing is a part of the redemption of Jesus, that God wills that every believer should have the right to claim it, and that the prayer of every child of God for healing will be heard. Ask this of the Word; it will answer you. According to the will of God, sickness is a discipline occasioned by sin (or shortcoming), and healing, granted to the prayer of faith, bears witness to His grace that pardons, that sanctifies, and that takes away sin.

September 26

Obedience and Health

There he made for them a statute and an ordinance, and there he proved them, and said, If thou wilt diligently hearken to the voice of the LORD thy God, and wilt do that which is right in his sight, and wilt give ear to his commandments, and keep all his statutes, I will put none of these diseases upon thee, which I have brought upon the Egyptians: for I am the LORD that healeth thee.
—Exodus 15:25–26

Israel was just released from Egypt when their faith was put to the test. God promised He would not put on the children of Israel any of the diseases that He had brought upon the Egyptians, as long as the Israelites would obey Him. They would be exposed to other trials. They might sometimes suffer hunger or have to contend with mighty foes, but sickness would not touch them. Had He not said, *"If thou wilt diligently hearken to the voice of the LORD thy God...I will put none of these diseases upon thee, which I have brought upon the Egyptians: for I am the LORD that healeth thee"*? Elsewhere He said, *"Ye shall serve the LORD your God,...and I will take sickness away from the midst of thee"* (Exodus 23:25). (See also Leviticus 7:12–16; 26:14–16; 28:15–61.)

This calls our attention to a truth of the greatest importance: the intimate relationship that exists between obedience and health; and between sanctification, which is the health of the soul, and divine healing, which ensures the health of the body. Both are comprised in the salvation that comes from God. Salvation is the redemption that the Savior has obtained for us; health is the salvation of the body, which also comes to us from the divine Healer; and, sanctification reminds us that true salvation and true health consist in being holy as God is holy. Thus it is in giving health to the body and sanctification to the soul that Jesus is really the Savior of His people.

Most Christians see nothing more in divine healing than a temporal blessing for the body, while in the promise of our holy God, its end is to make us holy. The call to holiness sounds stronger and clearer daily in the church. More and more believers are coming to understand that God wants them to be like Christ. The Lord is beginning, again, to make use of His healing virtue, seeking thereby to show us that, in our own day, the Holy One of Israel is still *"the LORD that healeth thee,"* and that it is His will to keep His people both in health of body and in obedience.

Job's Sickness and Healing

So went Satan forth from the presence of the LORD, and smote Job with sore boils from the sole of his foot unto his crown.
—Job 2:7

The veil that hides the unseen world is lifted for a moment in the mysterious history of Job. We see in it the temptations particular to sickness, and how Satan makes use of them to dispute with God, and to seek the perdition of the soul of man. God, on the other hand, seeks to sanctify it by the very same trial. In the case of Job, we see, in God's light, where sickness comes from, what result it should have, and how it is possible to be delivered from it.

Where does sickness come from? Opinions on this point differ vastly. Some hold that it is sent from God; others see it as the work of the Wicked One. Both are in error, as long as they hold their view to the exclusion of that held by the other party, while both are in the right if they admit that there are two sides to this question. Let us say, then, that sickness comes from Satan, but that it cannot exist without the permission of God. On the other hand, the power of Satan is that of an oppressor, who has no right to attack man, but whose claims on man are legitimate in that God decrees that he who yields himself to Satan places himself under his domination.

The history of Job illustrates this. His friends accused him, unjustly, of having committed sins of exceptional gravity, which caused his terrible suffering. This was, however, not the case, since God Himself had borne him witness that he was *"a perfect and an upright man, one that feareth God and escheweth evil"* (Job 2:3).

But in defending himself, Job went too far. Instead of humbling himself before the Lord, and recognizing his hidden sins, he attempted in all self-righteousness to justify himself. It was not until the Lord appeared to him that he came to say, *"I abhor myself, and repent in dust and ashes"* (Job 42:6).

If only the sick in our day understood that God has a distinct purpose in permitting their chastisement, and that as soon as it is attained—as soon as the Holy Spirit leads them to confess and forsake their sins and to consecrate themselves to the service of the Lord—the chastisement will no longer be needed. The Lord can and will deliver them!

Anointing in the Name of the Lord

Is any sick among you? let him call for the elders of the church; and let them pray over him, anointing him with oil in the name of the Lord.
—James 5:14

James' instructions to anoint the sick person with oil in the name of the Lord have given rise to controversy. Some have sought to infer that James had mentioned anointing with oil as a remedy to be employed. But since this prescription is made for all kinds of sickness, oil would have to possess a miraculous healing power. Let us see what the Scriptures tell us about anointing with oil, and what sense it attaches to the two words, *anointing* and *oil.*

It was the custom of the people in the East to anoint themselves with oil when they came out of the bath. We see, also, that all those who were called to the special service of God were to be anointed with oil. Thus the oil that was used to anoint the priests and the tabernacle was looked upon as *"most holy"* (Exodus 30:29). Wherever the Bible speaks of anointing with oil, it is an emblem of holiness and consecration. Nowhere in the Bible do we find any proof that oil was used as a medicine.

Anointing with oil is mentioned once in connection with sickness, but its place there was evidently as a religious ceremony and not as a medicine. Sometimes man feels the need of a visible sign, appealing to his senses, that may come to his aid to sustain his faith and enable him to grasp the spiritual meaning. The anointing, therefore, should symbolize to the sick one the action of the Holy Spirit who gives the healing.

Do we then need the anointing as well as the prayer of faith? The Word of God prescribes it. In order to follow God's Word, most of those who pray for healing receive the anointing. This is not so much because they regard it as indispensable, but to show that they are ready to submit to the Word of God in all things.

James, the head of the church of Jerusalem, faithful in preserving as far as possible the institutions of his fathers, continued the system of the Holy Spirit. And we also should regard it, not as a remedy, but as a pledge of the mighty virtue of the Holy Spirit, as a means of strengthening faith, a point of contact and of communion between the sick one and the members of the church who are called to anoint him with oil.

Full Salvation, Our High Privilege

**Son, thou art ever with me, and all that I have is thine.
—Luke 15:31**

We may talk a great deal about the father's love for the Prodigal Son, but when we think of the way he treated the elder brother, it brings to our hearts a truer sense of the wonderful love of the father.

In our parable, the elder son was always with his father and had two privileges: unceasing fellowship and unlimited partnership. But he was worse than the Prodigal Son, for, though always at home, he had never understood, received, or enjoyed these privileges. While the Prodigal Son was away from home, his elder brother was far from the *enjoyment* of home, even while living there.

Full salvation includes unceasing fellowship: *"Ever with me."* An earthly father loves his child and delights to make his child happy. *"God is love"* (1 John 4:8), and He delights to pour out His own nature on His people. Many people talk about God hiding His face, but there are only two things that ever caused God to do so—sin and unbelief. Nothing else can. *"God is love,"* and, speaking with all reverence, He can't help loving. We see His goodness toward the ungodly and His compassion on the erring. His fatherly love is manifested toward all His children.

Full salvation includes unlimited partnership: *"All that I have is thine."* The elder son complained of the father's gracious reception of the Prodigal while he had never been given a lamb to enjoy. The father, in tenderness, answered him, "Son, you were always in my house; you had only to ask and you would have been given everything you desired and required." And that is what our Father says to all His children.

But you are saying, "I am so weak; I cannot conquer my sins; I can't do anything." No, you cannot, but God can. For so long, He has been saying to you, "All that I have is yours. I have given it to you in Christ. All the Spirit's power and wisdom, all the riches of Christ, all the love of the Father—there is nothing that I have that is not yours."

I began by saying there are two classes of Christians: those who enjoy full salvation, and those who do not understand it. Well, if it is not clear to you, ask God to make it clear. Just let yourself go into the arms of God. Hear Him say, "Everything is yours."

You Are the Branches

Ye are the branches.
—John 15:5

What a simple thing it is to be a branch—the branch of a tree, or of a vine! The branch grows out of the vine and there it lives and bears fruit. It has no responsibility except receiving sap and nourishment from the root and stem.

If we only realized that our relationship to Jesus Christ, by way of the Holy Spirit, is like this! Instead of soul-weariness or exhaustion, our work would be a new experience, linking us to Jesus as nothing else can. I must understand, when I have to work, when I have to preach a sermon, or when I have to address a Bible class, that all the responsibility of the work is His. Christ desires that the very foundation of all your work should be this simple, blessed consciousness: Christ must care for everything.

Many a laborer has complained that he has too much work and not enough time for close communion with Jesus. What a sad thought that the bearing of fruit should separate the branch from the vine! That must be because we have looked at our work as something other than the branch bearing fruit.

Christians, you are the branches of the Lord Jesus Christ. Your heart may lack the consciousness of being a healthy, fruit-bearing branch, closely linked with Jesus. If you are not living in Him as you should be, then listen to Him saying, "I am the Vine. I will receive you, and I will draw you to Myself. I will bless you and strengthen you. I will fill you with My Spirit. I, the Vine, have taken you to be My branches. I have given Myself utterly to you; children, give yourselves utterly to Me. I became Man and died for you so that I might be entirely yours. Come and surrender yourselves entirely to be Mine."

Let our prayer be that He, the living Vine, will link each of us to Himself in such a way that we will walk victoriously, with our hearts singing, "He is my Vine, and I am His branch. I want nothing more, now that I have the everlasting Vine." Then, when you get alone with Him, worship and trust Him, love Him and wait for His love. "You are my Vine, and I am Your branch. It is enough; my soul is satisfied. Glory to Your blessed name!"

October

October 1

Abiding in Christ

He that saith he abideth in him ought himself also so to walk, even as he walked.
—1 John 2:6

Abiding in Christ and walking like Christ are two blessings of the new life presented here in their essential unity. The fruit of a life *in Christ* is a life *like Christ.*

To the first of these expressions, "abiding in Christ," we are no strangers. The wondrous parable of the vine and the branches, with the accompanying command, *"Abide in me, and I in you"* (John 15:4), has often been a source of rich instruction and comfort. And though we feel as if we have only imperfectly learned the lesson of abiding in Him, yet we have tasted something of the joy that comes when the soul can say, "Lord, You know all things. You know that I do abide in You." He also knows how often this fervent prayer still arises, "Blessed Lord, grant to me complete, unbroken abiding."

The second expression, "walking like Christ," is no less significant than the first. It is the promise of the wonderful power that abiding in Him will exert. As the fruit of our surrender to live wholly in Him, His life works so mightily in us that our walk—the outward expression of the inner life—becomes like His. The two are inseparably connected. The *abiding in* always precedes the *walking like* Him. Yet the desire to walk like Him must equally precede any large amount of abiding. Only then is the need for a close union fully realized. The heavenly Giver is free to bestow the fullness of His grace, because He sees that the soul is prepared to use it according to His design. When the Savior said, *"If ye keep my commandments, ye shall abide in my love"* (John 15:10), He meant this: "The surrender to walk like Me is the path to the full abiding in Me." Many will discover that this is the secret of their failure in abiding in Christ: they did not seek it with the idea of walking like Christ. The words of John invite us to look at the two truths in their vital connection and dependence on each other.

October

October 2

Just as He Has Done

For I have given you an example, that ye should do as I have done to you. —John 13:15

It was Jesus Christ, the beloved Redeemer of our souls, who spoke the words of our text. He had just humbled Himself to do the work of the slave by washing His disciples' feet. In doing so, His love demonstrated to the body the service that was lacking at the supper table. At the same time, He showed, in a striking symbol, what He had done for their souls in cleansing them from sin. In this twofold work of love, He set before them, just before parting, in one significant act, the whole work of His life as a ministry of blessing to body *and* soul. As He sat down, He said, *"I have given you an example, that ye should do as I have done to you."* All that they had seen in Him and experienced from Him is thus made the rule of their lives: "Even as I have done, you do also."

The words of the blessed Savior apply to us, too. To each one who knows that the Lord has washed away his sin, He commands with all the touching force of one who is going out to die, "Even as I have done to you, so do you also to others." Jesus Christ does indeed ask every one of us in everything to act just as we have seen Him do. What He has done to us, and still does each day, we are to do over again to others. In His humble, pardoning, saving love, He is our example; each of us is to be the copy and image of the Master.

At once, we think, "Alas, how seldom I have lived like Christ! How little I have even known that I was expected to live thus!" And yet, He is my Lord; He loves me, and I love Him. I must not entertain the thought of living in any other way than He would have me live. I must open my heart to His Word and fix my gaze on His example, until it exercises its divine power upon me and draws me with irresistible force to cry, "Lord, even as You have done, so will I do also."

October 3

As One Who Serves

If I then, your Lord and Master, have washed your feet; ye also ought to wash one another's feet.
—John 13:14

Y*e also ought to wash one another's feet"* are words that we want to fully understand. The form of a servant in which we see Him, the cleansing that was the objective of that service, the love that was its motivation—these are the three main thoughts.

First, let us look at the form of a servant. All was ready for the Last Supper, down to the water to wash the feet of the guests. But there was no slave to do the work. None of the Twelve thought of humbling himself. At once, Jesus rose, girded Himself with a towel, and began to wash their feet. Angels gazed with wonder! Christ, the Creator of the universe, chose the slave's place, took the soiled feet in His holy hands, and washed them.

In taking the form of a servant, Jesus proclaims the law of rank in the church of Christ. The higher one wishes to stand in grace, the more one must find his joy in being the servant of all. *"He that is greatest among you shall be your servant"* (Matthew 23:11). The higher I rise in the consciousness of being like Christ the deeper I will stoop to serve all around me.

The foot washing speaks of a double work—for the cleansing of the body, and for the saving of the soul. The follower of Jesus may not lose sight of this when commanded, *"Ye also ought to wash one another's feet."* Remembering that what is external is the gate to the inner spiritual life, he makes the salvation of the soul the first object in his ministry of love.

The spirit that will enable one to live such a life of loving service can be learned from Jesus alone. *"Having loved his own which were in the world, he loved them unto the end"* (John 13:1). Love never speaks of sacrifice. To bless the loved one, however unworthy, love willingly gives up all. It was love that made Jesus a servant. It is love that will make the servant's work such blessedness to us that we will persevere in it at all costs.

Live every day as the beloved of the Lord, in the experience that His love washes, cleanses, bears, and blesses you all the day long. His love flowing into you will flow out again from you, and make it your greatest joy to follow His example in washing the feet of others.

Our Head

Because Christ also suffered for us, leaving us an example, that ye should follow his steps...Who his own self bare our sins in his own body on the tree, that we, being dead to sins, should live unto righteousness. —1 Peter 2:21, 24

The call to follow Christ's example is so high that there is every reason to wonder, How can sinful men be expected to walk like Jesus? The answer that most people give is: "The command sets before us an ideal that is beautiful but unattainable."

The answer Scripture gives is different. It points us to the wonderful relationship in which we stand to Christ. The realization of this relationship between Christ and His people is necessary for everyone who is serious in following Christ's example. And what is this relationship? It is threefold. Peter wrote in the above passage of Christ as our Surety, our Example, and our Head.

Christ is our Surety. Christ suffered and died in our stead. He bore our sin and broke its curse and power. As Surety, He did what we could not.

Christ is also our Example. His suffering as my Surety calls me to a suffering like His as my Example. But is there not an impassable gulf between these two things, the suffering as Surety and the suffering as Example? No, there is a blessed third aspect of Christ's work that is the connecting link between Christ as Surety and Christ as Example.

Christ is also our Head. In this, His surety and His example have their unity. As a believer, I am spiritually one with Him. In this union, He imparts to me the power of His sufferings and death and resurrection. The very life that Christ lives works in the believer. Thus, he is dead, and has risen again with Christ.

To follow in His footsteps is a duty. Because it is a possibility, it is the natural result of the union between Head and members. It is only when this is understood that the blessed truth of Christ's example will take its right place. I have to gaze on His example so as to know and follow it. On the other, I have to abide in Him, and open my heart to the blessed workings of His life in me. As surely as He conquered sin and its curse *for me,* He will conquer it in its power *over me.* Because my Surety is also my Head, Christ as Example must and will be the rule of my life.

October 5

Suffering Wrongfully

For this is thankworthy, if a man for conscience toward God endure grief, suffering wrongfully. For what glory is it, if, when ye be buffeted for your faults, ye shall take it patiently? but if, when ye do well, and suffer for it, ye take it patiently, this is acceptable with God.
—1 Peter 2:19–20

Peter wrote, if anyone does wrong and is punished for it, to bear it patiently is no special grace. But if one does well, suffers for it, and takes it patiently, this is acceptable with God; such bearing of wrong is Christlike. In bearing our sins, Christ suffered wrong from man. Following His example, we must be ready to suffer wrongfully, too.

There is almost nothing harder to bear than injustice from our fellowmen. Besides the sense of pain, there is the feeling of humiliation and injustice, and the consciousness of our rights being violated. In what our fellowmen do to us, it is not easy to at once recognize the will of God. Let us study the example of Christ Jesus. From Him, we may learn what it was that gave Him the power to bear injuries patiently.

Christ believed in suffering as the will of God. He found in Scripture that the servant of God would suffer. He made Himself familiar with the thought, so that when suffering came, it did not take Him by surprise. When it came, His first thought was not how to be delivered from it but how to glorify God in it. This enabled Him to bear the greatest injustice quietly. He saw God's hand in it.

Christian, do you want to have strength to suffer wrong in the spirit in which Christ did? Accustom yourself, in everything that happens, to recognize the hand and will of God. Whether there is some great wrong done you, or some little offense that you meet in daily life, before you fix your thoughts on the person who did it, be still and remember, God allows me to come into this trouble to see if I will glorify Him in it. Let me first recognize and submit to God's will in it. Then, in the rest of soul that this gives, I will receive wisdom to know how to behave in it. With my eyes turned from man to God, suffering wrong is not as hard as it seems.

 October 6

Crucified with Him

I am crucified with Christ: nevertheless I live; yet not I, but Christ liveth in me....But God forbid that I should glory, save in the cross of our Lord Jesus Christ, by whom the world is crucified unto me, and I unto the world. —Galatians 2:20, 6:14

While the Lord was still on His way to the cross, the expression—taking up the cross—was the most appropriate to indicate the conformity to Him to which the disciple was called. But now that He has been crucified, the Holy Spirit gives another expression: to be crucified with Christ. One of the chief elements of likeness to Christ consists of being crucified with Him. Whoever wishes to be like Him must seek to understand the secret of fellowship with His cross.

Paul said, *"I am crucified with Christ; nevertheless I live; yet not I, but Christ liveth in me."* Through faith in Christ we become partakers of Christ's life that has passed through the death of the cross, and in which the power of that victorious death is always working. When I receive that life, I receive the full power of the death on the cross working in me in its never ceasing energy. *"I am crucified with Christ: nevertheless I live; yet not I, but Christ liveth in me."* The life I now live is not my own life. The life of the Crucified One is the life of the cross. Being crucified is a thing past.

I have been crucified with Christ; I have crucified the flesh. If I am crucified and dead with Him, then I am a partner in His victory. There is still a great work for me to do. But that work is not to crucify myself. I, the old man, was crucified. But what I have to do is to always treat it as crucified, and not to allow it to come down from the cross. I must keep the flesh in the place of crucifixion.

I gave myself to my crucified Savior, sin and flesh and all. But here a separation took place. In fellowship with Him, I was freed from the life of the flesh. In the innermost center of my being, I received new life: Christ lives in me. But the flesh, in which I remain condemned to death, is not yet dead. It is now my calling to see that the old nature is kept nailed to the cross. All its desires and affections cry out, "Come down from the cross. Save yourself and us." It is my duty to glory in the cross, to maintain the dominion of the cross with my whole heart, to make every uprising of sin dead, and not allow sin to have dominion.

October 7

Deny Yourself

We then that are strong ought to bear the infirmities of the weak, and not to please ourselves. Let every one of us please his neighbour for his good to edification. For even Christ pleased not himself; but, as it is written, The reproaches of them that reproached thee fell on me....Wherefore receive ye one another, as Christ also received us to the glory of God.
—Romans 15:1–3, 7

If any man will come after me, let him deny himself, and take up his cross, and follow me.
—Matthew 16:24

"*Christ pleased not himself.*" Referring to both God and man, this truth is the key of His life. In this, too, His life is our rule and example; we who are strong ought not to please ourselves.

To deny self is the opposite of pleasing self. When Peter denied Christ, he said, "'*I do not know the man*' (Matthew 26:72). I have nothing to do with Him and His interests. I do not wish to be counted His friend." Similarly, the true Christian denies himself, the old man. He says, "I do not know this old man. I will have nothing to do with him and his interests." And when shame and dishonor come upon him, or when anything happens that is not pleasant to the old nature, he simply says, "Do as you like with the old Adam. I will take no notice of it. Through the cross of Christ I am crucified to the world, the flesh, and self. To the friendship of this old man I am a stranger. I deny him to be my friend; I deny his every claim and wish. I do not know him."

The Christian who thinks only of his salvation from curse and condemnation cannot understand this. He finds it impossible to deny self. His life mainly consists of pleasing himself. The Christian who has taken Christ as his example cannot be content with this. The Holy Spirit has taught him to say, "I have been crucified with Christ, and so am dead to sin and self."

In fellowship with Christ, he sees the old man crucified, a condemned criminal. He is ashamed to know him as a friend. Because the crucified Christ is his life, self-denial is the law of his life. This self-denial extends over the whole domain of life. To the self-denying spirit, the will and glory of God and the salvation of man are always to be more important than our own interests or pleasure.

October 8

Self-Sacrifice for Others

Hereby perceive [know, RV] we the love of God, because he laid down his life for us: and we ought to lay down our lives for the brethren. —1 John 3:16

Self-sacrifice is of the very essence of true love. The very nature and blessedness of love consists in forgetting self, and seeking happiness in the loved one. Where there is a need in the beloved, love is impelled to offer up its own happiness for that of the other.

Who can say whether or not this is one of the secrets that eternity will reveal: that sin was permitted because otherwise God's love could never have been so fully revealed? The highest glory of God's love was manifested in the self-sacrifice of Christ. It is the highest glory of the Christian to be like his Lord in this. Without entire self-sacrifice, the new command, the command of love, cannot be fulfilled. Without entire self-sacrifice, we cannot love as Jesus loved. *"Be ye therefore imitators of God,"* said the apostle, *"...and walk in love, even as Christ also loved you, and gave himself up for us"* (Ephesians 5:1–2 RV).

It was this love that made His sacrifice acceptable in God's sight, a sweet-smelling savor. As His love exhibited itself in self-sacrifice, let your love prove itself to be conformable to His in the daily self-sacrifice for the welfare of others.

Even in the daily affairs of home life, in the conversations between husband and wife, Christ's self-sacrifice must be the rule of our walk. *"Husbands, love your wives, even as Christ also loved the church, and gave himself for it"* (Ephesians 5:25).

Especially notice the words of this text, *"Christ also loved you, and gave himself up for us, an offering and a sacrifice to God"* (Ephesians 5:2 RV). We see that self-sacrifice has two sides. Christ's self-sacrifice had a Godward as well as a manward aspect. It was *for us,* but it was *to God,* that He offered Himself as a sacrifice. In all our self-sacrifice, there must be these two sides in union, though the one may be more prominent than the other. It is only when we sacrifice ourselves to God that we will find the power for an entire self-sacrifice.

October 9

Not of the World

These are in the world....the world hath hated them, because they are not of the world....they are not of the world, even as I am not of the world.
—John 17:11, 14, 16

As he is, so are we in this world.
—1 John 4:17

If Jesus was not *of* the world, why was He *in* the world? The answer is that the Father had sent Him into the world. In these two expressions, *"in the world,"* and *"not of the world,"* we find the whole secret of His work as Savior, of His glory as the God-man.

He was in the world to fellowship with men, to enter into a loving relationship with them, and to struggle with the powers that rule the world. He was not of the world, witnessing against its sin and departure from God, in order to redeem all who belong to Him.

He was in the world and not of the world. To take one of these two truths and exclusively cultivate it is not so difficult. There are those who have taken *"not of the world"* as the only true Christianity, as when they seek to show their piety by severity in judging all that is in the world. Then there are those who stress *"in the world,"* who think that by showing that Christianity does not make us unfriendly or unfit to enjoy all that there is to enjoy, they will induce the world to serve God.

The follower of Jesus must combine both.

If he does not clearly show that he is *"not of the world,"* how will he convince the world of sin, prove to her that there is a higher life, or teach her to desire what she does not yet possess? Separation from the spirit of the world must characterize him.

And still, he must live as one who is *"in the world,"* placed here by God, among those who are of the world, to win their hearts and to communicate to them of the Spirit that is in him. He will not succeed by yielding, complying, and softening the realities of Christianity. No, he will succeed only by walking in the footsteps of Him who alone can teach how to be in the world and yet not of it. Only by a life of serving and suffering love, and in which, full of the Holy Spirit, he brings men into direct contact with the warmth and love of the heavenly life, can he be a blessing to the world.

October 10

In His Heavenly Mission

As thou hast sent me into the world, even so have I also sent them into the world.
—John 17:18

The Lord Jesus lived here on earth under a deep consciousness of having a mission from His Father to fulfill. He continually used the expression, "The Father has sent Me." He knew what the mission was. He knew that the Father had chosen Him and had sent Him into the world with the one purpose of fulfilling that mission. He knew the Father would give Him all that He needed for it. Faith in the Father having sent Him was the motive and power for all that He did.

For the Christian, it is no less important that he should know that he has a mission, what its nature is, and how he is to accomplish it. Our mission is like His in its purpose. Why did the Father send His Son? To make known His love and His will in the salvation of sinners. He was to represent the unseen Father in heaven, so that men on earth might know what the Father is like.

After the Lord had fulfilled His mission, He ascended into heaven. And now He has given His mission to His disciples, after having shown them how to fulfill it. They must so represent Him that, from seeing them, men can judge what He is. Every Christian must so be the image of Jesus that from them the world may know what Christ is like. Oh, my soul, take time to realize these heavenly thoughts. Our mission is like Christ's in its purpose—to show forth the holy love of heaven in earthly form.

Believer, the Lord, who knows you and your surroundings, has need of you, and has chosen you to be His representative in the circle in which you move. Fix your heart on this. He has fixed His heart on you and saved you, in order that you should bear and exhibit to those who surround you the very image of His unseen glory. Oh, think of the origin of your heavenly mission in His everlasting love, as His had its origin in the love of the Father. Your mission is, truly, just like His.

October 11

As the Elect of God

For whom he did foreknow, he also did predestinate to be conformed to the image of his Son, that he might be the firstborn among many brethren. —Romans 8:29

Scripture teaches us about personal election. It does this not only in single passages, but also in the whole history of its being worked out here in time through the counsels of eternity. We continually see how the whole future of God's kingdom depends on the faithful filling of His place by some single person. The only security for the carrying out of God's purpose is His foreordaining of the individual. In predestination alone, the history of the world and of God's kingdom, as of the individual believer, has its sure foundation.

There are Christians who cannot see this. They are so afraid of interfering with human responsibility that they reject the doctrine of divine predestination because it appears to rob man of his liberty of will. Scripture does not share this fear. It speaks in one place of man's free will as though there were no election. In another place, it speaks of election as though there were no free will. Thus, it teaches us that we must hold fast to both of these truths, even when we cannot understand them or make them harmonize. In the light of eternity, the solution of the mystery will be given. He who grasps both in faith will see that the stronger his faith is in God's everlasting purpose, the more his courage for work will be strengthened. While, on the other hand, the more he works and is blessed, the clearer it will become that all is of God.

For this reason, it is so important for a believer to make his election sure. Believer, take time and prayer to understand this truth, and let it exercise its full power in your soul. Let the Holy Spirit write it into your innermost being that you are *"predestinate*[d] *to be conformed to the image of his Son."* Let this be your purpose, too, in all your life—to show forth the image of your Elder Brother, that other Christians may be pointed to Him alone, may praise Him alone, and seek to follow Him more closely.

October 12

Doing God's Will

For I came down from heaven, not to do mine own will, but the will of him that sent me.
—John 6:38

In the will of God we have the highest expression of His divine perfection. In all nature, the will of God is done. For this, man was created with a free will, so that he might have the power to choose and do God's will; however, deceived by the Devil, man committed the great sin of doing his own rather than God's will.

Jesus Christ became man to bring us back to the blessedness of doing God's will. The great purpose of redemption was to make us and our wills free from the power of sin, and to lead us again to live and do the will of God. In His life on earth, He showed us what it is to live only for the will of God.

We must not think that this cost Him nothing. He says repeatedly, "Not My will, but the will of the Father," to let us understand that there was in very deed a denial of His own will. That man has a will other than God's is not sin. It is when he clings to his own will when it is seen to be contrary to the will of the Creator that sin occurs.

Child of God, one of the first marks of conformity to Christ is simple obedience to all the will of God. Begin by a willing and wholehearted keeping of the commands of God's holy Word. Go on to a yielding to everything that your conscience tells you is right, even when the Word does not directly command it. In this way, you will gain more direct insight into God's will. *"If any man will do his will, he shall know"* (John 7:17).

And if it ever appears too hard to live only for God's will, let us remember wherein Christ found His strength: it was because it was the Father's will that the Son rejoiced to do it. *"This commandment have I received of my Father"* (John 10:18). This made even the laying down of His life possible. Let it be our chief desire to say each day, "I am the Father's beloved child," and to think of each commandment as the Father's will.

October 13

In His Compassion

Then Jesus....said, I have compassion on the multitude.
—Matthew 15:32

Shouldest not thou also have had compassion on thy fellowservant, even as I had pity on thee?
—Matthew 18:33

On three different occasions Matthew said that our Lord was moved with compassion for the multitude. His whole life was a manifestation of the compassion with which He looked on the sinner, and of the tenderness with which He was moved at the sight of misery and sorrow. In this, He was the true reflection of our compassionate God, of the father who, moved with compassion toward his Prodigal Son, *"fell on his neck, and kissed him"* (Luke 15:20).

For the Lord Jesus, the will of God consisted not in certain things that were forbidden or commanded. No, He had entered into that which truly forms the very heart of God's will—to lost sinners, He would give eternal life.

Because God Himself is love, His will is that love should have full scope in the salvation of sinners. Jesus came down to earth in order to manifest and accomplish this will of God. He did not do this as a servant obeying the will of a stranger. In His personal life and in all His dispositions, He proved that the loving will of His Father to save sinners was His own.

Dear followers of Christ, let the will of the Father be to you what it was to your Lord. The will of the Father in the mission of His Son was the manifestation of divine compassion in the salvation of lost sinners. God's will is for us what it was for Jesus: the salvation of the perishing. It is impossible for us to fulfill that will except by having, bearing about, and showing in our lives the compassion of our God. The seeking of God's will must not be only denying ourselves certain things that God forbids and doing certain works that God commands; it must also consist in surrendering ourselves to have the same mind and disposition toward sinners as God has, and that we find our pleasure and joy alone in living for this. By the most personal devotion to each poor, perishing sinner around us, and by our helping them in compassionate love, we can show that the will of God is our will.

In His Oneness with the Father

Holy Father, keep through thine own name those whom thou hast given me, that they may be one, as we are....That they all may be one; as thou, Father, art in me, and I in thee, that they also may be one in us: that the world may believe that thou hast sent me. And the glory which thou gavest me I have given them; that they may be one, even as we are one: I in them, and thou in me, that they may be made perfect in one; and that the world may know that thou hast sent me, and hast loved them, as thou hast loved me.
—John 17:11, 21–23

What a treasure we have in this high priestly prayer in John 17! There the heart of Jesus is laid open to our view, and we see what His love desires for us. In this prayer, the mutual union of believers is more important than anything else. In His prayer for all who will in the future believe, this is the chief petition.

The Lord tells us plainly why He desires this unity so strongly. It is the only convincing proof to the world that the Father had sent Him. With all its blindness, the world knows that selfishness is the curse of sin. It is little help that God's children say that they are born again, that they are happy, or that they can prove that what the Scriptures teach is the truth. When the world sees a church from which selfishness is banished, then it will acknowledge the divine mission of Christ—a community of people who truly and heartily love one another.

How many believers do not even desire to be one even as the Father and the Son are one! They are so accustomed to a life of selfishness that they do not even long for such perfect love. They put off that union until heaven. And yet, the Lord was thinking of life on earth when He twice said, *"That the world may know."*

Beloved Christians, the oneness of Christ with the Father is our model: even as They are one, so must we be one. Let us love one another, serve one another, bear with one another, and live for one another. Our love is too small, but we will earnestly pray that Christ gives us His love wherewith to love. With God's love *"shed abroad in our hearts by the Holy Ghost"* (Romans 5:5), we will be so united as one that the world might know that it is indeed the truth that the Father sent Christ into the world, and that Christ has given to us the very life and love of heaven.

October 15

In His Dependence on the Father

Verily, verily, I say unto you, the Son can do nothing of himself, but what he seeth the Father do: for what things soever he doeth, these also doeth the Son likewise. For the Father loveth the Son, and showeth him all things that himself doeth: and he will show him greater works than these, that ye may marvel.
—John 5:19–20

Our relationship to Jesus is the exact counterpart of His to the Father. As the words of Jesus in John 5 describe the natural relationship between every father and son, they are applicable not only to the Only Begotten, but also to everyone who, in and like Jesus, is called a son of God.

There is no better way to think of the simple truth of the illustration than by thinking of Jesus learning His trade from His earthly father in the carpenter's shop. The first thing you notice is the entire dependence: *"The Son can do nothing of himself, but what he seeth the Father do."* Then you are struck by the implicit obedience that just seeks to imitate the father, *"for what things soever* [the Father] *doeth, these also doeth the Son likewise."* You then notice the loving intimacy to which the Father admits Him, keeping back none of His secrets: *"For the Father loveth the Son, and showeth him all things that himself doeth."* And, step-by-step, the Son will be led to all that the Father Himself can do: *"He will show him greater works than these, that ye may marvel."*

If we are to understand how Christ is truly to be our Example, we must fully believe in what our blessed Lord here reveals to us of the secrets of His inner life. He counted it no humiliation to wait on Him for His commands; rather, He considered it His highest blessedness to let Himself be led and guided by the Father as a Child.

My brethren, if you have so far only known a little about this life of conscious dependence and simple obedience, begin today. Let your Savior be your Example in this. It is His blessed will to live in you, and in you to be again what He was here on earth. Offer yourself to the Father this day to do nothing of yourself but only what the Father shows you. Fix your gaze on Jesus as the Example and Promise of what you will be.

October 16

In His Love

A new commandment I give unto you, That ye love one another; as I have loved you, that ye also love one another.
—John 13:34

It is not the command of a law that convinces us of sin and weakness; it is a new command under a new covenant that is established upon better promises. It is the command of Him who asks nothing that He has not provided, and now offers to bestow. He says, "As I have loved you, even so, love one another. The measure, the strength, and the work of your love will be found in My love for you."

"As I have loved you"—these words give us the measure of the love with which we must love each other. He who desires to be like Christ must unhesitatingly accept this as his rule of life. He knows how difficult, how impossible, it often is to love people. Before going out to meet them in circumstances where his love may be tried, he goes in secret to the Lord. With his eyes fixed on his own sin and unworthiness, he asks how much he owes his Lord. He goes to the cross and seeks to fathom the love with which the Lord has loved him.

Christ Jesus longs for you in order to make you a very fountain of love. As conformity to the Lord Jesus must be the chief mark of your Christian walk, so love must be the chief mark of that conformity. Do not be disheartened if you do not attain it at once. Take time in secret to gaze on that image of love. Take time in prayer and meditation to fan the desire for it into a burning flame. Take time to survey all around you, whoever they may be, and whatever may happen, with this one thought, "I must love them." Christian, take time in loving communion with Jesus, your loving example, and you will joyfully fulfill this command, too, to love as He did.

October 17

In His Praying

And in the morning, rising up a great while before day, he went out, and departed into a solitary place, and there prayed.
—Mark 1:35

In His life of secret prayer, my Savior is also my Example. He could not maintain the heavenly life in His soul without continually separating Himself from man and communing with His Father. The heavenly life in me has the same need of entire separation from man—the need not only of single moments, but also of time enough for fellowship with the Father in heaven.

The event that so attracted the attention of His disciples happened at the beginning of His public ministry, and they wrote it down. (See Mark 1:21–38.) After a day full of wonders at Capernaum, the crowd in the evening became even greater in number. It was late before they got to sleep. And as the disciples rose early in the morning, they found that Jesus was gone. In the silence of the night, He had gone out to seek a place of solitude in the wilderness. When they found Him there, He was still praying.

Why did my Savior need those hours of prayer? Did the Father not, in the depths of His heart, enjoy unbroken communion with Him? Yes, that hidden life was indeed His portion. But that life, as subject to the law of humanity, had need of continual refreshing from the Fountain. Just because it was strong and true, it could not bear the loss of direct and constant communion with the Father.

If you and I want to be like Jesus, we must especially contemplate Jesus as He prayed alone in the wilderness. What He did and spoke to man was first spoken and lived through with the Father. In communion with Him, the anointing with the Holy Spirit was each day renewed. He who desires to be like Him in His walk and conversation must simply begin by following Jesus into solitude. Even though it might cost the sacrifice of sleep, of business, of fellowship with friends, *the time must be found to be alone with the Father.* In our secret chamber, with closed door, God must be found every day and our fellowship with Him renewed. If Christ needed it, how much more do we! What it was to Him, it will be for us.

October 18

In His Use of Scriptures

All things must be fulfilled, which were written in the law of Moses, and in the prophets, and in the psalms, concerning me.
—Luke 24:44

What the Lord Jesus accomplished here on earth He owed greatly to His use of the Scriptures. In them, He found the way in which He had to walk, the food and the strength from which He could work, and the weapon by which He could overcome every enemy.

In the temptation in the wilderness, it was by His *"It is written"* (Matthew 4:4) that He conquered Satan. In His conflicts with the Pharisees, He continually appealed to the Word, asking, *"Have ye not read?"* (See, for example, Matthew 12:3, 5; Mark 12:10, 26; Luke 6:3.) *"Is it not written?"* (See Mark 11:17; John 10:34.) In His fellowship with His disciples, it was always from the Scriptures that He proved the necessity and certainty of His sufferings and resurrection: *"How then shall the scriptures be fulfilled?"* (Matthew 26:54). And during His last sufferings, it is in Scripture that He pours out the complaint of being forsaken, and then again commends His Spirit into the Father's hands.

Jesus was Himself the living Word. He had the Spirit without measure. If anyone could have done without the written Word, it would have been Him. And yet, we see that it is everything to Him. More than anyone else, He thus shows us that the life of God in human flesh and the Word of God in human speech are inseparably connected.

In Christ's use of Scripture, the most remarkable thing is this: He found Himself there. He saw His own image and likeness, and He gave Himself to the fulfillment of what He found written there. It is especially in His example that we must find our own image in the Scriptures. To be *"changed into the same image from glory to glory, even as by the Spirit of the Lord"* (2 Corinthians 3:18), we must gaze in the Scripture on that image as our own. In order to accomplish His work in us, the Spirit teaches us to take Christ as our Example and to gaze on His every feature as the promise of what we can be.

October 19

In Forgiving

Forbearing one another, and forgiving one another, if any man have a quarrel against any: even as Christ forgave you, so also do ye.
—Colossians 3:13

In the life of grace, forgiveness is one of the first blessings we receive from God. The redeemed saint can never forget that he is a forgiven sinner. Nothing works more mightily to awaken his joy than the experience of God's forgiving love.

If we read our Lord's words in Matthew 6:12, 15; 18:21–25; and Mark 11:25, we will understand how inseparably God's forgiveness of us and our forgiveness of others are united. After the Lord was ascended to grant forgiveness of sins, the Scriptures say of Him just what He had said of the Father, that we must forgive as He does. As our text expresses it, *"Even as Christ forgave you, so also do ye."*

It is not difficult to find the reason for this. When forgiving love comes to us, it seeks to win us for its own, to take possession of us, and to dwell in us. And when it has thus come down to dwell in us, it is still seeking to do its work toward us, in us, and through us, leading and enabling us to forgive those who sin against us. So much so that we are told that not to forgive is a sure sign that one has himself not been forgiven. He who only seeks forgiveness but has not truly accepted forgiving love to rule his heart, proves that God's forgiveness has never really reached him. He who, on the other hand, has really accepted forgiveness, will have, in the joy with which he forgives others, a continual confirmation that his faith in God's forgiveness of himself is a reality.

Beloved followers of Jesus, learn that as forgiveness of your sins was one of the first things Jesus did for you, forgiveness of others is one of the first that you can do for Him. Before there is a question of forgiveness of others, let your heart be filled with love for Christ, love for the brethren, and love for your enemies. Rejoice in how glad you are to let its light shine through you on others. How blessed a privilege it is to be able to thus bear the image of your beloved Lord!

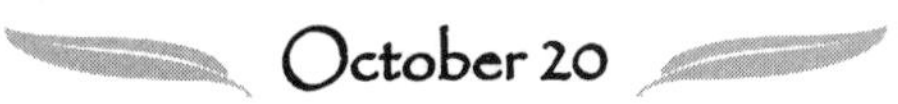

October 20

In Beholding Him

But we all, with open face beholding as in a glass the glory of the Lord, are changed into the same image from glory to glory, even as by the Spirit of the Lord.
—2 Corinthians 3:18

Moses spent forty days on Mount Sinai in communion with God. When he came down, his face shown with divine glory. It was so evidently God's glory that Aaron and the people feared to approach him (Exodus 34:30). In this we have an image of what takes place in the New Testament. When we behold the glory of God in Christ, in the mirror of the Holy Scriptures, His glory shines on us and fills us until it shines out from us again.

The heavenly Father shows us His divine glory in the face of Jesus because He knows that, by gazing on it, we will be conformed to the same image. Continually look to the divine glory as seen in Christ. What is the special characteristic of that glory? The chief marks of the image of the divine glory in Christ are His humiliation and His love.

There is the glory of His humiliation. When you see how the eternal Son emptied Himself and became man, and how as Man He humbled Himself as a servant and was obedient even unto the death of the cross (Philippians 2:7–8), you have seen the highest glory of God.

The glory of His love is inseparable from this. The humiliation leads you back to the love as its origin and power. It is from love that the humiliation gains its beauty. But this love was a hidden mystery until it was manifest in Christ Jesus.

Do you want to be like Christ? Gaze on the glory of God, that is to say, do not look only to the words in which His glory is seen, but look to Jesus Himself, the living Christ. Look into His very eyes, into His face, as a loving Friend, as the living God.

Beholding Jesus and His glory, you can confidently expect to become like Him. Gaze on and adore the glory of God in Christ; you will be changed with divine power from glory to glory. In the power of the Holy Spirit, the mighty transformation will be worked, your desires will be fulfilled, and becoming like Christ will be the blessed, God-given experience of your life.

October 21

In His Humility

In lowliness of mind let each esteem other better than themselves....Let this mind be in you which was also in Christ Jesus: who, being in the form of God, thought it not robbery to be equal with God: but made himself of no reputation, and took upon him the form of a servant, and was made in the likeness of men: and being found in fashion as a man, he humbled himself, and became obedient unto death, even the death of the cross.
—Philippians 2:3, 5–8

In this passage, we have a summary of all the most precious truths of the blessed Son of God. First, there is His majestic divinity: *"in the form of God"; "equal with God."* Then comes the mystery of His incarnation in that word of deep meaning: "[He] *made himself of no reputation."* The Atonement follows with the humiliation, obedience, suffering, and death: *"He humbled himself, and became obedient unto death, even the death of the cross."* And all is crowned by His glorious exaltation: *"God also hath highly exalted him"* (v. 9). Christ as God, Christ becoming man, Christ as Man in humiliation working out our redemption, and Christ in glory as Lord of all: such are the treasures of wisdom this passage contains.

We must be like Christ in His self-emptying and self-humiliation. The first great act of self-denial, in which, as God, He emptied Himself of His divine glory and laid it aside, was followed by the humbling of Himself as Man in His death on the cross. And in this twofold humiliation, Scripture very simply says that we must be like Christ.

The blessedness of a Christlike humility is unspeakable. It is of great worth in the sight of God. As Scripture states, *"God resisteth the proud, but giveth grace unto the humble"* (James 4:6). In the spiritual life, it is the source of rest and joy. To the humble all God does is right and good. Humility is always ready to praise God for the least of His mercies. Humility does not find it difficult to trust. It submits unconditionally to all that God says.

Oh, what a glorious calling for the followers of Christ! To be sent into the world by God to prove that there is nothing more divine than self-humiliation. The humble man glorifies God, leads others to glorify Him, and will at last be glorified with Him. Who would not want to be humble like Jesus?

In the Likeness of His Death

For if we have been planted together in the likeness of his death, we shall be also in the likeness of his resurrection....For in that he died, he died unto sin once: but in that he liveth, he liveth unto God. Likewise reckon ye also yourselves to be dead indeed unto sin, but alive unto God through Jesus Christ our Lord.
—Romans 6:5, 10–11

In Romans 6, we are taught what it is to be one with Christ in the likeness of His death. Let everyone who truly longs to be like Christ seek to correctly know what the likeness of His death means.

Christ had a double work to accomplish in His death. The one was to work out righteousness for us. The other was to obtain life for us. *Dying for sin* means that God laid our sin upon Him, and through His death, atonement is made for sin before God. *Dying to sin* refers to a personal relationship through His death; the connection in which He stood to sin was entirely dissolved. During His life, sin had great power to cause Him conflict and suffering. Death ended all of this. Sin no longer had the power to tempt or to hurt Him. Death had completely separated Him and sin. Christ died to sin.

Like Christ, the believer has also died to sin—he is one with Him in the likeness of His death. The Christian who does not understand this always imagines that sin still has power over him and that he must sometimes obey it. But he thinks this because he does not know that he, like Christ, is dead to sin. If He only believed his language would be, "Christ has died to sin. Sin has nothing more to say to Him. He is freed from its power. The same is true of me as a believer. The new life that is in me is entirely dead to sin. Like Christ, sin has no right or power over me whatever. I am freed from it; therefore, I do not need to sin."

O Christian, know the exceeding greatness of God's power that works in you. It was in the power of eternity that Christ, in His death, wrestled with the powers of hell and conquered them. You have part with Christ in His death; you have part in all the powers by which He conquered. Yield yourself joyfully and believingly to be led more deeply into the conformity to Christ's death. Then you can do nothing other than become like Him.

October 23

In the Likeness of His Resurrection

Therefore we are buried with him by baptism into death: that like as Christ was raised up from the dead by the glory of the Father, even so we also should walk in newness of life. For if we have been planted together in the likeness of his death, we shall be also in the likeness of his resurrection. —Romans 6:4–5

"The likeness of his death" is followed by *"the likeness of His resurrection."* To speak only of the likeness of His death gives a one-sided view of following Christ. The power of His resurrection gives us strength to go on from that likeness of His death. Being dead with Christ refers more to the death of the old life to sin that we abandon. Being risen with Christ refers to the new life through which the Holy Spirit expels the old.

We have already seen how our Lord's life, before His death, was a life of weakness. Sin had power over Him and over His disciples. But with the resurrection, all was changed. His resurrection life was full of the power of eternity. He had conquered death and sin not only for Himself, but also for His disciples, so that He could make them partakers of His Spirit and His heavenly power.

When the Lord Jesus now makes us partakers of His life, it is not the life that He had before His death, but the resurrection life that He won through death, a life that has already conquered hell, the devil, the world, and the flesh.

To most Christians this is a mystery; therefore, their lives are full of sin, weakness, and defeat. They believe in Christ's resurrection. They think that He had to rise again to continue His work in heaven as Mediator. But they have no idea that He rose again so that His resurrection life might now be the very power of their daily lives.

Your calling is to live like Christ. You have already been made one with Him in the likeness of His resurrection. The only question now is whether or not you are willing to surrender your whole life so that He may manifest resurrection power in every part of it. I beg you, offer yourself unreservedly to Him, with all your weakness and unfaithfulness. Believe that, as His resurrection was a wonder above all expectation, so He as the Risen One will still work in you exceeding abundantly above all you could think or desire. (See Ephesians 3:20.)

October 24

Conformable to His Death

That I may know him, and the power of his resurrection, and the fellowship of his sufferings, being made conformable unto his death.
—Philippians 3:10

We know that the death of Christ was the death of the cross. We know that the death of the cross is His chief glory. The distinguishing characteristic by which He is separated here on earth and in heaven from all other persons is this one: He is the Crucified Son of God. Of all the characteristics of conformity, this must necessarily be the chief and most glorious one: conformity to His death.

This is what made it so attractive to Paul. What had been Christ's glory and blessedness must have been his glory, too. He knew that the most intimate likeness to Christ is conformity to His death. What that death had been to Christ it would be to him, as he grew conformed to it.

Christ's death on the cross had been the end of sin. Conformity to Christ's death is the power to keep us from the power of sin. As I, by the grace of the Holy Spirit, am kept in my position as crucified with Christ, and live out my crucifixion life as the Crucified One lives it in me, I am kept from sinning. Christ's death on the cross was the entrance to the power of the resurrection life.

In our spiritual life, we often have to mourn the breaks, failures, and intervals that prove to us that there is still something lacking that prevents the resurrection life from asserting its full power. The secret is here: there is still some subtle self-life that has not yet been brought into the perfect conformity of Christ's death.

Therefore, look to the Crucified One. Gaze on Him until you have seen how He Himself draws near to live in you and breathe through your being His crucifixion life. It was through the eternal Spirit that He offered Himself unto God. By that Holy Spirit, Jesus Himself maintains in each soul who can trust Him for it, the power of the cross as an abiding death to sin and self. It is a never ceasing source of resurrection life and power. Therefore, once again, look to Him, the living, crucified Jesus.

Giving His Life for Men

But it shall not be so among you: but whosoever will be great among you, let him be your minister; and whosoever will be chief among you, let him be your servant: even as the Son of man came not to be ministered unto, but to minister, and to give his life a ransom for many.
—Matthew 20:26–28

Hereby perceive we the love of God, because he laid down his life for us: and we ought to lay down our lives for the brethren.
—1 John 3:16

In speaking of the likeness of Christ's death, and of being made conformable to it, there is one danger to which even the earnest believer is exposed. That danger is seeking after these blessings for one's own sake. He would never attain the close conformity to Jesus' death he hoped for. He would be leaving out that which is essential in the death of Jesus. To be made conformable to Christ's death implies a dying to self.

To the question of how far we are to go in living for, loving, serving, and saving men, the Scriptures do not hesitate to give the unequivocal answer: we are to go as far as Jesus did, even to the laying down of our lives. We are to consider this the entire purpose for which we are redeemed and are left in the world. Like Christ, the only thing that keeps us in this world is to be the glory of God in the salvation of sinners. Scripture does not hesitate to say that it is in His path of suffering, as He goes to work out atonement and redemption, that we are to follow Him.

As the most essential thing in likeness to Christ is likeness to His death, so the most essential thing in likeness to His death is the giving up of our lives to win others to God. It is a death in which all thought of saving self is lost in that of saving others. Let us pray for the light of the Holy Spirit to show us this. We must learn to feel that we are in the world just as Christ was, to give up self, to love and serve, to live and die, *"even as the Son of man came not to be ministered unto, but to minister, and to give his life a ransom for many."* Oh, that God would allow His people to know that they do not belong to themselves, but to God and to their fellowmen. Even as Christ lived, they are to live only to be a blessing to the world.

October 26

In His Meekness

Behold, thy King cometh unto thee, meek.
—Matthew 21:5

Learn of me; for I am meek and lowly in heart: and ye shall find rest unto your souls.
—Matthew 11:29

The first of these two verses is written about our Lord Jesus on His way to the cross. It is in His sufferings that the meekness of Jesus is especially manifested. Meekness is the opposite of all that is hard, bitter, or sharp. It refers to the disposition that makes us compassionate toward others.

Perhaps none of the virtues of God's Son is more seldom seen in those who ought to be examples. There are many servants of Jesus in whom much love for souls and much zeal for God's will are visible and yet who continually fall short in this area. This occurs most often when they are offended unexpectedly. They are carried away by anger and have to confess that they have lost the perfect rest of soul in God! There is no virtue, perhaps, for which some have prayed more earnestly than meekness. They would give anything if, in their relationships with their spouses, children, or business associates, they could always exhibit the meekness and gentleness of Christ.

For everyone who longs to possess this spirit, Christ's word is full of comfort and encouragement: *"Learn of me; for I am meek."*

Without ceasing, the word sounds in our ears as our Lord's answer to all the sad complaints of His redeemed ones concerning the difficulty of restraining temper. O my brethren, why is Jesus—your Jesus, your life, and your strength—the meek and lowly One, if not to impart to you, to whom He so wholly belongs, His own meekness?

Therefore, only believe! Believe that Jesus is able to fill your heart with His own spirit of meekness. Believe that Jesus Himself will accomplish in you the work that you have in vain endeavored to do. Welcome Him to dwell in your heart. Expect Him to reveal Himself to you. Learn that He is meek and lowly of heart, and you will find rest for your soul.

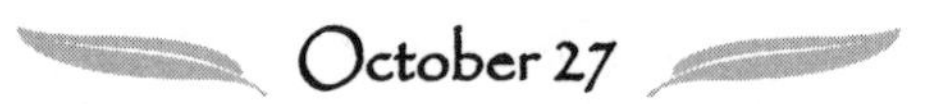

October 27

Abiding in the Love of God

As the Father hath loved me, so have I loved you: continue ye in my love. If ye keep my commandments, ye shall abide in my love; even as I have kept my Father's commandments, and abide in his love.
—John 15:9–10

Our blessed Lord not only said, *"Abide in me"* (John 15:4), but also, *"Abide in my love."* To reveal this life in His love to us in all its divine beauty and blessedness, Jesus tells us that His love for us, in which we are to abide, is just the same as the Father's love for Him, the love in which He abides. Surely, if anything were necessary to make the abiding in His love more wonderful and attractive, this ought to do so. *"As the Father hath loved me, so have I loved you: continue ye in my love."*

We are the beloved of Jesus. As the Father loved Him, He loves us. And what we need is to take time and to worship and wait until we see the infinite love of God in all its power and glory streaming forth on us through the heart of Jesus. It is seeking to make itself known, receiving complete possession of us, and offering itself as our home and resting place. Oh, if the Christian would only take the time to let this wondrous thought fill him, "I am the beloved of the Lord. Jesus loves me every moment, just as the Father loved Him." Then how our faith would grow, and we would believe that we are loved as Christ was.

Oh, this Christlike obedience, leading to a Christlike abiding in the divine love! To attain it, we must study Christ more. He emptied Himself, humbled Himself, and became obedient. (See Philippians 2:8.) May He empty and humble us, too! We must yield ourselves to be taught obedience by Him. We need to listen to what He has told us about how He did nothing of Himself, but only what He saw and heard from the Father. Entire dependence on the Father was the root of His obedience and the secret of His knowledge of the Father's deeper secrets. (See John 5:19–20.) God's love and man's obedience are like the lock and key fitting into each other. It is God's grace that has fitted the key to the lock; it is man who uses the key to unlock the treasures of love.

Led by the Spirit

**And Jesus being full of the Holy Ghost returned from Jordan, and was led by the Spirit into the wilderness.
—Luke 4:1**

**For as many as are led by the Spirit of God, they are the sons of God.
—Romans 8:14**

From His very birth, the Lord Jesus had the Spirit dwelling in Him. But there were times when He needed special communications of the Spirit with the Father. Thus it was with His baptism. The descent of the Holy Spirit on Him—the baptism of the Spirit, given in the baptism with water: He was filled with the Spirit. He returned from the Jordan full of the Holy Spirit and experienced more manifestly than ever the leading of the Spirit. Even as Jesus was filled with the Spirit and then led by the Spirit, so must we also be filled with the Spirit and led by the Spirit.

And this blessing is ours as it was His. Jesus, who was Himself baptized with the Spirit to set an example of how we are to live, has ascended into heaven to baptize us into likeness with Himself. What God demands from His children He first gives. He demands entire likeness to Christ because He will give us, as He did Jesus, the fullness of the Spirit. We must be filled with the Spirit.

It is Jesus who baptizes with the Spirit. All that He requires of us is the surrender of faith to receive what He gives. The surrender of faith. What He asks is whether or not we are indeed in earnest to follow in His footsteps, and for this to be baptized of the Spirit. Do not let there be any hesitation as to our answer.

Remember, the fullness of the Spirit is yours in Jesus. It is a gift that you accept and hold in faith, even when you do not feel its presence. The feeling may be weakness, fear, and much trembling, and yet the speaking, working, and living may be in demonstration of the Spirit and of power. (See 1 Corinthians 2:3–4.)

Live in the faith that the fullness of the Spirit is yours, and you rejoice every day in the blessed trust that the care of your spiritual life is in the hands of the Holy Spirit the Comforter. With the Spirit of life in Christ Jesus dwelling within, the likeness of the life of Christ Jesus will shine around.

October 29

In His Life Through the Father

I live by the Father: so he that eateth me, even he shall live by me. —John 6:57

What a blessed word we have as our text, to assure us that His life on earth and ours are really like each other: "I live because of the Father, so he who feeds on Me will live because of Me." If you desire to understand your life in Christ, you have only to contemplate what the Father was for Him, and how He worked in Him. Christ's life in and through the Father is the image and the measure of what your life in and through the Son may be.

As Christ's life was a life hidden in God in heaven, so must ours be. When He emptied Himself of His divine glory, He laid aside the free use of His divine attributes. He thus needed, as a man, to live by faith. He needed to wait on the Father for such communications of wisdom and power as it pleased the Father to impart to Him. He was entirely dependent on the Father; His life was hidden in God. Not in virtue of His own independent Godhead, but through the operations of the Holy Spirit, did He speak and act as the Father from time to time taught Him.

Exactly so, must your life be hidden with Christ in God. Christ calls you to a life of faith and dependence, because it is the life He Himself led. He is willing now to live over again His life in you, to teach you also to live in no other way. He knew that the Father was His life, that He lived through the Father, and that the Father supplied His need moment by moment. And now, He assures you that, as He lived through the Father, even so you will live through Him. Let your heart be filled with the thought of this fullness of life, which is prepared for you in Christ, and will be abundantly supplied as you need it.

Do not think of your spiritual life as something that you must watch over and nourish with care and anxiety. Rejoice every day that you need not live on your own strength, but in your Lord Jesus, even as He lived through His Father.

October 30

In Glorifying the Father

Father, the hour is come; glorify thy Son, that thy Son also may glorify thee....I have glorified thee on the earth.
—John 17:1, 4

Herein is my Father glorified, that ye bear much fruit; so shall ye be my disciples.
—John 15:8

The glory of an object is that its intrinsic worth answers perfectly to all that is expected of it. That excellence may be so hidden that the object has no glory to those who behold it. To glorify is to remove every hindrance, and so to reveal the full worth and perfection of the object that its glory is acknowledged by all.

The highest perfection and deepest mystery of the Godhead is His holiness. In it, righteousness and love are united. It is this holiness that is the glory of God. For this reason the two words are often found together. So in the song of Moses: *"Who is like thee, glorious in holiness?"* (Exodus 15:11). So in the song of the seraphim: *"Holy, holy, holy, is the LORD of hosts: the whole earth is full of his glory"* (Isaiah 6:3). And so in the song of the Lamb: *"Who shall not...glorify thy name? For thou only art holy"* (Revelation 15:4). As has been well said, "God's glory is His manifested holiness; God's holiness is His hidden glory."

Jesus came to earth that He might glorify the Father, and so that He might again show forth that glory that sin had so entirely hidden from man. Man himself had been created in the image of God, so that God might lay His glory upon him—that God might be glorified in him. Jesus came to restore man to his high destiny. He laid aside the glory that He had with the Father, and came in our weakness and humiliation, so that He might teach us how to glorify the Father on earth. Man cannot contribute any new glory to God, above what He has: he can serve only as a mirror in which the glory of God is reflected. God's holiness is His glory. As this holiness of God is seen in mankind, God is glorified.

Let us take time to take in this wondrous thought: our daily lives, down to their most ordinary acts, may be transparent with the glory of God. Let our whole life be animated by this principle, growing stronger until our watchword has become: all to the glory of God.

October 31

In His Glory

We know that, when he shall appear, we shall be like him; for we shall see him as he is. And every man that hath this hope in him purifieth himself, even as he is pure.
—1 John 3:2–3

God's glory is His holiness. To glorify God is to yield ourselves so that God may show forth His glory in us. It is only by yielding ourselves to be holy, to let His holiness fill our lives, that His glory can shine forth from us. The one work of Christ was to glorify the Father. Our one work is, like Christ's, by our obedience, testimony, and life to make known our God as *"glorious in holiness"* (Exodus 15:11).

When the Lord Jesus had glorified the Father on earth, the Father glorified Him with Himself in heaven. This was not only His just reward, but was also a necessity in the very nature of things. The law holds good for us, too. A heart that yearns and thirsts for the glory of God, that is ready to live and die for it, becomes prepared and fitted to live in it. *Living to* God's glory on earth is the gate to *living in* God's glory in heaven. If with Christ we glorify the Father, the Father will with Christ glorify us, too.

If here on earth we have given ourselves to have God's glory take possession of us, and if God's holiness and His Holy Spirit dwell and shine in us, then our human nature, with all our faculties, created in the likeness of God, will have poured into and transfused through it the purity, the holiness, the life, and the very brightness of the glory of God.

Nothing can be made manifest in that Day that does not have a real existence here in this life. If the glory of God is not our life here, it cannot be hereafter. It is impossible. Only he who glorifies God here can God glorify hereafter. Man is the image and glory of God. It is as you bear the image of God here, as you live in the likeness of Jesus—who is *"the brightness of his glory, and the express image of his person"* (Hebrews 1:3)—that you will be made ready for the glory to come. If we are to be as the image of the heavenly Christ in glory, we must first bear the image of the earthly Christ in humility.

November

November 1

The God of Our Salvation

Truly my soul waiteth upon God: from him cometh my salvation.
—Psalm 62:1

If salvation comes from God and is entirely His work, it follows that our first and highest duty is to wait on Him and do that work that pleases Him. Waiting then becomes the only way to truly know the God of our salvation. All the difficulties that are keeping us back from full salvation have their cause in this one thing: the defective knowledge and practice of waiting upon God.

The deep need for this waiting on God lies equally in the nature of man and the nature of God. God, as Creator, formed man to be a vessel in which He could show forth His power and goodness. Man was not to have, in himself, a fountain of life or strength or happiness. The ever-living One was each moment to communicate to man all that he needed.

When he fell from God, he was still absolutely dependent on Him. There was not the slightest hope of his recovery but in God. It is God alone who began the work of redemption. It is God alone who continues and carries it on each moment. Even in the regenerate man, there is no power of goodness in himself. Waiting on God is just as indispensable, and must be just as continuous, as the breathing that maintains his natural life.

It is because Christians do not know their relationship to God as absolute poverty and helplessness that they have no sense of absolute dependence or of the blessedness of continually waiting on God. But, once a believer begins to consent to it, waiting on God becomes his brightest hope and joy. God unceasingly working and His child unceasingly waiting and receiving—this is the blessed life.

"Truly my soul waiteth upon God: from him cometh my salvation." First, we wait on God for salvation. Then, we learn that salvation is only to bring us to God and teach us to wait on Him. Then, we find what is better still, that waiting on God is itself the highest salvation. It is ascribing to Him the glory of being All; it is experiencing that He is All to us. May God teach us the blessedness of waiting on Him!

November 2

The Keynote of Life

I have waited for thy salvation, O Lord.
—Genesis 49:18

It is not easy to say in what exact sense Jacob used these words in the midst of his prophecies in regard to the future of his sons. But, they certainly do indicate that his expectation was from God alone. It was God's salvation he waited for, a salvation that God had promised and alone could work out. Jehovah, the everlasting God, would show them what His saving power does. The words point forward to that wonderful history of redemption that is not yet finished, and to the glorious future in eternity to which it is leading. They suggest to us how there is no salvation but God's salvation, and how waiting on God for that is our true blessedness.

Let us think of ourselves and the glorious salvation God has worked out for us in Christ and is now going to perfect in us by His Spirit. Let us meditate until we realize that every participation of this great salvation, from moment to moment, must be the work of God Himself. God cannot part with His grace or goodness or strength as an external thing that He gives us. No, He can only give it, and we can only enjoy it, as He works it Himself directly and unceasingly. And, the only reason that He does not work it more effectually and continuously is that we do not let Him. We hinder Him either by our indifference or by our self-effort, so that He cannot do what He wants to do.

What He asks of us, in the way of surrender, obedience, desire, and trust, is all comprised in this one word: waiting on Him, waiting for His salvation. It combines the deep sense of our entire helplessness and our perfect confidence that our God will work all in His divine power.

Our heart is the scene of a divine operation more wonderful than creation. We can do as little toward the work as toward creating the world, except as God works in us to will and to do. God only asks us to yield, to wait upon Him, and He will do it all. Let us meditate and be still until we see how blessed it is that God alone do all. Our soul will sink down in deep humility to say, *"I have waited for thy salvation, O Lord."* And the deep, blessed background of all our praying, *"Truly my soul waiteth upon God"* (Psalm 62:1).

November 3

The True Place of Man

These wait all upon thee; that thou mayest give them their meat in due season. That thou givest them they gather: thou openest thine hand, they are filled with good.
—Psalm 104:27–28

This psalm is in praise of the Creator of the birds and the beasts of the forest, of the young lions, of the great sea, where things exist, both small and great beasts. And, it sums up the whole relationship of all creation to its Creator, and its continuous and universal dependence upon Him, in the one word, *"these wait all upon thee"*! Just as much as it was God's work to create, it is His work to maintain. The whole creation is ruled by the one unalterable law of waiting upon God!

The word is the simple expression of that for the sake of which alone man was brought into existence, the very groundwork of his constitution. The one object for which God gave life to mankind was that in them He might prove and show forth His wisdom, power, and goodness. He would be, each moment, their life and happiness, and pour forth unto them the riches of His goodness and power. And just as this is the very place and nature of God, to be unceasingly the supplier of every want, so the very place and nature of man is nothing but this: to wait upon God and receive from Him what He alone can give, what He delights to give.

"These wait all upon thee; that thou mayest give them." It is God who gives all: let this faith enter deeply into our hearts. Before we fully understand all that is implied in our waiting upon God, and before we have even been able to cultivate the habit, let the truth enter our souls. Waiting on God, unceasing and entire dependence upon Him, is, in heaven and earth, the only true faith, the one unalterable and all-comprehensive expression for the true relationship to the ever blessed One in whom we live.

Let us resolve at once that it will be the one characteristic of our life and worship, a continual, humble, truthful waiting upon God. We may rest assured that He who made us for Himself, that He might give Himself to us and in us, will never disappoint us. In waiting on Him, we will find rest and joy and strength, and the supply of every need.

For Supplies

The LORD upholdeth all that fall, and raiseth up all those that be bowed down. The eyes of all wait upon thee; and thou givest them their meat in due season.
—Psalm 145:14–15

Psalm 104 is a psalm of Creation, and the words, *"These wait all upon thee"* (v. 27), were used with reference to the animal creation. Here, we have a psalm of the kingdom, and *"the eyes of all wait upon thee"* appears especially to point to the needs of God's saints, who fall and are heavy laden. What the universe and the animal creation does unconsciously, God's people are to do voluntarily. Man is to be the interpreter of nature. He is to prove that there is nothing more blessed in the exercise of our free will than to use it in waiting upon God.

If any army marches out into an enemy's country, and news is received that it is not advancing, the question is asked, What is the cause of the delay? The answer will very often be: "waiting for supplies." Without these, it dare not proceed. It is likewise in the Christian life: at every step, we need our supplies from above. And, there is nothing so necessary as to cultivate that spirit of dependence on God, which refuses to go on without the needed supply of grace and strength.

If the question is asked whether this is anything different from what we do when we pray, the answer is that there may be much praying with very little waiting on God. In praying, we are often occupied with our own needs, and with our own efforts. In waiting upon God, the first thought is of the God upon whom we wait. We enter His presence and feel we need just to be quiet, so that He, as God, can overshadow us with Himself. God longs to reveal Himself, to fill us with Himself. Waiting on God gives Him time to come to us in His divine power.

Before you pray, bow quietly before God, remember and realize who He is, how near He is, how certainly He can and will help. When praying, let there be intervals of silence, reverent stillness of soul, in which you yield yourself to God, in case He may have other things He wishes to teach or to work in you. Learn to say of every want and every lack of grace: I have waited too little upon God, or He would have given me in due season all I needed.

For Instruction

Show me thy ways, O LORD; teach me thy paths. Lead me in thy truth, and teach me: for thou art the God of my salvation; on thee do I wait all the day. —Psalm 25:4–5

I spoke of an army entering an enemy's territories. The answer to the question as to the cause of delay was: "waiting for supplies." The answer might also have been: "waiting for instructions," or "waiting for orders." If the last dispatch had not been received, with the final orders of the commander, the army dared not move. It is even so in the Christian life—as deep as the need of waiting for supplies is that of waiting for instructions.

See how beautifully this comes out in Psalm 25. The writer knew and loved God's laws exceedingly, and he meditated in that law day and night. But, this was not enough. He knew that for the right spiritual understanding of the truth, and for the right personal application of it to his own particular circumstances, he needed a direct, divine teaching.

The psalm has at all times been a very special one because of its reiterated expression of the felt need of the divine teaching and of the childlike confidence that that teaching would be given. Study the psalm until your heart is filled with the two thoughts: the absolute need and the absolute certainty of divine guidance. And with these, how entirely it is in this connection that he speaks, *"On thee do I wait all the day."* Waiting for guidance, waiting for instruction, is a very blessed part of waiting upon God.

The special surrender to the divine guidance in our seasons of prayer must cultivate, and be followed up by, the habitual looking upward *"all the day."* As simple as it is to walk all day in the light of the sun, so simple can it become to a soul, practiced in waiting on God, to walk all day in the enjoyment of God's leading. What is needed to help us to such a life is just one thing: the real knowledge and faith of God as an every ready source of wisdom and goodness, longing much to be to us all that we can possibly require. If we only believed that He waits to be gracious, that He waits to be our life and to work in us—how this waiting on God would become our highest joy, the natural and spontaneous response of our hearts to His great love!

For All Saints

**Let none that wait on thee be ashamed.
—Psalm 25:3**

Let us now think of the great company of God, and the saints throughout the world who are all waiting on Him, and join in the fervent prayer: *"Let none that wait on thee be ashamed."*

Just think for a moment of the many waiting ones who need that prayer, how many are weary and feel as if their prayers are not answered. Think of how many servants of God, ministers, missionaries, or teachers, whose hopes have been disappointed, and whose longing remains unsatisfied. And then, too, think of how many who have heard of a life of perfect peace, of strength and victory, and who cannot find the path. With all these, it is only that they have not yet learned the secret of waiting upon God.

If this intercession for all who wait on God becomes part of our waiting on Him for ourselves, we will help to bear each other's burdens, and so fulfill the law of Christ. (See Galatians 6:2.)

There will be introduced into our waiting on God that element of unselfishness and love, which is the path to the the fullest communion with God. Love to believers and love to God are inseparably linked. In God, the love to His Son and to us are one: *"That the love wherewith thou hast loved me may be in them"* (John 17:26). In Christ, the love of the Father to Him, and His love to us, are one: *"As the Father hath loved me, so have I loved you"* (John 15:9). In us, He asks that His love to us be ours to our brothers and sisters: *"That ye love one another; as I have loved you"* (John 13:34). And how can we, day by day, prove and cultivate this love except by praying daily for each other? Christ did not seek to enjoy the Father's love for Himself; He passed it all on to us. All true seeking of God will be inseparably linked with the thought and the love of our brothers and sisters in prayer for them.

Blessed Father, let none who wait on You be ashamed; not one. Some are weary, and the time of waiting appears long. Some are feeble and scarcely know how to wait. Some are so entangled in the their prayers and their work, they think that they can find no time to wait continually. Father, teach us all how to wait! Teach us to think of and pray for each other. Father, let none who wait on You be ashamed! For Jesus' sake. Amen.

November 7

A Plea in Prayer

Let integrity and uprightness preserve me; for I wait on thee.
—Psalm 25:21

For the third time in this psalm we have the word *wait.* As in verse 5, *"on thee do I wait all the day,"* so here, the believing supplicant appeals to God to remember that he is waiting on Him, looking for an answer. It is a great thing for a soul not only to wait upon God, but to be filled with such a consciousness that its whole spirit and position is that of a waiting one. It can, in confidence, say, "Lord, You know I wait on You!" It will prove a mighty plea in prayer, giving ever-increasing boldness of expectation to claim the promise, "Those who wait on Me will not be ashamed!"

The prayer in connection with which the plea is put forth here is one of great importance in the spiritual life. If we draw near to God, it must be with a true heart. There must be perfect integrity in our dealing with God. As we read in the next psalm, *"Judge me, O LORD; for I have walked in mine integrity....As for me, I will walk in mine integrity"* (Psalm 26:1, 11), there must be perfect uprightness of single-heartedness before God for His righteousness is for the upright in heart. (See Psalm 36:10.) The soul must allow nothing sinful, nothing doubtful, if it is indeed to receive His full blessing. This can only be done with a heart wholly and singly given up to His will. The whole spirit that animates us in the waiting must be, *"let integrity and uprightness"*—You know I am looking to You to work them perfectly in me—let them *"preserve me; for I wait on thee."*

And, if at our first attempt to truly live the life of fully and always waiting on God, we begin to discover how much that perfect integrity is lacking, this will just be one of the blessings that the waiting was meant to work. A soul cannot seek close fellowship with God without a very honest and entire surrender to His will. If it is true that God alone is goodness and joy and love, if it is true that our highest blessedness is in having as much of God as we can, if it is true that Christ has redeemed us wholly for God and made a life of continual abiding in His presence possible, nothing less ought to satisfy us than to be ever breathing this blessed atmosphere, *"I wait on thee."*

Be Strong and Of Good Courage

Wait on the Lord; be strong, and let thine heart take courage; yea, wait thou on the LORD.
—Psalm 27:14 (RV)

The psalmist has just said, *"I had fainted, unless I had believed to see the goodness of the LORD in the land of the living"* (v. 13). If not for his faith in God, his heart would have fainted. But, in the confident assurance in God that faith gives, he urges himself and us to remember one thing above all—to wait upon God. *"Wait on the LORD: be strong, and let thine heart take courage; yea, wait thou on the LORD."* One of the chief needs in our waiting upon God is a quiet, confident persuasion that it is not in vain. Have courage and believe that God will hear and help.

"Be strong, and let thine heart take courage." These words are frequently found in connection with some difficult enterprise, in prospect of the combat with the power of strong enemies, and the insufficiency of all human strength. Is waiting on God a work so difficult that such words are needed: *"Be strong, and let thine heart take courage"*? Yes, indeed. The deliverance for which we often have to wait is from enemies, in whose presence we are so weak. The blessings for which we plead are all unseen heavenly, supernatural, divine realities.

Our souls are so little accustomed to hold fellowship with God; the God on whom we wait so often appears to hide Himself. We who have to wait are often tempted to fear that we do not wait enough, that our faith is too feeble, that our desire is not as upright or as earnest as it should be. Amid all these causes of fear or doubt, how blessed to hear the voice of God: *"Wait on the LORD: be strong, and let thine heart take courage; yea, wait thou on the LORD."* Let nothing in heaven or earth or hell keep you from waiting on your God in full assurance that it cannot be in vain.

Come, and however feeble you feel, just wait in His presence. Come with all that is dark and cold in you into the sunshine of God's holy, omnipotent love. Sit and wait there, with the one thought: here I am, in the sunshine of His love. God will do His work in you. Oh, trust Him fully! *"Wait on the LORD: be strong, and let thine heart take courage; yea, wait thou on the LORD."*

With the Heart

Be strong, and let your heart take courage, all ye that hope in the LORD.
—Psalm 31:24 (RV)

The words are nearly the same as in our last meditation. But I gladly avail myself of them again to stress a much needed lesson for all who desire to truly learn what waiting on God is. The lesson is this: it is with the heart that we must wait upon God. *"Let your heart take courage."* All our waiting depends on the state of the heart. We can advance no further into the holy place of God's presence, than our heart is prepared for it by the Holy Spirit. *"Let your heart take courage, all ye that hope in the LORD."*

The truth appears so simple that some may ask, "Do not all admit this? Where is the need of insisting on it so specially?" Because many Christians have no sense of the great difference between Christianity of the mind and Christianity of the heart. They do not know how infinitely greater the heart is than the mind. It is this that causes much of the feebleness of our Christian life. And it is only as this is understood that waiting on God will bring its full blessing. Proverbs 3:5 says, *"Trust in the LORD with all thine heart; and lean not unto thine own understanding."* In all faith, we have to use these two powers. The mind has to gather knowledge from God's Word and prepare the food by which the heart is to be nourished. But, here is the danger of our leaning to our own understanding of divine things.

People imagine that if they are occupied with the truth, the spiritual life will, as a matter of course, be strengthened. This is by no means the case. It is with the heart that man believes and comes into touch with God. It is in the heart that God has given His Spirit to be the presence and the power of God in us. It is the heart that must trust, love, worship, and obey. My mind is unable to create or maintain the spiritual life within me. The heart must wait on God for Him to work in me.

"Let your heart take courage, all ye that hope in the LORD." Present it before Him as that wonderful part of your spiritual nature in which God reveals Himself. Give your whole heart, with its secret workings, into God's hands continually. He wants the heart. He takes it and, as God, dwells in it.

In Humble Fear and Hope

Behold, the eye of the LORD is upon them that fear him, upon them that hope in his mercy; to deliver their soul from death, and to keep them alive in famine. Our soul waiteth for the LORD: he is our help and our shield. For our heart shall rejoice in him, because we have trusted in his holy name. Let thy mercy, O LORD, be upon us, according as we [wait for] thee.
—Psalm 33:18–22

God's eye is upon His people; their eyes are upon Him. In waiting upon God, our eyes, looking up to Him, meet His looking down upon us. This is the blessedness of waiting upon God, that it takes our eyes and thoughts away from ourselves and occupies us with our God. Let us consider this wonderful meeting between God and His people, and notice what we are taught here of them on whom God's eye rests, and of Him on whom our eye rests.

"The eye of the LORD is upon them that fear him, upon them that hope in his mercy." Fear and hope are generally thought to be in conflict with each other. In the presence and worship of God, they are found side by side in perfect harmony. And this is so, because in God Himself all apparent contradictions are reconciled. Righteousness and peace, judgment and mercy, infinite power and infinite gentleness, a majesty that is exalted above all heaven, and a condescension that bows very low, meet and kiss each other.

There is a fear that has torment, that is cast out by perfect love. (See 1 John 4:18.) But, there is a fear that is found in the very heavens. In the song of Moses and the Lamb they sing, *"Who shall not fear thee, O Lord, and glorify thy name?"* (Revelation 15:4). And out of the very throne the voice came, *"Praise our God, all ye his servants, and ye that fear him"* (Revelation 19:5). Let us in our waiting ever seek to *"fear this glorious and fearful name, THE LORD THY GOD"* (Deuteronomy 28:58). The deeper we bow before His holiness in holy fear and awe, in deep reverence and self-abasement, even as the angels veil their faces before the throne, the more His holiness will rest upon us. Then, we will be filled to have God reveal Himself. The deeper we enter into the truth *"that no flesh should glory in his presence"* (1 Corinthians 1:29), will it be given us to see His glory. *"The eye of the LORD is upon them that fear him."*

Patiently

Rest in the LORD, and wait patiently for him...Those that wait upon the LORD, they shall inherit the earth.
—Psalm 37:7, 9

"Ye have need of patience" (Hebrews 10:36). *"Let patience have her perfect work, that ye may be perfect and entire"* (James 1:4). Such words show us what an important element, in the Christian life, patience is. And nowhere is there a better place for cultivating it than in waiting on God. There we discover how impatient we are. We confess that we are impatient with men and circumstances, or with ourselves and our slow progress in the Christian life. If we truly set ourselves to wait upon God, we will find that it is with Him we are impatient, because He does not at once do our bidding. It is in waiting upon God that our eyes are opened to believe in His sovereign will. Then, we will see that the sooner we absolutely yield to it, the more surely His blessing can come to us.

"It is not of him that willeth, nor of him that runneth, but of God that showeth mercy" (Romans 9:16). We have as little power to strengthen our spiritual life as we had to originate it. We *"were born, not...of the will of the flesh, nor of the will of man, but of God"* (John 1:13). Even so, our willing and running, our desire and effort, avail nothing; all is *"of God that showeth mercy."*

All the exercises of the spiritual life, our reading and praying, our willing and doing, have their value. But, they can go no farther than that they prepare us in humility to depend upon God Himself, and in patience to wait His good time. The waiting is to teach us our absolute dependence upon God's working, and to make us, in perfect patience, place ourselves at His disposal. They who wait on the Lord will inherit the land (see Psalm 37:34) and its blessing. The heirs must wait; they can afford to wait.

Seek not only the help, the gift; seek Himself; wait for Him. Give God His glory by resting in Him, by waiting patiently for Him. This patience honors Him greatly. It leaves Him, as God on the throne, to do His work. It lets God be God. If your waiting is for some request, wait patiently. If your waiting is more an exercise of the spiritual life seeking to have more of God, wait patiently. Rest in the Lord, be still before the Lord, and wait patiently. *"Those that wait upon the LORD, they shall inherit the earth."*

November 12

Keeping His Ways

Wait on the LORD, and keep his way, and he shall exalt thee to inherit the land.
—Psalm 37:34

If we desire to find a man we long to meet, we inquire as to the places in which he is to be found. When waiting on God, we need to be very careful that we keep His ways; outside of these we never can expect to find Him. *"Thou meetest him that rejoiceth and worketh righteousness, those that remember thee in thy ways"* (Isaiah 64:5). We may be sure that God is never to be found but in His way. There, by the soul who seeks and patiently waits, He is to be found. *"Wait on the LORD, and keep his way, and he shall exalt thee."*

"Wait on the LORD"—has to do with worship and disposition—*"and keep his way"*—deals with walk and work. The outer life must be in harmony with the inner; the inner must be the inspiration and the strength for the outer. If we do not keep His way, our waiting on Him can bring no blessing. The surrender to a full obedience to all His will is the secret of full access to all the blessings of His fellowship.

Notice how strongly this comes out in the psalm. It speaks of the evildoer who prospers in his way and calls on the believer not to worry himself. When we see men around us prosperous and happy while they forsake God's ways, and ourselves left in difficulty or suffering, we are in danger of gradually yielding to seek our prosperity in their path. *"Fret not thyself....Trust in the LORD, and do good....Rest in the LORD, and wait patiently for him....Cease from anger, and forsake wrath....Depart from evil, and do good....The LORD...forsaketh not his saints....The righteous shall inherit the land....The law of his God is in his heart; none of his steps shall slide"* (Psalm 37:1, 3, 7, 8, 27, 28, 29, 31).

And then follows—*wait* occurs for the third time in the psalm—"*Wait on the LORD, and keep his way."* Do what God asks you to do; God will do more than you can ask Him to do.

For More Than We Know

And now, Lord, what wait I for? My hope is in thee. Deliver me from all my transgressions.
—Psalm 39:7–8

There may be times when we feel as if we do not know what we are waiting for. There may be other times when we think we know, and when it would be good for us to realize that we do not know. God is able to do for us exceeding abundantly above what we ask or think. (See Ephesians 3:20.) And, we are in danger of limiting Him when we confine our prayers to our own thoughts of them. It is great at times to say, *"And now, Lord, what wait I for?"* I scarcely know; this only I can say, *"My hope is in thee."*

How we see this limiting of God in the case of Israel! When Moses promised them meat in the wilderness, they doubted, saying, *"Can God furnish a table in the wilderness?...He smote the rock, that the waters gushed out...can he give bread also? Can he provide flesh for his people?"* (Psalm 78:19–20). If they had been asked whether God could provide streams in the desert, they would have answered, Yes. But, when they thought of God doing something new, they limited Him. Their expectation could not rise beyond their experience, or their own thoughts of what was possible.

Even so, we may be limiting God by our conceptions of what He is able to do. Let us beware of limiting God in our prayers. Let us, therefore, cultivate the habit of waiting on God, not only for what we think we need, but for all that His grace and power are ready to do for us.

In every true prayer, there are two hearts in exercise. The one is your heart, with its little, dark, human thoughts of what you need and what God can do. The other is God's heart, with its infinite purposes of blessing. To which of these two ought the larger place be given in your approach to Him? Undoubtedly, to the heart of God. But, how little this is done. This is what waiting on God is meant to teach you. Confess how little you understand what God is willing to do for you, and say each time as you pray, *"And now, Lord, what wait I for?"* My heart does not know. *"My hope is in thee."* Wait on God to do more for you than you can ask or think.

The Way to the New Song

I waited patiently for the LORD; and he inclined unto me, and heard my cry….And he hath put a new song in my mouth, even praise unto our God.
—Psalm 40:1, 3

Listen to the testimony of one who can speak from experience of the outcome of waiting upon God. True patience is so foreign to our self-confident nature, it is so indispensable in our waiting upon God, it is such an essential element of true faith, that we would do well to once again meditate on what the Word has to teach us.

The word *patience* is derived from the Latin word for suffering. It suggests the thought of being under the constraint of some power from which we would gladly be free. At first, we submit against our will. Experience teaches us that when it is vain to resist, patient endurance is our wisest course. In waiting on God, it is of infinite consequence that we not only submit because we are compelled to, but because we joyfully consent to be in the hands of our blessed Father. Patience then honors God, and gives Him time to have His way with us. It is the highest expression of our faith in His goodness. It brings the soul perfect rest in the assurance that God is carrying on His work. It is the token of our full consent that God should deal with us in such a way and time as He thinks best. True patience is the losing of our self-will in His perfect will.

Such patience is needed for the true waiting on God. Such patience is the growth and fruit of our first lesson in the school of waiting. To many, it will appear strange how difficult it is to truly wait upon God. The great stillness of soul before God that sinks into its own helplessness and waits for Him to reveal Himself must be waited for. The deep humility that is afraid to let its own will work except as God works to will and to do requires patience. The meekness that is content to be and to know nothing except as God gives His light takes time. The entire resignation of the will that only wants to be a vessel in which His holy will can move and mold is not found at once. But, each will come in measure as the soul maintains its position, and continually says, *"Truly my soul waiteth upon God: from him cometh my salvation. He only is my rock and my salvation"* (Psalm 62:1–2).

November 15

For His Counsel

They soon forgat his works; they waited not for his counsel.
—Psalm 106:13

This refers to God's people in the wilderness. He had redeemed them and was prepared to supply their every need. But, when the time of need came, *"they waited not for his counsel."* They did not think that the almighty God was their Leader and Provider. They did not ask what His plans might be. They simply thought the thoughts of their own hearts, and provoked God by their unbelief.

How this has been the sin of God's people in all ages! In the land of Canaan, in the days of Joshua, the only three failures of which we read were owing to this one sin. In going up against Ai, in making a covenant with the Gibeonites, in settling down without going up to possess the whole land, *"they waited not for his counsel."* And so, even the advanced believer is in danger from this most subtle of temptations: taking God's Word, thinking his own thoughts of it, and not waiting for His counsel. Let us especially regard it not only as a danger to which the individual is exposed, but as one against which God's people, in their collective capacity, need to be on their guard.

Our whole relationship to God is ruled in this, that His will is to be done in us and by us. He has promised to make known His will to us by His Spirit. Our position is to be waiting for His counsel as the only guide of our thoughts and actions. In our church worship, in our meetings, in our gatherings as committees or helpers in any part of the work for God, our first object must always be to ascertain the mind of God. God always works according to the counsel of His will. The more that counsel of His will is sought, found, and honored, the more surely will God do His work for us and through us.

The great danger is that in our consciousness of having our Bible, in our past experience of God's leading, in our sound creed and our honest wish to do God's will, we trust in these and do not realize that with every step we need and may have a heavenly guidance. There may be elements of God's will, application of God's Word, experience of the leading of God, manifestations of the power of His Spirit, of which we know nothing as yet. God is willing to open up these to souls who are willing, in patience, to wait for Him to make it known.

And His Light in the Heart

I wait for the LORD, my soul doth wait, and in his word do I hope. My soul waiteth for the LORD more than they that watch for the morning: I say, more than they that watch for the morning.
—Psalm 130:5–6

How intensely the morning light is often waited for: by the mariners in a shipwrecked vessel; by an army that finds itself surrounded by an enemy. The morning light will show what hope of escape there may be. The morning may bring life and liberty. And so, the saints of God in darkness have longed for the light of His countenance, more than watchmen for the morning. They have said, *"My soul waiteth for the Lord more than they that watch for the morning."* Can we say that, too?

God is light. God is a sun. Paul said, *"God...hath shined in our hearts, to give the light"* (2 Corinthians 4:6). What light? *"The light of the...glory of God in the face of Jesus Christ"* (v. 6). Just as the sun shines its life-giving light into our earth, so God shines into our hearts the light of His glory in Christ His Son. Our hearts are meant to have that light filling them all day. They can have it because God is our sun, and it is written, *"Thy sun shall no more go down"* (Isaiah 60:20). God's love shines on us without ceasing.

Learn to wait on the Lord, more than watchers for the morning! All within you may be very dark. But, is that not the very best reason for waiting for the light of God? The beginnings of light may be just enough to discover the darkness, and painfully to humble you on account of sin. Can you not trust the light to expel the darkness? Do believe it will. Just bow in stillness before God, and wait on Him to shine into you. Say, in humble faith, God is light, infinitely brighter and more beautiful than that of the sun. God is light, here shining on my heart. I have been so occupied with the candles of my thoughts and efforts that I have never opened the shutters to let His light in. Unbelief has kept it out. The light does shine; the light will shine in me and make me full of light. And I will learn to walk all day in the light and joy of God. My soul waits on the light of the Lord, more than the watchers for the morning.

In Times of Darkness

And I will wait upon the LORD, that hideth his face from the house of Jacob, and I will look for him.
—Isaiah 8:17

Here we have a servant of God waiting upon Him on behalf of his people, from whom God was hiding His face. We may be walking in the light of God's countenance, and yet God may be hiding His face from people around us. Far from our being content to think that this is the just punishment of their sin, we are called with tender hearts to wait on God on their behalf. The privilege of waiting upon God brings great responsibility. Even as Christ at once used His place of privilege as intercessor, so we must use our access for our less favored brothers and sisters.

You worship with a certain congregation. Possibly, there is not the spiritual life or joy either in the preaching or the fellowship that you desire. There is so much error or worldliness, so much seeking after human wisdom and culture, or so much trust in ordinances and observances, that you are not surprised that God hides His face. It is no wonder that there is little power for conversion or true edification.

Then, there are branches of Christian work with which you are connected—Sunday school, men's fellowship, mission work—in which the feebleness of the Spirit's working indicates that God is hiding His face. You think, too, you know the reason. There is too much trust in men and money. There is too much self-indulgence. There is too little faith and prayer; too little of the spirit of the crucified Jesus. At times, you feel as if things are hopeless.

God can and will help. Let the spirit of the prophet come into you and set yourself to wait on God, on behalf of His erring children. Instead of the tone of judgment, realize your calling to wait upon God. If others fail in doing it, give yourself doubly to it. The deeper the darkness, the greater the need of appealing to the only Deliverer. The greater the self-confidence around you, that knows not that it is poor and wretched and blind, the more urgent the call to be at your post waiting upon God. Say on each new occasion, *"I will wait upon the LORD, that hideth his face from the house of Jacob."*

November 18

To Reveal Himself

And it shall be said in that day, Lo, this is our God; we have waited for him, and he will save us: this is the LORD; we have waited for him, we will be glad and rejoice in his salvation.
—Isaiah 25:9

In this passage are two thoughts. The one is that of God's people who have been unitedly waiting on Him. The other, that the fruit of their waiting has been that God has revealed Himself, that they could say, *"Lo, this is our God...this is the LORD."* The power and blessing of united waiting is what we need to learn.

This phrase is repeated twice, *"We have waited for him."* In time of trouble, the hearts of the people had been drawn together, and they had set themselves to wait for their God. Is this not just what we need in our churches? Are there not in the church of Christ evils to which no human wisdom is equal? Have we not formalism and worldliness, robbing the church of its power? Have we not culture and money and pleasure threatening its spiritual life? Are not the powers of the church utterly inadequate to cope with the powers of infidelity and wretchedness in the world? And, is there not, in the promise of God and in the power of the Holy Spirit, a provision made that can give the church the restful assurance that she is doing all God expects of her? And would not united waiting upon God for the supply of His Spirit most certainly seem the needed blessing? We cannot doubt it.

The object of a more definite waiting upon God in our gatherings would mean a deeper conviction that God must and will do all. It would require a more humble and abiding entrance into our deep need of entire and unceasing dependence upon Him. We must have a confident expectation that to those who wait on Him, God will, by His Spirit, give the secret of His acceptance and presence, and then, in due time, the revelation of His saving power. The great aim would be to bring everyone in a praying and worshipping company under a deep sense of God's presence, so that when they part there will be the consciousness of having met God Himself, of having left every request with Him, and of now waiting in stillness while He works out His salvation.

As a God of Judgment

Yea, in the way of thy judgments, O LORD, have we waited for thee....for when thy judgments are in the earth, the inhabitants of the world will learn righteousness.
—Isaiah 26:8–9

The LORD is a God of judgment: blessed are all they that wait for him.
—Isaiah 30:18

Mercy and judgment are forever together in God's dealings. In the flood, in the deliverance of Israel out of Egypt, in the overthrow of the Canaanites, we ever see mercy in the midst of judgment. The judgment punishes the sin, while mercy saves the sinner. Or, rather, mercy saves the sinner by means of the very judgment that came upon his sin. As we wait on God, we must expect Him as a God of judgment.

"In the way of thy judgments, O LORD, have we waited for thee." If we are honest in our longing for holiness, His holy presence will stir up and discover hidden sin. It will bring us low in the conviction of the evil of our nature, its opposition to God's law, and its inability to fulfill that law. The words will come true: *"Who may abide the day of his coming?...For he is like a refiner's fire"* (Malachi 3:2). In mercy, God executes His judgments upon sin, as He makes it feel its wickedness. Many try to flee these judgments. The soul that longs for God, and for deliverance from sin, bows under them in humility and in hope. In silence of soul, it says, *"Rise up, LORD, and let thine enemies be scattered"* (Numbers 10:35). *"In the way of thy judgments...have we waited for thee."*

Let no one who seeks to learn to wait on God wonder if at first the attempt to wait only reveals more sin. Let no one despair because unconquered sins, evil thoughts, or great darkness appear to hide God's face. Submit and sink down under the judgment of your sin. Judgment prepares the way and breaks out in mercy. It is written, *"Zion shall be redeemed with judgment"* (Isaiah 1:27). Wait on God, in the faith that His mercy is working out His redemption in the midst of judgment. Wait for Him; He will be gracious to you.

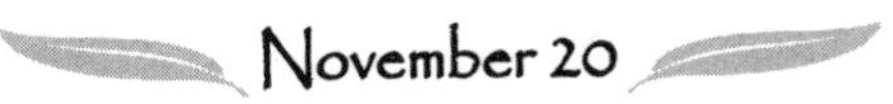

Who Waits on Us

And therefore will the LORD wait, that he may be gracious unto you, and therefore will he be exalted, that he may have mercy upon you: for the LORD is a God of judgment: blessed are all they that wait for him.
—Isaiah 30:18

We must not only think of our waiting upon God, but also of God's waiting upon us. The vision of Him waiting on us will give new inspiration to our waiting upon Him. It will give us confidence that our waiting cannot be in vain. If He waits for us, then we may be sure that we are welcome—that He rejoices to find those He has been seeking for. Let us seek even now to find out something of what it means. *"Therefore will the LORD wait, that he may be gracious unto you."* We will accept and echo back the message, *"Blessed are all they that wait for him."*

Look up and see the great God upon His throne. He has inconceivably glorious purposes concerning every one of His children to reveal in them His love and power. He waits with all the longings of a father's heart that He may be gracious unto you. And, each time you wait upon Him, you may look up and see Him ready to meet you. He is waiting so that He may be gracious unto you.

And you may ask, "How is it that even after I wait upon Him, He does not give the help I seek, but waits longer?" There is a double answer. The one is this: God is wise. He cannot gather the fruit until it is ripe. He knows when we are spiritually ready to receive the blessing. Waiting in the sunshine of His love will ripen the soul. Be assured that if God waits longer than you could wish, it is only to make the blessing doubly precious. Our times are in His hands. He will avenge His elect speedily. He will make haste for our help and not delay one hour too long.

The other answer points to what has been said before. The giver is more than the gift; God is more than the blessing. And our being kept waiting on Him is the only way for our learning to find our life and joy in Him. Oh, if God's children only knew what a privilege it is to be linked in fellowship with Him! *"Therefore will the LORD wait, that he may be gracious unto you."* His waiting will be the highest proof of His graciousness.

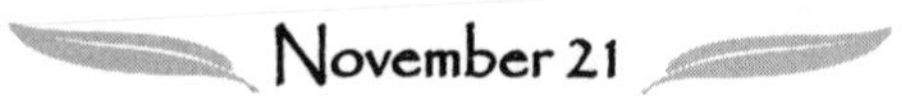

The Almighty One

But they that wait upon the LORD shall renew their strength; they shall mount up with wings as eagles; they shall run, and not be weary; and they shall walk, and not faint.
—Isaiah 40:31

Our waiting on God will depend greatly on our faith of what He is. In our text, we have the close of a passage in which God reveals Himself as the everlasting and almighty One. It is as that revelation enters into our soul that the waiting will become the spontaneous expression of what we know Him to be—a God altogether most worthy to be waited upon.

Listen to the words, *"Why sayest thou, O Jacob…My way is hid from the LORD…? Hast thou not known? hast thou not heard, that the everlasting God, the LORD, the Creator of the ends of the earth, fainteth not, neither is weary?"* (Isaiah 40:27–28). So far from it: *"He giveth power to the faint; and to them that have no might he increaseth strength. Even the youths shall faint…and the young men shall utterly fall"* (vv. 29–30). And consider that *"the glory of young men is their strength"* (Proverbs 20:29). All that is deemed strong with man shall come to nothing. *"But they that wait upon the LORD,"* on the Everlasting One, who does not faint, and is not weary, they *"shall renew their strength; they shall mount up with wings as eagles; they shall run, and"*—listen now, they will be strong with the strength of God, and, even as He, they will *"not be weary; and they shall walk, and"* even as He, they will *"not faint."*

Yes, *"they shall mount up with wings as eagles."* You know what eagles' wings mean. The eagle is the king of birds; it soars the highest into the heavens. Believers are to live a heavenly life, in the very presence and love and joy of God. They are to live where God lives; they need God's strength to rise there. It will be given to them that wait on Him.

You know how the eagles' wings are obtained. Only in one way—by the eagle birth. You are born of God. You have the eagles' wings. You may not have known it; you may not have used them; but God can and will teach you how to use them.

The Certainty of Blessing

And thou shalt know that I am the LORD: for they shall not be ashamed that wait for me.
—Isaiah 49:23

Blessed are all they that wait for him.
—Isaiah 30:18

What promises! How God seeks to draw us to waiting on Him by the most positive assurance that it never can be in vain; *"they shall not be ashamed that wait for me."* How strange that, though we so often have experienced it, we are yet so slow to learn that this blessed waiting must and can be the very breath of our life. Let us once again listen and meditate, until our heart says with new conviction, *"Blessed are all they that wait for him."*

We found in the prayer of Psalm 25: *"Let none that wait on thee be ashamed"* (v. 3). The very prayer shows how we fear that it might be true. Let us listen to God's answer, until every fear is banished, and we send back to heaven the words God speaks, "All they who wait for Me will *not* be ashamed." *"Blessed are all they that wait for him."*

The context of each of these two passages points us to times when God's church was in great straits, and to human eyes there were no possibilities of deliverance. But, God interposes with His word of promise, and pledges His almighty power for the deliverance of His people. And it is as the God who has undertaken the work of their redemption that He invites them to wait on Him, and assures them that disappointment is impossible.

We, too, are living in days in which there is much in the state of the church. Amid all we praise God for, there is, alas, much to mourn over! Were it not for God's promises, we might well despair. But, in His promises the living God calls us to wait on Him. He assures us we will not be put to shame. Oh, that our hearts might learn to wait before Him, until He Himself reveals to us what His promises mean. In the promises, He reveals Himself in His hidden glory! We will be irresistibly drawn to wait on Him alone. May God increase the company of those who say: *"Our soul waiteth for the LORD: he is our help and our shield"* (Psalm 33:20).

November 23

For Unlooked-for Things

For since the beginning of the world men have not heard, nor perceived by the ear, neither hath the eye seen, O God, beside thee, what he hath prepared for him that waiteth for him.
—Isaiah 64:4

The previous verses in Isaiah, especially Isaiah 63:15, refer to the low state of God's people. The prayer has been poured out, *"Look down from heaven"* (v. 15). *"Why hast thou…hardened our heart from thy fear? Return for thy servants' sake"* (v. 17). And 64:1–2, *"Oh that thou wouldest rend the heavens, that thou wouldest come down…as when the melting fire burneth…to make thy name known to thine adversaries!"* Then the plea from the past, *"When thou didst terrible things which we looked not for, thou camest down, the mountains flowed down at thy presence"* (v. 3). *"For"*—this is now the faith awakened by the thought of things we looked not for—*"neither hath the eye seen, O God, beside thee, what he hath prepared for him that waiteth for him."*

God alone knows what He can do for His waiting people. As Paul expounded and applied it: *"The things of God knoweth no man, but the Spirit of God"* (1 Corinthians 2:11). *"But God hath revealed them unto us by his Spirit"* (v. 10).

The need of God's people is as urgent in our days as it was in the time of Isaiah. There are now, as there was then, a few who seek after God with their whole hearts. But, if we look at Christendom as a whole, at the state of the church of Christ, there is infinite cause for beseeching God to rend the heavens and come down. Nothing but a special interposition of almighty power will avail. Unless God comes down *"as when the melting fire burneth…to make* [His] *name known to* [His] *adversaries"* (Isaiah 64:2), our labors are comparatively fruitless.

What is to be done? There is only one thing. We must wait upon God. And what for? We must cry, *"Oh that thou wouldest rend the heavens…*[and] *come down, that the mountains might flow down at thy presence"* (Isaiah 64:1). We must ask and expect, that God will do unlooked-for things. We must set our faith on a God of whom men do not know what He has prepared for them who wait for Him. The wonder-doing God, who can surpass all our expectations, must be the God of our confidence.

To Know His Goodness

The LORD is good unto them that wait for him.
—Lamentations 3:25

There is none good but God. (See Matthew 19:17.) His goodness is in the heavens. *"Oh how great is thy goodness, which thou hast laid up for them that fear thee"* (Psalm 31:19). *"O taste and see that the LORD is good"* (Psalm 34:8). And here is now the true way of entering into and rejoicing in this goodness of God—waiting upon Him. The Lord is good—even His children often do not know it, for they do not wait in quietness for Him to reveal it. But, to those who persevere in waiting, it will come true. *"The LORD is good unto them that wait for him."* If you want to fully know the goodness of God, give yourself to a life of waiting on Him.

At our first entrance into waiting upon God, the heart is mainly set on the blessings that we wait for. God graciously uses our needs and desires for help to educate us for something higher than we were thinking of. We were seeking gifts; He, the Giver, longs to give Himself. It is for this reason that He often withholds gifts, and that the waiting is made so long. He is constantly seeking to win the heart of His child for Himself. He wishes that we would not only say, when He bestows the gift, "How good is God!" but that before it comes, and even if it never comes, we should always be experiencing: *"The LORD is good unto them that wait for him."*

What a blessed life the life of waiting then becomes, the continual worship of faith, adoring, and trusting His goodness. Instead of only taking refuge in time of need, there comes a great longing to wait continually and all day. And, however duties and engagements occupy the time and the mind, the soul gets more familiar with the secret art of waiting. Waiting becomes the habit and disposition, the very second nature and breath of the soul.

Begin to see that waiting is not one among a number of Christian virtues. But, it expresses that disposition that lies at the root of the Christian life. It gives new power to our prayers and worship, because it links us, in unalterable dependence, to God Himself. And, it gives us the unbroken enjoyment of the goodness of God: *"The LORD is good unto them that wait for him."*

November 25

Quietly

It is good that a man should both hope and quietly wait for the salvation of the LORD.
—Lamentation 3:26

"Take heed, and be quiet; fear not, neither be fainthearted" (Isaiah 7:4). *"In quietness and in confidence shall be your strength"* (Isaiah 30:15). Such words reveal to us the close connection between quietness and faith. They show us what a deep need there is of quietness, as an element of waiting upon God. If we are to have our whole heart turned toward God, we must have it turned away from man, from all that occupies and interests, whether of joy or sorrow.

God is a being of such infinite greatness and glory, and our nature has become so estranged from Him, that it requires our whole heart and desires set upon Him, even in some little measure, to know and receive Him. Everything that is not God, that excites our fears or stirs our efforts or awakens our hopes or makes us glad, hinders us in our perfect waiting on Him. The message is one of deep meaning: *"Take heed, and be quiet"*; *"In quietness...shall be your strength"*; *"It is good that a man should...quietly wait."*

Scripture abundantly testifies how the very thought of God in His majesty and holiness should silence us: *"The LORD is in his holy temple: let all the earth keep silence before him"* (Habakkuk 2:20); *"Hold thy peace at the presence of the Lord GOD"* (Zephaniah 1:7); *"Be silent, O all flesh, before the LORD: for he is raised up out of his holy habitation"* (Zechariah 2:13).

As long as the waiting on God is chiefly regarded as an end toward more effectual prayer, this spirit of perfect quietness will not be obtained. But, when it is seen that waiting on God is itself an unspeakable blessedness—one of the highest forms of fellowship with God—the adoration of Him in His glory will of necessity humble the soul into a holy stillness, making way for God to speak and reveal Himself.

Though at first it may appear difficult to know how thus quietly to wait, with the activities of mind and heart for a time subdued, every effort after it will be rewarded. We will discover that it grows upon us, and the little season of silent worship will bring a peace and a rest that give a blessing all day.

November 26

In Holy Expectancy

Therefore I will look unto the LORD; I will wait for the God of my salvation: my God will hear me.
—Micah 7:7

Have you ever heard of a book, *Expectation Corners*? It tells of a king who prepared a city for some of his poor subjects. Not far from them were storehouses where everything they could need was supplied *if* they sent in their requests. But, there was one condition: they were to be on the lookout for the answer, so that when the king's messengers came with the answer to their petitions, they would be found waiting to receive them. The sad story is told of one person who never expected to get what he asked because he believed he was too unworthy. One day, he was taken to the king's storehouses; there, to his amazement, he saw all the packages that had been made up for him and sent. The king's messengers had been to his door but found it closed; he was not on the lookout. From that time on, he learned the lesson from Micah: *"I will look unto the LORD; I will wait for the God of my salvation: my God will hear me."*

A joyful expectancy is the essence of true waiting. This is not only in reference to the many requests every believer makes, but most to the one great petition that ought to be the chief thing every heart seeks—that the life of God in the soul may have full sway, that the heart may be *"filled with all the fulness of God"* (Ephesians 3:19). This is what God has promised. This is what God's people too little seek, because they do not believe it possible. This is what we ought to seek and dare to expect, because God is able and waiting to work it in us.

However, God Himself must work it. And for this end our working must cease. We must see how entirely it is to be the faith of the operation of God, who raised Jesus from the dead. Just as much as the resurrection, the perfecting of God's life in our souls is to be directly His work. And, waiting has to become, more than ever, a tarrying before God in stillness of soul, counting upon Him who raises the dead and calls the things that are not as though they were. (See Romans 4:17.)

For Redemption

Simeon....was just and devout, waiting for the consolation of Israel: and the Holy Ghost was upon him....Anna, a prophetess....spake of him to all them that looked for redemption in Jerusalem.
—Luke 2:25, 36, 38

Here we have the mark of a waiting believer. *"Just,"* righteous in all his conduct; *"devout,"* ever walking as in His presence; *"waiting for the consolation of Israel,"* looking for the fulfillment of God's promises: *"and the Holy Ghost was upon him."* This was the one mark of a godly band of men and women in Jerusalem. They were waiting on God, looking for His promised redemption. And now that the consolation of Israel has come, and the redemption has been accomplished, do we still need to wait? We do indeed. But, will not our waiting, who look back to it as come, differ greatly from those who looked forward to it as coming? It will, especially in two aspects. We now wait on God in the full power of the redemption, and we wait for its full revelation.

The Epistles teach us to present ourselves to God as *"dead indeed unto sin, but alive unto God through Jesus Christ"* (Romans 6:11), *"blessed...with all spiritual blessings in heavenly places in Christ"* (Ephesians 1:3). Our waiting on God may now be in the wonderful consciousness that we are accepted in the Beloved, that the love that rests on Him rests on us, and that we are living in the very presence and sight of God. In our waiting on God, let this be our confidence: in Christ we have access to the Father. How sure, therefore, we may be that our waiting cannot be in vain.

Our waiting differs, too, in that while they waited for a redemption to come, we see it accomplished and now wait for its revelation in us. Christ not only said, *"Abide in me"* (John 15:4), but also *"I in you"* (v. 4). The Epistles not only speak of us in Christ, but of Christ in us.

My life in Christ up there in heaven and Christ's life in me down here on earth—these two are the complement of each other. The waiting on God, which began with special needs and prayer, will increasingly be concentrated, as far as our personal life is concerned, on this one thing: Lord, reveal Your redemption fully in me; let Christ live in me.

For the Coming of His Son

[Be] ye yourselves like unto men that wait for their lord.
—Luke 12:36

Until the appearing of our Lord Jesus Christ: which in his times he shall show, who is the blessed and only Potentate, the King of kings, and Lord of lords.
—1 Timothy 6:14–15

Turned to God from idols to serve the living and true God; and to wait for his Son from heaven.
—1 Thessalonians 1:9–10

Waiting on God in heaven, and waiting for His Son from heaven—these two God has joined together. The waiting on God for His presence and power in daily life will be the only true preparation for waiting for Christ in humility and holiness. The waiting for Christ coming to take us to heaven will give the waiting on God its true tone of hopefulness and joy. The Father, who, in His own time, will reveal His Son from heaven, is the God who, as we wait on Him, prepares us for the revelation of His Son. The present life and the coming glory are connected in God and in us.

There is a danger of separating them. It is always easier to be engaged with the Christianity of the past or the future than to be faithful in the Christianity of today. As we look to what God has done in the past, or will do in time to come, the personal claim of present duty and submission to His working may be avoided. All you who say you wait for Christ's coming, be sure that you wait on God now. The same omnipotent love that is to reveal that glory is working in you even now to prepare you for it.

If you want to learn how to properly wait for His Son from heaven, live even now waiting on God in heaven. Waiting for Christ Himself is so different from waiting for things that may come to pass! The latter any Christian can do; the former, God must work in you every day by His Holy Spirit. Therefore, all you who wait on God, look to Him for grace to wait for His Son from heaven in the Spirit which is from heaven. And, you who want to wait for His Son, wait on God continually to reveal Christ in you.

For the Promise of the Father

He charged them not to depart from Jerusalem, but to wait for the promise of the Father.
—Acts 1:4 (RV)

In speaking of the saints in Jerusalem at Christ's birth—with Simeon and Anna—we saw how the call to waiting is no less urgent now than it was then. We wait for the full revelation in us of what came to them, but what they could scarcely comprehend. In one sense, the fulfillment can never come again as it came at Pentecost. In another sense, and that in as deep a reality as with the first disciples, we need to wait daily for the Father to fulfill His promise in us.

The Holy Spirit is not a person distinct from the Father in the way two persons on earth are distinct. The Father and the Spirit are never separate from each other. The Father is always in the Spirit; the Spirit works nothing but as the Father works in Him. Each moment, the same Spirit that is in us is in God, too. And, he who is most full of the Spirit will be the first to wait on God most earnestly. The Spirit in us is not a power at our disposal. Nor is the Spirit an independent power, acting apart from the Father and the Son. The Spirit is the real, living presence and the power of the Father working in us. Therefore, he who knows that the Spirit is in him waits on the Father for the full revelation and experience of the Spirit's indwelling.

What new meaning and promise does this give to our lives of waiting! It teaches us to continually keep the place where the disciples tarried at the footstool of the throne. It reminds us that, as helpless as they were to meet their enemies, or to preach to Christ's enemies until they were endued with power, we, too, can only be strong in the life of faith, or the work of love, as we are in direct communication with God and Christ. They must maintain the life of the Spirit in us. This assures us that the omnipotent God will, through the glorified Christ, work in us a power that can bring unexpected things to pass, impossible things. Oh, what the church will be able to do when her individual members learn to live their lives waiting on God—when together, with all of self and the world sacrificed in the fire of love, they unite in waiting with one accord for the promise of the Father, once so gloriously fulfilled, but still unexhausted!

Continually

Therefore turn thou to thy God: keep mercy and judgment, and wait on thy God continually.
—Hosea 12:6

Continuity is one of the essential elements of life. Interrupt it for a single hour in a man, and it is lost. God wants me to be, and God waits to make me; I want to be, and I wait on Him to make me, every moment, well pleasing in His sight. If waiting on God is the essence of true faith, the maintenance of the spirit of entire dependence must be continuous. The call of God, *"wait on thy God continually,"* must be obeyed.

This continual waiting is indeed a necessity. To those who are content with a feeble Christian life, it appears to be a luxury beyond what is essential to be a good Christian. But, all who are praying the prayer, "Lord, make me as holy as a pardoned sinner can be made! Keep me as near to You as it is possible!" feel that it is something that must be had. They feel that there can be no unbroken fellowship with God waiting continually on the Lord.

The continual waiting is a possibility. Many think that with the duties of life it is out of the question. They cannot always be thinking of it. Even when they wish to, they forget.

They do not understand that it is a matter of the heart and that what the heart is full of occupies it, even when the thoughts are otherwise engaged. A father's heart may be continuously filled with intense longing for a sick wife or child at a distance, even though pressing business requires all his thoughts. In the midst of occupations and temptations, it can wait continually.

Do not limit God in this by your thoughts of what may be expected. In His very nature, God, as the only Giver of life, cannot do anything other than work in His child every moment. Do not look only at the one side: "If I wait continually, God will work continually." No, look at the other side. Place God first and say, "God works continually; every moment I may wait on Him continually." Take time until the vision of your God working continually, without one moment's intermission, fills your being. Your waiting continually will then come of itself. Full of trust and joy, the holy habit of the soul will be, *"on thee do I wait all the day"* (Psalm 25:5). The Holy Spirit will keep you ever waiting.

December

The Morning Hour

My voice shalt thou hear in the morning, O LORD; in the morning will I direct my prayer unto thee, and will look up.
—Psalm 5:3

The Lord GOD...he wakeneth morning by morning, he wakeneth mine ear to hear as the learned.
—Isaiah 50:4

Morning has always been considered the time best suited for personal worship by God's servants. Most Christians regard it as a privilege to devote the beginning of the day to seek fellowship with God. Whether they think of a whole hour or half an hour or a quarter of an hour, they agree with the psalmist when he said, *"My voice shalt thou hear in the morning, O LORD."*

A well-known Christian leader has said, "Next to receiving Christ as Savior and claiming the baptism of the Holy Spirit, we know of no act that brings greater good to ourselves or others than the determination to keep the morning watch and spend the first half hour of the day alone with God." At first glance this statement appears too strong. The determination to keep the morning watch hardly appears sufficiently important to be compared to receiving Christ and the baptism of the Holy Spirit. However, it is true that it is impossible to maintain a Christian walk in the leading and power of the Holy Spirit, without daily fellowship with God. The morning watch is the position in which the surrender to Christ and the Holy Spirit can be fully maintained.

The morning watch must not be regarded as an end in itself. It is to serve to secure the presence of Christ for the whole day. To abide in Him, kept by Him, doing His will—this cannot be an irregular practice if we are truly devoted to Him.

The believer who has made devotion to Christ his watchword will find in the morning hour the place where his holy calling is renewed. During this quiet time, his will is fortified to walk worthy of his calling. (See Ephesians 4:1.) His faith is rewarded by the presence of Christ who is waiting to meet him and take charge of him for the day. *"We are more than conquerors through him that loved us"* (Romans 8:37). A living Christ waits to meet us.

Fellowship with the Father

But thou, when thou prayest, enter into thy closet, and when thou hast shut thy door, pray to thy Father which is in secret.
—Matthew 6:6

Man was created for fellowship with God. God made him in His own image, so that he would be capable of enjoying God, entering into His will, and delighting in His glory. Because God is the all-pervading One, man could have lived in the enjoyment of this unbroken fellowship.

Sin robbed us of this fellowship. Nothing but this fellowship can satisfy the heart of either man or God. It was this fellowship that Christ came to restore. Fellowship with God is the consummation of all blessedness on earth as it is in heaven. This blessing comes when we experience the promise, *"I will never leave thee, nor forsake thee"* (Hebrews 13:5), and when we can say, "The Father is always with me."

This fellowship with God is meant to be ours all day long, whatever the circumstances surrounding us. The ability to maintain close fellowship with God will depend entirely upon the intensity with which we seek Him in the hour of secret prayer. The one essential thing in the morning watch is fellowship with God.

Our Lord teaches us the inner secret of prayer: *"Shut thy door,* [and] *pray to thy Father which is in secret."* When you are in secret, you have the Father's presence and attention. Of more importance than all your requests is this one thing: the living assurance that your Father sees you and that you have now met Him face-to-face. You are now enjoying actual fellowship with Him.

Christian, there is a terrible danger to which you stand exposed in your inner chamber of prayer. You are in danger of substituting prayer and Bible study for living fellowship with God.

Your needs and your desire to pray humbly, earnestly, and believingly may so occupy your mind that the light of His countenance and the joy of His love cannot enter you. Your Bible study may so interest you that the very Word of God may become a substitute for God Himself. The greatest hindrance to fellowship is anything that keeps the soul occupied instead of leading it to God Himself. We go out into the day's work without the power of an abiding fellowship because the blessing was not secured in our morning devotions.

Unbroken Fellowship

But thou, when thou fastest, anoint thine head, and wash thy face; that thou appear not unto men to fast, but unto thy Father which is in secret: and thy Father, which seeth in secret, shall reward thee openly.
—Matthew 6:17–18

When they saw the boldness of Peter and John....they took knowledge of them, that they had been with Jesus.
—Acts 4:13

And it came to pass, when Moses came down from mount Sinai...that Moses wist not that the skin of his face shone while he talked with him. And when Aaron and all the children of Israel saw Moses, behold, the skin of his face shone; and they were afraid to come nigh him...till Moses had done speaking with them, he put a veil on his face.
—Exodus 34:29–30, 33

The transition from fellowship with God to interaction with our fellowmen is difficult. If we have met God, we long to maintain His presence. Yet when we go out to the breakfast table, the presence of our families and material things take over, and we begin to lose what we gained in our quiet time. Let us strive to learn how our conversations with people may be, instead of a hindrance, a help to the life of continual fellowship with God.

The story of Moses with the veil on his face teaches us that close and continued fellowship with God will in due time leave its mark and manifest itself to those around us. Just as Moses did not know that his face shone, we will be unaware of the light of God shining from us.

This same lesson was taught by our Lord when He said we should not draw attention to ourselves when fasting, *"that thou appear not unto men to fast."* Expect God to make others know that His grace and light are upon you.

The story of Peter and John confirms the same truth: they had been with Jesus not only while He was on earth, but as He entered into the heavenlies. They simply acted out what the Spirit taught them. Even their enemies could see by their boldness *"that they had been with Jesus."*

Prayer and the Word of God

And when Moses was gone into the tabernacle of the congregation to speak with him, then he heard the voice of one speaking unto him from off the mercy seat...and he spake unto him.
—Numbers 7:89

In regard to the connection between prayer and the Word in our private devotion, this expression has often been quoted: "When I pray, I speak to God; when I read the Bible, God speaks to me." This verse in the history of Moses is one in which this thought is beautifully brought out. When Moses went in to pray and to wait for instructions, he found One waiting for him. What a lesson for our morning watch!

A prayerful spirit is the spirit to which God will speak. A prayerful spirit will be a listening spirit, waiting to hear what God says. In true communion with God, His presence and the part He takes must be as real as my own.

Moses separated himself from the people and went to the place where God was to be found. Jesus has told us where that place is. He calls us to enter into our closet, shut the door, and pray to the Father who is in secret. (See Matthew 6:6.) Any place where we are really alone with God can be for us the secret of His presence. To speak with God requires a heart in full expectation of meeting God personally. Those who go there to speak to God will hear the voice of One speaking to them.

Prayer and the Word are inseparably linked together; power in the use of either depends upon the presence of the other. The Word gives me *matter* for prayer, telling me what God will do for me. It shows me the *path* of prayer, telling me how God wants me to come to Him. It gives me the *power* for prayer, the assurance that I will be heard. And it brings me the *answer* to prayer, as it teaches what God will do for me. Prayer prepares the heart for receiving the Word from God Himself, for the teaching of the Spirit to give the spiritual understanding of it, for the faith that is made partaker of its mighty working.

Prayer and the Word have one common center—God. Prayer seeks God; the Word reveals God. Make God the object of your desire. Prayer and the Word will be a blessed fellowship with God, the interchange of thought and love and life, a dwelling in God and God in us. Seek God and live!

Becoming a Man or Woman of God

Moses the man of God blessed the children of Israel.
—Deuteronomy 33:1

"*The man of God*"! How much this name means! He is a man who comes from God. He walks with God and carries the mark of His presence. His whole being is ruled by the glory of God, and he involuntarily causes men to think of God. In his heart the life of God has taken its rightful place. His one desire is that God should have a place of prominence in men's hearts throughout the world.

God seeks these individuals so that He may fill them with Himself and send them into the world to help others to know Him. Moses was such a man of God that people naturally spoke of him this way—*"Moses the man of God."*

The thought of a man like Moses leads us beyond our own personal needs. He was so closely linked to God that men instinctively gave this as his chief characteristic—*"the man of God."* This thought brings us out into public life and suggests the idea of the impression we make upon others. We can be so full of God's holy presence that, when others see us, this name will come to mind—*"the man of God."*

These are the kinds of men and women the world and God equally need. Why is this? Because the world, by sin, has fallen away from God. Because in Christ the world has been redeemed for God. God has no way of showing people what they ought to be except through men and women of God. Man was created for God, so that God might live, work, and show forth His glory in him and through him. God was to be his all in all.

When the redemption of Christ was completed in the descent of the Holy Spirit into the hearts of men, this indwelling was restored, and God regained possession of His home. A person can give himself completely to the presence of the Holy Spirit, not only as a power working in him, but also as God dwelling in him. Then he can become, in the deepest meaning of the word, *"a man of God."* (See John 14:16, 20, 23, and 1 John 4:13, 16.)

It is in the secret prayer habit of daily life that we learn to know our God, His fire, and our power with Him. May we know what it is to be a man or woman of God and what it implies.

The Power of God's Word

The word of God, which effectually worketh also in you that believe.
—1 Thessalonians 2:13

The value of a man's words depends upon what I know about him. If a man promises to give me half of all he has, it greatly matters whether he is a poor man or a millionaire. One of the first requirements for fruitful Bible study is the knowledge of God as the Omnipotent One and of the power of His Word.

The power of God's Word is infinite. *"By the word of the LORD were the heavens made....For he spake, and it was done; he commanded, and it stood fast"* (Psalm 33:6, 9). God's power works in His Word. God's Word has creative power and calls into existence the very thing of which it speaks.

The Word of the living God is a living Word, and it gives life. It can call into existence and make alive again what is dead. Its quickening power can raise dead bodies, can give eternal life to dead souls. All spiritual life comes through it, for we are born of incorruptible seed *"by the word of God, which liveth and abideth for ever"* (1 Peter 1:23).

The Word has power to illuminate our darkness; in our hearts it will bring the light of God and the knowledge of His will. The Word can fill us with courage to conquer every enemy. The Word will cleanse, sanctify, and work in us faith and obedience. It will become in us the seed of every trait in the likeness of our Lord. It will make all that is in the Word true in us and so prepare our hearts to be the habitation of the Father and the Son.

What a change would come over our relationship with God's Word and to the morning watch if we really believed this simple truth! Let us begin our training for that ministry of the Word by proving its power in our own experience. Let us begin to seek to learn the great faith lesson, the mighty power of God's Word.

The Word of God is true because God Himself will make it true in us. We have much to learn regarding what hinders that power, much to overcome to be freed from these hindrances, and much to surrender to receive that power. But all will be right if we study our Bibles with the determination to believe that God's Word has omnipotent power in our hearts to accomplish every blessing of which it speaks.

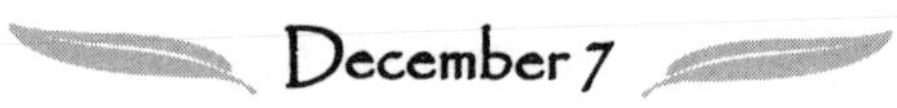

December 7

The Word Is a Seed

The kingdom of heaven is like to a...seed.
—Matthew 13:31

I think that in all of nature, the best illustration for the Word of God is that of the seed. The points of resemblance between the two are quite evident. There is the apparent insignificance of the seed—a little thing as compared with the tree that springs from it. There is the life, enclosed and dormant within a husk. There is the need for suitable soil, without which growth is impossible. There is the slow growth, with its length of time calling for long patience. And there is the fruit, in which the seed reproduces and multiplies itself. In all these respects, the seed teaches us precious lessons as to our use of God's Word.

A seed bears a fruit that contains the same seed for new reproduction. In the same way, the Word will not only bring you the fruit it promised, but that fruit will become a seed that you carry to others to give life and blessing.

Not only the Word, but *"the kingdom of heaven is like to a...seed."* The kingdom's attributes come as a hidden seed in the heart of the regenerate person. Christ is a seed. The Holy Spirit is a seed. The exceeding greatness of the power (see Ephesians 1:19) that works in us is a seed. The hidden life is there in the heart, but it is not always felt in its power. The divine glory is there, to be counted on and acted on even when not felt, to be waited for in its springing forth and its growth.

As this central truth is firmly grasped and held as the law of all heavenly life on earth, the study of God's Word becomes an act of faith, surrender, and dependence on the living God. I believe humbly, almost tremblingly, in the divine seed that is in the Word, and I believe in the power of God's Spirit to make it true in my life and experience. I yield my heart hungrily and entirely to receive this divine seed. I wait on God in absolute dependence and confidence to give the increase in a power above anything we can ask or think. (See Ephesians 3:20.)

Knowing and Doing God's Word

[Jesus] said, Yea rather, blessed are they that hear the word of God, and keep it.
—Luke 11:28

If any man will do his will, he shall know.
—John 7:17

Some time ago I received a letter from an earnest Christian asking me for some hints to help him in Bible study. He wanted some guidelines as to how to begin, so that he could better understand and know the Bible. The very first thing I said to him is this: in your Bible study everything will depend on the spirit in which you approach it.

In worldly things a man is ruled by the goals he sets for himself. It is no different with the Bible. If your aim is simply to know the Bible well, you will be disappointed. If you think that thorough knowledge of the Bible will necessarily be a blessing, you are mistaken. To some it is a curse; to others it is powerless—it does not make them either holy or happy. To some it is a burden; it depresses them instead of quickening them or lifting them up.

What should be the real objective of the Bible student? Because God's Word is food, bread from heaven, the first reason for Bible study is a hunger for righteousness—a desire to do God's will.

This is what the Bible teaches us: *"Blessed are they that hear the word of God, and keep it."* There is no blessedness in hearing or knowing God's Word apart from keeping it.*"If any man will do his will, he shall know."* According to this, all true knowledge of God's Word depends upon there first being the will to do it. God will unlock the real meaning and blessing of His Word only to those whose will is set upon doing it. I must read my Bible with one purpose: *"Whatsoever he saith unto you, do it"* (John 2:5).

When you ask God to lead you into the treasures of His Word, do it as one who presents himself *"a living sacrifice"* (Romans 12:1), ready to do whatever God says with deep humility. To enjoy your food you must first be hungry. The first requirement for Bible study is a simple longing to find out what God wants you to do and the determination to do it. *"If any man will do his will, he shall know"*—the Word of God will be opened to him.

Becoming a Doer of the Word

But be ye doers of the word, and not hearers only, deceiving your own selves...not a forgetful hearer, but a doer of the work, this man shall be blessed in his deed.
—James 1:22, 25

It is a terrible delusion to delight in hearing the Word and yet not do it. Multitudes of Christians listen to the Word of God regularly and yet do not do it. If their own children were to hear but not do what they said, they would be greatly disturbed. However, the delusion is so complete that some never know they are not living good Christian lives. What deludes us in this way?

One cause for this delusion is that people often mistake hearing the Word for religion or worship. The mind delights in having truth explained, and their imaginations are pleased with clever illustrations. To an active mind, knowledge gives pleasure. A man may study electricity for the enjoyment the knowledge gives him, without the least intention of applying it practically. Some people go to church, enjoy the preaching, and yet do not do what God asks. The unconverted and the converted man alike are content to continue listening and saying, yet still doing the things they should not do.

Another reason for this delusion centers on our private Bible reading. The reading of the Bible is often regarded as a duty. We spend our five or ten minutes in the morning, reading thoughtfully and trying to understand what we have read. It is a duty faithfully performed that eases the conscience. We do not realize how this attitude of duty can cause us to become hardened toward God's Word. To avoid this delusion, we must approach our daily Bible reading with the desire to do and be all that God would have us to be. *"But be ye doers of the word, and not hearers only, deceiving your own selves."*

This delusion must be conquered during our morning quiet time. This new approach may disturb our regular Bible reading schedule. However, the important thing is that we decide to do what we read. Our Lord Jesus said, *"If any man will do his will, he shall know of the doctrine, whether it be of God"* (John 7:17). If we delight in God's law and set our wills on doing it, then we can receive divine illumination. Without this will to do, our knowledge has little value. It is simply head knowledge.

Keeping Christ's Commandments

**If ye know these things, happy are ye if ye do them.
—John 13:17**

The joy and the blessing of God's Word is only to be known by doing it. This subject is of such importance in the Christian life, and in our Bible study, that I must ask you to return to it once more. Let us this time just take the one expression "keeping the Word," or "keeping the commandments."

In Jesus' farewell address to His disciples, He emphasized the importance of keeping His commandments.

> *If ye love me, keep my commandments. And…he shall give you another Comforter.* (John 14:15–16)
>
> *He that hath my commandments, and keepeth them, he it is that loveth me: and he…shall be loved of my Father.* (v. 21)
>
> *If a man love me, he will keep my words: and my Father will love him.* (v. 23)
>
> *If ye abide in me, and my words abide in you, ye shall ask what ye will, and it shall be done unto you.* (John 15:7)
>
> *If ye keep my commandments, ye shall abide in my love.* (v. 10)
>
> *Ye are my friends, if ye do whatsoever I command you.* (v. 14)

Study and compare these passages until the words enter your heart and work the deep conviction that keeping Christ's commandments is the condition of all spiritual blessing. It is necessary for the coming of the Holy Spirit and His actual indwelling, and for the manifestation of Christ in our lives.

Power in prayer depends on the keeping of the commandments. The power to claim these blessings in faith day by day requires obedience. The will of God, delighted in and done, is the only way to the heart of the Father and His only way to our hearts.

The Word Is Life

And out of the ground made the LORD God to grow...the tree of life also in the midst of the garden, and the tree of knowledge of good and evil.
—Genesis 2:9

There are two ways of knowing things. The one is by thought or idea—"I know about a thing." The other is by living—"I know by experience." An intelligent blind man may know all that science teaches about light by having books read to him. A child who has never thought about what light is knows more about light than the blind scholar. The scholar knows all about it by thinking. The child knows it in reality by seeing and enjoying it.

This is also true in Christianity. The mind can form thoughts about God from the Bible and know all the doctrines of salvation, while the inner life does not know the power of God to save. This is why we read, *"He that loveth not knoweth not God; for God is love"* (1 John 4:8). He may know all about God and love, but unless he loves, he does not know God. Only love can know God.

God's Word is the Word of Life. *"Out of* [the heart] *are the issues of life"* (Proverbs 4:23). The life of a person can be strong, even when mental knowledge is limited. On the other hand, knowledge can be the object of diligent study and great delight, while the person's life is not affected by it.

It is only by experiencing God and His goodness that we can receive true knowledge. The knowledge of the intellect cannot quicken or revive. *"Though I...understand all mysteries, and all knowledge;... and have not charity, I am nothing"* (1 Corinthians 13:2).

It is in our daily Bible reading that this danger must be met and conquered. We need the intellect to hear and understand God's Word in its human meaning. But we need to know that the possession of the truth by the intellect can only benefit us when the Holy Spirit makes it life and truth in the heart. We need to yield our hearts and wait on God in quiet submission and faith to work in us by that Spirit. As this becomes a holy habit, our intellects and hearts will work in perfect harmony. Each movement of the mind will be accompanied by the corresponding movement of the heart, waiting on and listening for the teaching of the Spirit.

The Heart and the Intellect

Trust in the LORD with all thine heart; and lean not unto thine own understanding.
—Proverbs 3:5

The main purpose of the book of Proverbs is to guide in the path of wisdom and understanding. The writer of Proverbs warned us to distinguish between trusting our own understanding and seeking the spiritual understanding that God gives.

"Trust in the LORD with all thine heart; and lean not unto thine own understanding." In all our seeking after knowledge and wisdom, in all our plans for studying the Word, we have two powers at work: the intellect that knows things from the ideas we form, and the heart that knows them by experience as they become part of our wills and desires. One of the main reasons Bible teaching and Bible knowledge bear little fruit in the lives of Christians is because we trust in our own understanding.

Many people argue that God gave us our intellect, and without it there is no possibility of knowing God's Word. This is true, but in the Fall our whole human nature was disordered. The will became enslaved and our understanding was darkened. Most people acknowledge that even the believer does not have in himself the power of a holy will and needs the daily renewing of Jesus Christ. They admit that the believer does not have the power to love God and his neighbor unless it is given to him by the Holy Spirit. But most people do not realize that the intellect is equally ruined spiritually and incapable of understanding spiritual truth.

It was this desire for knowledge that led Eve astray and was the outcome of the temptation. To think that we can take the knowledge of God's truth for ourselves out of His Word is still our greatest danger. We need to realize the terrible danger of self-confidence and self-deception and to see the need for this warning: *"Trust in the LORD with all thine heart; and lean not unto thine own understanding."*

Instead of trusting your understanding, come with your heart to the Bible and trust God. Let your whole heart be set upon the living God as the Teacher when you enter your prayer closet. Then you will find good understanding. God will give you an understanding heart, a spiritual understanding.

God's Thoughts and Our Thoughts

**For as the heavens are higher than the earth,
so are...my thoughts than your thoughts.
—Isaiah 55:9**

On earth the words of a wise man often mean something different from what the hearer understands them to mean, especially upon first hearing. How natural, then, that the words of God, as He communicates them, mean something infinitely higher than we understand at first. We must remember this because it will cause us to search for the fuller meaning of God's Word as He meant it. It will give us confidence to hope that there is fulfillment in life beyond our highest thoughts.

God's Word has two meanings. The one is the meaning that originated in the mind of God, making human words the bearer of divine wisdom, power, and love. The other is our partial, distorted understanding of God's Word. Although such words as *the love of God, the grace of God,* and *the power of God* may seem very true and real to us, there is still an infinite fullness in the Word that we have not yet known. How strikingly this is put in our text from Isaiah: *"As the heavens are higher than the earth."* Our faith in this fact is so clear that no one would dream of trying with his little arms to reach the sun or the stars. And now God says, *"My thoughts* [are higher] *than your thoughts."* Even when the Word has given us God's thoughts and our thoughts have tried to understand them, they still remain as high above our thoughts as the heavens are higher than the earth.

God wants to make His Word true in us. The Holy Spirit is already in us to reveal the things of God. In answer to our humble prayer, God will give insight into the mystery of God—our wonderful union and likeness to Christ, His living in us, and our being as He was in this world.

If our hearts thirst, a time may come when, by a special communication of His Spirit, all our yearnings will be satisfied. Christ will take possession of the heart, and what was of faith will now become an experience. Then we will realize that, *"as the heavens are higher than the earth,"* His thoughts are higher than our thoughts.

True Meditation

Blessed is the man...[whose] delight is in the law of the LORD; and in his law doth he meditate day and night.
—Psalm 1:1–2

Let the words of my mouth, and the meditation of my heart, be acceptable in thy sight, O LORD, my strength, and my redeemer.
—Psalm 19:14

God's Word only works when the truth it brings to us has stirred the inner life and reproduced itself in trust, love, or adoration. When the heart has received the Word through the mind and has had its spiritual powers exercised, the Word is no longer void, but has done what God intended it to do.

It is in meditation that the heart takes hold of the Word. We must remember that the heart is the will and the emotions. The meditation of the heart implies acceptance, surrender, and love. *"Out of* [the heart] *are the issues of life"* (Proverbs 4:23). Whatever the heart truly believes, it receives and allows to rule the life. The intellect gathers and prepares the food on which we are to feed. In meditation the heart takes it in and feeds on it.

The art of meditation needs to be cultivated. Just as we need to be trained to concentrate our mental powers to think clearly, a Christian needs to meditate until he has formed the habit of yielding his whole heart to every word of God.

How can this power of meditation be cultivated? The Word is meant to bring us into His presence and fellowship. Take the Word as from God Himself with the assurance that He will make it work in your heart. In Psalm 119, the word *meditate* is mentioned seven times, each time as a prayer addressed to God: *"I will meditate in thy precepts"* (v. 15); *"Thy servant did meditate in thy statutes"* (v. 23); *"O how love I thy law! it is my meditation all the day"* (v. 97). Meditation is turning our hearts toward God and seeking to make His Word a part of our lives.

"Let the words of my mouth, and the meditation of my heart, be acceptable in thy sight, O LORD, my strength, and my redeemer." Let this be your aim, that your meditation may be part of the spiritual sacrifice you offer. Let this be your prayer and expectation, that your meditation may be the living surrender of the heart to God's Word in His presence.

Having a Childlike Spirit

I thank thee, O Father, Lord of heaven and earth, because thou hast hid these things from the wise and prudent, and hast revealed them unto babes. —Matthew 11:25

The wise and prudent are those who have confidence in their reasoning ability in their pursuit of spiritual knowledge. The babes are those whose chief work is not the mind and its power, but the heart and its emotions. Ignorance, helplessness, dependence, teachableness, trust, and love—these are the qualities God seeks in those whom He teaches. (See Psalm 25:9, 12, 14, 17, 20.)

One of the most important parts of our devotions is the study of God's Word. In order to receive the Word in the Spirit, we must wait for the Father to reveal its truth in us. We must have that childlike attitude to which the Father loves to impart the secrets of His love. With the wise and prudent, the most important thing is head knowledge. From them God hides the true spiritual meaning of the very thing they think they understand. With babes it is not the head and its knowledge, but the heart and its emotions that are important. Because they have a sense of humility and trust, God reveals to them the very thing they know they cannot understand.

In order to receive a revelation of God, we must first have this childlike spirit. We all know the first thing a wise workman does is to see that he has the proper tools and that they are in proper order. He does not consider it lost time to stop his work and sharpen the tools. Similarly, it is not lost time to let the Bible study wait until you see whether you are in the right position—waiting for the Father's revelation with a childlike spirit. If you feel that you have not read your Bible in this spirit, confess at once the self-confident spirit. Pray for the childlike spirit, and then believe you have it. Although it may be suppressed, it is in you. You can begin at once as a child of God to experience it.

This childlike spirit is in you as a seed in the new life. It must rise and grow in you as a birth of the indwelling Spirit. Live as a newborn babe, *"desire the sincere milk of the word"* (1 Peter 2:2).

Beware of trying to assume this state of mind only when you want to study Scripture. It must be the permanent habit of your mind, the state of your heart. Only then can you enjoy the continual guidance of the Spirit.

Learning of Christ

Take my yoke upon you, and learn of me; for I am meek and lowly in heart: and ye shall find rest unto your souls. —Matthew 11:29

All Bible study, in order to be fruitful, should be learning of Christ. The Bible is the schoolbook, and Christ is the teacher. It is He who opens the understanding, the heart, and the seals. (See Luke 24:45; Acts 16:14; Revelation 5:9.) He is the living eternal Word, the written words are the human expression. Christ's presence and teaching are the secret of all true Bible study. The written Word is powerless, except as it brings us to the living Word.

No one has ever thought of accusing our Lord of not honoring the Old Testament. In His own life He proved that He loved it because it came out of the mouth of God. He always pointed the Jews to it as the revelation of God and the witness to Himself. But with the disciples, it is remarkable how frequently He spoke of His own teaching as what they most needed and had to obey.

The Jews had their self-made interpretation of the Word, and made it the greatest barrier between themselves and Him of whom it spoke. Christians often do this, too. Our human understanding of Scripture, fortified by the authority of the church or our own denomination, becomes the greatest hindrance to Christ's teachings. Christ the living Word seeks first to find His place in our hearts and lives, to be our only Teacher. From Him we will learn to honor and understand Scripture.

"Learn of me; for I am meek and lowly in heart." Our Lord gives us the secret of His own inner life that He brought down to us from heaven. This secret that He wants us to learn from Him is found in the words, *"I am meek and lowly in heart."* It is the one virtue that makes Him the Lamb of God, our suffering Redeemer, our heavenly Teacher and Leader. It is the one attitude that He asks us to learn from Him—out of this all else will come.

For Bible study and our entire Christian lives, this is the one condition we need to truly learn of Christ. He, the Teacher, meek and lowly in heart, wants to make you what He is, because that is salvation. As a learner you must come and study and believe in Him, the meek and lowly One. You must seek to learn of Him how to be meek and lowly, too.

December 17

Christ, Your Teacher

Take my yoke upon you, and learn of me; for I am meek and lowly in heart: and ye shall find rest unto your souls.
—Matthew 11:29

The first virtue of a pupil is a willingness to be taught. What does this imply? He must have an awareness of his own ignorance, a readiness to give up his own way of thinking. He must look at things from the teacher's standpoint. He must have a quiet confidence that the master knows and will show him how to learn to know, too. The meek and lowly spirit listens to know what the teacher's will is and how to carry it out. If a pupil has this kind of spirit, it must be the teacher's fault if the student does not learn.

Why is it that, with Christ as our Teacher, there is so much failure and so little real growth in spiritual knowledge? Why is there so much hearing and reading of the Bible, so much profession of faith in it as our only rule of life, and yet such a lack of the manifestation of its spirit and its power? Why is there so much honest, earnest application in the prayer closet and in Bible study, but so little of the joy and strength God's Word can give?

These questions are ones of extreme importance. There must be some reason why there are so many disciples of Jesus who think they honestly desire to know and do His will, and yet, by their own confession, they are not holding forth the Word of Life as a light in the world. If the answer to this question could be found, their lives would be changed.

"Take my yoke upon you, and learn of me; for I am meek and lowly in heart: and ye shall find rest unto your souls." Many people have taken Christ as Savior but not as Teacher.

This teachable spirit that refuses to know or do anything in its own wisdom is to be the spirit of our entire lives, every day and all day long. In the morning hour this spirit is to be cultivated, and deliverance from self is to be achieved. It is there, while occupied with the words of God, that we need daily to realize that these words have value only as they are opened up by the personal teaching of Christ. We daily need this experience so that, as the living Lord Jesus takes charge of us, His teaching can be received. It is during this quiet time that we must cultivate the teachable spirit that takes up His yoke and learns from Him.

The Life and the Light

**In the beginning was the Word, and the Word was with God, and the Word was God....In him was life; and the life was the light of men.
—John 1:1, 4**

**He that followeth me shall not walk in darkness, but shall have the light of life.
—John 8:12**

Because Christ was God, He could be the Word of God. Because He had the life of God in Himself, He could be the Revealer of that life. And so, as the living Word, He is the life-giving Word. The written Word can be made of no effect when we trust human wisdom for an understanding of it. The written Word must be accepted as the seed in which the life of the living Word lies hidden. When it is quickened by the Holy Spirit, it can become to us the Word of Life. Our communion with God's written Word must be inspired and regulated by faith in the eternal Word, who is God.

This same truth comes out in the expression that follows: the life is the light. When we see a light shining, we know that there is a source of that light in some form. This is also true in the spiritual world. There must be life before there can be light. There can be reflected light from a dead or dark object. There can be borrowed light without life. But true life alone can show true light. He who follows Christ will have the light of life.

The one great lesson the Spirit seeks to enforce in regard to God's Word is this: only as Scripture is received out of the life of God into our lives can there be any real knowledge of it. The Word is a seed that bears within it the divine life. When it is received in the good soil of a heart that hungers for life. It will reproduce in our lives the very life of God, the likeness and character of the Father and the Son through the Holy Spirit.

Ask the Father for the Holy Spirit to make the Word living and active in your heart. Hunger for the will of God as your daily food. Thirst for the living spring of the Spirit within you. Receive the Word into your will, your life, your joy—the life it brings will give the light with which it shines.

Principles of Bible Study

Blessed is the man....[whose] delight is in the law of the LORD; and in his law doth he meditate day and night.
—Psalm 1:1–2

There is a desire in the church for more Bible study. Evangelists like D. L. Moody and others have proven what power there is in preaching drawn directly from God's Word and inspired by the faith of its power. Christians have asked, "Why can't our ministers speak in the same way, giving the very Word of God more emphasis?" Many young ministers have come away from seminary confessing that they were taught everything except the knowledge of how to study the Word or how to help others study it. In some churches, the desire has been expressed to supply this need in the training of ministers. Yet it has been difficult for men with theological training to return to the simplicity of God's Word. This simplicity is necessary in order to teach younger men the way to make Scripture the one source of their knowledge and teaching.

The Word brings us into the most intimate fellowship with God—unity of will and life. In the Word, God has revealed His whole heart and all His will. In His law and precepts, He tells us what He wants to do for us. As we accept that will in the Word as from God Himself and yield ourselves to its working, we learn to know God in His will.

In Holy Scripture we have the very words in which the holy God has spoken and in which He speaks to us. Today these words are full of the life of God. God is in them and makes His presence and power known to those who seek Him in them. To those who ask and wait for the teaching of the Holy Spirit who dwells within us, the Spirit will reveal the spiritual meaning and power of the Word. The Word is thus meant every day to be the means of the revelation of God Himself to the soul and of fellowship with Him.

Have we learned to apply these truths? The Word tells us to seek God, to listen for God, to wait for God. God will speak to you; let God teach you. All we hear about more Bible teaching and study must lead to this one thing. We must be Christians in whom the Word is never separated from the living God Himself. We must live as Christians to whom God speaks every day and all day long.

Your Position in Christ

Set your affection on things above...for ye are dead, and your life is hid with Christ in God.
—Colossians 3:2–3

When entering God's presence in the morning hour, the Christian must realize where he stands in relation to God. Each person who claims access and an audience with the Most High must have a living sense of the place he has in Christ before God.

Who am I? Who is it that comes to ask God to meet me and spend the whole day with me? I am one who knows that I am in Christ and that my life is *"hid with Christ in God."* In Christ I died to sin and the world. I am now taken out of them, separated and delivered from their power. I have been raised together with Christ; and in Him, I live unto God. My life is *"hid with Christ in God."*

Yes, this is who I am. I am one who longs to say, "Christ is my life." The longing of my soul is for Christ, revealed by the Father Himself within the heart. Nothing less can satisfy me. My life is *"hidden with Christ."* He can be my life in no other way than as He is in my heart. Christ is the Savior from sin, the gift and instrument of God's love. Christ is my indwelling Friend and Lord.

If God should ask, "Who are you?" I would reply, "I live in Christ and Christ in me. Lord, You alone can make me know and be all that this truly means."

I am sure you realize how important the morning hour is to secure God's presence for the day. During that time, you take a firm stand on the foundation of redemption. Accept what God has bestowed on you in Christ. Be what God has made you to be. Confess your position in Christ. In a battle, much depends upon an unshakable position. Take your place where God has placed you.

The very attempt to do this may at times interfere with your ordinary Bible study. This will be no loss. Your daily Christian walk depends on knowing who your God is and who you are as His redeemed one in Christ. When you have learned the secret, it will, even when you do not think of it, be the strength of your heart, both in going in before God and going out with Him to the world.

December 21

The Will of God

**Thy will be done in earth, as it is in heaven.
—Matthew 6:10**

The will of God is the living power to which the world owes its existence. Through that will, the world is what it is. The world is the manifestation of that divine will in its power and goodness. The world has only what God has willed it to have. Creation does what it was destined for; it shows forth the glory of God. *"Thou art worthy, O Lord, to receive glory…for thou hast created all things, and for thy pleasure they are and were created"* (Revelation 4:11).

The unfallen angels consider it their highest honor to be able to will and do exactly what God wills and does. The glory of heaven is that God's will is done there. The sin and misery of fallen angels and men consists simply in their having turned away from and having refused to do the will of God.

Redemption is the restoration of God's will to its place in the world. To this end, Christ came and showed how man has only one thing to live for: to do the will of God. Christ said, *"I come to do thy will, O God"* (Hebrews 10:9). He showed us how there was one way of conquering self-will—by obeying God's will even unto death.

God's redeeming will is now able to do in fallen men what His creating will had done in nature. In Christ, God has revealed the devotion to and the delight in His will that He asks and expects of us. In Christ, God works our wills to make us able and willing to do all His will.

He Himself *"worketh all things after the counsel of his own will"* (Ephesians 1:11), to *"make you perfect in every good work to do his will, working in you that which is wellpleasing in his sight"* (Hebrews 13:21). As this is revealed by the Holy Spirit we begin to acquire an insight into the prayer, *"Thy will be done in earth, as it is in heaven."* Then the true desire is awakened in us.

It is essential to the believer that he realize his relationship to God's will and its claim on him. How few believers say, "My desire is to be in complete harmony with the will of God. I feel my one need is to maintain my surrender, to do what God wills me to do. By God's grace, every hour of my life can be lived in the will of God—doing His will as it is done in heaven."

Feeding on the Word

Thy words were found, and I did eat them; and thy word was unto me the joy and rejoicing of mine heart.
—Jeremiah 15:16

This verse teaches us three things. First, that the finding of God's Word comes only to those who diligently seek it. Second, the eating means personally taking hold of the Word for our own sustenance. *"Man shall not live by bread alone, but by every word that proceedeth out of the mouth of God"* (Matthew 4:4). Third, we also learn about the rejoicing: *"The kingdom of heaven is like unto treasure hid in a field; the which when a man hath found, he hideth, and for joy thereof goeth and selleth all that he hath, and buyeth that field"* (Matthew 13:44).

Eating is here the central thought. It is preceded by the searching and finding. It is accompanied and followed by the rejoicing. It is the only aim of the one; it is the only cause of the other. In the secrecy of the inner chamber, much depends on this.

To realize the difference between this and the finding of God's words, compare the corn a man may have stored in his granary with the bread on his table. All the diligent labor he has put into sowing and harvesting his grain cannot profit him unless he eats the bread. Do you see the application of this to your Scripture study in the morning quiet time? You need to find God's words and master them by careful thought, so as to have them stored in your mind for your own use. In this work there may often be the joy of harvest or of victory—the joy of treasure secured or difficulties overcome. Yet we must remember that this finding and possessing the words of God is not the actual eating of them.

The fact that a farmer possesses good, wholesome corn will not nourish him. Similarly, the fact of being deeply interested in the knowledge of God's Word will not of itself nourish your soul. *"Thy words were found"*—that happened first. *"And I did eat them"*—that brought the joy and rejoicing.

It is such feeding on the Word that will enable you to say, *"And thy word was unto me the joy and rejoicing of mine heart."* George Müller said that he learned not to stop reading the Word each day until he felt happy in God. Then he felt prepared to go out and do his day's work.

The Power of Daily Renewal

Though our outward man perish, yet the inward man is renewed day by day.
—2 Corinthians 4:16

According to his mercy he saved us, by the washing of regeneration, and renewing of the Holy Ghost.
—Titus 3:5

With every new day, the life of nature is renewed. As the sun rises again with its light and warmth, the flowers open, birds sing, and life is everywhere stirred. As we rise, we feel that we have gathered new strength for the duties of the day.

Our inner life needs daily renewal, too. It is only by fresh nourishment from God's Word and communion with God in prayer, that the vigor of the spiritual life can grow. Our outward man may perish and work may exhaust us, yet the inner man can be *"renewed day by day."*

A quiet time with the Word and prayer are the means for daily renewal. To be effective, these means must be empowered by the Holy Spirit. In Titus, we are taught that we have been *"saved...by the washing of regeneration, and renewing of the Holy Ghost."* These two expressions are not a repetition. Regeneration is one act, the beginning of the Christian life. The renewing of the Holy Spirit is a work that is carried on continuously.

In Ephesians 4:22–23, while the words *"put off...the old man"* indicate an act done once for all, the words *"be renewed in the spirit of your mind"* are in the present tense and point to a progressive work. Even so in Colossians 3:10, we read, "[You] *have put on the new man, which is renewed in knowledge after the image of him that created him."* We can count on the blessed Spirit for the daily renewal of the inner man in the inner chamber.

In our devotions, everything depends upon maintaining the true relationship to the third person of the Trinity. It is only through the Holy Spirit that the Father and the Son can do their work, and through whom the Christian can do his work. This may be expressed in two simple words, *faith* and *surrender.*

Your Inner Life

Ye fools, did not he that made that which is without make that which is within also?
—Luke 11:40

The outward is the visible expression of the hidden, inward life. The outward is generally known before the inward. Through it the inward is developed and reaches its full perfection. The apostle Paul said, *"Howbeit that was not first which is spiritual, but that which is natural; and afterward that which is spiritual"* (1 Corinthians 15:46). To maintain the right relationship between the inward and the outward is one of the secrets of the Christian life.

If Adam in the Garden had not listened to the Serpent, his trial would have resulted in the perfecting of his inward life. Adam did not seek his happiness in the hidden, inward life of a heart in which God's command was honored. Instead, he fixed his desire on the world around him, on the pleasure that the knowledge of good and evil could give him.

All false religion, from idolatry to the corruption of Christianity, has its root in this desire. Deception takes place when the outward—that which pleases the eye, the mind, or the taste—takes the place of truth in the inward.

Christianity is a matter of the heart—a heart into which God has sent forth the Spirit of His Son, a heart in which the love of God is poured out (see Romans 5:5) and true salvation is found. The inner chamber, with its secret communion with the Father who *"seeth in secret"* (Matthew 6:4), is the training school for the inner life. The daily use of the inner chamber will make the inner, hidden life strong.

In religion the great danger is giving more interest to outward experiences than to inward reality. It is not the intensity of your Bible study, or the frequency of your prayers or works that make for a true spiritual life. We need to realize is that God is a Spirit. There is also a spirit within us who can know and receive Him.

Look in your heart, and your heart will find its Savior, its God. If you see and feel nothing of God, it is because you seek Him in books, in church, in outward religious exercises. You will not find Him there until you have first found Him in your heart. Seek Him in your heart, and you will never seek in vain, for He dwells there in His Holy Spirit!

Holidays and Your Quiet Times

**If the goodman of the house had known what hour the thief would come, he would have watched, and not have suffered his house to be broken through.
—Luke 12:39**

How leisure time is spent greatly affects our characters. It has been said that "leisure hours are the hinge on which true education turns." It is true that developing a person's character is more important than training the mind and abilities. While a teacher can do much to stimulate and guide a student, every child has to work out his own character. It is in the leisure hours, when he is free from rules and observation, that a child shows what his true character is. This statement can also be applied to Christianity.

At Bible college, students will take time for their daily devotions as part of their regular routine. Their minds are geared for systematic work. They set aside time for devotions just as they do time for a class or private study.

When the time for vacation or a holiday comes and students are free to do exactly as they please, many find that the morning fellowship with God interferes with their holiday pleasure. The question of how we spend our leisure time is very important. It is then that we turn freely and naturally to what we love most.

A teacher in America is reported to have said, "The greatest difficulty with which we have to contend is the summer vacation. Just when we have brought a child to a good point of discipline, we lose him. When he comes back in the autumn, we have to begin and do it all over."

The sudden relaxation of habits and the subtle thought that perfect freedom to do as one likes means perfect happiness cause many young students to backslide in their Christian walks. The attainment of months may be lost by the neglect of a week. The spirit of the morning watch means unceasing vigilance all day and every day.

Do not think of asking for a holiday from this communion with God. Cherish holidays for the special time they give you to study beyond your ordinary Bible study course. Cherish your holidays for the opportunity of more fellowship with the Father. Instead of holidays becoming a snare, make them a blessed time for victory over self and the world, of increase in grace and strength.

Renewed in God's Image

Ye...have put on the new man, which is renewed in knowledge after the image of him that created him.
—Colossians 3:9–10

If so be that ye have heard him, and have been taught by him...be renewed in the spirit of your mind; and...put on the new man, which after God is created in righteousness and true holiness.
—Ephesians 4:21, 23–24

In every pursuit it is essential to have the goal clearly defined. It is not enough that there is movement—we need to know that the movement is headed in the right direction. When we are in partnership with another person, we need to know that our goals are the same. If our daily renewal is to attain its objective, we need to know clearly what its purpose is.

"Ye...have put on the new man, which is renewed in knowledge." The divine life, the work of the Holy Spirit within us, is no blind force. We are to be workers together with God. (See 2 Corinthians 6:1.) Our cooperation is to be intelligent and voluntary. *"The new man...is renewed in knowledge,"* day by day. There is a knowledge that natural understanding can draw from the Word, but it is without life and power. It has none of the real truth and substance that spiritual knowledge brings. Only the renewing power of the Holy Spirit gives true knowledge. This involves an inward tasting, a living experience of the very things of which the words are but the images. *"The new man...is renewed in knowledge."* However diligent our Bible study may be, true knowledge is gained only as spiritual renewal is experienced.

The morning hour is the time for our daily renewing by the Holy Spirit into the image of God as righteousness and holiness. We need a time of meditation and prayer to get our hearts set upon God's purposes. We need a true vision of how the inward man can be renewed day by day into the very likeness of God. Let nothing less be your aim. The image of God, the life of God, is in you, and His likeness can be seen in you. Let all your trust in Him mean nothing less than finding His likeness formed in you by the renewing of the Holy Spirit.

Let this be your daily prayer—to be renewed according to the image of Him who created you.

Renewed and Transformed

**For which cause we faint not; but though our outward man perish, yet the inward man is renewed day by day.
—2 Corinthians 4:16**

**And be not conformed to this world: but be ye transformed by the renewing of your mind.
—Romans 12:2**

It is not an easy thing to be a mature Christian. It cost the Son His life. It is God's part to create a new man in every believer and to maintain that life with the daily care of the Holy Spirit.

When the new man is put on, it is our responsibility to see that the old man is put off. All the attitudes, habits, and pleasures of our own nature are to be put away. If a man is to come after Christ, he must deny himself and take up his cross. (See Matthew 16:24.) He must forsake all and follow Christ in the path in which He walked. The Christian must cast away not only all sin, but everything that may cause him to sin. He is to hate his own life, to lose it, if he is to live in the power of eternal life. It is a serious thing, far more serious than most people think, to be a true Christian.

The full experience of the life of Christ in our persons and our work for others depends on our fellowship in His suffering and death. There can be no renewal of the inward man without the sacrifice, the perishing of the outward man.

Only as the spirit of this world is recognized, renounced, and cast out can the Spirit enter in. Then the Holy Spirit can do His blessed work of renewing and transforming. The world and whatever is of the worldly spirit must be given up. Whatever is of self must be lost. This daily renewal of the inward man is very costly if we are trying to do it in our own strength. When we really learn that the Holy Spirit does everything, and by faith give up the struggle, the renewing becomes the simple, healthy, joyful growth of the heavenly life in us.

The inner chamber then becomes the place we long for every day. Day by day, we yield ourselves afresh to the Lord who has said, *"He that believeth on me…out of his belly shall flow rivers of living water"* (John 7:38). The renewing of ourselves by the Holy Spirit becomes one of the most blessed truths of the daily Christian life.

To Be Made Holy

Sanctify them through thy truth: thy word is truth.
—John 17:17

In His great intercessory prayer, our Lord spoke of the words that the Father had given Him, of passing them on to His disciples, and of their having received and believed them. It was their keeping these words that would enable them to live the life and do the work of true disciples. Receiving the words of God from Christ and keeping them are the signs and power of true discipleship.

"Sanctify them through thy truth: thy word is truth." The great objective of God's Word is to make us holy. No diligence or success in Bible study will really profit us unless it makes us humbler and holier. In our use of Holy Scripture, this must be our main objective. The reason there is often so much Bible reading with so little real result in a Christlike character is that *"salvation through sanctification of the Spirit and belief of the truth"* (2 Thessalonians 2:13) is not truly desired.

This holiness through the Word must be sought and waited for from God in prayer. It is necessary to know God's Word and meditate on it; to set our hearts upon being holy and to make this our primary objective in studying the Word. But all this is not enough. Everything depends upon our asking the Father to sanctify us through the Word. It is God who makes us holy by the Spirit of holiness who dwells within us. He works in us the very mind and attitudes of Christ who is our sanctification.

"There is none holy as the Lord" (1 Samuel 2:2). All holiness is His, and He makes things holy by His holy presence. The tabernacle and temple were not holy by cleansing, separation, or consecration. They became holy by the incoming and indwelling God. God makes us holy through His Word bringing Christ and the Holy Spirit into us. The Father can do this only as we wait before Him and give ourselves to Him. When we pray by faith, "Sanctify me through Your truth. Your Word is truth," our knowledge of God's Word will truly make us holy.

The morning watch is a sacred time. It is the time devoted to the yielding of ourselves to God's holiness, sanctified through the Word. Remember, the one aim of God's Word is to make us holy. Let this be our prayer, "Father, sanctify me through Your truth."

Teachings from Psalm 119

O how love I thy law! It is my meditation all the day....Consider how I love thy precepts....I love them exceedingly.
—Psalm 119:97, 159, 167

There is one portion of Holy Scripture devoted to teaching us the place that God's Word should have in our lives. It is the longest chapter in the Bible, and in almost every one of its 176 verses the Word is mentioned. Anyone who really wants to know how to study his Bible should make a careful study of this psalm. It is possible you have never read it through as a whole. Take time to read it through and understand its main ideas. If you find it difficult to do this by reading it once, read it again.

Take note of the names that refer to God's Word. Note the verbs expressing how we should feel in regard to the Word. Count how many times the writer speaks in the past tense of his having observed and delighted in God's testimonies. Notice how many times he expresses in the present tense how he rejoices in and esteems God's law. Consider how, in the future tense, he vows to observe God's precepts to the end. See how more than a hundred times he presents himself before God as one who honors His law.

Notice how the whole psalm is a prayer spoken to God. All the psalmist has to say about the Word of God is spoken to the face of God. He believes that it is pleasing to God and good for his own soul to connect his meditation on the Word by prayer with the living God Himself.

The Word of God becomes to him the inexhaustible material for having communion with God. As we gradually gain insights into these truths, we will discover new meaning from the individual verses. When we take a whole paragraph with its eight verses, we will find how they help to lift us into God's presence. We will be lifted into the life of obedience and joy that says, *"I have sworn, and I will perform it, that I will keep thy righteous judgments"* (v. 106). *"O how love I thy law! It is my meditation all the day."*

Let us seek to have the kind of devotional life that this psalm reveals. Let God's Word every day lead us to God. Let our prayers be followed by the vow that, as God revives, we will obey His commandments. Let all that God's Word brings to us make us more earnest in longing to carry that Word to others.

Abiding in Christ

Abide in me, and I in you.
—John 15:4

Jesus is set before us as a man among us doing a work here on earth and continuing that work in heaven. But many Christians never advance beyond an external Lord, in whom they trust for what He has done and is doing. They know little of the true mystery of Christ in us as an indwelling Savior.

The former, simpler view is that of the first three gospels. The more advanced view is found in the gospel of John. The former is the aspect of truth presented in the doctrine of justification. The latter is the teaching concerning the union of the believer with Christ and his continual abiding as taught in John and the epistles to the Ephesians and Colossians.

This abiding in Christ must be more than a truth you hold in its right place in your gospel doctrine. It must be a matter of experience that inspires your faith in Christ and relationship with God. To be in Christ, to abide in Christ, is not a matter of intellectual faith, but a spiritual reality.

The full manifestations of God and His saving love can come in no other way than by indwelling. To the degree our hearts are given to Him in faith and our wills are given in active obedience, He comes in and abides in us. We can say, because we know, *"Christ liveth in me"* (Galatians 2:20).

If we are to live with Christ in us and we in Him, then we must be renewed and strengthened in our personal relationships with God in the morning watch. Our access to God, our expectation from God must all be in living fellowship with Christ. If you feel that you want to realize God's presence more fully, come to God in Christ. Think how Jesus, a man on earth, drew near to the Father in deep humility and dependence, in full surrender and obedience. We must come in His spirit, in union with Jesus.

Seek to take the place before God that Christ has taken in heaven, that of redemption, victory, and of full entrance to glory. Do it by faith in His indwelling power in you here on earth. Expect your approach to God to be accepted according to your heart's surrender and acceptance in Christ. Then you will be led on in the path in which Christ, living in you and speaking in you, will be truth and power.

The Trinity and You

For this cause I bow my knees unto the Father of our Lord Jesus Christ...That he would grant you, according to the riches of his glory, to be strengthened with might by his Spirit in the inner man; that Christ may dwell in your hearts by faith; that ye, being rooted and grounded in love, may be able...to know the love of Christ, which passeth knowledge, that ye might be filled with all the fulness of God. Now unto him that is able to do exceeding abundantly above all that we ask or think, according to the power that worketh in us, unto him be glory in the church by Christ Jesus throughout all ages, world without end. Amen.

—Ephesians 3:14, 16–21

Many Christians understand that it is necessary in the Christian life to give special attention to the three persons of the blessed Trinity. They often feel it difficult to combine the various truths into one and to know how to worship the Three-in-One. Our text reveals this wonderful relationship and the perfect unity.

We have the Spirit within us as the power of God, and yet He does not work according to our wills or His own. It is the Father who grants us to be strengthened *"by his Spirit in the inner man."* It is the Father who does *"exceeding abundantly above all that we ask or think, according to the power that worketh in us."* The Spirit within us makes us more dependent on the Father. The Spirit can only work as the Father works through Him. We need to combine trusting awareness of the Holy Spirit indwelling us with a dependent waiting on the Father to work through Him.

As you study and compare these passages, notice especially how practical this truth of the Holy Trinity is. Scripture teaches us little about its mystery in the divine nature, but refers only to God's work in us and our faith and experience of His salvation.

True faith in the Trinity will make us strong, alert Christians. The divine Spirit will make Himself one with our inner beings. The blessed Son will dwell in us, as the way to perfect fellowship with God. The Father, through the Spirit and the Son, will work His purpose so that we are filled with all the fullness of God.

Let us bow our knees to the Father! Then the mystery of the Trinity will be known and experienced.

About the Author, Andrew Murray

Andrew Murray (1828–1917) was an amazingly prolific Christian writer. He lived and ministered as both a pastor and author in the towns and villages of South Africa. Some of Murray's earliest works were written to provide nurture and guidance to Christians, whether young or old in the faith; they were actually an extension of his pastoral work. Once books such as *Abide in Christ, Divine Healing,* and *With Christ in the School of Prayer* were written, Murray became widely known, and new books from his pen were awaited with great eagerness throughout the world.

He wrote to give daily practical help to many of the people in his congregation who lived out in the farming communities and could only come into town for church services on rare occasions. As he wrote these books of instruction, Murray adopted the practice of placing many of his more devotional books into thirty-one separate readings to correspond with the days of the month.

At the age of seventy-eight, Murray resigned from the pastorate and devoted most of his time to his manuscripts. He continued to write profusely, moving from one book to the next with an intensity of purpose and a zeal that few men of God have ever equaled. He often said of himself, rather humorously, that he was like a hen about to hatch an egg; he was restless and unhappy until he got the burden of the message off his mind.

During these later years, after hearing of pocket-sized paperbacks, Andrew Murray immediately began to write books to be published in that fashion. He thought it was a splendid way to have the teachings of the Christian life at your fingertips, where they could be carried around and read at any time of the day.

One source has said of Andrew Murray that his prolific style possesses the strength and eloquence that are born of deep earnestness and a sense of the solemnity of the issues of the Christian life. Nearly every page reveals an intensity of purpose and appeal that stirs men to the depths of their souls. Murray moves the emotions, searches the conscience, and reveals the sins and shortcomings of many of us with a love and hope born out of an intimate knowledge of the mercy and faithfulness of God.

For Andrew Murray, prayer was considered our personal home base from which we live our Christian lives and extend ourselves to others. During his later years, the vital necessity of unceasing prayer in the spiritual life came to the forefront of his teachings. It was then that he revealed the secret treasures of his heart concerning a life of persistent and believing prayer.

Countless people the world over have hailed Andrew Murray as their spiritual father and given credit for much of their Christian growth to the influence of his priceless devotional books.

Absolute Surrender

Andrew Murray

If our hearts are willing to surrender everything into God's hands, there is no end to what He will do for us—no end to the blessings He will bestow. Andrew Murray's wise counsel will enable you to take a giant step closer to God as you begin your journey into perfect peace and trust. Discover the joys of *Absolute Surrender* to our loving Father today.

ISBN: 978-0-88368-093-3 • Mass Market • 144 pages

The Holiest of All
(updated edition)
Andrew Murray

It is only the full and perfect knowledge of what Christ is and does for us that can bring us into a full and perfect Christian life. In this updated edition of Andrew Murray's classic commentary on the book of Hebrews, the author explores how you can have a life of joy, destroy Satan's power, and progress in your walk with God so that you will always live in victory and inherit the Bible's promises. Come into the Holy of Holies and abide with *The Holiest of All.*

ISBN: 978-0-88368-523-5 • Trade • 576 pages

Whitaker
House

THE
PRACTICE
OF
God's
PRESENCE
A N D R E W
Murray

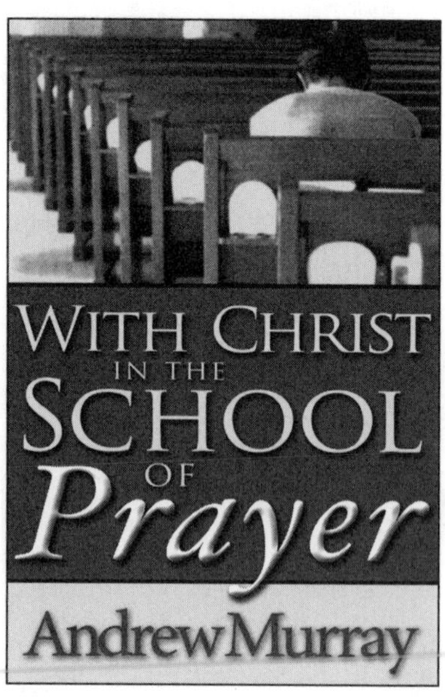

With Christ in the School of Prayer
Andrew Murray

Few books have had as much impact in calling the church to prayer as Andrew Murray's classic, *With Christ in the School of Prayer.* As you saturate yourself in the timeless wisdom found here, you will discover how to prepare yourself for effective participation in the great privilege Christ has extended to believers—to join with Him in intercessory prayer.

ISBN: 978-0-88368-106-0 • Mass Market • 240 pages

WHITAKER
HOUSE

Andrew Murray on Prayer
Andrew Murray

Combining seven of Andrew Murray's most treasured works on prayer, this book will give you biblical guidelines for effective communication with God. Discover essential keys to developing a vital prayer life, including how to receive clear direction from the Lord, see your unsaved loved ones come to Christ, and overcome temptation. Lovingly explained, the principles presented here will permanently transform your prayer life!

ISBN: 978-0-88368-528-0 • Trade • 656 pages

Whitaker House

Books by Andrew Murray

Abide in Christ
Absolute Surrender
Andrew Murray Devotional
Andrew Murray on Prayer
Andrew Murray on the Holy Spirit
The Blessings of Obedience
The Blood of the Cross
Covenants and Blessings
The Deeper Christian Life
Divine Healing
An Exciting New Life
Experiencing the Holy Spirit
God's Best Secrets
The Holiest of All
How to Strengthen Your Faith
Humility
The Master's Indwelling
The Ministry of Intercession
The Power of the Blood of Christ
The Practice of God's Presence
Prayer Guide
The Prayer Life
Raising Your Children for Christ
Reaching Your World for Christ
The Secret of Intercession
The Secret of Spiritual Strength
Secrets of Authority
The Spirit of Christ
The True Vine
Waiting on God
With Christ in the School of Prayer
With Wings As Eagles